McGRAW-HILL'S
OUR NATION, OUR WORLD

MEETING PEOPLE

School, Self, Families, Neighborhood, and Our Country

GOING PLACES

People in Groups, Filling Needs in Communities and on Farms

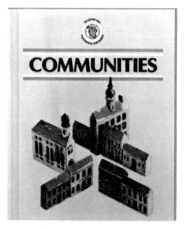

COMMUNITIES

Geography and History of Cities in the United States, Canada, and Mexico

EARTH'S REGIONS

Geography and Ways of Living on Five Continents, Studying the 50 States

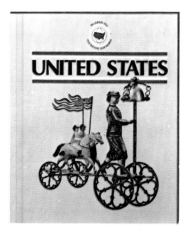

UNITED STATES

Chronological History of the United States, North America Today

THE WORLD

World History, Ancient Civilizations, Important Nations Today

1

CONSULTANTS

BONNIE AMASON
A.M. Davis Elementary School
Richmond, Virginia

DR. L. JO ANNE BUGGEY
Educational Consultant
Minneapolis, Minnesota

MILDRED CROWELL
Jamestown Academy
Williamsburg, Virginia

CORA DVERSDALL
Parkview Elementary School
Oklahoma City, Oklahoma

DON FELICE
Falling Creek Middle School
Richmond, Virginia

JUDY A. FISHER
Dennis Elementary School
Oklahoma City, Oklahoma

CAROLYN FITZGERALD
Powhatan Middle School
Powhatan, Virginia

SANDY HANNINGTON
Central Elementary School
Yukon, Oklahoma

CAROLYN HERBST
Eli Whitney Vocational High School
Brooklyn, New York

DR. RONALD J. HERMANSEN
Staff Assistant, Social Studies
Granite School District
Salt Lake City, Utah

DR. LEONORE HOFFMANN
City University of New York
Former Director, Federal Projects
Modern Language Association

SISTER M. JEANNETTE, I.H.M.
Archdiocese of Philadelphia
Philadelphia, Pennsylvania

ELAINE S. JONES
Woodinville, Washington

SISTER SHARON KERRIGAN
Diocese of Joliet
Joliet, Illinois

HERELYNN KIDD
Shedeck Elementary School
Yukon, Oklahoma

MARY S. McDADE
St. Joseph's School
Petersburg, Virginia

JEAN McGRADY
Western Oaks Elementary School
Bethany, Oklahoma

SISTER GLENN ANNE McPHEE
Archdiocese of Los Angeles
Los Angeles, California

ELAINE MAGNUSON
Canyon Creek Elementary School
Bothell, Washington

SHERRILL MILLER
Seattle, Washington

FRED PEFFER
Central Elementary School
Yukon, Oklahoma

SUZANNE PHELPS
Traub Elementary School
Midwest City, Oklahoma

BETSY PIERCE
Hamilton-Holmes Elementary School
King William, Virginia

SUSIE REYNOLDS
Overholser Elementary School
Bethany, Oklahoma

JOANNE ROBERTSON
Redmond, Washington

SISTER ANN SCHAFER
St. Luke's School
Seattle, Washington

KENNETH SUNDIN
Hollywood Hill Elementary School
Woodinville, Washington

JANE THOMAS
Robious Middle School
Midlothian, Virginia

NORA WASHINGTON
Byrd Primary School
Hadensville, Virginia

RONALD GRIGSBY KIRCHEM
Editorial Consultant and Contributing Writer

Editor in Chief: Leonard Martelli
Senior Editor: Alma Graham
Editing and Styling: Mary Ann Jones
Photo Editing Supervision: Rosemary O'Connell
Production Supervision: Salvador Gonzales
Assistant Editors: James Allan Bartz, Ronald J. Bogus
Photo Editor: Alan Forman
Design by: Function Thru Form Inc.
Cover Design by: Blaise Zito Associates
Cover Photography by: Bill Holland
Photo Credit: From the Collection of Bill Holland

2

THE WORLD

BY Leonard Martelli, Alma Graham,
June Tyler, Rosemary Messick,
Cleo Cherryholmes, Gary Manson

WEBSTER DIVISION, McGRAW-HILL BOOK COMPANY

New York   St. Louis   San Francisco   Auckland   Bogotá   Düsseldorf
Johannesburg   London   Madrid   Mexico   Montreal   New Delhi
Panama   Paris   São Paulo   Singapore   Sydney   Tokyo   Toronto

LIST OF MAPS AND CHARTS

FUN FACTS AND STRANGE FACTS

WHERE WE ARE IN TIME AND PLACE

SEPARATE TIME LINES

ISBN 0-07-039946-8

CONTENTS

1777

1795

1912

1959

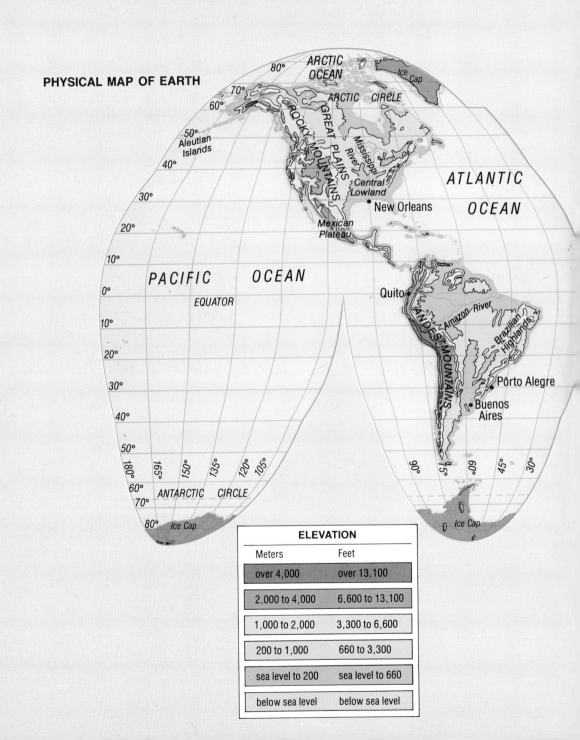

PHYSICAL MAP OF EARTH

ARCTIC OCEAN

Ice Cap

80°

70°

60°

ARCTIC CIRCLE

50°

Aleutian Islands

40°

ROCKY MOUNTAINS

GREAT PLAINS

Mississippi River

30°

Central Lowland

New Orleans

ATLANTIC OCEAN

20°

Mexican Plateau

10°

PACIFIC OCEAN

0°

EQUATOR

Quito

10°

Amazon River

ANDES MOUNTAINS

Brazilian Highlands

20°

30°

Pôrto Alegre

40°

Buenos Aires

50°

180° 165° 150° 135° 120° 105°

90° 75° 60° 45° 30°

60°

ANTARCTIC CIRCLE

70°

80° Ice Cap

Ice Cap

ELEVATION	
Meters	Feet
over 4,000	over 13,100
2,000 to 4,000	6,600 to 13,100
1,000 to 2,000	3,300 to 6,600
200 to 1,000	660 to 3,300
sea level to 200	sea level to 660
below sea level	below sea level

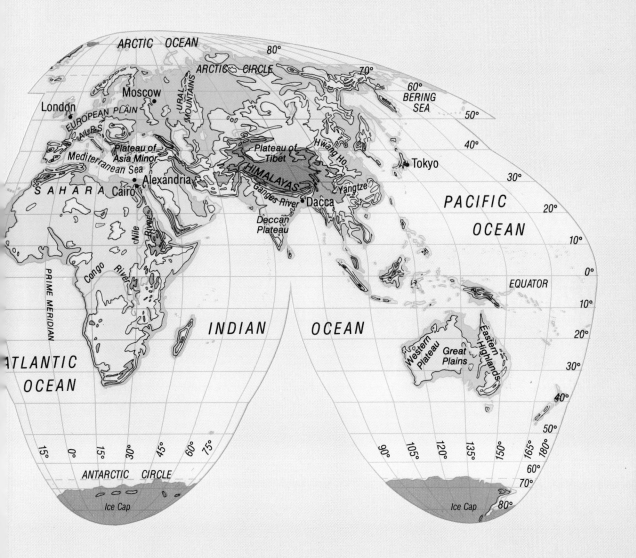

ARCTIC OCEAN

80°

ARCTIC CIRCLE

70°

60°
BERING
SEA

50°

Moscow

URAL MOUNTAINS

London

EUROPEAN PLAIN

ALPS

Plateau of
Asia Minor

Mediterranean Sea

Plateau of
Tibet

Hwang Ho

40°

Tokyo

30°

S A H A R A   Cairo   Alexandria

HIMALAYAS

Ganges River   Dacca

Yangtze

PACIFIC

OCEAN

20°

Nile River

Deccan
Plateau

10°

Congo River

0°

EQUATOR

10°

PRIME MERIDIAN

INDIAN   OCEAN

20°

Western
Plateau

Great
Plains

Eastern
Highlands

30°

ATLANTIC

OCEAN

40°

50°

15°   0°   15°   30°   45°   60°   75°

90°   105°   120°   135°   150°   165°   180°

60°

70°

ANTARCTIC   CIRCLE

Ice Cap

80°

Ice Cap

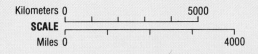

Kilometers 0   5000

SCALE

Miles 0   4000

ATLAS

POLITICAL MAP OF EARTH

1 Belize
2 Jamaica
3 Dominican Republic
4 Trinidad and Tobago
5 Antigua and Barbuda
6 Austria
7 Czechoslovakia
8 Hungary
9 Albania
10 Denmark
11 West Germany
12 East Germany
13 Netherlands
14 Belgium
15 Switzerland
16 Benin
17 Central African Republic
18 São Tomé and Príncipe
19 Djibouti
20 Equatorial Guinea
21 Gambia
22 Ghana
23 Guinea
24 Guinea-Bissau
25 Seychelles
26 Cyprus
27 Lebanon
28 Kuwait
29 Qatar
30 United Arab Emirates

31 Tuvalu
32 Nauru
33 Solomon Islands
34 Kiribati

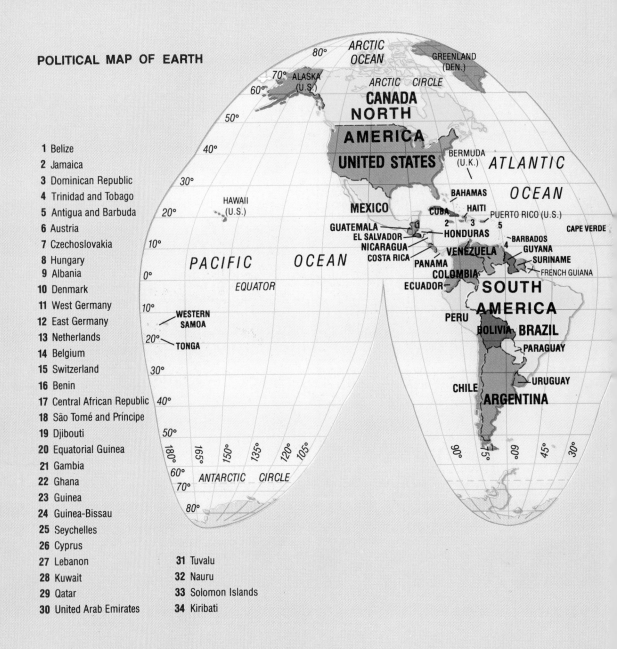

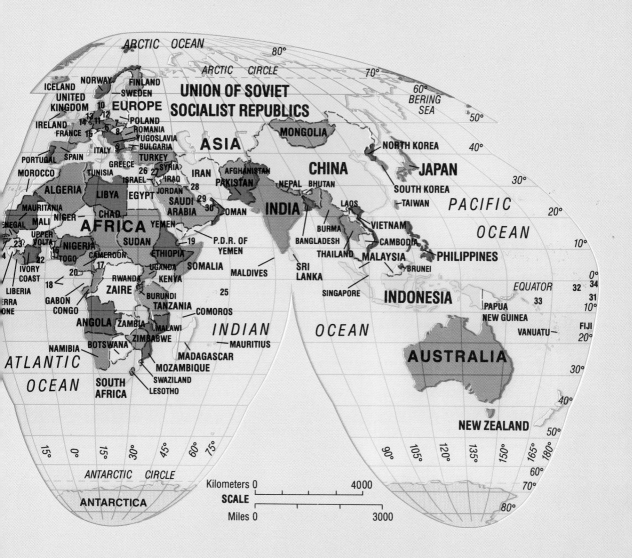

ARCTIC OCEAN 80°

ARCTIC CIRCLE 70°

ICELAND NORWAY FINLAND 60°
UNITED SWEDEN BERING
KINGDOM 10 EUROPE UNION OF SOVIET SEA
IRELAND 12 POLAND SOCIALIST REPUBLICS 50°
14 11 6 13 ROMANIA MONGOLIA NORTH KOREA 40°
FRANCE 15 5 8 YUGOSLAVIA ASIA
9 7 BULGARIA CHINA JAPAN
PORTUGAL SPAIN ITALY GREECE TURKEY SOUTH KOREA 30°
MOROCCO TUNISIA 26 27 SYRIA AFGHANISTAN TAIWAN PACIFIC
ISRAEL IRAQ IRAN PAKISTAN NEPAL BHUTAN
ALGERIA LIBYA EGYPT JORDAN 28 INDIA LAOS OCEAN 20°
MAURITANIA CHAD SAUDI 29 OMAN BURMA VIETNAM
NIGER ARABIA 30 BANGLADESH CAMBODIA 10°
SENEGAL MALI AFRICA YEMEN THAILAND PHILIPPINES
UPPER 19 P.D.R. OF MALAYSIA
23 VOLTA NIGERIA SUDAN YEMEN SRI BRUNEI 0°
4 22 TOGO CAMEROON ETHIOPIA SOMALIA MALDIVES LANKA EQUATOR 32 34
IVORY 20 17 UGANDA SINGAPORE INDONESIA 33 31
COAST RWANDA KENYA PAPUA 10°
LIBERIA 18 ZAIRE BURUNDI 25 NEW GUINEA
GABON TANZANIA VANUATU FIJI
ONE CONGO COMOROS AUSTRALIA 20°
ANGOLA ZAMBIA MALAWI
NAMIBIA BOTSWANA ZIMBABWE INDIAN OCEAN 30°
ATLANTIC MADAGASCAR MAURITIUS
MOZAMBIQUE 40°
OCEAN SOUTH SWAZILAND
AFRICA LESOTHO NEW ZEALAND 50°

15° 0° 15° 30° 45° 60° 75° 90° 105° 120° 135° 150° 165° 180° 60°

ANTARCTIC CIRCLE 70°

ANTARCTICA Kilometers 0   4000 80°
SCALE
Miles 0   3000

11

ATLAS

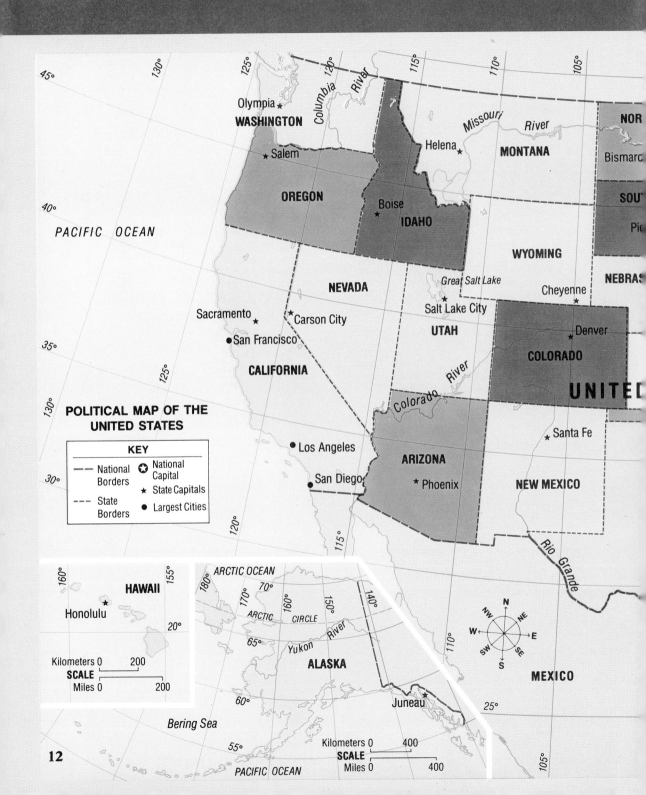

POLITICAL MAP OF THE
UNITED STATES

KEY

— — National Borders	⊛	National Capital
– – State Borders	★	State Capitals
	●	Largest Cities

PACIFIC OCEAN

45°
40°
35°
30°

130°
125°
120°
115°
110°
105°

Olympia ★
WASHINGTON
★ Salem
OREGON

Columbia River

Helena ★
MONTANA
Missouri River

NOR
Bismarc

SOU
Pie

Boise ★
IDAHO

WYOMING

NEBRAS

NEVADA
Great Salt Lake
Cheyenne ★

Sacramento ★
Carson City ★
● San Francisco

Salt Lake City ★
UTAH

Denver ★
COLORADO

CALIFORNIA

Colorado River

UNITED

● Los Angeles

Santa Fe ★

San Diego ●
ARIZONA
Phoenix ★

NEW MEXICO

Rio Grande

HAWAII
160°
155°
Honolulu ★
20°

Kilometers 0   200
SCALE
Miles 0   200

ARCTIC OCEAN
180°
70°
170°
160°
150°
140°
ARCTIC
CIRCLE
65°
Yukon River
ALASKA
60°
Juneau ★
55°

Kilometers 0   400
SCALE
Miles 0   400

Bering Sea
PACIFIC OCEAN

N
NW   NE
W   E
SW   SE
S

MEXICO
25°
110°
105°

1 LOOKING AT EARTH

Lesson 1: Our Planet

FIND THE WORDS

planet   orbit   moon
solar system   axis   North Pole
South Pole   equator
hemisphere   solstice
equinox   tropic of Cancer
tropic of Capricorn   tropic zone
tropics   Arctic Circle
Antarctic Circle   polar zone
temperate zone

Imagine you are an astronaut. You have just blasted off on a trip to the moon. As you look back at Earth, you see the view above. This is what the astronauts on *Apollo 16* saw as they left Earth to travel into space.

Earth is a planet. A **planet** is a world that moves around a star. It moves in a special path called an **orbit.** Nine planets move around the star we call the sun. Earth is one of these nine planets.

Some of the planets circling our sun have moons. A **moon** is a body that moves around a planet. A moon moves around a planet just as a planet moves around a star. Earth has only one moon. Some planets have more. The sun, the planets, and the moons make up our **solar system.**

Solar means "of the sun." Look at the picture of the solar system below. It shows which planets are closest to the sun. It also shows which planets are farthest away. It also shows the sizes of the various planets as compared with one another.

Planets get their light and heat from the sun. Some planets are so close to the sun that they are very hot. Others are so far away that they are cold. Find the hottest planets in the picture. Then find the coldest ones.

Earth is the third planet from the sun. It is neither too hot nor too cold for people, animals, and plants. Earth also has the air, water, and food needed to support life as we know it.

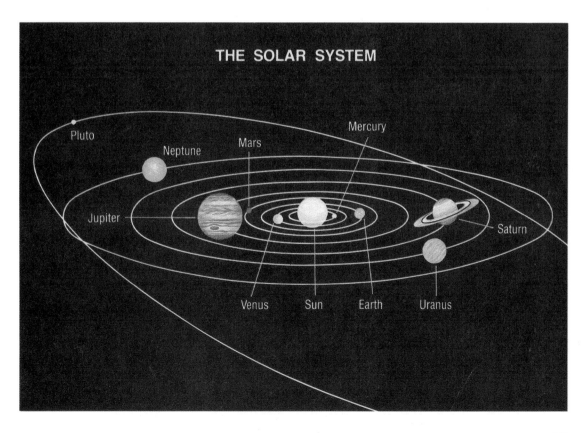

THE SOLAR SYSTEM

Pluto
Neptune
Mars
Mercury
Jupiter
Saturn
Venus
Sun
Earth
Uranus

On Earth, we divide time into years, months, and days. A year is the time it takes Earth to make one full trip around the sun. A month is the time it takes our moon to make one full trip around Earth. Look at the diagram below. It shows how the lighted part of the moon changes in size and shape as the moon moves around Earth.

A day is the time it takes Earth to spin around once on its axis. Earth's **axis** is an imaginary line that runs from the North Pole to the South Pole. The **North Pole** is the most northern point on Earth. The **South Pole** is the most southern point on Earth.

Earth turns on its axis from west to east. Because of this, the sun seems to rise in the east and set in the west. When the sun rises, the part of Earth where you live is turning toward the sun. When the sun sets, your part of

Earth is turning away from it.

Earth makes one full turn on its axis every 24 hours. As Earth spins on its axis, only one side of it faces the sun at a time. The side lit by the sun has day. The side turned away from the sun has night. Day and night are not always the same length. This is because Earth's axis is tilted at an angle in relation to the sun.

Earth is divided in the middle by an imaginary line called the **equator.** The two halves of Earth are called **hemispheres** (HEM uh SFIRZ). *Hemi* means "half" and *sphere* means "round ball." The half of Earth north of the equator is the Northern Hemisphere. The half south of the equator is the Southern Hemisphere.

Look at the picture on page 18. On June 22, the North Pole is tilted toward the sun. At that time, much of the sun's light and heat are falling on the northern

The moon itself is always the same size. But the lighted part gets larger and smaller during the month.

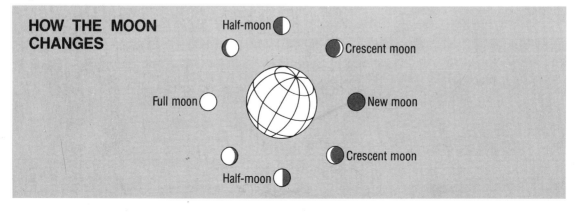

HOW THE MOON CHANGES — Half-moon — Crescent moon — Full moon — New moon — Half-moon — Crescent moon

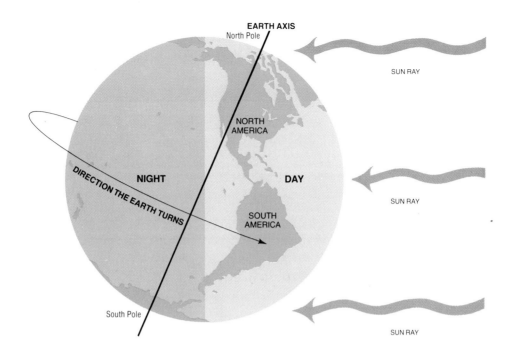

EARTH AXIS
North Pole

SUN RAY

NORTH
AMERICA

DIRECTION THE EARTH TURNS

NIGHT

DAY

SUN RAY

SOUTH
AMERICA

South Pole

SUN RAY

part of Earth. There are more hours of daylight. The weather is warm or hot. It is summer in the Northern Hemisphere.

At the same time, the South Pole is tilted away from the sun. The southern part of Earth is getting less of the sun's light and heat. There are more hours of darkness. The weather is cool or cold. It is winter in the Southern Hemisphere.

On December 22, the opposite is true. This is because Earth moves around the sun. The tilt of Earth always stays the same. But

Earth can be divided into Northern and Southern Hemispheres.

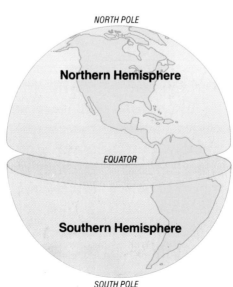

NORTH POLE

Northern Hemisphere

EQUATOR

Southern Hemisphere

SOUTH POLE

THE SEASONS

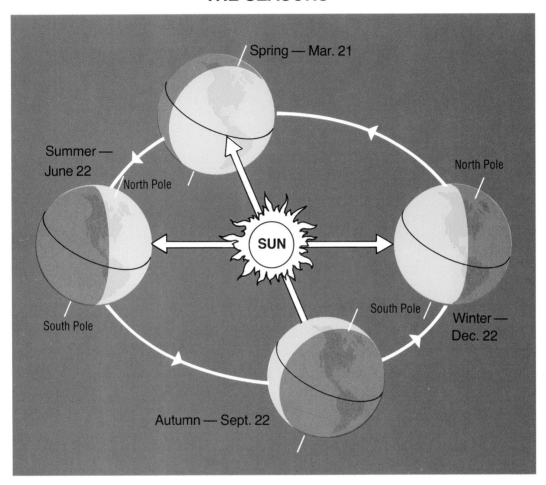

Spring — Mar. 21

Summer — June 22

North Pole

SUN

South Pole

North Pole

South Pole

Winter — Dec. 22

Autumn — Sept. 22

as Earth moves around the sun, the tilt changes steadily *in relation to the sun.* When Earth has moved halfway around the sun, the tilt is the opposite in relation to the sun. Now the South Pole is tilted toward the sun. It is summer in the Southern Hemisphere and winter in the Northern Hemisphere.

June 22 and December 22 are **solstices.** These are the dates of the year on which the day and the night are longest or shortest. On these dates, the tilt of Earth is greatest in relation to the sun.

On June 22, the day is longest and the night is shortest in the Northern Hemisphere. The day is shortest and the night is longest in the Southern Hemisphere. June 22 is the summer solstice and the beginning of summer in the Northern Hemisphere. June 22 is the winter solstice and the beginning of winter in the Southern Hemisphere. See the picture above.

On December 22, the day is shortest and the night is longest in the Northern Hemisphere. The day is longest and the night is shortest in the Southern Hemisphere. December 22 is the winter solstice and the beginning of winter in the Northern Hemisphere. December 22 is the summer solstice and the beginning of summer in the Southern Hemisphere.

As Earth moves around the sun, the lengths of day and night are equal on two dates. These dates, March 21 and September 22, are the **equinoxes** (EE kwuh NOK sez). On these dates, the Earth is tilted the least in relation to the sun. March 21 is the **vernal equinox,** or spring equinox, and the beginning of spring in the Northern Hemisphere. March 21 is the **autumnal equinox**, or fall equinox, and the beginning of autumn in the Southern Hemisphere. September 22 is the autumnal equinox and the beginning of autumn in the Northern Hemisphere. September 22 is the vernal equinox and the beginning of spring in the Southern Hemisphere.

The part of Earth close to the equator is never tilted away from the sun. At the equator, day and night are always of equal length. The lands near the equator get much light and heat from the sun all year. Except in the highlands, the weather is always hot.

North of the equator is an imaginary line called the **tropic of Cancer.** This line is parallel to the equator. The tropic of Cancer is the most northern place at which the sun is ever directly overhead. The sun is directly overhead along the tropic of Cancer at noon on June 22. As you have learned, June 22 is the summer solstice in the Northern Hemisphere.

South of the equator is a line similar to the tropic of Cancer. It is called the **tropic of Capricorn.** This line is also parallel to the equator. The tropic of Capricorn is the most southern place at which the sun is ever directly overhead. The sun is directly overhead along the tropic of Capricorn at noon on December 22. As you have learned, December 22 is the summer solstice in the Southern Hemisphere.

The area of Earth between the tropic of Cancer and the tropic of Capricorn is called the **tropic zone.** It is also called the **tropics.** The weather is usually hot in the tropic zone.

Between the tropic of Cancer and the North Pole is another imaginary line, the **Arctic Circle.** The area between this circle and the North Pole is often called the Arctic. Between the tropic of Capricorn and the South Pole is a similar imaginary line, the **Antarctic Circle.** The area between this circle and the South Pole is often

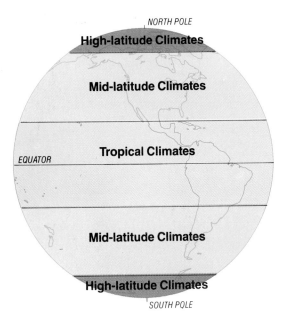

NORTH POLE

High-latitude Climates

Mid-latitude Climates

EQUATOR

Tropical Climates

Mid-latitude Climates

High-latitude Climates

SOUTH POLE

The temperate zones have milder weather than the tropic zone and the polar zones.

called the Antarctic. The Arctic is near the North Pole. The Antarctic is near the South Pole. As a result, they are both called **polar zones.** These zones get little heat from the sun. In the polar zones, the weather is always cool or cold.

Near the equator, the weather is hot. Near the poles, the weather is cold. But between the equator and the poles, the weather is milder. The area between the tropic of Cancer and the Arctic Circle is called a **temperate zone.** The area between the tropic of Capricorn and the Antarctic Circle is also called a temperate zone. *Temperate* means "mild." In the temperate zones, the weather is not as hot as in the tropics nor as cold as in the polar zones.

The weather does not change much at the equator or at the poles. It is always hot near the equator and cold near the poles. But, in the temperate zones, there are changes in the weather. In the temperate zones, the year is divided into four nearly equal parts, called seasons.

The four seasons are winter, spring, summer, and autumn (or fall). Each season has its own kind of weather. The weather depends mainly on the position of Earth and the sun. Of course, the seasons are opposite in the two hemispheres. When it is winter in the Northern Hemisphere, it is summer in the Southern Hemisphere. When it is spring in the Northern Hemisphere, it is autumn in the Southern Hemisphere, and so on. Just think, in Australia, Christmas and New Year's Day come at the beginning of summer!

The weather in different places in one country may be different during the same season. This can be the case even when the places are in the same region. But the pattern of summer, winter, spring, and autumn is true for most places. You will soon learn that things like bodies of water and the height of the land can affect the weather.

Your part of Earth is only one place among many. More than 4 billion people live on our planet.

In Sydney, Australia, people go to the beach in January.

The air, water, and land can support many living things in very different ways. To understand how people live as they do and why, you must learn more about Earth itself.

REVIEW

WATCH YOUR WORDS

1. The ____ divides Earth into two hemispheres.
   axis   equator   tropic of Cancer

2. A____moves around a star.
   planet   moon   solar system

3. The day and night are longest or shortest at the____.
   tropics   equinoxes   solstices

4. The ____ is the area between the tropic of Cancer and the tropic of Capricorn.
   polar zone   temperate zone   tropic zone

5. Earth makes a full turn on its ____ every 24 hours.
   axis   equinox   solstice

CHECK YOUR FACTS

Look at the Picture

6. How many planets are there in the solar system?

7. Which planets are between Earth and the sun?

Look at the Lesson

8. What is December 22 in the Northern Hemisphere?

9. What are the names of the two equinoxes?

10. How many temperate zones are there?

THINK ABOUT IT

Suppose Earth did not tilt on its axis. How would the day be different? How would the seasons be different?

Lesson 2: Landforms and Bodies of Water

Earth has many different environments. An **environment** is made up of all the surroundings in a place. An environment includes the land and the water. It includes the weather and the climate. It includes all the plants and animals that live in a place. It also includes the things people have done to change a place.

In this lesson, you will study two parts of Earth's environment, the lands and the waters. Land has different shapes called **landforms.** Mountains, hills, plains, and plateaus are landforms. Land can be different in other ways as well. Some lands are covered by ice and snow most of the year. Other lands are covered by thick forests where it rains every day. Some lands are covered with sand. Other lands have fertile soil in which many food crops can grow. Though Earth's lands can be very different, people manage to live on almost every one of them.

Earth has seven major land masses. These large areas are called **continents.** Every continent except Antarctica has one or more nations on it. A **nation** is an area with an independent government. The United States is one of the nations on the continent of North America. Look at the map on pages 10 and 11. Find out what other large nations make up most of the North American continent.

The other continents are South America, Europe, Asia, Africa, Australia, and Antarctica. Scientists believe that, long ago, Earth had only two large land masses. These later split up to make the continents as we know them today. Look at the map again. Find two continents not connected to any others. Find the continent that has the South Pole.

You are going to study six of these continents this year. These are Europe, Asia, Africa, Australia, North America, and South America. You will not study Antarctica.

The land areas of Earth are surrounded by large bodies of water called **oceans.** Over 70 percent of Earth's surface is covered by water. Two of the oceans are very large. One is the Atlantic Ocean. The other is the Pacific

LANDFORMS

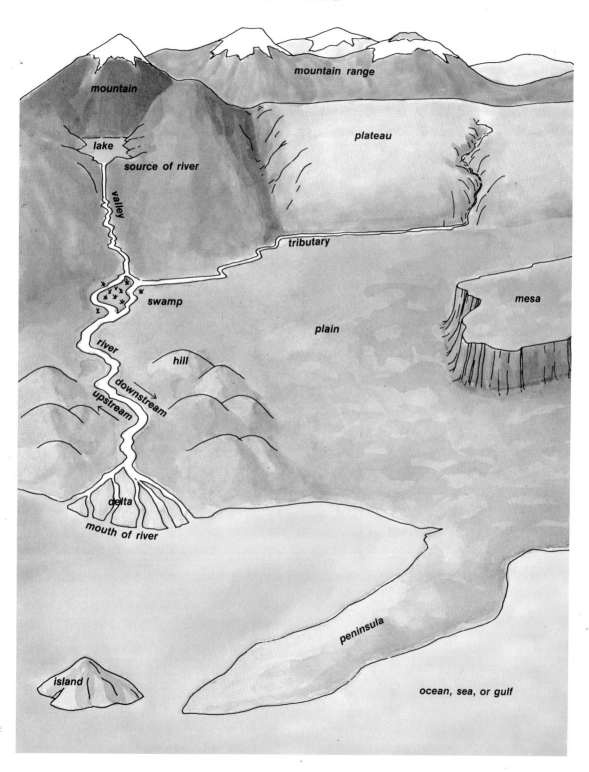

Ocean. Find Earth's four oceans on the map on pages 10 and 11. Oceans are important areas on Earth. They provide people with food and minerals. People also use ships to travel on the water.

Earth's oceans are not all alike. The Atlantic Ocean, for example, is far stormier than the Pacific Ocean. Indeed, *pacific* means "peaceful." The Indian Ocean has much warmer water than the Arctic Ocean. These are only some of the ways in which the oceans of Earth are very different.

The continents of Earth are very different from one another, too. Even within a single nation on one continent, there are many differences between areas. Think of the United States. It has the highlands of the Rocky Mountains. It has the lowlands of Death Valley in California. The United States has great rivers and large lakes. Think of the Mississippi River and Lake Superior. Flat plains cover much of the midwestern and western parts of the country. There are dusty deserts, such as the Mojave (moh HAH vee) Desert in California. There are large swamps, such as the Everglades in Florida.

The continents are very different. However, the same kinds of landforms and bodies of water are found on every continent. For example, there are rivers and lakes in many places. A **river** is a long, narrow body of water. Rivers drain water from the land. Almost all flow into another body of water, such as an ocean. A **lake** is a body of water surrounded by land. Rivers and lakes supply fresh water and food. They are used by people for travel and for transporting goods. Large numbers of people often live along rivers and around lakes.

Some continents have fewer rivers than others. Look at the map on pages 8 and 9. On which continents would fresh water be hard to find?

Lakes, like rivers, are of many sizes. Some lakes are very large. For example, Lake Baikal (by KAWL) in the Union of Soviet Socialist Republics, or Soviet Union, is huge. Almost all lakes help support life.

Continents have land of different elevations, or heights. The **elevation** of land is its height above the level of the surface of the ocean. This level is known as **sea level. Mountains** are the places on Earth with the highest elevations. They are places where Earth's surface has been pushed up at some time in the past. Some mountains are newer and more jagged, like the Alps in Europe. Other mountains are older and more rounded, like the Appalachians in the United States.

Sometimes, there are large flat areas in the mountains. These are called **plateaus** (pla TOHZ). Even though plateaus are at a high elevation, they are still flat. On the map on pages 8 and 9, find some plateaus.

Between mountains, there are areas of low land. These are called **valleys.** The word *valley* is also used for the area drained by a river. Sometimes, far from the mountains, the land is nearly flat. These flat lands are called **plains.** Much of Western Europe is a plain. So is most of the central part of the United States.

Some of the mountains and plateaus of Earth are good places for growing food and raising cattle. But, as a rule, valleys and plains are more favorable landforms for people. A much less favorable area is the desert. A **desert** is a very dry area. Parts of such a place are often covered with sand. There is little moisture in a desert. Thus, plant life is scarce. Life in a desert is often a struggle for food and water. But it is possible for people to live in a desert. People can learn to change their way of life to suit the environment where they live.

REVIEW

WATCH YOUR WORDS

1. Rivers and____supply fresh water.
   oceans   plateaus   lakes

2. A____is a high, flat area.
   valley   plateau   mountain

3. Each continent except Antarctica has one or more____.
   nations   oceans   deserts

4. The ____ includes all the surroundings in a place.
   landform   environment
   sea level

5. A____is a very dry area.
   plain   plateau   desert

CHECK YOUR FACTS

Look at the Map (See pages 10–11)

6. How many nations are on the continent of Australia?

7. Name two oceans in addition to the Atlantic and the Pacific.

Look at the Lesson

8. How many continents are there?

9. List some ways in which people use rivers and lakes.

10. What do plateaus and plains have in common?

THINK ABOUT IT

Many scientists believe the continents were once joined. Look at the map of the world on pages 8 and 9. What places can you find where the continents might fit together?

Lesson 3: Climates

FIND THE WORDS

climate   North Atlantic Drift
tundra   continental   subarctic
humid continental   steppe
marine   humid subtropical
Mediterranean   tropical grassland
tropical rain forest   highlands

You have learned that an environment is made up of all the surroundings in a place. You have studied the major landforms and bodies of water of Earth. Another important part of an environment is climate. **Climate** is the kind of weather an area usually has over a long period of time. Think of climate as the pattern of the weather.

There are many kinds of climates on Earth. Since climates are not the same everywhere, there are great differences in weather from area to area. Look at the map on pages 28 and 29. It shows some of the major climates of our planet.

The climate of a region is partly the result of its location on Earth. The nearer an area is to one of the poles, the colder you might expect it to be. But the location of a region is not the only thing that determines its climate. There are other things that can make a climate less extreme. An area far north of where you live may be less cold than you might expect. Another area near the equator may be less hot than you might guess.

Look at the map again. Europe lies farther north than much of North America. So you might expect Europe to have a generally colder climate than North America. But the climate in some parts of Europe is warmer than you might think. A current of warm water in the Atlantic Ocean flows toward Europe. This current is called the **North Atlantic Drift.** It warms the coast of Western Europe. The Mediterranean Sea warms Southern Europe.

Being near a large body of water affects the climate of an area in other ways. Nearness to water affects the amount of rainfall. There may be more rain near water than farther inland. There are fewer very high or very low temperatures when land is close to water. This is because the temperature of water changes very slowly. A body of water stays warmer in winter and colder in summer than air does. As a result, it keeps the temperature on nearby land from changing as much as it otherwise might.

HIGH-LATITUDE CLIMATES

Climate	Winter	Summer	What is it like?
Ice cap	bitterly cold	cold	covered with permanent, thick ice
Tundra	bitterly cold, dry	cold, dry	always cold and dry; some hardy plants and animals

MID-LATITUDE CLIMATES

Climate	Winter	Summer	What is it like?
Mediterranean	mild, wet	warm, dry	a pleasant climate to live in
Humid subtropical	mild, wet	hot, wet	long summers and short winters
Marine	mild, wet	mild, wet	usually not too cold or too hot at any time of year
Continental	cold, wet	mild to hot, but wet	weather changes quickly; very hot in summer and cold in winter
Steppe (continental grasslands)	hot to cold, some rainfall	hot, some rainfall	weather changes quickly; enough rain for grasses to grow
Desert	hot to cold, but dry	hot and dry	not many plants grow except those that can store water

LOW-LATITUDE (TROPICAL) CLIMATES

Climate	Winter	Summer	What is it like?
Tropical grasslands (savanna)	hot, dry	hot, wet	always hot; covered with thick grasses and some trees
Rain forest	hot, wet	hot, wet	always hot with much rain; thickly covered with trees and smaller plants

Note: Highland areas have various local climates.

CLIMATES OF EARTH

ARCTIC CIRCLE

TROPIC OF CANCER

EQUATOR

ANTARCTIC CIRCLE

CLIMATES

Ice Cap: covered with permanent thick ice

Tundra: cold and dry all year

Continental: mild to hot wet summer, cold wet winter

Marine: mild wet summer, mild wet winter

Highlands: various local climates

Steppe: hot summer, hot to cold winter, variable rainfall

Desert: hot summer, hot to cold winter, dry all year

Humid Subtropical: hot wet summer, mild wet winter

Mediterranean: warm dry summer, mild wet winter

Tropical Grasslands: hot wet summer, hot dry winter

Rain Forest: hot and wet all year

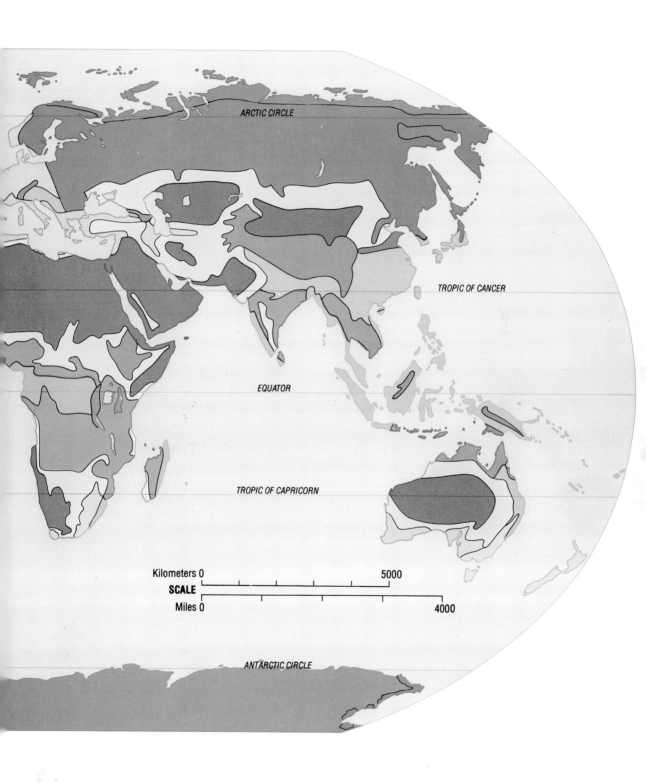

ARCTIC CIRCLE

TROPIC OF CANCER

EQUATOR

TROPIC OF CAPRICORN

Kilometers 0   5000
SCALE
Miles 0   4000

ANTARCTIC CIRCLE

29

The patterns of wind also affect climate. For example, winds can bring cold air from the North Pole down into the United States. Or winds may bring warm air up from the Gulf of Mexico.

Climate also depends on the elevation of the land. Highlands are cooler than lowlands. Suppose you are very near the equator. If the area is low, the climate may be very hot. But if you are high up on a mountain, the climate may be very cool. The tops of some mountains in the tropics are covered by snow. This happens because the air becomes thinner as you go up. Thin air holds less heat.

The climates of Earth have special names. Some of these names are taken from the names of certain regions. These regions have special kinds of weather, landforms, and natural plants.

The **tundra** is a treeless plain of the Arctic region around the North Pole. The tundra has cold, dry weather throughout the year. On the tundra, the ground is frozen most of the time.

Below the tundra is a large region with a **continental** climate. The more northerly parts of the continental area are sometimes said to have a **subarctic** climate. *Subarctic* means "below the arctic." In subarctic areas, it is cool or warm in summer. Winters there

are cold. Subarctic areas get more moisture than the tundra.

The more southerly parts of the continental area are sometimes said to have a **humid continental** climate. Summer there is mild to hot, with much rain. In winter, the weather is cold and wet.

The **steppes** (STEPS) are very large plains. They are also called continental grasslands. Steppes stretch from the European part of the Soviet Union into central Asia. Such areas have hot to cold winters and hot summers. There is some rain in both winter and summer.

In areas with a **marine** (muh REEN) climate, the weather is mild and wet all year. *Marine* means "of the sea." It is the ocean that keeps the weather from getting too hot or too cold. The ocean also supplies moisture that causes fog and rain. The Pacific Northwest of the United States has a marine climate.

North of the tropics is the **humid subtropical** climate area. *Subtropical* means "less than tropical." The weather there is not so hot as in the tropics. Winters are mild and wet. Summers are hot and wet. Much of the southern United States has a humid subtropical climate.

Areas with a **Mediterranean** climate have warm, dry summers and mild, wet winters. This kind of climate is named for the lands around the Mediterranean Sea, which have such a climate. In Italy and Spain, for example, the climate is Mediterranean.

You have learned that a desert is a very dry and sometimes sandy area. There is little rainfall in a desert. Winters there are hot to cold, and summers are always hot. Often, the temperature falls sharply at night and rises greatly during the day.

Two climate areas are common near the equator. **Tropical grasslands** are also called savannas. They are plains covered with thick grasses and some trees. The weather there is hot and dry in winter and hot and wet in summer. **Tropical rain forests** have hot, wet weather all year long. The ground there is thickly covered with trees and smaller plants.

Highlands are areas high above sea level. In them, the climate changes greatly from place to place. There is no set pattern.

Earth has many different kinds of environments. Some are easy to live in. Others create hardships for people. Every environment includes certain shapes of the land. Every environment also includes water resources. The third major part of an environment is the climate. This is the pattern of the weather.

REVIEW

WATCH YOUR WORDS

1. Italy and Spain have a____climate.
   marine   desert   Mediterranean

2. On the ____ , the ground is frozen most of the time.
   tundra   desert   steppes

3. The____are large plains.
   drifts   steppes   highlands

4. The____have no set climates.
   deserts   steppes   highlands

5. ____is the pattern of the weather.
   Climate   North Atlantic Drift   Mediterranean

CHECK YOUR FACTS

Look at the Map

6. What continents have areas of tundra?

7. Where is the world's largest desert area?

8. Where is the world's largest highland area?

Look at the Lesson

9. What is climate a part of?

10. The climate of Europe is (warmer/colder) than you might expect.

THINK ABOUT IT

What climate areas might be hard for people to live in? Give some reasons for each of your choices.

Lesson 4: Resources of Earth

FIND THE WORDS

resource   limited   petroleum

Resources are anything on Earth that people can use. Resources are all around us. We ourselves can be resources. People with skills, knowledge, or strength are resources. Resources can include soil, water, minerals, sunlight, or trees. Just about anything you can name that is useful in one way or another can be a resource. Think about the resources that you use or see each day. Include your home, your parents, the food you eat, and the clothes you wear. Include the school building in which you learn and the roads you travel on. Even this book you are reading is a resource!

Sometimes people say that resources are **limited.** This means that there is just so much of a thing. When that is gone, there will not be any more. This is only partly true. People make resources. They learn a new way to use a material. Or they find a way to use something that was not useful before. Before people knew how to use it, **petroleum,** or oil, was not considered a resource. It

Strip mining of coal is done on Earth's surface. Machines dig up the soil and rock that cover a coal deposit. Then other machines scoop out the coal. Coal is a limited resource. It can be used up. But strip-mined land can be saved if people put back the soil and plant grass and trees.

RESOURCES OF SOUTH AMERICA AND CENTRAL AMERICA

RESOURCES

- Sugar Cane
- Bananas
- Petroleum
- Coffee
- Beef Cattle
- Iron Ore
- Copper
- Cotton
- Cacao
- Corn
- Sheep
- Tin
- Wheat
- Silver

SCALE

Kilometers 0 — 1000

Miles 0 — 500 — 1000

Petroleum is found under the land and the oceans. This rig is used to drill an oil well in the ocean floor. Then pipes are used to bring the oil to the surface.

was thought of as black, sticky, bad-smelling stuff that seeped from the ground in some places. But people learned how to use it for energy. They learned to make plastics and cloth from it. It is true that the supply of petroleum will probably be used up someday. But people will probably find something else to meet the needs that petroleum fills today.

So when we talk about resources, we are talking about what is useful to people today. In the year 2000, we might be talking about something else. The map on page 33 shows some resources of South America. In the future, this resource map might look different. But the map shows some of the resources people need today. Notice that some parts of South America are rich in resources. Others are not.

REVIEW

WATCH YOUR WORDS

1. Anything people use is a_____.
   mineral   resource   petroleum
2. It is only partly true that resources are_____.
   useful   limitless   limited

CHECK YOUR FACTS

3. Can people themselves ever be a resource?

4. Was petroleum always considered a resource?
5. Are resources spread evenly over Earth?

THINK ABOUT IT

Imagine that the supply of petroleum is used up. What other sources of energy might people use in its place?

Lesson 5: Changes on Earth's Surface

FIND THE WORDS

**earthquake   lava   volcano
tidal wave   ring of fire   erode
sediment   glacier**

Imagine that you wake up suddenly during the night. Your bed, your room, your whole house are shaking violently. There is a loud roar. You jump out of bed. But you cannot stand up. The floor is moving up and down rapidly. Then your mother and father rush into your room. Together, you go to the front doorway. You hold onto the door frame for support. Outside, you hear a loud crash. A tree must have fallen.

"Earthquake!" you hear someone yell. Then the shaking stops. The ground is still again. You look around. Your whole neighborhood seems different.

Earthquakes

The surface of Earth is made up of huge blocks of rock that are balanced against each other. When one of these blocks moves even a little, this causes the surface of the land to move. This movement can be fast. It can be up and down or side to side. When there are build-ings on the moving land, they can be greatly damaged. People inside the buildings can be killed. These quick movements of Earth's surface are called **earthquakes.** Earthquakes occur in many parts of the world. Look at the map on page 36. It shows the parts of Earth where earthquakes are most likely to happen. It also shows where volcanoes are located. Earthquakes and volcanoes are often found in the same areas.

A powerful earthquake struck Alaska in 1964. You can see the kind of damage it did to the buildings and the street.

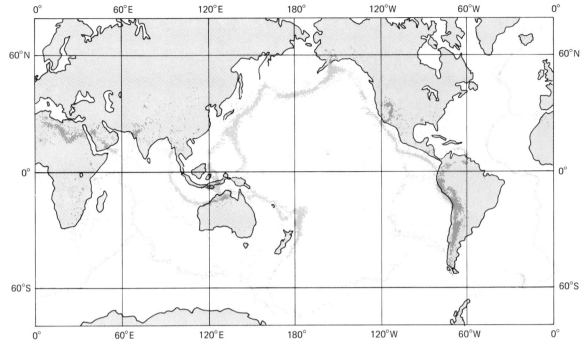

The colored dots on this map show where most earthquakes happen and volcanoes erupt. Find the ring of fire around the Pacific.

STRANGE FACTS

The place is San Francisco, California. The time is April 18, 1906. The event is an earthquake. It strikes at 5:13 A.M., while people are still sleeping. Streets begin to split apart. Buildings crumble. Electric wires fall down. Under the streets, the gas lines break. This causes fires to break out all over the city. But water pipes have burst, too. There is no water to put the fires out. They burn on for three days. In that time, many people lose their homes. Some lose their lives or lose their loved ones, for 700 people die.

The people of San Francisco rebuilt their city in less than 10 years. But people cannot control the forces in the Earth beneath their feet. An earth- quake can strike without warning. Some earthquakes have been predicted. But people still do not know how to prevent them.

Volcanoes

Deep within Earth is rock so hot that it has melted. This melted rock, called **lava** (LAHV uh), makes its way to the surface through cracks in the rock. It can shoot out of an opening in the earth called a **volcano**. Volcanoes can pour forth steam. They can cover the surrounding land with lava or ash. When this happens, we say the volcano *erupts*. Melted rock can build up around a volcano, forming a mountain. If the mountain is in the ocean, its top may form an island. In 1883, a volcano actually blew up an island in the East Indies! A huge wave, called a **tidal wave**, killed 36,000 people on islands nearby.

There are two big belts of volcanoes on Earth. One goes around the Pacific Ocean. It is called the **ring of fire.** The other goes across Asia, through the Mediterranean Sea, and into the Atlantic Ocean.

Water, Wind, and Ice

Running water **erodes**, or washes away, the land. Rain falls on the land and carries bits of soil away with it. As the rain collects into streams and then rivers, it carries more and more soil. This soil is called **sediment.** Rivers drop this sediment along their banks. They also drop it where they empty into the oceans. Thus, by washing away sediment and

In 1963, the island of Surtsey rose up out of the Atlantic Ocean near Iceland. It is the top of a volcano. You can see it erupting here.

A glacier is a river of ice with a bottom like sandpaper. As it moves, it grinds and polishes the rock beneath it. This glacier in Alaska has cut a path in the mountains.

37

dropping it elsewhere, water changes the shape of the land. Most of the changes on Earth's surface are caused by water.

Wind blows dust, soil, and sand across the surface of Earth. Mostly in dry areas, the wind can move fine sediment. This can change the shape of the land. But wind is not nearly as important as water in changing Earth's surface.

Ice can also change the shape of the land. High up in mountainous areas, huge, slowly moving masses of ice are sometimes found. These are called **glaciers** (GLAY shurz). Glaciers are formed when snow falls on an area but does not melt. At times in the past, Earth's climate cooled. Then huge glaciers formed on the continents. These huge masses of ice ground down the land as they moved. They dug out large basins. The Great Lakes in North America were formed this way. If you live in an area once covered by a glacier, you might find rounded rocks with smooth surfaces. These were ground down by glaciers.

The land is changed by people, too. They mine it for minerals. They level it for buildings. They build dams to store water. Farmers plow and terrace the earth. But so far, water, wind, and ice have made most changes in the land. They change Earth slowly.

REVIEW

WATCH YOUR WORDS

1. Rivers drop____along their banks.
   lava   sediment   glaciers

2. Great, slowly moving masses of ice are____.
   tidal waves   volcanoes   glaciers

3. ____comes from volcanoes.
   Lava   Sediment   Glacier

4. Quick movements of Earth's surface are called____.
   tidal waves   glaciers   earthquakes

5. ____ sometimes erupt and shoot out lava or ash.
   Tidal waves   Volcanoes
   Earthquakes

CHECK YOUR FACTS

Look at the Map

6. Where in the United States are earthquakes and volcanoes most likely to occur?

7. What parts of Earth are mostly free of earthquakes and volcanoes?

Look at the Lesson

8. Where are the two big belts of volcanoes?

9. What causes most changes on Earth's surface?

10. How were the Great Lakes formed?

TRY SOMETHING NEW

Write a report on earthquakes or volcanoes. Use an encyclopedia or other source suggested by your teacher.

CHAPTER REVIEW

WATCH YOUR WORDS

1. Earth turns on its ____. It also moves around the sun in an____.
   equator   orbit   axis   equinox

2. The day or night is longest at the ____. Day and night are equal at the____.
   seasons   tropics   solstices
   equinoxes

3. The ____ lies between the tropic of Cancer and the tropic of Capricorn.
   tropic zone   temperate zone
   polar zone

4. The height of land above the oceans is its____.
   sea level   mountain   elevation

5. A ____ is an area with an independent government.
   landform   nation   continent

6. The ground is often frozen in the ____.
   steppes   desert   tundra

7. The ____ is weather over a long period of time.
   climate   environment   landform

8. ____ are anything people can use.
   Sediments   Resources   Landforms

9. Water ____ the land.
   orbits   elevates   erodes

10. A ____ can grind down the land.
    glacier   earthquake   volcano

CHECK YOUR FACTS

11. How many planets are there in our solar system?

12. Name the two hemispheres separated by the equator.

13. How many continents does Earth have? Name them.

14. Name the four oceans.

15. What is the difference between plateaus and plains?

16. What ocean current warms Europe?

17. In a marine climate, the weather is (dry/wet) all year.

18. Petroleum (was/was not) always considered a resource.

19. Name two things that change Earth's surface quickly.

20. Name three things that change Earth's surface slowly.

USE YOUR MAPS

21. Look at the map of the world on pages 10 and 11. On what three oceans does the United States border?

22. What ocean does *not* touch the United States?

23. Look at the climate map on pages 28 and 29. What is another name for steppes?

24. Look at the natural resources map on page 33. In what parts of South America is petroleum found?

25. Look at the map on page 36. In what ocean do the most earthquakes and volcanoes occur?

THINK ABOUT IT

26. The moon always turns the same face toward Earth. Suppose the same side of Earth was always turned toward the sun. What effect might this have on the climate?

27. Suppose you lived at the equator. Would you be concerned about the seasons? Why, or why not?

28. What kind of landform do you live on? What kind would you most like to live on? Tell why.

29. What kind of climate does your area have? What kind do you think you might like best?

30. Are there any volcanoes that you know of in your area? To your knowledge, has your area had an earthquake recently?

2 ALL ABOUT MAPS

Lesson 1: Earth and the Globe

FIND THE WORDS

globe   intersection   meridian
line of longitude   parallel
line of latitude   grid   degree
circumference
degree of longitude
prime meridian
degree of latitude

A **globe** is a model of Earth as the planet really is. Like Earth itself, a globe is shaped like a sphere. You already know that *sphere* means "round ball." On the surface of a globe is a drawing of Earth's surface. This drawing shows you where all the land and water on Earth are located. With a globe, you can learn many other things about Earth as well.

Look at the picture below. It shows a globe divided into hemispheres. You already know that a hemisphere is half of a sphere. Since a globe is a sphere, a hemisphere is also half of a globe. A hemisphere on a globe stands for half of the surface of Earth.

In the last chapter, you learned about the equator. This imaginary line runs east and west around the middle of Earth. It divides Earth into two hemispheres. These are, as you probably remember, the Northern Hemisphere and the Southern Hemisphere. But there is another way to divide Earth. Suppose that a line runs north and south around Earth through the North Pole and the South Pole. This imaginary line also divides Earth into two hemispheres. These are the Eastern Hemisphere and the Western Hemisphere.

At the equator, Earth can be divided into the Northern Hemisphere and the Southern Hemisphere. Along a meridian, Earth can be divided into the Eastern Hemisphere and the Western Hemisphere.

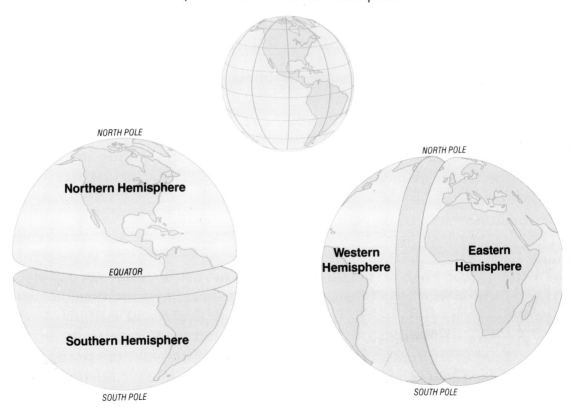

NORTH POLE

Northern Hemisphere

EQUATOR

Southern Hemisphere

SOUTH POLE

NORTH POLE

Western Hemisphere

Eastern Hemisphere

SOUTH POLE

Think about what it means to divide Earth twice this way. Every part of Earth is in two of the four hemispheres. A place is in either the Northern Hemisphere or the Southern Hemisphere. The same place is also in either the Eastern Hemisphere or the Western Hemisphere.

Look at a globe. The top and bottom of a globe have markings showing where the North Pole and the South Pole are. Note that there are also lines running in different directions. Some run from north to south. They stretch from the North Pole at the top of the globe to the South Pole at the bottom. Other lines run from east to west across a globe. They run in the same direction as the equator.

These imaginary lines are drawn to help you find places on a globe. Every place on Earth is at or near a point where two of these lines cross each other. The point where the two lines meet is called an **intersection.**

The lines that run north and south from pole to pole are **meridians** (muh RID ee unz). Meridians are also called **lines of longitude.** The lines that run east and west, in the same direction as the equator, are **parallels.** Parallels are also called **lines of latitude.** The parallels and meridians cross to form a grid that covers the whole globe.

A **grid** is a pattern of lines. If you know how to use this grid, you can find any place on Earth.

Each of the meridians and parallels has a number. This number is so many degrees. A **degree** is the unit into which the circumference (sur KUM fur uns) of a circle is divided. The **circumference** of a circle is its outside edge. Every circle is divided into 360 degrees. The symbol for a degree is °.

The numbers on the meridians measure **degrees of longitude.** These are degrees east or west of the **prime meridian.** This line, zero degrees (0°) longitude, passes through Greenwich (GREN ich), England. The numbers east of the prime meridian are called degrees east longitude. The numbers west of the prime meridian are called degrees west longitude.

Look at the map on pages 10 and 11. It is a flat world map with the parallels and meridians shown. Find the prime meridian. Now find the line that shows 15° west longitude. It passes through Iceland. The line 15° east longitude passes through several nations in Africa. Name them.

The numbers on the parallels measure **degrees of latitude.** These are degrees north or south of the equator. The equator, itself, is at zero degrees (0°) latitude. The numbers north of the equator are called degrees north latitude. The North Pole is at 90° north latitude. Degrees south of the equator are called degrees south latitude. The South Pole is at 90° south latitude.

Look at the map on pages 10 and 11 again. In Europe, the line 40° north latitude passes through Portugal, Spain, Italy, and Greece. Find 70° north latitude. It passes through Norway and the Soviet Union. Most of Europe lies be-tween these two latitudes.

On pages 8 and 9, find the city of Moscow in the Soviet Union. Notice that it is about midway be-tween the lines 50° and 60° north latitude. It is actually at about 56° north latitude. Notice that it is also close to the line 45° east lon-gitude. It is actually at about 38° east longitude. Moscow can be said to be located at 56° north lat-itude and 38° east longitude.

REVIEW

WATCH YOUR WORDS

1. Meridians are also____.
   lines of latitude   parallels
   lines of longitude

2. Parallels are also____.
   lines of latitude   meridians
   lines of longitude

3. The____is at zero ° longitude.
   equator   circumference
   prime meridian

4. The circumference of a circle is divided into 360____.
   degrees   meridians   parallels

5. The equator is at zero____.
   meridian   ° latitude   ° longitude

CHECK YOUR FACTS

Look at the Maps (pages 8–9, 10–11)

6. What two continents are in both the Northern Hemisphere and Southern Hemisphere?

7. What continent is in both the Eastern Hemisphere and Western Hemisphere?

8. What European city is located very near 50° north latitude, 0° east longitude?

Look at the Lesson

9. What important line passes through Greenwich, England?

10. At what degree of latitude is the South Pole located?

THINK ABOUT IT

Look at a globe. What happens to the distances between the lines of longi-tude as they near the poles? What hap-pens to the lengths of the lines of latitude as they near the poles?

Lesson 2: What Are Maps?

FIND THE WORDS

detail   map   dimension
two-dimensional
three-dimensional
distorted   projection
cylindrical projection
Mercator projection
interrupted projection
homolosine projection
conic projection

A globe is a true model of Earth. But a globe cannot fit into a book. It would not be easy to carry a globe around with you. A globe would not be helpful if you wanted to give someone directions to a place near your home. A globe does not show the **details,** or small parts. For these reasons, people use maps.

A **map** is a drawing that shows all of Earth or a part of it. A globe, like the Earth, is round. A map, however, is flat. Thus, it is not as accurate as a globe.

A map is like this page you are reading. Both have flat surfaces. The map and the page can show only two **dimensions,** or sizes. One of these is length. Length is the distance from the top of the page to the bottom. The other is width. Width is the distance from one side of the page to the other. Flat surfaces are **two-dimensional.**

Now close the book and look at it. You can see that it has a third dimension. It has height or depth. Height is the thickness of the book. The book is **three-dimensional.** Earth and a globe are both three-dimensional. There is no problem showing the round Earth on the round globe. But showing part of the round surface of Earth on the flat surface of a map is difficult. What is shown on the map will not be exactly what is on Earth. It will not be as accurate as what can be shown on a globe. There is no way to show a rounded surface accurately on a flat surface.

If a map shows just a small part of Earth's surface, it does not change the shape too much. Look at the drawings of Iceland and Greenland on page 45. They show what happens when small and large parts of Earth's surface are flattened. When a large section like Greenland is flattened, its shape and size are **distorted.** That means they are not accurate.

Showing the rounded surface of Earth on the flat surface of a map is called **projection.** There are many kinds of projections. Each is

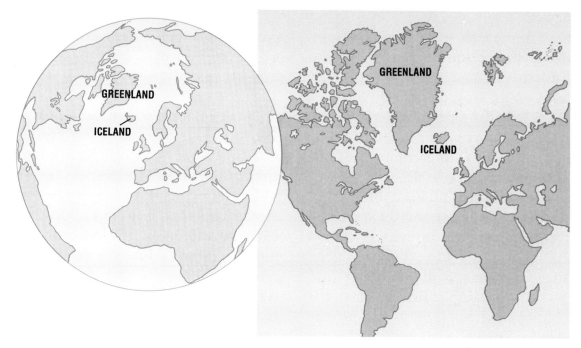

Iceland is small. Its size and shape look much the same on a globe and on a map. But Greenland is a much larger section of Earth's surface. Its size and shape are distorted when it is flattened out.

A conic projection is good for showing parts of Earth that are at or near the same latitude. Most of the United States lies between 30° and 50° north latitude.

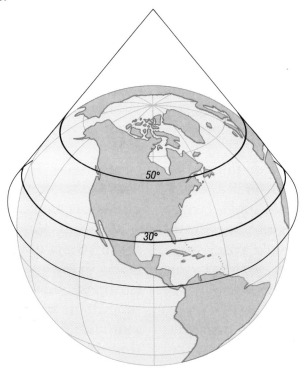

an attempt to solve one problem. Some projections make it easy to find directions. Some distort the land areas. Some distort the water areas. And some leave off some parts so that other parts can be accurate. Two different projections are shown on page 47.

One important kind of projection is **cylindrical** (suh LIN dri kul) **projection.** It can be understood in the following way. Take a large sheet of paper. Roll the paper into a cylinder. A cylinder has the shape of a tin can without the ends. Put the paper cylinder around the globe. The cylinder should touch the globe at the equator. Suppose you had a clear globe and put a light at its center. The light would project the markings on the globe's surface onto the paper. This projection would be very accurate where the globe and paper touch at the equator. It would be very inaccurate at the poles.

Mercator (mur KAY tur) **projection** is one kind of cylindrical projection. Look at the drawing of the Mercator projection on page 47. Notice that Greenland looks larger than South America. Yet, South America is actually ten times bigger than Greenland. A Mercator projection is good for showing direction, though.

On a Mercator map, the meridians, or lines of longitude, and the parallels, or lines of latitude, are all straight lines. The meridians are all parallel to one another. That means they are equally far apart along their whole lengths. The distance between each meridian and the next one is always the same, too. The parallels are also all parallel to one another. However, the distance between each parallel and the next one is not the same. When the meridians and parallels cross, they form right angles (90°). A Mercator map is not good for measuring distances or sizes, except near the equator.

Another kind of projection is **interrupted projection.** *Interrupted* means "not continuous." A map with interrupted projection does not show continuous outlines for all areas of Earth. Look at the second map on page 47. It is a kind of interrupted projection called **homolosine** (hoh MOL uh SYN) **projection.** The map outline is interrupted over certain ocean areas. This means that parts of the oceans were left out. But the land areas, the continents, are shown almost as they look on a globe.

Another kind of projection is **conic** (KON ik) **projection.** It is made like a cylindrical projection. However, instead of a cylinder, a cone is used. A cone is shaped like a funnel. A map with conic projection is very accurate where the

MERCATOR PROJECTION

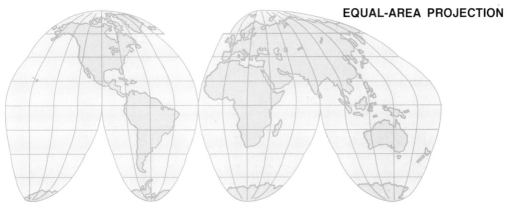

On a Mercator projection, lines of longitude do not meet at the poles. They remain parallel. Near the poles, extra land and water are added.

EQUAL-AREA PROJECTION

A homolosine projection is a kind of equal-area map. It leaves out parts of the oceans to make the land areas more nearly right.

cone touches the globe. A conic projection is shown on page 45.

There are three things you should remember while looking at a map. Some parts of the map will be accurate pictures of Earth, just as a globe is. Some parts of the map are larger than they should be. Some parts are smaller than they should be. Compare the different map projections.

We use latitude and longitude to find places on a map. Look at the map of the United States on pages 12 and 13. Find your own state. What are the latitude and longitude of your state's capital city? Compare the map and a globe. Does the map give an accurate picture? Or does it seem to be distorted?

We use maps because they are easier to handle than globes. Maps also give us pictures of small areas that cannot be shown on a globe. But always remember that the round Earth becomes distorted when it is made flat on a map.

Maps of the world did not always show Earth as we know it. To many early mapmakers, the world was limited to lands around the Mediterranean Sea. Their known world included only three continents: Europe, Asia, and Africa.

Until the 1500s, many people believed that Earth was flat. Past a certain point in the ocean, they thought they would sail off the edge of the world. They also believed that sea monsters lurked in the deep, waiting to swallow up their ships.

This early Dutch map was drawn around 1570. By then, Europeans had discovered the Western Hemisphere. But North and South America are strangely shaped. In 1570, these continents had not been fully explored. They could not yet be photographed from space. But at least, they were there on the map—sea monsters and all!

REVIEW

WATCH YOUR WORDS

1. A map is ___.
   two-dimensional
   three-dimensional   homolosine

2. A Mercator projection is ___.
   three-dimensional   cylindrical
   conic

3. A homolosine projection is ___.
   cylindrical   conic   interrupted

4. ___ is a way of showing the round Earth on a flat map.
   Dimension   Projection   Detail

5. A globe is ___.
   cylindrical   two-dimensional
   three-dimensional

CHECK YOUR FACTS

6. List two reasons why a globe is not always useful.

7. Why is a map less accurate than a globe?

8. Name three kinds of projection.

9. In a Mercator projection, the distance between each parallel and the next one (is/is not) the same.

10. What is often left out in an interrupted projection?

THINK ABOUT IT

What shape would Earth have to have for maps to be accurate?

Lesson 3: More about Maps

Three important sources of information on a map are the key, the direction arrow or compass, and the scale.

Suppose you want to study a certain city. One way would be to look at a photograph of the city taken from an airplane. Such a view from the air is called an aerial photograph. One is shown on page 50. Now look at the map on page 51. The map shows the things in the photograph. But the map shows those things in a different way.

The markings on the map are symbols. **Symbols** are signs that stand for things. The symbols on the map stand for the buildings and roads in the photo. Match places in the photograph with the symbols on the map.

A map **key** tells what each symbol on the map stands for. Find the key on the map of the city. Then find the symbol for schools. Locate the schools on the map. Follow the same steps to find the hospitals.

Maps also help you find directions. To learn the directions, find the **direction arrow** on the map.

There will almost always be at least one arrow marked "north" or "N." This arrow points to the North Pole. Sometimes, the map will have four crossed arrows. These arrows point in the directions of north, south, east, and west. Sometimes, the arrows show directions between the four main ones. For example, NE, for northeast, would be midway between north (N) and east (E). A group of direction arrows is a **compass**.

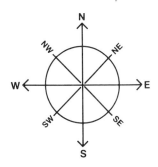

Another important symbol on a map is its scale. Every map is much smaller than the area it shows. So, to be shown on a map, a large area has to be drawn quite small. We say that the area is drawn to scale. The **scale** is marked on the map. It shows how much a certain distance on the map equals in real distance on Earth. By using a ruler, you can measure the distance on the map in centimeters or inches. You can then use the scale to change the

map distance into the real distance in kilometers or miles.

You can use maps in many ways—if you can read them. You can find and give directions. You can locate places and measure distances. You can understand the symbols used on the maps. You will look at maps many times in the years ahead. That is why it is important to learn now how to understand what maps tell you.

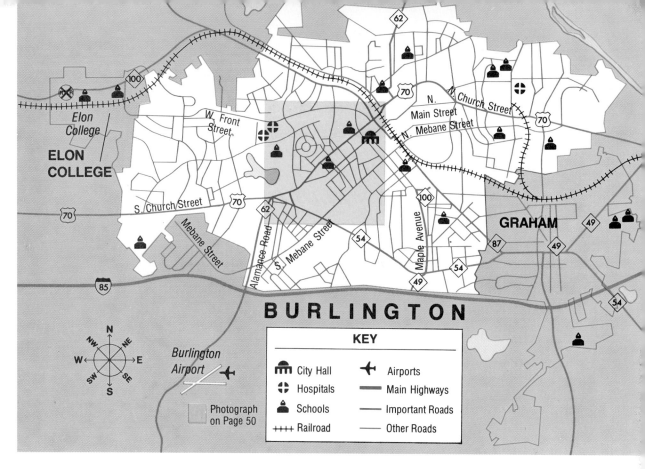

KEY

🏛 City Hall   ✈ Airports

✚ Hospitals   ▬ Main Highways

🔺 Schools   — Important Roads

+++ Railroad   — Other Roads

Burlington Airport ✈

Photograph on Page 50

REVIEW

WATCH YOUR WORDS

1. The ____ shows how much real distance a map distance stands for.
   symbol   compass   scale

2. The ____ points north.
   direction arrow   key   scale

3. Many direction arrows make a ____ .
   symbol   compass   key

4. The signs on a map that stand for things are ____ .
   keys   scales   symbols

5. The ____ tells what the symbols stand for.
   key   scale   compass

CHECK YOUR FACTS

6. List some symbols that might be found on a city map.

7. How can you find out what symbols on a map mean?

8. How can you find directions on a map?

9. What does SW on a compass stand for?

10. How can you read distances on a map?

THINK ABOUT IT

Suppose a map does not have a direction arrow or compass. How can you guess which way is north?

Lesson 4: Maps as Tools

FIND THE WORDS

**distribution map   political map
border   boundary   capital
physical map   street map
road map   highway map**

Maps are tools. They can be used in many ways. They can give you many different kinds of information. A street map can help you find your way to a place you want to visit. A highway map shows you the direction and distance from one city to another.

Some maps can show the amount of certain things in different places. For example, a map can show the amount of rain that falls in a year in different parts of a nation. A map may show where wheat grows in different parts of a continent. Such maps are called **distribution maps.** *Distribution* means "dividing into parts or shares." So a distribution map shows where things are divided and scattered in a given area or over the whole Earth.

Look at the map of resources of Central and South America on page 33. This map is a distribution map. The map on pages 28 and 29 shows the world's climates. Look at the map on pages 56 and 57. It shows the number of people per square kilometer or mile on Earth. These, too, are kinds of distribution maps. Distribution maps are very valuable. From such maps, you can get much information. And the information you get will be easier to understand than long lists of facts and figures.

A **political map** shows the nations of the world. It can also show parts of nations, such as states. Such a map shows the borders of nations or of their parts. A **border** is a line that divides one nation or part of a nation from another. A border is also called a **boundary.**

A political map can show borders in several ways. It can show lines for borders. It can show nations or their parts in different colors. Or it can do both.

A political map also usually shows cities and towns. These include **capital** cities, where the center of government for a nation or state is located. Capitals are often marked with stars.

A **physical map** shows what the surface of Earth or parts of it are like. It can show mountains, valleys, and plains. A physical map can have different colors for land of different heights. For example, lowlands might be shown in green, highlands in brown.

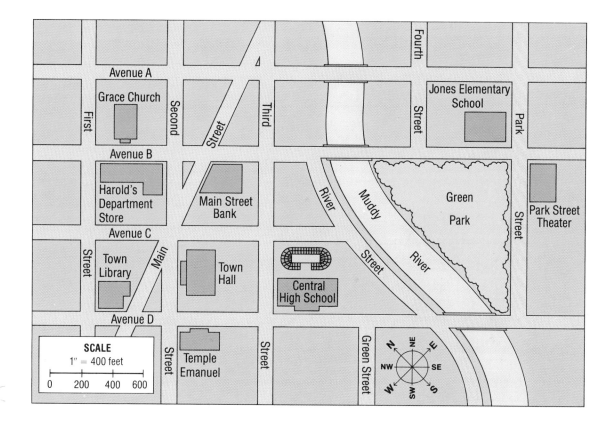

If you want to know where a particular nation is located, you use a political map. A physical map shows what the surface of a given nation is like. Many maps give both political and physical information. Look at the map of India on page 290. Find the capital city. Find the Himalayas.

Street maps are used often by most of us. A **street map** shows the highways, roads, and streets of a small area. It also often shows other large things, such as parks and big buildings. A street map may be a simple sketch, like the one on this page. Such a map

might help you find a friend's house. A street map may have many details. Such a map might help you find the athletic stadium in a city you visit. A street map tells you where the place you want to find is located. It tells you in what direction you must go to find it. It tells you how far you must travel to reach it.

When you begin to drive an automobile, you will use **road maps.** These are also called **highway maps.** Such a map tells you the distance to a place you want to visit. The map helps you find the best route to travel. Look at the

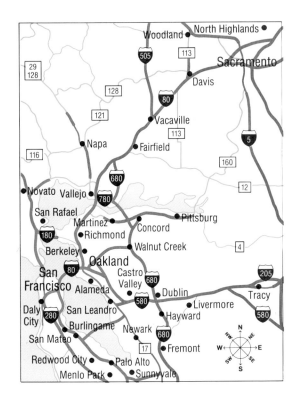

road map on the left. Trace the best route from Sacramento to San Francisco. Road maps give other valuable information. They show where large parks and other interesting areas are located. They may list bridge crossings and tolls.

Some maps make it easier to understand history. There are maps that show where great battles were fought. Other maps show the borders of nations in the past.

Maps are tools. Information of all kinds is shown on maps. Both when you are in school and when you are working, maps can help you solve problems.

REVIEW

WATCH YOUR WORDS

1. Highway maps are the same as _____ .
   distribution maps   street maps
   road maps

2. A _____ city is where the center of the government is located.
   political   capital   distribution

3. A _____ map shows borders.
   physical   political   distribution

4. A _____ map shows what Earth's surface is like.
   physical   political   capital

5. A _____ map shows the amount of something in different places.
   physical   political   distribution

CHECK YOUR FACTS
Look at the Maps (See pages 10–11, 33, and 54)

6. What nations border on the United States?

7. Is cotton grown in eastern or western South America?

8. Suppose you were making a trip from San Francisco to Sacramento. In what direction would you travel?

Look at the Lesson

9. What kind of map shows climates?

10. What three things does a street map tell you about the place you want to find?

THINK ABOUT IT

Physical maps can show many details of Earth's surface in addition to those listed in the lesson. What other kinds of details can you think of?

CHAPTER REVIEW

WATCH YOUR WORDS

1. Lines of longitude are ____ . Lines of latitude are ____ .

   degrees   meridians   parallels   intersections

2. A map is ____ . A globe is ____ .

   interrupted   homolosine   two-dimensional   three-dimensional

3. A ____ is made up of several direction arrows.

   key   scale   compass

4. A ____ map shows what Earth's surface is like. A ____ map shows borders and cities.

   distribution   political   capital   physical

5. The center of government is in the ____ city.

   capital   political   distribution

CHECK YOUR FACTS

6. Name Earth's four hemispheres.

7. What is the number of a parallel or meridian called?

8. From what line are meridians measured? From what line are parallels measured?

9. Why is a globe more accurate than a map?

10. What kind of projection is a Mercator map?

11. What is special about a homolosine projection?

12. How can you find out what the symbols on a map mean?

13. How can you tell what map distance equals in real distance?

14. What kind of map shows where natural resources are located?

15. How can you tell whether a city is a capital?

CLOSE THE MAP GAP

16. Draw a globe. Show the location of the following: North Pole, South Pole, equator, Northern Hemisphere, Southern Hemisphere

17. Draw a globe. Put the equator and the prime meridian on it. Show some lines of latitude and longitude.

18. Draw a map that shows how the lines of longitude and latitude run in a Mercator projection.

19. Draw a map of an imaginary city. Show some main streets, a few parks, some major buildings, an airport, and a railroad. Label all these things. Use symbols and a key. Include a direction arrow and a scale.

20. Draw a map of an imaginary continent, Atlantis, with one nation. Show that it borders on the Atlantic Ocean. Add its capital, Atlanta. Show some other cities. Show some rivers, lakes, mountains, and a desert. Label all the different things you show. Also include a key, a scale, and a compass.

THINK ABOUT IT

21. If a circle has 360 degrees, why then are there only up to 90 degrees of latitude and up to 180 degrees of longitude?

22. At what three places on Earth could you stand in three hemispheres at once?

23. Suppose Earth were flat, as people once believed. How would this affect the accuracy of maps?

24. Why do you think a conic projection is more accurate than a cylindrical projection?

25. If a river's course changes, many maps may have to be changed. What other kinds of changes can you think of that would affect maps?

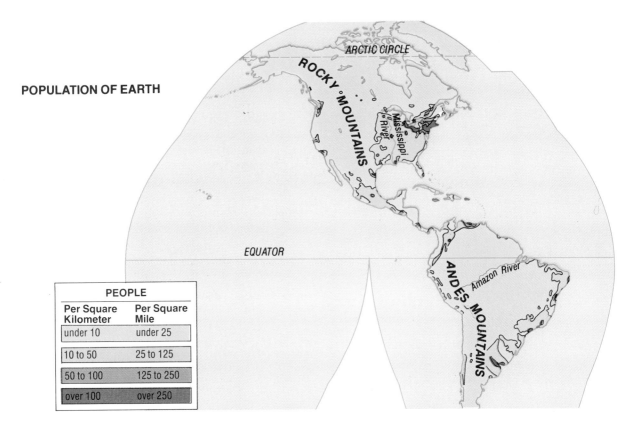

POPULATION OF EARTH

PEOPLE	
Per Square Kilometer	Per Square Mile
under 10	under 25
10 to 50	25 to 125
50 to 100	125 to 250
over 100	over 250

CHAPTER 3 PEOPLE AND EARTH

Lesson 1: Where People Live

FIND THE WORDS

population   irrigation

On pages 56 and 57, you see a very important and useful kind of distribution map. It is a population map of Earth. The **population** is the number of people in an area. A population map shows you where people live. You can see there are large numbers of people in certain places on Earth. In other places, there are few people. Notice that in the far north of North America and Europe, there are not many people. Yet in Western Europe, India, and parts of

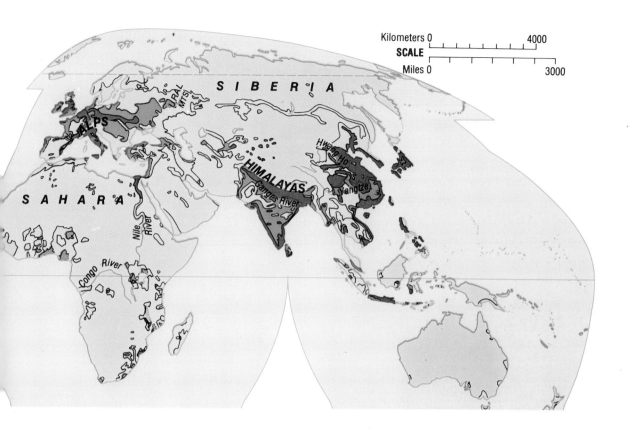

Kilometers 0   4000
SCALE
Miles 0   3000

SIBERIA
URAL MTS.
ALPS
HIMALAYAS
Hwang Ho
Yangtze
Ganges River
SAHARA
Nile River
Congo River

China, there are huge numbers of people. Notice that, according to the map key, the map shows persons per square kilometer and square mile. This does not mean that people are scattered evenly over the land. It means that this is an average.

But why are people so unevenly spread over Earth? Why do they crowd together on only a small part of Earth's surface? There are many reasons.

To find some answers, let's look at each place where few people live. Look at North Africa. Few people live in much of that area because much of the land there is desert. The weather is hot and dry. Little or no rain falls. There is no way for large numbers of people to live. They cannot grow food or build large cities because these things depend on water. There are also deserts on the Arabian Peninsula and in central Asia, the western United States, and central Australia. These, too, are areas with few people. Check the climate map on pages 28 and 29. Can you find any deserts where many people live?

Some parts of Earth are too cold for people. The land is not useful. It may be frozen part of the year. Look at the climate map again. Few people live in the Arctic. No one lives in Antarctica. A few scientists work there.

Some parts of Earth are hot and wet. The land is thickly covered with trees and other plants. The soils are poor. These are tropical rain forests. Find the Amazon River valley in South America. Find the Congo River valley in central Africa. People find the hot and wet weather in tropical rain forests uncomfortable. It is difficult to grow crops in the poor soils. Large numbers of people cannot live in these areas.

Notice also that large numbers of people do not live in the mountain areas of Earth. Look at the population map again. Notice that few people live in the mountains of Asia, North America, or Europe. People find it difficult to live in the mountains because the land is steep. Only in the valleys or on the high plateaus of mountain areas can people make a living.

So large areas of Earth are not useful to people. People tend to live on the plains or in hilly areas. They tend to live in wide river valleys. There, the land is usually fertile. Large amounts of food can be grown. Look at the map on pages 8 and 9. There are plains in Western Europe, in northern and eastern India, and in eastern China. Notice that these are all areas with a great many people.

In time, people may discover ways to bring water to all the deserts. Supplying water to land is called **irrigation.** People may be able to learn to live in colder areas or to make more use of them. But until then, people will remain crowded on a small part of Earth's surface.

REVIEW

WATCH YOUR WORDS

1. A map that shows where people live is a(n)____map.
   irrigation   tropical   population

2. Supplying water to land that needs it is called____.
   population   irrigation   elevation

CHECK YOUR FACTS

3. People (are/are not) spread evenly over Earth.

4. Name four kinds of places where few people live.

THINK ABOUT IT

Besides Antarctica, on what huge areas of Earth's surface do no people live?

Lesson 2: People and Culture

All over Earth, people have the same basic needs. They need air, water, food, clothing, and shelter. They need these things just to stay alive. People also need a place where they can feel safe and have the company of other people. How we fill our needs is part of the way we live.

All over Earth, people fill their needs in different ways. They eat different kinds of food. They dress in different ways. They build different kinds of homes. They live in different kinds of groups.

In this book, we will be studying people and the ways they live. When we study the ways people live, we are studying their culture. A **culture** is all the things that make up a group's way of living. There are four main parts of culture. They are a group's beliefs, tools and skills, organization, and communication.

Beliefs

Beliefs are all the things a group of people thinks are right or wrong, good or bad. A group's religion is included among its beliefs. So also are its ideas about how people should live and act toward one another. Beliefs can include ideas about government. They can also include the ways goods and services are produced and divided up among people.

For example, people in a Communist nation may believe that religion is not important. They may feel that the government should own all the businesses. They may believe that the government should run everything and tell people what to do or what not to do. But people in a nation like the United States may have entirely different beliefs. They may believe that religion is very important. They may feel that individuals should run the government and own all businesses. They may believe that people should do as they please as long as they do not harm others or break laws.

Tools and Skills

All over Earth, people use tools. A **tool** is an object that helps people do work. In one place, people might farm with a simple wood plow pulled by an ox. In another, they might farm with steel tractors and plows.

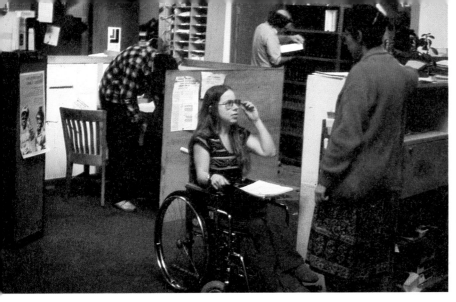

Tools help people make better use of their skills. Using good tools, people can work faster and get more done. Special kinds of tools help people overcome handicaps. A wheelchair is such a tool. It takes skill to operate one.

Whenever people use tools, they are showing skills. A **skill** is the knowledge of how to do something well. In particular, the cities of Earth have many people with tools and the skills to use them.

Organization

All cultures in the world have many different kinds of groups of people. **Organization** refers to the ways groups are gathered and run. Organized groups come in many sizes. A **family** is a group of people related by blood or marriage. Families are small, but they are very important in a culture. In the next lesson, you will study nations. These can be very large organized groups.

Organized groups, no matter what their size, have some things in common. They have rules that apply to the members of the group. They have leaders who make and enforce these rules. They have ways of teaching the rules to new members.

Take religion, for example. You have read that religion is a set of beliefs. These include beliefs about a god or gods. They include beliefs about the ways the god or gods should be worshiped or served. But a religion is more than this. It is also an organized group. In addition to beliefs, a religious group has rules. A religious group also has leaders. These might include bishops, priests, ministers, or rabbis. Religious groups also have ways of teaching their beliefs and rules to new members. A **religion** is an organized group of people with common beliefs about a god or gods.

Teaching the rules to new members is important in all groups. This is called **education.** Through education, a group makes sure that it will live on after the older members die. However, education involves much more than teaching rules. It usually means passing on everything known to a group. In particular, this includes teaching new members how to do things.

Education might be very simple. It might just mean that older people teach the young how to hunt, fish, farm, cook, or sew. Education might also be very complicated. Young people often spend years in large schools with many teachers and books.

Communication

Communication involves passing information from one person to another. Communication can take many forms. It can include the way you look at someone or how you move your hands. Spoken words are the most common form of communication. Words and the ways they are used make up a **language.** Speech can be communicated through telephones, radio, television, and movies. Words can also be changed into symbols, or signs, and written down. The alphabet of letters you learned to

A newspaper or magazine is a medium of communication. These journals give news about Nigeria.

read and write when you started school is a set of symbols. Numbers are also symbols. Written symbols can be found on signs and posters and in books, magazines, and newspapers.

People of the same culture all use the same language. They use language to pass on beliefs and knowledge about tools and skills. Rules are stated in language, and leaders use language to enforce them. Language holds a culture together and allows it to live on. Without communication, no culture or other organized group could exist. So studying how people communicate will tell us much about them.

As we study people in different parts of Earth, we should always ask ourselves these four groups of questions:

1. What do these people believe?
2. What tools do these people use? What skills do they have?
3. How are these people organized? What kind of government do they have? What kind of religion do they have? How do they produce and divide up goods and services?
4. How do these people communicate with each other? What kind of literature do they have? What kinds of arts do they have?

REVIEW

WATCH YOUR WORDS

1. ___ is teaching knowledge and rules to new members of a group.
   Religion   Culture   Education
2. An organized group with common beliefs about a god or gods is a ___ .
   religion   culture   family
3. ___ is made up of words and the ways they are used.
   Communication   Culture   Language
4. A(n) ___ is an object that helps people do work.
   tool   skill   organization
5. A ___ is the knowledge of how to do something well.
   tool   skill   belief

CHECK YOUR FACTS

6. People fill their needs in (the same/ different) ways.
7. What are the four main parts of culture?
8. What three things do all organized groups have in common?
9. Why is education important in groups?
10. An organized group (could/could not) exist without communication.

THINK ABOUT IT

It has been said that it is their tools and language that make people human. Do you think this is true? Why, or why not?

Lesson 3:   Nations of Earth

FIND THE WORDS

territory   citizen   government
democracy   communism
socialism   military   monarchy
sovereignty

Almost 150 nations occupy the land of Earth. They range in size from the Soviet Union to Vatican City. The Soviet Union stretches thousands of miles across the continents of Europe and Asia. Vatican City covers only a few blocks in Rome, Italy. Some countries have only a few thousand people. Others, like China, have hundreds of millions. But no matter what their size, Earth's nations all have several things in common. These are territory, population, government, and sovereignty. Each of these is discussed below.

Territory

Each nation on Earth occupies a particular land area, or **territory.** Whether it is large or small, that nation claims a certain space for itself. Look at a map of Earth on pages 10 and 11. You will see borders marking off the land of each nation. But do not think that national borders do not change. For example, look at the map on page 64. It shows the nations of Europe as they were before World War I. The names and borders of several European nations have changed between 1914 and now.

Population

In addition to territory, each nation has a population. Each nation claims that the people who live within its borders are its citizens. A **citizen** is a person who is a member of a particular nation.

In some nations, almost all the people may belong to one culture group. They may speak the same language and have similar beliefs. They may eat the same foods and dress in the same ways. In other nations, the people may belong to very different culture groups. Even within the same nation, people may speak different languages. They may eat different foods and dress in different ways. They may even look very different.

Government

Every nation on Earth has a government of one kind or another. **Governments** are made up of people who make the laws and rules for a nation. In each nation, governments allow the people a certain amount of freedom. Some governments allow the people more freedom than others do.

EUROPE BEFORE WORLD WAR I

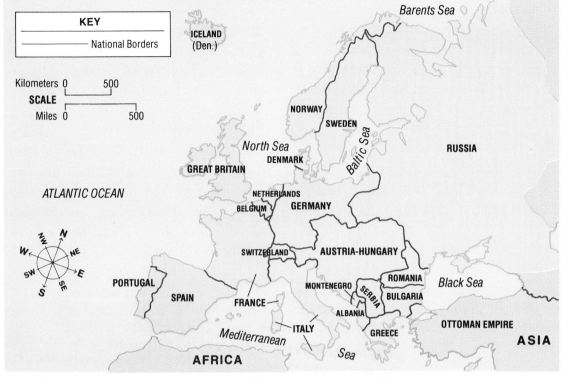

Before World War I, some nations had different names and different amounts of territory. Poland, Czechoslovakia, and Yugoslavia did not yet exist. Austria-Hungary included parts of Poland, Czechoslovakia, Romania, Yugoslavia, and Italy. The Ottoman Empire (later Turkey) included much land in Asia and a small part of Europe.

There are many different kinds of governments. Some are elected by the people, like the government of the United States. Such a government is said to be democratic. **Democracy** is rule by the people. In general, people have the most freedom under democratic governments. Other governments are chosen by only some of the people, like a Communist government. **Communism** is the belief that property should be owned by all people in common. As the first step toward communism, Communist governments have established socialism. Under **socialism**, the government owns and runs all businesses.

Some governments are made up of soldiers. These are called **military** governments. Other governments are led by monarchs. **Monarchy** is rule by one person.

This person inherits the position, keeps it for life, and passes it on to descendants. Monarchs usually have such titles as emperor, king, queen, prince, or grand duke. Some nations are monarchies in form but democracies in action. The United Kingdom of Great Britain and Northern Ireland is such a nation. There, the king or queen reigns, but the people rule.

Sovereignty

Every nation has **sovereignty** (SOV uh run tee) in its own territory. This means that a nation is the highest and final authority in its area. In theory, no other nation can tell it what to do on its own land. In fact, however, a nation is often influenced by other nations. This happens even within its own territory.

REVIEW

WATCH YOUR WORDS

1. ___ is rule by the people.
   Communism   Monarchy
   Democracy

2. ___ is the belief that property should be owned in common.
   Communism   Socialism
   Democracy

3. The people who make the laws and rules for a nation make up the ___ .
   military   government   sovereignty

4. ___ means that a government is the highest and final authority in its territory.
   Monarchy   Democracy
   Sovereignty

5. ___ governments are made up of soldiers.
   Military   Communist   Citizen

CHECK YOUR FACTS

6. What four things do all nations have in common?

7. National borders (do/do not) change.

8. Is there ever more than one culture group in a nation?

9. Under socialism, who owns and runs the businesses?

10. Is a sovereign nation ever influenced by another nation in its own territory?

THINK ABOUT IT

You have read that Great Britain is both a monarchy and a democracy. Can you think of any other nations that combine two or more forms of government?

Lesson 4: Rich Nations, Poor Nations—Part 1

FIND THE WORDS

income   developed
industrialized   manufactured
less-developed   developing

You probably live in a house or apartment with several rooms. Your home has heat, running water, a bathroom, and a kitchen with a stove and refrigerator. You and other members of your family have clothes for winter and summer. Your family probably has a television set and a car. You do not worry about where your next meal is coming from. You know you will have enough to eat. You can expect to live to be about 70 years old. About 4 out of every 10 people on Earth live about the same way you do.

If you had been born in another part of the world, you might live in a house with only one room. The floor would be the ground. The walls would be made of mud brick. The roof would be made of tin or straw. The house would have no running water. It would have no bathroom or kitchen. Most of the time, your

How does this Bolivian village differ from a United States suburb?

family would cook outside over a fire. Each member of your family might have only a little rice for meals. Sometimes, you would go to bed hungry. If some disaster like a flood happened, you could starve to death. You could expect to live to be only about 40 or 50 years old. About 6 out of every 10 people on Earth live this way.

Some people live in rich nations. The United States is a rich nation. That does not mean that everyone in the United States is rich. Certainly there are poor people. But the average person in the United States lives well.

Some people live in poor nations. That does not mean that everyone in those nations is poor. It means that most people are poor. There are probably no nations on Earth that do not have some people who are rich.

How do we know which countries are rich? How do we know which countries are poor? There are several ways to measure this. One important way is to look at **income,** or wealth. We find out how much income a nation creates each year for each of its citizens. This does not mean that each person gets the same amount. It

NATIONAL INCOME

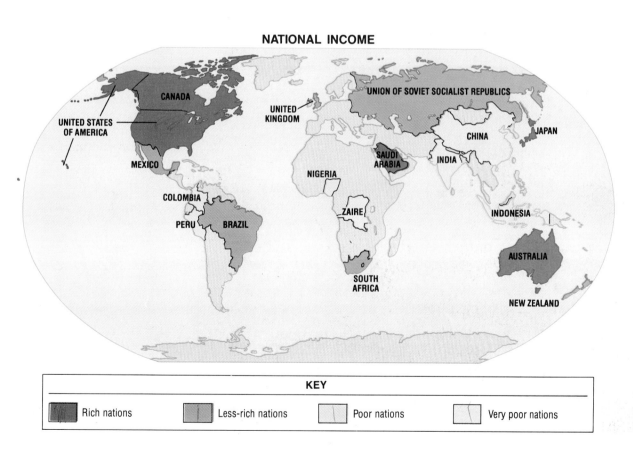

KEY

Rich nations   Less-rich nations   Poor nations   Very poor nations

means that we first add up all the income created in the nation in a year. We then divide by the total number of people in the nation. Some people may really get very little. A few people may get most of the income. But at least we have a measure of the wealth of the nation as a whole.

Look at the map on page 67. The key shows you rich nations, less-rich nations, poor nations, and very poor nations. Study the map. Where are most rich nations located? On what continents? In what hemisphere? Where are most poor nations located? Where are the poorest nations? Look at the population map on pages 56 and 57. Are there rich nations with dense populations? Where? Are there poor nations with dense populations? Where?

Rich nations are sometimes called **developed,** or **industrialized,** nations. These terms mean that the nation can produce many **manufactured** goods. These are things made in factories. These goods could be automobiles, television sets, clothing, trucks, steel, furniture, shoes, glass, or books. Poor nations are usually called **less-developed,** or **developing,** nations. Less-developed nations may have few factories.

REVIEW

WATCH YOUR WORDS

1. ____ is the wealth created in a nation.
   Industry   Manufacturing   Income

2. ____goods are made in factories.
   Developed   Manufactured
   Developing

3. Rich nations are____.
   developed   manufactured
   developing

4. Poor nations are____.
   developed   industrialized
   developing

5. *Developed* means the same as____.
   manufactured   industrialized
   developing

CHECK YOUR FACTS

6. About how long can a person in a rich nation expect to live?

7. In poor nations, all people (are/are not) poor.

8. Describe an important way to measure a nation's wealth.

9. How are many goods produced in rich nations?

10. Poor nations often have (many/few) factories.

THINK ABOUT IT

Today, rich nations have many factories. However, before the 18th century, no nation had much manufacturing. What do you think life was like for most people then?

Lesson 5: Rich Nations, Poor Nations—Part 2

There are many other ways besides income to measure how rich or poor a nation is. In this lesson, we will look at three ways. These are the work people do, what food they eat, and how long they can expect to live.

In most rich nations, not many people are farmers. Most people work in offices, factories, or stores. Some people help manufacture goods. Others provide services for other people. For example, people who work in hospitals, schools, government, or transportation provide services. Most people live in cities. Thus, they do not grow their own food.

In poor nations, most people are farmers. Mostly, they grow only the food they eat. They are completely dependent on the land.

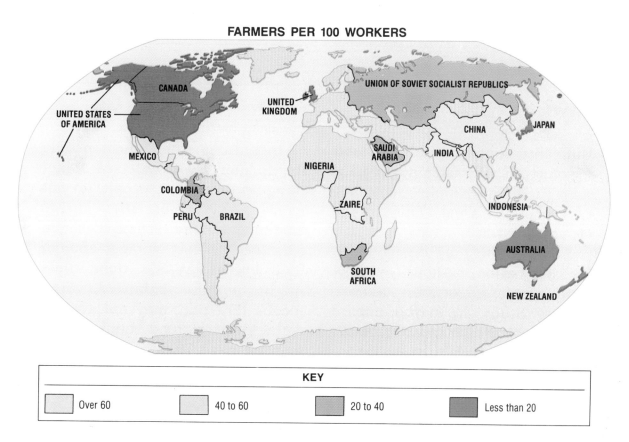

FARMERS PER 100 WORKERS

KEY			
Over 60	40 to 60	20 to 40	Less than 20

AMOUNT OF FOOD

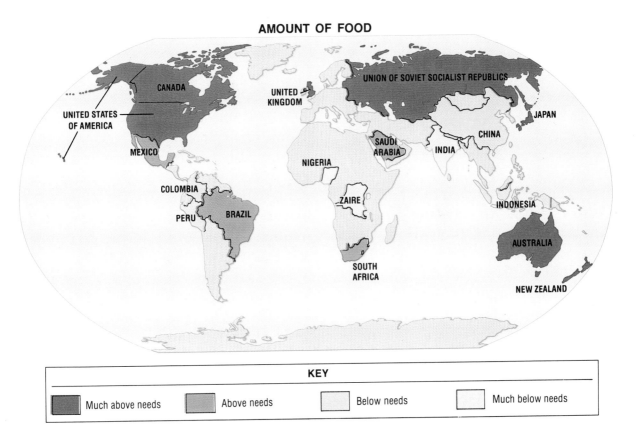

KEY

■	Much above needs	▨	Above needs	▢	Below needs	▢	Much below needs

The rains might not fall. A flood or some other disaster might happen. Then, the people might not have enough to eat. They might starve to death.

Look at the map on page 69. For each nation, it shows you how many people out of every 100 are farmers. Study the map. Compare it to the income map on page 67. Are the nations with the lowest incomes also the nations where most people are farmers?

In nations where most people are farmers, you will see something strange. Most people do not have a good diet. **Diet** is the amount and kind of food a person eats. People may not get enough food every day. Or their diets might not be **balanced.** That means that they may not get the right kinds of food. Look at the map on page 70. In what nations do people get more food than they need to maintain health? In what

LIFE EXPECTANCY

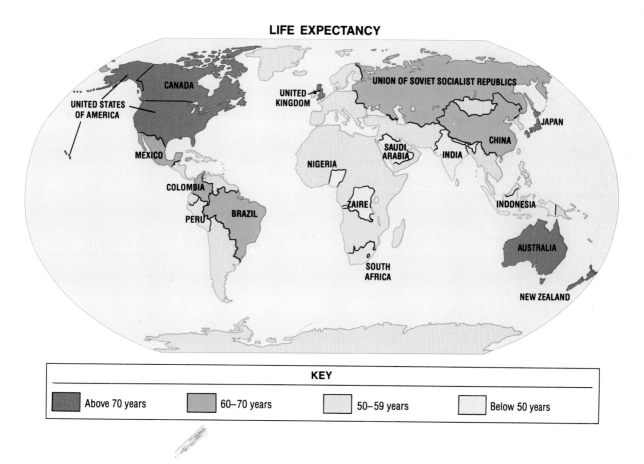

KEY

	Above 70 years		60–70 years		50–59 years		Below 50 years

nations do people get less food than they need to stay healthy?

Finally, let's look at the number of years a person born in a nation can expect to live. A person born in the United States today can expect to live more than 70 years. This is called a person's **life expectancy.** Usually, when people have a long life expectancy, it means several things. It means they have a good diet. They have good clothing and shelter. They have good medical care. When people have a short life expectancy, it means just the opposite. It means their diet may be poor. They may have poor clothing and shelter. They may have little medical care.

Look at the map on this page. It shows you the life expectancy of the people in a number of nations. In which nations on the map is the life expectancy highest? In which nations is it lowest?

FUN FACTS

Today, we think of money as metal coins and paper bills. Money may also be a personal check or a plastic credit card. But in another time or place, money might be something quite different. On islands in the Pacific, money has been as light as bird feathers. It has been as heavy as disks of stone.

In earlier times, money was often useful in itself. Money might be cattle, oxen, sheep, goats, or pigs. It might be furs, hides, or cloth. It might be nuts or dried fish. It might be metal tools, such as knives, spades, or hoes. It might even be gunpowder for battle.

Other things were valued as money more for beauty than usefulness. Shells, beads, and bracelets were prized as ornaments. The precious metals gold and silver came to be valued most. They were often made into coins. But the Incas of Peru used gold and silver only for decoration. They did not use money at all. To them, wealth was workers, animals, crops, and fertile land.

Roman soldiers once got a ration of salt. Later, they were given an allowance of money to buy the salt. Their salt money was called a *salārium*. It gave us our word *salary*. Now, to be "worth one's salt" is to be good at one's work and worth one's pay.

Elephants were once the standard of money in Ceylon. In ancient Greece, a certain weight of gold was worth an ox. The Latin word for wealth, *pecūnia*, meant "wealth in cattle." It gave us our word *pecuniary* (pi KYOO nee EHR ee), which means "having to do with money."

The Chinese were the first people to use paper money. Marco Polo was surprised to see it when he traveled to China from Italy in the 1200s. A piece of paper had no value in itself. People in Europe did not want this kind of money. They did not begin to use paper bank notes until the 1600s.

Paper money came to Canada in an unusual way. In 1685, the supply of cash from France to its Canadian colony ran short. To pay French soldiers there, the government used a new form of money—playing cards! The governor signed each card on the back.

REVIEW

WATCH YOUR WORDS

1. In the United States, the ___ is more than 70 years.
   diet   balance   life expectancy

2. ___ is the amount and kind of food a person eats.
   Diet   Balance   Life Expectancy

CHECK YOUR FACTS

3. List three ways besides income to measure how rich or poor a nation is.

4. What does it mean to say that a diet is balanced?

5. What kinds of things shorten life expectancy?

THINK ABOUT IT

The United States is a rich nation. But some groups of Americans have life expectancies below 70 years. What might that say about their way of living?

72

CHAPTER REVIEW

WATCH YOUR WORDS

1. Supplying water to land is___.
   dieting   communication   irrigation
2. ___ is passing information from one person to another.
   Organization   Communication   Population
3. Nations have territories, populations, governments, and___.
   democracy   monarchy   sovereignty
4. Nations with many factories are___.
   industrialized   developing   balanced
5. A diet with the right kinds of food is___.
   military   developed   balanced

CHECK YOUR FACTS

6. Why do few people live in the far north of North America?
7. In what kinds of areas do many people live?
8. What is culture?
9. List three things that all organized groups have in common.
10. What is the largest nation? What is the smallest?
11. What does it mean to say that each nation has sovereignty?
12. What two words are often used to describe rich nations?
13. What two words are often used to describe poor nations?
14. What do most people do for a living in poor nations?
15. What does it mean to say that a person has a good diet?

USE YOUR MAPS

16. Look at the population map on pages 56 and 57. Do more Australians live along the coast or in the interior?
17. Look at the climate map on pages 28 and 29. Name some climates found in the far north.
18. Compare the map of Europe before World War I (page 64) with the map of the world today (pages 10–11). Find three nations that existed before World War I that do not exist now.
19. Look at the maps on pages 67, 70, and 71. How does the United States rate in income, in diet, and in life expectancy?
20. Look at the map on page 69. How many out of every 100 people in the United States are farmers?

THINK ABOUT IT

21. Today, most people live in areas with fertile land. Do you think people will ever be spread more evenly over Earth? Why, or why not?
22. Are all groups of people organized? Can you think of any that are not?
23. What kinds of problems can a nation have if it has more than one culture group?
24. Do you know of any people in the United States who live like most people in poor nations?
25. In rich nations, many people live in cities and work in buildings. In poor nations, many people are farmers who work on the land. Discuss how these two ways of life might affect the following: government, education, communication, transportation.

UNIT REVIEW

WATCH YOUR WORDS

Use the words below to fill in the blanks. Use each term only once.

axis	earthquakes	hemispheres	longitude	resources
climates	elevations	highlands	map	scale
compass	erodes	key	orbit	temperate
continents	globe	landforms	planet	tropic
degrees	grid	latitude	projection	volcanoes

Earth is a(n) ___ . It moves in a(n) ___ around the sun. Each day, Earth spins on its ___ . The equator divides Earth into two ___ . Between the tropic of Capricorn and the tropic of Cancer is the ___ zone. The weather changes in the ___ zones.

Earth's surface has ___ and oceans. The land has different shapes, called ___ . Land is also at different ___ above sea level. Earth has different weather patterns called ___ . But in the ___ , there are no set weather patterns. The lands of Earth include many natural ___ . The surface of Earth changes quickly because of ___ and ___ . More slowly, it ___ away.

A ___ is a model of Earth. A ___ is a flat picture on which Earth's curved surface is shown by ___ . Places on Earth are located by lines of ___ and lines of ___ . Both of these are measured in ___ . They cross to form a ___ that helps you find places. The symbols on maps are listed in a ___ . The ___ on a map shows direction. The ___ on a map shows distance.

CHECK YOUR FACTS

1. What are the two days called on which day and night are equal? What are the two days called on which day or night is longest?

2. Which continent has no nations? Which has only one nation?

3. What are the large plains in the Soviet Union called?

4. What is the source of lava?

5. What is the belt of volcanoes around the Pacific Ocean called?

6. How many degrees are there in every circle?

7. What kind of projection is a Mercator map?

8. What does a star on a map usually mean?

9. What kind of map shows how things are spread over Earth?

10. What kind of map shows borders of nations?

11. Name four kinds of areas where few people live.

12. How can the desert be made more useful for people?

13. List the four main parts of culture.

14. Name two kinds of written symbols.

15. About how many nations are there?

16. What four things do all nations have in common?

17. How can the income of nations be compared?

18. Out of every 10 persons on Earth, about how many live in rich nations?

19. Poor nations usually have (more/fewer) farmers.

20. Poor people usually live (longer/shorter) lives.

CLOSE THE MAP GAP

21. Draw a globe. Show the location of the following: equator, tropic of Cancer, tropic of Capricorn, Arctic Circle, Antarctic Circle.

22. Draw a globe and a cone that show how a conic projection is made.

23. Draw a street map that would show someone how to get from your home to your school. Label all streets you show. Include a direction arrow and a scale. Show and label landmarks that would help someone find the way.

24. Draw a map of an imaginary nation. Show the borders of the nation and its parts. Show and label states, a capital, and cities. Include a key, a scale, and a compass.

25. Draw a map that shows the distribution of widgets (imaginary goods) in the United States.

USE YOUR MAPS

26. Look at the maps on pages 70 and 71. Find the diet level and life expectancy for the following nations:
    a. United States
    b. Soviet Union
    c. China
    d. Brazil
    e. Nigeria

THINK ABOUT IT

27. Tasmania is an island off southern Australia. Suppose you were making a trip there during your summer vacation. What kinds of clothes might you pack to take with you?

28. Does it ever snow at the equator? If so, where?

29. How might natural resources and national income be related?

30. What is the capital of the United States? Has this city always been the capital?

31. Do all people use the same symbols for writing?

TRY SOMETHING NEW

32. Using a flashlight and a globe, show your class the effects of Earth's tilt.

33. Write a report about summer far north, in the Land of the Midnight Sun.

34. Make a list of all the things you can think of that change with the seasons.

35. Make a list of all the different kinds of landforms and bodies of water near where you live.

36. Make a list of natural resources in your area.

PUT IT ALL TOGETHER

Make a chart that shows exactly where you live. Include the names of your community, county, state, nation, continent, hemispheres, and planet.

UNIT 2

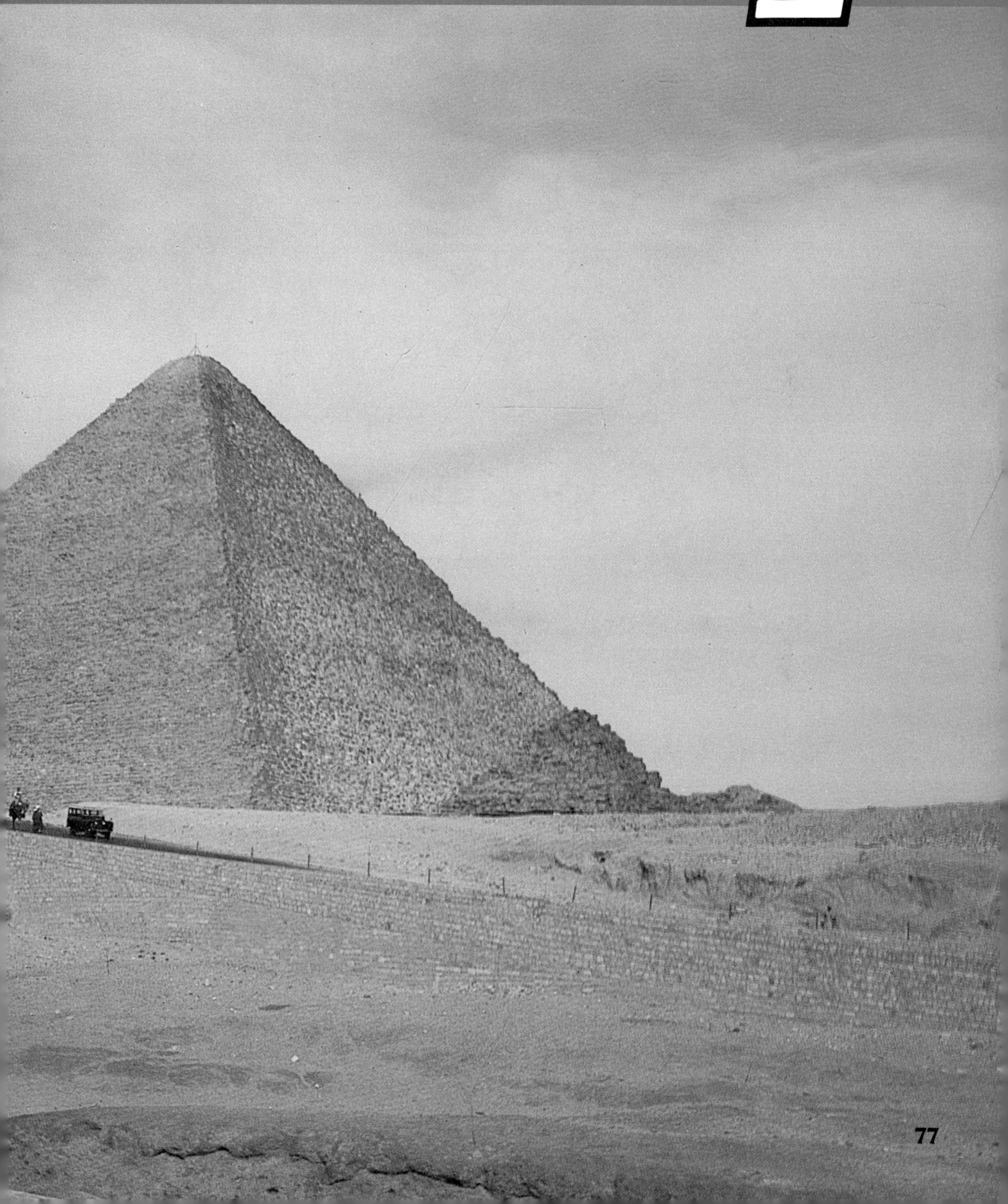

CHAPTER 1 PEOPLE BUILD CITIES

Lesson 1: Why We Learn about the Past

FIND THE WORDS

history	historic	prehistory
prehistoric	ruins	archaeologist

People have always wanted to know about the past. Children like to remember and talk about fun things they did. They like to hear stories about their parents' lives. People wonder about what happened before they were born.

Sometimes, people learn about the past to solve a problem they have now. They might ask questions like these: How did we get into this mess? What can we do to get out of it?

You can learn about the past in many ways. The most important way is by studying written records. About 5000 years ago, people learned to write down what had happened to them. Perhaps a

78

trader wanted a record of things that had been bought or sold. Famous kings and queens wanted their deeds recorded. They wanted people in the future to know how great they were.

History is the written record of the past. The period since people learned to write is called **historic** times. The period before people learned to write is often called **prehistory.** In addition, it is known as **prehistoric** (PREE hiss TOR ik) times. *Pre* means "before."

We can learn much about the past from written records. But many things were never written. And most writings from the past have been lost. However, we can still learn much about the past from other things people have left behind. In some places, there are ruins of cities built thousands of years ago. **Ruins** are the remains of things built in the past. They are often in bad shape. But they can still tell us many things about the people who built them.

People who dig up and study old ruins are called **archaeologists** (AHR kee AHL uh jists). Studying ruins adds to what we know about historic times. But the remains of buildings and other things are *all* we know of prehistoric peoples. These things give us many clues about the ways people lived before they learned to write.

As you might guess, the farther we go back into history, the less we know for sure about what happened. We have to make more and more guesses. We know a lot about what happened 50 years ago. We know less about what happened 500 years ago. We know even less about what happened 5000 years ago. In general, the longer ago something happened, the less we can know about it.

REVIEW

WATCH YOUR WORDS

1. ___ is the period before people learned to write.
   History   Prehistory   Archaeology
2. ___ is the written record of the past.
   History   Prehistory   Archaeology
3. ___dig up and study old ruins.
   Historians   Prehistorians
   Archaeologists

CHECK YOUR FACTS

4. Ruins (can/cannot) tell us much about people in the past.
5. The further we go back into history, the (more/less) we know about what happened.

TRY SOMETHING NEW

Ask your parents to tell you what they know about the history of your family.

Lesson 2: Prehistoric People

FIND THE WORDS

domesticate   pottery   bronze

In prehistoric times, people learned many useful things. They learned to make and use tools and weapons of stone. They learned to use fire for heat, protection, and cooking. They learned to grow food. They learned to **domesticate** (duh MESS ti KAYT), or tame, certain animals.

Before people learned these things, they lived very simple lives. They lived in small groups. They cared for their children. They took shelter from the cold, wind, and rain in any place they could find. Few prehistoric people lived more than 30 years.

For food, prehistoric people gathered what they could find. They picked berries and fruit from trees and bushes. They dug up roots to eat. They took eggs from birds' nests and honey from bees' hives. They also hunted for meat and fish. Mostly, they killed small animals. But sometimes, they worked together to kill large animals. When they could do this, they had food for several days. They stayed in one place only as long as the food there lasted. When it was used up, they moved on to another place to find food.

Prehistoric people spent their time providing for their needs. During the day, they gathered food and hunted. When it grew dark, they went to their shelters. The night held many terrors for prehistoric people. They had no light except for fires they built. They feared animals that hunted at night. They were also afraid of thunder, lightning, and storms. That was because they did not understand what these things were.

But even these early people were different from animals. Prehistoric people walked upright on their legs. That way, their arms were free. They had a thumb and

These axes were made by prehistoric people.

This painting shows how one artist thought a group of prehistoric people might have looked.

fingers, so they could hold things in their hands. Since their arms were free and their hands flexible, prehistoric people could use tools. They could defend themselves with weapons, such as spears and clubs. They could carry heavy loads. They could do many different kinds of work.

Prehistoric people also had large brains. They could store in their brains memories of what they had learned in the past. They also learned to speak. Thus, they could tell each other the things they had learned. As a result, knowledge was passed on from parents to children.

We do not know why or how prehistoric people learned the things they did. They may have learned about fire from lightning. Lightning sometimes set forests or grasslands on fire. People saw that fire frightened animals and gave heat. They may have learned to cook food by eating animals that had been trapped in a grass fire.

Perhaps they liked the taste. They might also have noticed that cooked food did not spoil as quickly as raw food did.

People may have learned to domesticate animals by raising baby animals. They might have found small dogs or goats that had become separated from their parents. Or they might have taken them deliberately. People may also have trapped a herd of animals in a valley. After a time, the trapped animals had become domesticated.

Growing food was another important skill that prehistoric people learned. They may have eaten some fruit and thrown the seeds on the ground. Days later, they may have noticed that the seeds had grown into little plants. Still later, they may have noticed that the plants had produced new fruits.

Prehistoric people in different parts of the world learned the same skills. People living in places thousands of miles apart knew

At the American Museum of Natural History in New York is this model of a village built by prehistoric people.

how to use tools, weapons, and fire. They learned how to domesticate animals and grow food.

Toward the end of prehistoric times, many people had settled into villages. About 150 people lived in each of these small settlements. The village people built homes of wood and dried mud. They kept herds of animals and grew crops for food. The herds and crops provided a steady supply of food. Now, people did not have to spend all their time hunting and gathering food. They had more time for other things. They had time to invent many new things.

People began to make better tools, such as axes. They made fine weapons, such as spears and bows and arrows. They learned how to make **pottery**, things formed from clay. They learned how to make thread from animal hair. They used the thread to make cloth. They learned to use metals, such as copper and gold. From copper, they made tools. From gold, they made jewelry. Later, they learned to use **bronze**, a mixture of copper and tin.

REVIEW

WATCH YOUR WORDS

1. ___is made from clay.
   Bronze   Pottery   Gold

2. ___is a mixture of copper and tin.
   Bronze   Pottery   Jewelry

CHECK YOUR FACTS

3. Name two kinds of animals that people learned to domesticate.

4. Prehistoric people in different parts of the world (did/did not) learn the same skills.

5. People settled in villages toward the (beginning/end) of prehistoric times.

THINK ABOUT IT

Imagine that you find yourself alone on an island. You have to provide for your own needs. What things would you need? How would you get them?

Lesson 3: The Beginning of Civilization

FIND THE WORDS

civilization   ancient   society
fertile

You know that a culture is a group's way of living. You know that the way a group is organized is part of its culture. A **society** is a large, organized group of people that lasts for a long time. Societies have traditions, a culture, and institutions. Often, a society is also a nation.

In this unit, you will look at some societies of the distant past. You will see how they had important effects on the way we live today. In the rest of this book, you will learn about societies of the present. You will study how they came to be the way they are today.

Civilization Develops

All people have a culture. But not all cultures develop into civilizations. A **civilization** is a highly developed form of culture. The word *civilization* comes from the Latin word *civis,* which means "city." So the main thing about a civilization is that it has cities. People first developed civilizations when they began to build and live

Above: The ruins of this ancient Sumerian city are on the banks of the Euphrates River in Syria. *Below:* This golden helmet was made for a prince in Ur, an ancient Sumerian city.

in cities. They had advanced in many ways by that time. The peoples and civilizations of long ago are called **ancient** (AYN shunt), or very old.

The River Valleys

People began to build cities and develop civilizations in four river valleys. These valleys lay in four different parts of the world. The earliest civilization arose in Mesopotamia (MESS uh puh TAY mee uh). This word means "the land between two rivers." Mesopotamia is an area of flat land between the Tigris (TY griss) and Euphrates (yoo FRAY teez) rivers in Southwest Asia. Today, most of this area is in the nation of Iraq. Civilizations also developed in the valleys of the Nile River in Egypt, of the Indus River in northwestern India, and of the Hwang Ho (HWAHNG HOH), or Yellow River, in northern China. Look at the map on page 85. Find these four great river valleys.

These river valleys also had certain things in common. They all had fertile land. **Fertile** (FUR tul) land is soil that is good for growing crops. In each area, the land was flooded every year. These floods watered and enriched the soil. In most of these areas, the rainfall was low or undependable. The people who lived there had to bring water to their fields. As you have learned, this is called irrigation. The rivers provided a dependable supply of irrigation water.

Irrigation was the key to the growth of civilization. One person or even one family could not control the flow of a river. People had to work together to do so. Whole villages and groups of villages had to cooperate. People had to learn to do new things and to help each other. First, they had to plan and lay out the system of irrigation. They had to build dams to control the water. They had to dig ditches to move it to where it was needed. They had to find ways to lift the water from the river to fields that were higher up. They also needed a calendar to tell them when the floods would come. That way, they could get ready for them.

Just think what all this means. Building an irrigation system is a big job. People had to have good, strong tools to help them do the heavy work. They had to draw plans and write down records. They needed leaders to direct the work. You can easily see how irrigation did more than help crops grow. It helped civilization grow, as well.

Irrigation brought many advances and improved the food supply. Since there was now extra food, some people could live in cities. They could get their food

WHERE WE ARE IN TIME AND PLACE

ANCIENT CIVILIZATIONS

3500 B.C.	3100 B.C.	3000 B.C.	2700 B.C.	2500 B.C.	2050 B.C.
Sumerian civilization begins in Mesopotamia	Upper Egypt and Lower Egypt unite	Bronze Age begins in Sumeria	Old Kingdom begins in Egypt	Civilization begins in Indus Valley	Middle Kingdom begins in Egypt

1890 B.C.	1570 B.C.	1500 B.C.	750 B.C.	550 B.C.	332 B.C.	30 B.C.
Babylonian Empire begins in Mesopotamia	New Kingdom begins in Egypt	Civilization begins in China	Assyrian Empire begins	Persian Empire begins	Alexander the Great conquers Egypt	Egypt becomes part of Roman Empire

CRADLES OF CIVILIZATION

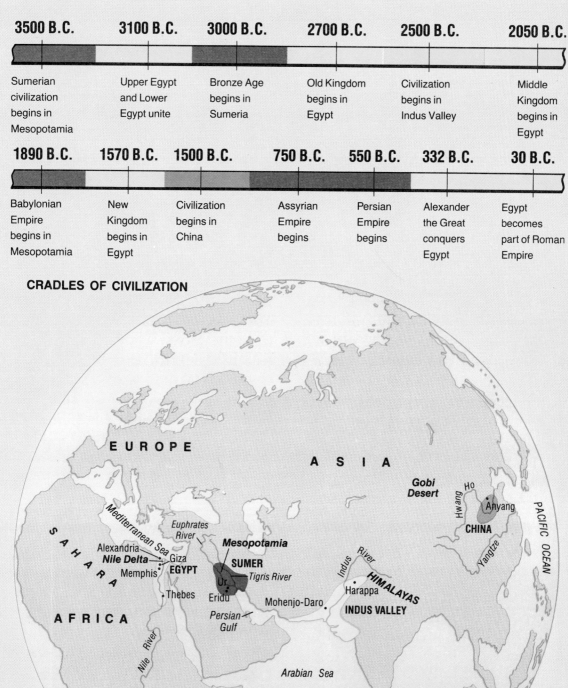

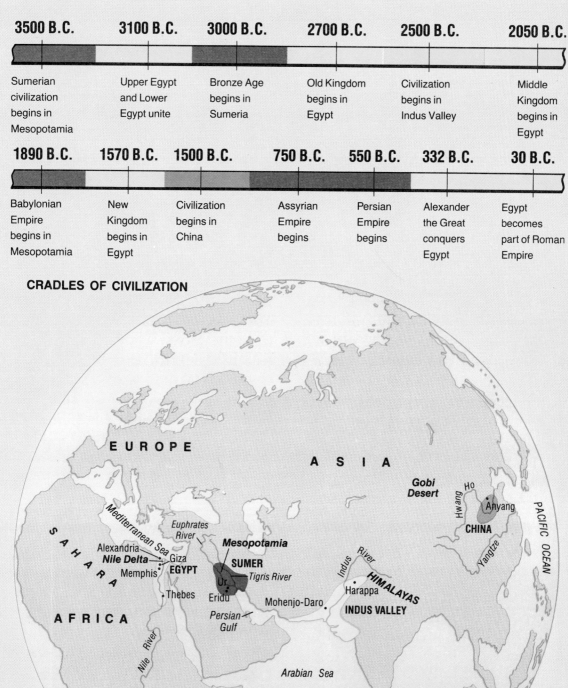 image includes the following labels: EUROPE, ASIA, Gobi Desert, Ho, Hwang, Anyang, CHINA, PACIFIC OCEAN, Yangtze, Mediterranean Sea, Euphrates River, Mesopotamia, SUMER, Tigris River, Indus River, HIMALAYAS, Alexandria, Nile Delta, Giza, EGYPT, Memphis, Ur, Eridu, Mohenjo-Daro, Harappa, INDUS VALLEY, SAHARA, Thebes, AFRICA, Nile River, Persian Gulf, Arabian Sea

Even today, some people in the Middle East still irrigate their fields like people did in ancient times.

from nearby farms. They could do other work instead of spending all their time raising food.

Cities themselves helped the ancient civilizations advance even further. Systems had to be created for supplying the people in cities with food and water. Systems were needed to carry away wastes from the cities. Cities had to be protected from attack. Powerful governments arose to help fill these needs. The governments were able to run big projects. They were strong enough to defend the cities. They began to collect taxes. With this money, they could pay skilled workers, soldiers, priests, and scholars. So cities became the heart of civilization.

REVIEW

WATCH YOUR WORDS

1. A ___ is a highly developed form of culture.
   civilization   society   village
2. ___ land is good for farming.
   Desert   Fertile   Cultured
3. ___ is bringing water to farmland from somewhere else.
   Agriculture   Fertilizing   Irrigation

CHECK YOUR FACTS

4. All cultures (do/do not) develop into civilizations.
5. Where did the earliest civilization arise?

THINK ABOUT IT

Why do you think civilization arose in similar places around the world?

Lesson 4: A City-State Civilization Begins in Sumer

FIND THE WORDS

delta	bank	dike	canal
alloy	city-state		temple
ziggurat	stylus		cuneiform
empire	emperor		empress

About 3500 B.C., the first civilization in the world was developing in Mesopotamia. One culture group lived there in an area called Sumer (SOO mur) or Sumeria (soo MEHR ee ah). These people were the Sumerians. Ur and Eridu were their main cities.

In Mesopotamia, the Tigris and Euphrates rivers flow toward each other. Together, they have created a large delta where they enter the Persian (PUR zhun) Gulf. In a **delta,** a river spreads out into many mouths. It lays down soil it carries, which builds up land. Sumer was located in the delta of the Tigris and Euphrates rivers.

Sumer does not seem to be a good place for a civilization to start. In summer, it is hot and dry in that area. Plants often turn brown and die. There is little rain. Most of it falls in the winter, when few crops grow. So the rain is of little use to farmers.

Each spring, the Tigris and Eu-phrates rivers flood their valleys. This happens between April and June. Snow melts in the mountains to the north. This water swells the rivers, which overflow. Finally, the water drains into the Persian Gulf. But the floods leave a new layer of rich soil on the land. This raises the level of the land a little. But in some years, there is much less water than in others.

The Sumerians solved these problems. They decided to build dikes along the **banks,** or sides, of the rivers. **Dikes** are walls, usually made of dirt, that make the river-banks higher. Dikes help keep water in the river.

The dikes the Sumerians built protected their homes and crops from the floods. They also helped them grow crops without rain. In the summer, when there was little rain, they could cut holes in the dikes. Water would then flow out onto the land near the river.

The Sumerians also dug long **canals,** or waterways, to carry the water to their fields. This was fairly easy to do because the land in Mesopotamia is flat. With canals, land that did not get enough rain could now be used to grow crops. Irrigation made much more farming possible.

The Sumerians grew grains, such as wheat and barley, in their irrigated fields. They grew vegetables, such as onions and beans. Dates and other fruits were also grown.

The grains were especially important. Grains were used to feed sheep, goats, pigs, and cattle. The cattle were used to pull plows. With their good soil, dependable water supply, and cattle, the Sumerians soon grew more grain than they needed for themselves. They began to sell their extra grain to others. This grain trade helped the cities of Sumer grow. They grew very quickly between 3500 and 3100 B.C.

The extra food also allowed more people to do work other than farming. They began to make special things, such as pottery and bricks. The potter's wheel was invented at this time. This tool helps a potter make smooth, even shapes very quickly. Much pottery was made in Sumer.

The Bronze Age began about 3000 B.C. The Sumerians combined copper with tin to make bronze. This **alloy** (AL oi), or mixture of metals, was stronger than either of the pure metals. The stronger metal was used to make many new things. Among them were better weapons, like swords.

Good weapons were important to the Sumerians. They had a great need to protect themselves from their enemies. The land of Sumer had no natural barriers like mountain ranges or deserts. Because of this, invaders were a constant threat.

Ruling the Cities

Each Sumerian city was really a small, independent country made up of the city and the surrounding area. Such a nation is called a **city-state.** Each city-state had its own ruler. The city-states struggled for power and trade. They often fought over the rights to land and water.

At first, priests ruled the city-states. The priests were powerful because of their special relationship to the Sumerian gods. The Sumerians believed that the land was owned by the gods. They thought the gods had made each city and its people. The people were supposed to serve the gods. The priests ruled in name of the gods. The Sumerians also believed that the gods caused the good and bad things that happened to them. They felt they needed the priests to plead with the gods for help.

The priests were also scholars. They knew how to measure land, tell time, and use a calendar. They knew how to write, and they kept the written records.

This is the Ziggurat at Ur.

The Ziggurat

Each city-state had a chief god. The Sumerians believed that this god protected their city-state. They built a large **temple,** or religious building, in the center of the city to honor the god. This temple was usually the largest building in the crowded city. It had many stories. Each story was a little smaller than the one below it. This formed a high platform. On top of the highest story was the actual temple. Only priests could enter there. The whole temple building was called a **ziggurat** (ZIG oo RAT).

Inside the small temple was a statue of the chief god. The Sumerians believed that their gods were like human beings. So they tried to please them by offering them good food, wine, and beautiful clothing. They played music for them. The Sumerians believed that, in return for these gifts, the gods told the high priests what should be done in the cities. The messages came in the form of dreams.

The ziggurat was much more than a place of worship. On the lower stories were libraries and storerooms. There were also places for the male and female priests to live. There were shops for workers. There might be a school nearby.

Using a potter's wheel is a skill learned in ancient times.

Writing

The Sumerians were the first people to develop a writing system. The Sumerian writing system spread widely through Southwest Asia. It was the basis of most of the writing systems used today.

The Sumerians used special symbols to record words and numbers. A **stylus** (STY luss), or sharp stick, was used to cut the symbols into wet clay tablets. The tablet was then baked or dried to preserve the marks. The Sumerian system of writing is called **cuneiform** (kyoo NEE uh FORM). This

name means "wedge." Cuneiform strokes are broad at one end and pointed at the other.

The Sumerians used cuneiform writing mainly for business. They also wrote down personal matters, such as marriage contracts, to avoid disputes.

Kings Become Powerful

In times of peace, the Sumerians were easily able to solve their major problem of controlling floods and irrigating their fields. But the problem of defending themselves against invaders was more serious. Each city-state feared neighboring city-states. The Sumerians were also afraid of the peoples who lived around them. The rich cities of Sumer were attractive prizes for these peoples.

There were constant invasions in Sumer. As a result, the high priests lost power. The Sumerians began to depend on strong soldiers to protect them. Before this, the priests had paid and commanded the army. Now, the highest military leader became king. He had complete control of the government. The king's most important job was to see that the walls that protected the city were kept in good repair. He was also in charge of the army. Some kings used their armies to try to conquer other city-states of Sumer.

By 2000 B.C., the Sumerian city-states had become weaker. They were invaded time after time. A people called the Babylonians (BAB uh LOH nee unz) took over Sumer and the lands around it. Sumer became part of Babylonia. Still later, Babylonia was conquered by the Assyrians (ah SIR ee unz). The Assyrians built a huge empire. An **empire** is a large and powerful nation that usually includes many different peoples. Male rulers of empires are called **emperors.** Female rulers of empires are called **empresses.** By 550 B.C., the Persians had conquered the area. The Persian Empire was one of the largest empires in the world up to that time.

The hanging gardens of Babylon were one of the wonders of the ancient world.

REVIEW

WATCH YOUR WORDS

1. ＿＿form at the mouth of rivers.
   Dikes Canals Deltas

2. A(n)＿＿is a mixture of metals.
   alloy copper stylus

3. A(n)＿＿is a large and powerful nation with many different peoples.
   alloy empire city-state

4. A(n)＿＿is a religious building.
   temple empire cuneiform

5. The Sumerians built＿＿in the centers of their cities.
   banks empires ziggurats

CHECK YOUR FACTS

6. What two large rivers flow through Mesopotamia?

7. Name some crops the Sumerians grew.

8. In about what year did the Bronze Age begin?

9. Between the city-states of Sumer, there was usually (peace/war).

10. Who ruled in Sumer first, the kings or the priests?

THINK ABOUT IT

Why was the invention of writing important? List as many reasons as you can.

Lesson 5: Ancient India and China

FIND THE WORDS

citadel   palace   dynasty
ancestor   peasant

The Indus Valley

Today, the Indus River runs through the nations of India and Pakistan. It flows from the high mountains of the Himalayas down to the Arabian Sea. The valley of the Indus was one of the places where civilization began.

Sometime after 2500 B.C., the people of the Indus valley became civilized. They had advanced from a simple farming society to a society with cities and organized government. Two major cities developed in this area: Harappa (huh RAP uh) and Mohenjo-Daro (moh HEN joh DAHR oh). There were also a number of smaller towns.

The two main cities seem to have been designed by the same group of architects. Their buildings are solid and practical rather than beautiful. Each city had a large **citadel** (SIT uh DEL), or fort, surrounded by thick walls. These walls were 12 meters (40 feet) thick and were made of baked clay bricks. They kept out invaders and flood waters. Within the citadel was a **palace.** This is a large building in which a ruler lives. The palace had deep bathing pools, rooms for storing extra food, and a temple.

Outside the citadel walls were

This is a child's pull toy found in one of the ancient cities of the Indus Valley.

the houses of the common people. The houses were very much alike. They were several stories tall and made out of brick. The rooms were grouped around an inside courtyard. The houses and streets had covered brick drains for carrying away wastes. Not until Roman times were these to be equalled. Each city also had several public wells. Shops lined the streets.

The ancient cities of the Indus valley are very impressive. But most people still made their living by farming. They raised grains, such as wheat, barley, and sesame. They also grew melons, dates, and peas. They planted cotton. They had discovered how to spin thread and how to weave and dye cloth. The use of cotton cloth is one of India's great gifts to the world.

The Indus peoples also raised animals. Cattle, sheep, goats, water buffaloes, and perhaps even elephants were among these. The Indus peoples were the first to domesticate birds such as chickens.

In addition to making cloth, skilled workers in the Indus valley made large amounts of pottery. They also worked with ivory, bones, and metals such as gold, silver, and bronze.

The Indus peoples left many samples of their writing. They made seals of soapstone for marking documents. Thousands of these seals—decorated with figures and writing—have been discovered. But so far, no one knows how to read the writing. If we ever learn what it means, we may find out much more about how the Indus people lived.

China

China was largely cut off from the other ancient civilizations. Look at the map on page 85.

Northern China is very cold in winter. Through this area flows the great Hwang Ho, or Yellow River. The Hwang Ho begins in the high mountain ranges to the west. It twists and turns through northern China, creating a broad valley. In the spring, the snows melt in the mountains. This causes the mighty river to overflow its banks. The flood waters also carry rich, yellow soil. This is deposited each year in the Hwang Ho valley. Like the Sumerians, the people who settled in the Hwang Ho valley came to depend on this yearly flood.

Civilization in China

The first farming communities in China developed about 4000 B.C. in the Hwang Ho valley. The people of this area had tamed dogs and pigs. They were skilled at making pottery. They learned to

These two vases were made in ancient China. The one on the left is from prehistoric times. The one on the right is from the Shang period. Notice how the vase on the right is more finely made.

use the water of the river to irrigate their land. About 2000 B.C., rice was introduced into the area. It soon became the most important food. By 1500 B.C., the farming communities near the Hwang Ho had become civilized. Walls now protected many villages.

The Chinese learned to make silk cloth. They used the thread from cocoons spun by silkworms. They also invented a kind of writing based on pictures. After 1500 B.C., many records were written in China. The Chinese also began to create beautiful art.

By this time, most of the Hwang Ho valley was ruled by the Shang dynasty. A **dynasty** (DY nuh stee) is a family of rulers. The

Shangs governed from their capital city, Anyang. This city was located in the northern part of the Hwang Ho valley. The power of the Shang leaders was only strong around their capital. They had to depend on local chieftains in areas farther away. These regions included the rest of the Hwang Ho valley and land as far south as the Yangtze (YANG TSEE) River. These local rulers were largely independent. However, they respected the Shang rulers as religious leaders.

Under the Shang rulers, the Chinese people did not develop a sense of unity as a nation. They felt united only because they spoke the same language and shared the same way of life.

Life under the Shangs

During the Shang period, the Chinese began to worship their ancestors. **Ancestors** are the people from whom someone is descended. Ancestor worship became a very important part of Chinese religion and culture. The Chinese believed that after people died, their spirits lived on to guide and protect their descendants. The ruling family tried to communicate with the spirits of their ancestors when a problem arose. This became an important custom. It spread to the nobility and the common people.

At times, human beings were even sacrificed to the dead. This might take place on special occasions such as a funeral. The victims were slaves, prisoners-of-war, or, sometimes, relatives or friends of a dead ruler.

The capital city of the Shangs, Anyang, was shaped like a rectangle. It was protected by a thick mud wall. The ruler's palace was in the center of the city. Around it lived nobles and skilled workers. These workers made beautiful pottery and statues. They created art and weapons from bronze.

But most of the Chinese people did not live in cities. They were **peasants.** These are people who farm small plots of land. The Chinese peasants lived in villages across the land. They raised cattle, dogs, pigs, and chickens. They grew grains, such as wheat, millet, and rice. In many ways, their lives were like those of the peasants in Sumer and the Indus valley. Life was very hard for these people. The climate of northern China was dry. The farmers had to depend on the Hwang Ho for irrigation. They could not have large farms. The peasants worked their small plots of land with hoes and spades.

REVIEW

WATCH YOUR WORDS

1. A(n)____is a family of rulers.
   ancestor citadel dynasty

2. A____is a fort.
   palace citadel dynasty

3. ____are small farmers.
   Peasants Ancestors Dynasties

CHECK YOUR FACTS

4. What kind of cloth did the ancient people of India invent?

5. Ancient China had (many/few) contacts with other civilizations.

THINK ABOUT IT

In the days of the ancient civilizations, how did most people still live?

Lesson 6: Ancient Egypt

What the Tigris and Euphrates were to Sumer, the Indus to India, and the Hwang Ho to China, the Nile was to Egypt. The great river flows from highlands deep within Africa through the desert called the Sahara (suh HAR uh). In the south, the Nile valley is called Upper Egypt. For a few miles on either side of the river, the land is rich and can be irrigated. The rest is desert. In the north, the Nile flows through its delta into the Mediterranean Sea. The delta area is called Lower Egypt.

About 3100 B.C., Menes (MEE neez), the King of Upper Egypt, conquered Lower Egypt. Thus, the country was brought together. This was the true beginning of Egyptian history. For 3000 years thereafter, Egyptian life and culture grew richer but did not change greatly.

From 3100 B.C. to 30 B.C., Egypt was ruled by 32 dynasties, or families of kings. The Egyptian kings were called **pharaohs** (FEHR ohz). They were considered to be gods as well as kings. The Egyp-tians also worshiped many other gods. Temples and their priests were very important in Egypt.

As in other ancient civiliza-tions, the power of Egypt's rulers rested on their control of a great river. Each year, the Nile was swollen by rains in Central Africa. Its floods had to be held back. The water and the silt it carried had to be used to irrigate and enrich the fields. The Egyptians, too, built great irrigation systems.

All power was in the hands of the pharaohs. They were assisted by advisers, who were usually priests. The pharaohs governed through local districts called **nomes.** Each nome was made up of many villages.

Most Egyptians were farmers who lived in villages. Using the water of the Nile, they grew two or three crops a year. They raised grains, such as barley and wheat, and also fruits and vegetables. Oxen pulled the farmers' plows.

The few cities were centers of government and religion. Great palaces and temples stood at their centers. The small huts of workers were crowded around the large public buildings. Wealthy people built homes on **estates** (eh STAYTS), or large farms, outside the towns.

These are two of the Great Pyramids at Giza.

Under the first two dynasties that ruled after 3100 B.C., Egyptian culture advanced rapidly. The Egyptians developed a form of picture writing that is known as **hieroglyphics** (HY ruh GLIF iks). They wrote on **papyrus** (puh PY russ), a paper made from reeds. The pharaohs began building great tombs for themselves. Menes, the first pharaoh, built a great capital city, later called Memphis. Memphis lay where Upper and Lower Egypt met. It was surrounded by huge walls.

During the third dynasty, about 2700 B.C., a period called the Old Kingdom began. Pharaoh Zoser had his architect, Imhotep, build him a great tomb. It was the Step Pyramid, the world's first great stone building. A **pyramid** (PIR uh mid) is a triangular building with four sides. Zoser's pyramid had setbacks, like Sumerian ziggurats.

Tombs were important to the pharaohs because the Egyptians believed in life after death. They wanted to take with them all they would need in the afterlife. They tried to preserve, or save, their dead bodies for their afterlife. They developed special methods for doing this. The preserved bodies of the ancient Egyptians are called **mummies.**

The pharaohs of the fourth dynasty built the first true pyramids in the 2500s. The most famous of these are the three Great Pyramids at Giza (GEE zuh), near Memphis. Building the largest pyramid involved moving 2,300,000 blocks of stone. Each block weighed about 2½ tons. The building of the Great Pyramids strained Egypt's resources. Later pharaohs built great tombs for themselves. However, none were as large as the Great Pyramids.

The power of the pharaohs slowly grew weak. For almost a hundred years, Egypt had several kings at once. Then, about 2050 B.C., the king of the city of Thebes (THEEBZ) in Upper Egypt reunited the country. This was the beginning of the period known as the Middle Kingdom. During this period, for the first time, the Egyptians had strong contacts with Asia and the lands around the eastern Mediterranean. But an Asian people, the Hyksos (HIK SAHSS), conquered northern Egypt about 1700 B.C. They ruled there for more than a century. The Hyksos introduced horses to Egypt.

About 1570 B.C. the king of Thebes defeated the Hyksos. He reunited Egypt again. This marked the beginning of the New Kingdom. The pharaohs of the New Kingdom fought wars in Africa and Asia. They won lands that increased Egypt's territory. They had their tombs carved out of rock in the Valley of the Kings, near Thebes.

In later years, Egypt came to be ruled by Libyans, Ethiopians, and Persians. Alexander the Great drove away the Persians in 332 B.C. He founded the great city of Alexandria, west of the Nile delta. Alexandria became the capital of Egypt.

After Alexander's death, Egypt was ruled by a Greek dynasty called the Ptolemies (TOL uh meez). Under the Ptolemies, Egypt became an important center of Greek culture. But the culture of ancient Egypt also continued. The Ptolemaic dynasty came to an end with the death of Queen Cleopatra in 30 B.C. Egypt then became part of the Roman Empire.

REVIEW

WATCH YOUR WORDS

1. A(n)____is a large farm.
   nome   pyramid   estate

2. The kings of ancient Egypt were called____.
   pharaohs   pyramids   mummies

3. Egyptian writing was called____.
   pharaohs   hieroglyphics   papyrus

CHECK YOUR FACTS

4. What body of water has dominated Egypt's history?

5. Name the two main parts of ancient Egypt.

THINK ABOUT IT

Ancient Egypt was conquered by outside groups many times. Yet its culture changed very little. How can this be so?

CHAPTER REVIEW

WATCH YOUR WORDS

1. ____times came before____times.
   prehistoric historic ancient
   dynastic

2. Archaeologists study____.
   ruins technology dynasties

3. To tame animals is to____them.
   ruin domesticate irrigate

4. Land that is good for farming is____.
   fertile domesticated irrigated

5. ____means very old.
   Palatial Hieroglyphic Ancient

6. A(n)____is a sharp stick.
   stylus ziggurat alloy

7. ____ are built on the ____, or sides, of rivers to hold back the water.
   banks dikes canals deltas

8. A____is a waterway.
   stylus canal delta

9. ____ was the system of writing in ancient Sumer.
   Cuneiform Hieroglyphics Papyrus

10. A(n) ____ is a female ruler of an empire. A(n) ____ is a male ruler of an empire.
    dynast empress emperor
    ancestor

CHECK YOUR FACTS

11. Which civilization is older, Sumer or ancient China?

12. What buildings in Sumer and ancient Egypt are similar?

13. China (was/was not) a unified nation under the Shang rulers.

14. What were local districts called in ancient Egypt?

15. Pyramids (were/were not) built throughout the history of ancient Egypt.

USE YOUR MAPS

16. Look at the map of ancient civilizations on page 85. Which one was far from the others?

17. Along what rivers was each of the ancient civilizations centered?

18. Look at the map of ancient empires on page 103. Which empires ruled in Mesopotamia?

19. Which ancient empires included part of Europe?

20. Which were the two largest ancient empires?

THINK ABOUT IT

21. Discuss the role of religion in ancient Sumer, China, and Egypt.

22. List some ways in which religion and government were connected in ancient civilizations.

23. Is farming still important to civilization? Give reasons for your answer.

24. In what ways was domesticating wild animals important to early peoples?

TRY SOMETHING NEW

25. Using an encyclopedia, write a report on the anicent pyramids of Central America.

CHAPTER 2
ANCIENT GREECE AND ROME

Lesson 1: The History of Classical Greece

FIND THE WORDS

oligarchy   tyrant   slave   helot
jury   Hellenistic

The Greeks of long ago greatly influenced Europe, the United States, and much of the rest of the world. Our theater, literature, architecture, art—all these owe much to the Greeks. They affected our views of history, philosophy, and science. We even owe many of our sports to them! The ancient Greeks set standards of beauty and learning that are still important today.

Ancient Greece was centered on the mainland of southeastern Europe and on nearby islands. The Greeks also lived in parts of Asia Minor and elsewhere in the Mediterranean world. Look at the map on page 103. You can see that Greece was near other ancient civilizations of Asia and Africa. The

Greeks borrowed many ideas from these other cultures. They changed these ideas and added to them, producing a great civilization.

The mainland of Greece is mountainous. Overland travel there was difficult. But the Mediterranean Sea was a great highway for the ancient Greeks. It let them trade with other ancient peoples. It also allowed them to borrow and lend ideas.

When most people think of ancient Greece, they think of the period called the Classical Age. Classical Greece reached its height about 450 B.C. But there were advanced cultures in Greece hundreds of years before that time. There was a major culture, the Minoan (mi NOH un) culture, on the island of Crete (KREET) south of the mainland of Greece. A second culture, the Mycenaean (MY suh NEE un) culture, rose on the Greek mainland somewhat later. These earlier cultures were the foundation for the civilization of Classical Greece.

By 800 B.C., a new civilization was arising in Greece. But it was not centered in one place, as the Minoan and Mycenaean cultures had been. Instead, it was scattered throughout the country. Look at the map on page 103. You can see that Greece has a very complicated geography. The Greek mainland is very irregular in shape.

Mountains divide one part of it from another. There are many small islands off the coast. Greece's geography did not encourage unity. Instead, little settlements surrounded by farms grew into city-states. By 500 B.C., there were almost 300 independent city-states. These lay on the Greek mainland, on the islands of the Aegean Sea, and on the coast of Asia Minor.

Government in the Greek City-States

Each city-state decided how it would be governed. At first, monarchy, or rule by one person, a king, was the usual system. The early Greeks believed that their kings were descended from the gods. Gradually, however, the forms of government changed in Greece.

Important families and people who owned large amounts of land became more powerful in the government. These small groups tried to make decisions for all the people in a city-state. Often, these people believed their rule was a form of service to the other members of the community. Such rule by only a few is called **oligarchy** (OL uh GAHR kee). Many people, however, did not think that this system was the best kind of government. Often, there were revolts against the oligarchies. A single ruler, known as a **tyrant** (TY runt), often took over until order was restored. The word *tyrant* later came to mean not only a ruler who had all the power, but one who ruled harshly.

By 500 B.C., a few city-states had adopted democracy, or rule by the people. This form of government gave each citizen of a city-state a role in making decisions for the community. But, not everyone who lived in a city-state was considered a citizen. For example, women could not take part in government. The many **slaves,** people who were owned by others, had no rights at all. Still, many more people participated in government under Greek democracy than ever before in history.

In all the Greek city-states, there was a deep respect for the law. Laws in Greece were meant to help people live together in peace. Usually, the laws had been approved by the citizens. Greek laws tried to protect every citizen.

The Greek city-states developed in different ways. Perhaps the greatest contrast was between the two most famous city-states, Sparta and Athens.

Sparta

In Sparta, each person's life was controlled by the government. The government leaders made the laws and enforced them. Sparta did not develop democracy.

Sparta lay in the Peloponnesus (PEL uh puh NEE suss), the southern part of the Greek mainland. The Dorians, who had conquered this area, had forced the people already there to work for them. They called these workers **helots** (HEL utz). Helots were peasants who were tied to the land. In the 700s B.C., the Spartans also conquered more territory in Messenia (muh SEE nee uh), an area to the west. One reason that Sparta did not become a democracy was that its rulers were always afraid of revolts among the peoples they had conquered.

Sparta's system of government dated from about 600 B.C. There was an assembly of citizens, but it had little power. Sparta was ruled by a small group called the Council of Elders. The Council of Elders made the laws, which were then approved by the assembly.

Only about 10 percent of the people in Sparta were considered citizens. Most of the inhabitants were helots. They had few rights. Helots could not become citizens. Indeed, they were little more than slaves.

From birth to death, life in Sparta was controlled by the government. The government wanted only the "best" people to become citizens. As a result, babies born weak or deformed were killed.

Children were not allowed to live with their families for very long. Boys were sent to military camps at the age of 7. There, they learned how to play sports and games and how to handle themselves in battle.

Spartan girls were trained to work at home. They were encouraged to become strong, healthy mothers. Most wanted to grow up and have sons who could go to war for Sparta.

Not surprisingly, the Spartans were good soldiers. Sparta had great military power. In the 500s B.C., Sparta formed the Peloponnesian (PEL uh puh NEE zhun) League. This was a group of city-states that included Sparta and its neighbors. The league helped make Sparta more powerful.

Athens

The city-state of Athens was very different from Sparta. Much of what we associate with Classical Greece really came from Athens. Athens rose on the coastal plain of the Greek mainland after the decline of the Myceneans. The city was dominated by its highest hill, the Acropolis (ah KROP uh liss). Forts for protection and temples in which to worship the gods were built on the Acropolis.

Athens was first ruled by kings. Then, from the 700s to the 500s B.C., it was governed by an oligarchy called the Council of Nobles. This group chose one of its members to serve as chief magistrate. This person was the most important official in the government.

In 621 B.C., the council passed

ANCIENT EMPIRES

KEY

- Cities
- Egyptian Empire about 1470 B.C.
- Assyrian Empire about 670 B.C.
- Greek city-states in the 600s B.C.
- Persian Empire about 500 B.C.
- Empire of Alexander the Great in 323 B.C.
- Carthaginian Empire in the 200s B.C.

new laws that many Athenians considered harsh. One law forced people who could not pay their debts to become the slaves of the people whom they owed. Within a short time, many small landowners had been made slaves. Rebellion seemed at hand.

Some of the nobles hoped to prevent a revolt. In 594 B.C., they asked a man called Solon (SOH lun) to become chief magistrate. Solon was wise and kind. His first act was to cancel the farmers' debts. He also stopped the practice of making debtors into slaves.

Solon put other reforms into effect. He made the council larger. Now not only nobles, but also large landowners, were members. This group became the Council of 400. The council wrote the laws. All citizens voted on them.

The rulers who followed Solon in Athens continued to increase the role of the people in the government of the city-state.

The Persian Wars

The Persian Empire, which rose in Southwest Asia, threatened the independence of the Greek city-states. By 500 B.C., many of the Greek cities in Asia Minor were ruled by the Persians. Darius, the Persian ruler, wanted to extend his empire into lands north of Greece. If the Persians conquered them, they would surround the center of Greece. To keep this from happening, the Athenians tried to help the Greek cities in Asia Minor.

Darius was so angry at this move by the Athenians that he tried to attack Athens. He sent a fleet of warships. But it was destroyed by a storm at sea. A second Persian attack resulted in the Battle of Marathon in 490 B.C. The Athenians defeated the Persians only 40 kilometers (25 miles) from Athens.

The Persians did not give up after their defeat at Marathon. Xerxes (ZURK seez), the son of Darius, tried to attack Greece again in 480 B.C. Xerxes brought a huge army of 250,000 and a fleet of 600 ships to Greece. This time, the Athenians asked Sparta for help. The two city-states fought together against their enemy.

The Persians landed near Thermopylae (thur MOP uh lee), a narrow pass in the Greek mountains. There, 6000 Spartans died fighting them. The Greeks thought they would do best against the Persians at sea. A great battle was fought off the island of Salamis (SAL uh miss). The Persians had three times as many ships as the Athenians. But the Athenian ships were lighter and easier to handle. The Persian fleet was defeated. After other battles, the Persian threat to Greece came to an end in 479 B.C.

On the Acropolis, a big hill in Athens, are ruins of the ancient city.

Athens' Golden Age

After the Persian Wars until 431 B.C., Athens was at the height of its power. This era is often called the Golden Age of Athens. It is also known as the Age of Pericles (PEHR uh KLEEZ) after a great Athenian leader of the time.

During this period, Athens was the leading city-state of Greece. One reason for this was its powerful navy. After the Persian Wars, the Greek city-states formed the Delian (DEE lee un) League. This group joined together in hopes of protecting Greece from any future attack. Athens quickly became its leader. The headquarters of the league were on the island of Delos (DEE lahss). However, its navy was made up mostly of Athenian ships.

During the Age of Pericles, Athens was a democracy. Athenian citizens voted to approve or reject laws and to choose leaders. This voting took place in large meetings. All adult men in Athens could vote, whether or not they owned property.

Laws in Athens were made by the Assembly. This group met about 40 times a year, or about once every 10 days. Any citizen could speak and vote at these meetings. Any subject could be discussed. This was much like the town meetings held in New England today.

All citizens were eligible to serve on juries. A **jury** is a group of citizens that helps decide a case brought to trial. Each Athenian

This old picture shows Alexander's army in battle.

jury had 500 members. The members were paid for their service on the jury. This was intended to prevent anyone from bribing them.

Pericles was the leader of Athens from 461 to 429 B.C. During this time, the Parthenon, a great temple to the goddess Athena (uh THEE nuh), was built on the Acropolis. The arts and literature also reached new heights.

Education was very important in ancient Athens. By law, all boys had to be educated. There were no public schools, however. Instead, parents hired others to teach their sons. Usually, boys went to school between the ages of 6 and 16. They studied such subjects as ge-

ometry, astronomy, geography, and public speaking. They learned to play musical instruments. They developed their bodies by boxing, wrestling, and running.

Girls were trained only in how to keep a good home. However the Athenians felt that this should include learning how to read and write and how to play musical instruments. Athenian women were also taught to weave cloth and make pottery.

The Peloponnesian War

Athens dominated the Delian League. The Athenians forced the people of the other Greek city-states to pay taxes to them. These city-states began to resist Athenian rule. Between 431 and 404 B.C. Sparta led the other city-states against Athens in the Peloponnesian War.

During the war, Athens lost the support of the other city-states. Sparta developed a fleet that could fight the Athenian navy. The Athenians were forced to surrender in 404 B.C. Sparta then took control of much of Greece. Spartan rule, as you might imagine, was harsh.

Alexander the Great

North of Greece lay Macedonia. This land was greatly affected by Greek culture. In the 300s B.C., Philip II, a great military leader, became the ruler of Macedonia. In 338 B.C., Philip fought with the Greeks and defeated them.

Philip died in 336 B.C. His son, Alexander, became the ruler of Macedonia. Alexander soon attacked Persia. He defeated the Persian armies. Alexander's troops marched through the Mediterranean world. Soon, the empire of Alexander stretched to India.

Alexander the Great died in 323 B.C. His empire did not outlast him for long. It was soon divided into three main parts by his generals. But Greek culture was spread even further throughout the ancient world as a result of Alexander's conquests. The period from 323 B.C. to 30 B.C. is known as the Hellenistic Age. **Hellenistic** (HEHL uh NISS tik) means "Greek-like."

Greek civilization dominated the lands around the eastern Mediterranean during the Hellenistic Age. Later, this region was ruled by Romans, Arabs, and Turks. But the influence of the ancient Greeks can still be seen there.

REVIEW

WATCH YOUR WORDS

1. ____is rule by a few.
Democracy   Monarchy   Oligarchy

2. A ____ is a person owned by another person.
slave   helot   servant

3. The____Age followed Alexander.
Greek   Hellenistic   Roman

CHECK YOUR FACTS

4. In ancient Greece, women (could/could not) vote.

5. Sparta was (more/less) democratic than Athens.

THINK ABOUT IT

List some ways in which Greek democracy was like our own. In what ways was it different?

Lesson 2: Gifts from the Greeks

FIND THE WORDS

epic   philosophy   philosopher

When you think of the size of Earth, the city-state of Athens—and even all of ancient Greece—seems very small. Ancient Greek times and the Golden Age of Athens were but brief periods in the world's long history. Yet, out of those small places and those short periods came ideas that affect our lives today.

Theater and Literature

The ancient Greeks were the first people to write plays. They presented them in great outdoor theaters. Some of these theaters still exist.

Most early Greek literature was poetry. The epic poem was invented by the Greeks. An **epic** is a long poem that tells a story.

Later Greeks also wrote fine works of prose. The most important Greek prose was works of philosophy. But Greek historians

Greek plays were performed in this ancient outdoor theater. This ruin is in present-day Turkey.

also set high standards for writing about the past.

Philosophy

The very word *philosophy* is Greek. **Philosophy** (fi LAHS uh fee) means "love of wisdom." So philosophy is the study of ideas. It involves questions of right and wrong. It is also the study of truth and falsehood. All these things were important to the Greeks.

The ancient Greeks asked many important questions. They wanted to know why people acted as they did. They tried to learn what a person's role in life was. They tried to find out how people could affect their own lives.

The Greeks did not agree on the answers to the questions they asked. There were several important groups of **philosophers,** or people who study philosophy. The three most important Greek philosophers were Socrates (SOK ruh TEEZ), Plato (PLAY toh), and Aristotle (AR iss TOT ul).

History

The idea of written history began with the Greeks. The first important Greek historian was Herodotus (hi ROD uh tus). He wrote about the Persian Wars.

Thucydides (thoo SID uh DEEZ) was the greatest Greek historian. He wrote about the Peloponnesian War.

This ancient stone carving shows Persephone, a figure from Greek myths.

Politics

One of the greatest gifts of the Greeks to the world was the concept of democracy. Their idea that citizens should take part in government was very important. Never before in history had average citizens had the right to vote and hold public office.

The Greek idea that citizens have a right to take an active part in government still survives. In some New England towns, people still practice Greek-style democracy. There, every citizen of the town has the right to speak and to vote at town meetings.

Science

The ancient Greeks took many of their scientific ideas from older cultures. To these, they added new ideas. Much of modern science is based on Greek thought. In particular, the Greeks affected mathematics, physics, astronomy, and medicine.

Architecture and Art

The main styles of Greek architecture were Doric, Ionic (eye ON ik), and Corinthian. You can still see these styles in some buildings today. Greek buildings were simple and finely balanced. Their beauty has seldom been equalled since.

The ancient Greeks were superb artists. Much pottery and some sculpture has survived from their times to ours. Though often damaged, many of these works of art are still incredibly beautiful.

Sports

Have you ever watched the modern Olympic (oh LIM pik) games on television? They are based on games held in ancient times at Olympia in Greece. To the ancient Greeks, these contests gave people a chance to come together and compete peacefully. The Olympic games were intended to bring some unity to the city-states. A laurel wreath and a statue were given to each winner.

The sports of running, jumping, boxing, and wrestling were founded by the Greeks. They believed in the motto "a sound mind in a sound body." Today, this tradition continues in the idea of the scholar-athlete. That is a person who does well both in studies and in sports.

Greece and Rome

The power of Greece declined in the last centuries before the birth of Christ. To the west, the people of the city of Rome were building an empire. Their empire would dominate the Mediterranean world for centuries. They laid the foundations for the Europe of the Middle Ages and after. But Roman civilization was, in large part, based on the civilization of ancient Greece.

REVIEW

WATCH YOUR WORDS

1. A(n)____is a long poem.
   lyric epic novel
2. ____means "love of wisdom."
   Philosopher Poet Philosophy

CHECK YOUR FACTS

3. Name the three most important Greek philosophers.

4. Name two Greek historians.
5. What are the main styles of Greek architecture?
6. What sports were founded by the Greeks?

THINK ABOUT IT

Have you ever read any Greek literature or seen any Greek plays? If so, what have you read or seen?

Lesson 3: The Early History of Rome

FIND THE WORDS

legend	patrician	Senate
senator	plebeian	republic
consul	dictator	tribune
	legion	

Rome and the Etruscans

About 1000 B.C., people from the area near the Black and Caspian seas moved into the lands along the Tiber (TY bur) River in Italy. These people were called Latins. They became farmers and lived in small villages.

About 900 B.C., the Etruscans (i TRUSS kunz) settled between the Arno and Tiber rivers. Find these areas on the map on page 113. The Etruscans probably came from Asia Minor. Gradually, they expanded their territory. By 700 B.C., Etruscan lands stretched east to the Apennines (AP uh NYNZ) Mountains. They reached north to the Po River valley and south to the seaport of Naples (NAY pulz).

Paintings, pottery, and other objects have been found in Etruscan tombs. These show that the Etruscans had a civilization that

In this drawing, Romulus returns from a battle in triumph.

combined parts of Southwest Asian and Greek cultures. They had a written language. They were also fine builders.

There is a **legend,** or old story, that tells how Rome began. No one knows how much of it is true, but it makes a good story all the same. According to the legend, Rome was started by twin brothers named Romulus (RAHM yuh lus) and Remus (REE mus). As children, they were supposed to have been thrown into a river by their mother. They were rescued by a female wolf, who raised them. Their father was supposed to have been Mars, the Roman god of war. In about the year 753 B.C., the brothers founded a city on Palatine (PAL uh TYN) Hill, above the Tiber River. Romulus later killed Remus. The city was called Rome after Romulus.

Archaeologists do agree that Rome was founded in the mid-700s B.C. They believe a group of Etruscans settled there. Gradually, the city spread to six other nearby hills along the Tiber River. A fort was built on one of the seven hills of Rome, Capitol Hill.

The legend says that Romulus was the first king of Rome. In any case, we are sure that the early government was a monarchy. As the Etruscans extended their rule throughout Italy, Rome became part of their territory. The last three kings of Rome were Etruscans. During the Etruscan period, Rome grew larger and stronger. Its people also became more civilized. They borrowed ideas from the Etruscans. These were ideas that the Etruscans, in turn, had borrowed from the Greeks.

The Roman people were divided into two groups. Those who belonged to wealthy and important families were called **patricians** (puh TRISH unz). They were the nobles. The heads of patrician families made up a group called the **Senate.** The **senators,** as the members of this group were called, gave advice to the king. The king was elected from among the senators. The other families of Rome were called **plebeians** (pli BEE unz). They were the common people. At first, the plebeians had no say in the government.

The Etruscan kings became harsh rulers. In 509 B.C., the people of Rome rebelled against their Etruscan king. That ended Etruscan rule in Rome. The monarchy also came to an end. The Romans formed a kind of government called a republic. The word *republic* comes from Latin, the language of the Romans. Literally, it means "the people's thing." A **republic** is a government without a monarch. It can be an oligarchy or a democracy, depending on how many people rule.

WHERE WE ARE IN TIME AND PLACE

HISTORY OF ROME

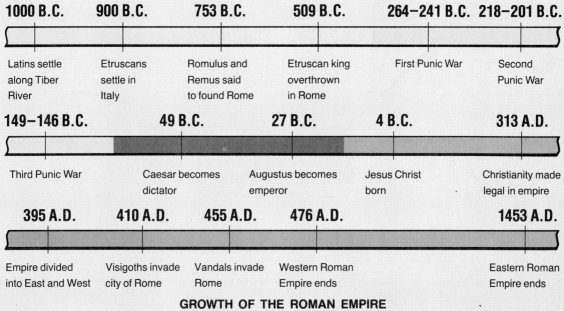

1000 B.C.	900 B.C.	753 B.C.	509 B.C.	264–241 B.C.	218–201 B.C.

Latins settle along Tiber River | Etruscans settle in Italy | Romulus and Remus said to found Rome | Etruscan king overthrown in Rome | First Punic War | Second Punic War

149–146 B.C.	49 B.C.	27 B.C.	4 B.C.	313 A.D.

Third Punic War | Caesar becomes dictator | Augustus becomes emperor | Jesus Christ born | Christianity made legal in empire

395 A.D.	410 A.D.	455 A.D.	476 A.D.	1453 A.D.

Empire divided into East and West | Visigoths invade city of Rome | Vandals invade Rome | Western Roman Empire ends | Eastern Roman Empire ends

GROWTH OF THE ROMAN EMPIRE

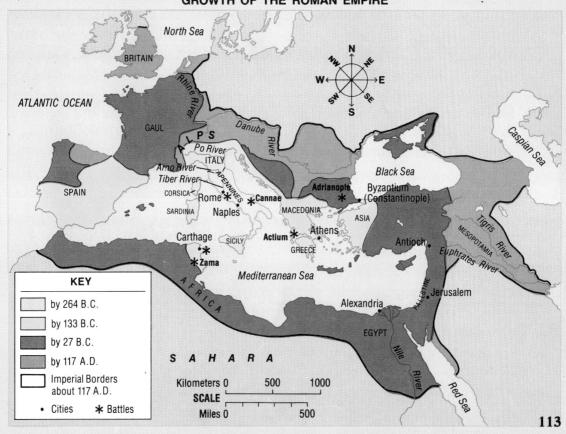

KEY

- by 264 B.C.
- by 133 B.C.
- by 27 B.C.
- by 117 A.D.
- Imperial Borders about 117 A.D.
- • Cities   * Battles

SCALE
Kilometers 0   500   1000
Miles 0   500

113

The Roman Republic

At first, the Roman Republic was an oligarchy, ruled by the powerful few. Gradually, the Roman people came to have more and more say in their government.

To replace the king, the Senate of Rome first chose two **consuls.** They were to serve as rulers and chief judges. The Senate continued to advise the consuls, as it had the king. The senators also continued to make the major decisions.

Gradually, the system of government changed in Rome. The patricians lost some of their power in the government. By 287 B.C., the government of the Roman Republic was organized in the way described below.

The laws were carried out by the two consuls elected by the Senate. These consuls also controlled the army and navy. In times of trouble, a **dictator** (DIK tay tur), or ruler with total power, could be elected for up to 6 months.

Consuls served for a year. Then, they returned to the Senate. Former consuls might become *censors*, or guardians of the public morals.

Plebeians were represented in the government. They had their own assembly. The assembly elected officials called **tribunes** (TRIB YOONZ). The job of the tribunes was to protect the plebeians from the consuls and to represent the common people. According to Roman law, no one could interfere with a tribune. Anyone breaking this law could be put to death. Tribunes could try lawbreakers to see if they were guilty or innocent.

The tribunes gained a great deal of power over the years. They could stop any act of a consul involving a plebeian. All they had to do was say "*veto*" (VEE toh), which meant "I forbid." Tribunes could ask the Senate to meet to consider various questions. They could affect the actions of the Senate by threatening to veto them.

Expansion under the Republic

Freed from Etruscan rule, Rome began to expand its territories. First, people in neighboring city-states became part of the Roman Republic. As each new area was taken, the Romans allowed the conquered peoples to become citizens of Rome. Eventually, Rome conquered all of Italy. Thus, all the people of Italy became Roman citizens.

Rome's expansion was not completely peaceful. In 270 B.C., Rome became involved in a dispute among the Greek city-states in southern Italy. This led to conflict between Rome and Carthage (KAHR thij), a powerful city-state in North Africa.

Rome had developed a powerful army. It was organized into **legions** (LEE junz). These were groups of about 6000 foot soldiers.

Between 264 and 146 B.C., Carthage and Rome fought three wars. These are called the Punic (PYOO nik) Wars.

In the First Punic War, Rome gained control of Sicily. Within a few years, Rome also took over the large Mediterranean islands of Sardinia (sahr DIN ee uh) and Corsica (KOR si kuh).

The Carthaginians did not accept their defeat by the Romans. In 218 B.C., they began the Second Punic War. Hannibal, a great Carthaginian general, led an invasion of Italy. In the Battle of Cannae (KAN ee) in 216 B.C., Hannibal's army defeated the Romans. But the Carthaginians were not able to capture Rome. The Roman general Scipio (SKIP ee OH) then led an attack on Carthage. At Zama, in 202 B.C., Hannibal's army was defeated. An uneasy peace followed.

The Third Punic War began in 149 B.C. A Roman army invaded North Africa. The Romans surrounded Carthage and cut off its food supply. After many of the Carthaginians had starved to death, the city fell in 146 B.C. Carthage had been defeated for the last time. Its territory became the Roman province of Africa.

STRANGE FACTS

Hannibal of Carthage was one of the greatest generals in history. Hannibal carried the Second Punic War into Italy by marching over the Alps. His army included about 60,000 troops, 6000 horses, and 38 elephants!

It was an amazing feat. In the cold and snow of winter, Hannibal's soldiers climbed steep paths covered with ice. Hostile people who lived in the mountains rolled heavy stones down on them from above. Both men and animals lost their footing and plunged to their deaths. Yet about half of Hannibal's forces made it to Italy. The Romans were shocked and surprised. No one had believed that such an army could cross the Alps.

In Italy, Hannibal led his troops to

great victories. He won the great Battle of Cannae. But never was he able to capture the city of Rome, itself.

The Romans built roads to connect all parts of their empire. In this way, they could move armies quickly from place to place.

After the Second Punic War, the Roman armies began to move to the east. They had conquered Macedonia and Greece and made them Roman provinces by the end of the Third Punic War. Beginning in 133 B.C., the Romans started to take over lands in Southwest Asia. By 100 B.C., Rome controlled all the lands around the Mediterranean Sea except Egypt. And Egypt was friendly to the Romans. Look at the map on page 113. You can see how far Roman power grew.

REVIEW

WATCH YOUR WORDS

1. In Roman society, ____ were higher than____.
   republics   plebeians   Senates   patricians

2. In ancient Rome, the ____ gave advice to the ruler.
   republics   plebeians   Senate

3. A ____ is a government without a monarch.
   republic   kingdom   Senate

4. The ____ were rulers and chief judges in Rome.
   tribunes   legions   consuls

5. The ____ represented the common people in the government of Rome.
   tribunes   plebeians   consuls

CHECK YOUR FACTS

6. What group ruled Rome in its early years?

7. Was the early Roman republic a democracy or an oligarchy?

8. Who had the right of veto, the tribunes or the consuls?

9. With what city-state did the Roman Republic fight three wars?

10. In 100 B.C., what important Mediterranean land did Rome not yet control?

THINK ABOUT IT

How could one city like Rome come to dominate the whole Mediterranean world?

Lesson 4: The Roman Empire

From 133 B.C. on, there was much fighting in the Roman Republic. As the leaders struggled for power, many Romans were killed. Out of these struggles emerged one of Rome's—and the world's—great leaders, Julius Caesar (JOOL yus SEE zur).

Gaius Julius Caesar was born about 100 B.C. into a patrician family of Rome. During the first 40 years of his life, Caesar held many positions in the Roman government. The kinds of jobs he had and the way he did them made him popular with the common people of Rome.

Caesar had long been working with Crassus, a wealthy Roman. In 60 B.C., Crassus and Caesar joined with Pompey (POM pee), a very popular general, to form the First Triumvirate. **Triumvirate** (try UM vur it) means "ruling body of three men." The First Triumvirate was a private partnership set up by the three men to further their own interests. It succeeded very well.

In 59 B.C., Caesar was elected consul. In this position, he was able to get laws that Pompey desired passed. He also was able to get Crassus a contract to collect taxes in the provinces. Caesar soon left Rome to become governor of Gaul (now France).

The Romans knew that Caesar was a good political leader. But he turned out to be a great general as well. He led the Roman legions in many battles in Gaul, losing only twice in 9 years. During this time, he extended Roman rule throughout Gaul.

While Caesar was winning great victories in Gaul, Pompey and Crassus remained in Rome. Crassus died in 53 B.C. Pompey began to fear that Caesar was becoming too powerful. He began to favor the party of the senators and to try to undermine Caesar.

In 49 B.C., Pompey persuaded the Senate to call Caesar back from Gaul and take away his army. Caesar, however, refused to return to Rome. Instead, he led one of his legions across the Rubicon (ROO bi kon), a small river that divided Gaul from Italy. This amounted to a declaration of war against Pompey. Ever since, the phrase "crossing the Rubicon" has meant a turning point in life.

It took Caesar only 60 days to win control of all of Italy. But it took him several years to defeat all of Pompey's armies.

In 49 B.C., Caesar had been made dictator and consul. He was also made tribune for life. He already controlled the state religion. After the final defeat of Pompey's forces, Caesar was made dictator for life.

As ruler of Rome, Caesar accomplished many things. He adopted a new calendar, eliminating many errors. The Julian calendar was widely used until modern times. He put an end to much of the corruption in the provincial governments. He reorganized city governments in Italy and appointed honest officials. Caesar also appointed able people to office, even if they had previously opposed him. He extended Roman citizenship to more people in the conquered provinces.

A group of senators, led by Brutus and Cassius (KASH us), plotted to kill Caesar. On March 15, 44 B.C., Caesar was attacked and stabbed to death as he entered the Senate to speak. Rome was once again without a leader. Years of fighting were to follow.

Octavian

Octavian (ahk TAY vee un), Caesar's great-nephew and adopted son, was only 18 at the time of Caesar's death. He soon returned to Rome from Greece. Octavian joined with Mark Antony, Caesar's great friend, and Lepidus. They set up the Second Triumvirate. Octavian and Antony defeated the armies of Brutus and Cassius, Caesar's killers. The Second Triumvirate then held the power in Rome.

Although Octavian was young when Caesar died, he soon became a powerful and great ruler. And Octavian's power continued to grow. Antony tried to challenge him for control of all of Rome's empire. But Octavian's forces defeated those of Antony and Queen Cleopatra of Egypt at Actium in 31 B.C. From then on, Octavian was the single ruler of Rome's vast lands.

Augustus

In 27 B.C., the Senate gave Octavian the name *Augustus* (aw GUSS tuss), meaning "majestic." Augustus ruled wisely. He controlled the government in Rome. But he let the conquered territories rule themselves to a great degree. However, all the provinces had Roman governors.

Augustus became consul, tribune, and high priest. In this way, he controlled the whole government. He also took the title of *princeps* (preen KEHPS), meaning "first in rank." This gave him the right to speak first in the Senate on any topic. From this title

The picture on the right shows a bridge and aqueduct built by the Romans. It is still standing in France today. The family of Augustus, the Roman Emperor, is shown in the stone carving below.

comes our word *prince*. Augustus is considered the first emperor of Rome. Later emperors came to use the names *Caesar* and *Augustus* as titles.

The Emperor Augustus developed a group of officials responsible only to him to carry out the business of government. These people were much like government officials today. Augustus restored the rule of law to the Roman Empire. He organized the empire so

that it would run smoothly. Under his rule, many roads and bridges were built to connect the various parts of the empire. **Aqueducts** (AK wuh DUKTZ), or raised pipes, were built to carry water to towns and cities. Some Roman roads, bridges, and aqueducts were so well-built that they are still used today, 2000 years later.

Augustus began a period of peace in the empire that was to last for more than 200 years. This period was called the *Pax Romana*, the Roman peace. During this time, the peoples of the Roman Empire lived in safety. Their civilization became ever richer.

Emperors after Augustus

After Augustus died in 14 A.D., there was another struggle for control of the government. There was no set way of passing on power from one ruler to another in the Roman Empire.

Several of the emperors who followed Augustus were not very good rulers. Yet Augustus had set up such a good system of government that the empire survived no matter who the ruler was.

From 96 to 180 A.D., Rome had some excellent emperors. By this time, the Roman Empire included more than 100 million people.

The empire stretched east to the Euphrates River, west to the Atlantic Ocean, north to the Danube and Rhine rivers, and south to the Sahara. Trace its borders on the map on page 113. But about this time, the Roman Empire was beginning to have serious problems. Trade between the provinces declined. Many people were unable to find work. The value of money dropped. Goods cost more to buy. Despite his title, the emperor was often actually controlled by the army.

This is the Supreme Court building in our country. It is built in the style of Greek and Roman buildings.

In this ancient wall painting, a Roman woman is playing a musical instrument.

The job of emperor of Rome was not very secure from this time on. From 180 to 284 A.D., there were 29 Roman emperors. Only four of these died natural deaths. All the others were killed in struggles for power.

The Emperor Diocletian (DY uh KLEE shun) tried to restore order to the empire between 284 and 305 A.D. He made very strict rules. But he did not succeed in stopping the decline of Rome. The empire was beginning to fall apart.

REVIEW

CHECK YOUR FACTS

1. Who were the members of the First Triumvirate?

2. Where did Caesar prove he was a good general?

3. Who were the members of the Second Triumvirate?

4. Who was the first emperor of Rome?

5. What was the *Pax Romana?*

TRY SOMETHING NEW

Look up the words *kaiser* and *czar* in the dictionary. From what word do they both come?

Lesson 5: The Rise of Christianity

FIND THE WORDS

Judaism   catacomb   bishop
apostle   pope

Jesus and Christianity

One of the most important events in world history occurred in the Roman Empire. Jesus Christ was born in the town of Bethlehem in Judea (joo DEE uh), a province of Rome. Jesus was the founder of Christianity, one of the world's great religions.

The calendar used in most of the world dates from what was erroneously thought to be the year of Jesus' birth. The letters *B.C.* mean "before Christ." The letters *A.D.* stand for the Latin words *anno Domini* (AN oh   DOM un NY), meaning "in the year of the Lord." After this system was in use, historians discovered that Jesus was actually born about 4 years earlier than had been thought, or in about 4 B.C.

Jesus was born to a Jewish family. He lived his early life in the town of Nazareth. Little is known about these years. The New Testament, the Christian part of the Bible, tells the story of Jesus' last years. The New Testament writers describe the religious ideas he preached in Palestine. He did not begin to preach until he was about 30.

Jesus' teachings differed somewhat from the traditional Jewish beliefs. Some Jewish leaders began to fear Jesus as he gathered more followers. Even the Romans who governed Palestine came to fear him. When Jesus was 33, he was put to death in Jerusalem by the Romans. But the ideas of Jesus Christ lived on. They were written down in the New Testament and became the basis of Christianity. This was a new religion, but one with deep roots in **Judaism**, the Jewish religion.

Christianity Grows

Jesus' followers, known as Christians, spread his new religion throughout the Roman Empire after his death. More and more people far from Palestine became Christians.

The Roman governors and officials expected the Christians to behave like the other peoples of the empire. They were required to burn incense before the image of the emperor on certain days. They were made to serve in the army. They were supposed to give all their support and loyalty to the emperor.

But the Christians refused to do many of these things. They said that they could not serve both Rome and God. During the early years, Christians were often arrested and put into prison. Many were punished or even killed for their beliefs.

The Emperor Diocletian was sure that the Christians wanted to seize the empire. He ordered their churches and property burned. He outlawed the Christian religion. Anyone found worshiping Christ could be put to death. But the church survived by going underground. To go underground means to hide from public view. In Roman times, this often meant going literally under the ground. One of the best places for holding secret church services was in the **catacombs,** underground tombs just outside Rome.

The Emperor Constantine (KON stun teen) decided that the Christians should be allowed to practice their religion. He made the Christian church equal to all other religions in the empire in 313 A.D. This encouraged the further growth of Christianity. Finally, the Emperor Theodosius (THEE uh DOH shus) made Christianity the official religion of the Roman Empire during his rule from 379 to 395 A.D. All other religions were forbidden.

The Colosseum (KOL uh SEE um) in Rome was a big stadium. Here many Christians were put to death.

The Emperor Constantine was a strong ruler. This carving is in a museum in Rome.

Christianity was now growing stronger as the Roman Empire was becoming weaker. The church bought land and built churches and other religious buildings. It began to care for the sick and the poor. It even began to act like a government.

The Christian church came to be ruled by religious leaders called **bishops.** The bishop of Rome became the most important leader of the church. That was because he was in the capital city of the Roman Empire. The Roman bishop was also thought to be the successor of St. Peter. Peter had been one of Christ's first followers, who were called **apostles** (uh POSS ulz). Peter was considered Christ's chief apostle. He was believed to have been the very first bishop of Rome. In 445 A.D., the bishop of Rome claimed to be the ruler of the whole Christian church. From that time on, the Roman bishop was called the **pope.** The parts of the Christian church ruled by the pope came to be called the Roman Catholic Church.

The popes began to play an important role in the government of Rome and of Italy. For example, when the Huns threatened to attack Rome, the pope held talks with their leader. The church became deeply involved in the lives of all the peoples of Europe.

REVIEW

WATCH YOUR WORDS

1. The first followers of Jesus Christ were called____.
   bishops apostles popes

2. The parts of the Christian church were ruled by leaders called____.
   bishops apostles popes

3. The bishop of Rome came to be called the____.
   catacomb apostle pope

CHECK YOUR FACTS

4. What does B.C. mean? A.D.?

5. Which Roman emperor made Christianity legal? Which emperor made it the official religion?

Lesson 6: The Fall of the Roman Empire

FIND THE WORDS

**barbarian   mercenary
monastery   monk**

In its later years, the Roman Empire was so large, and its problems so great, that it became very difficult to govern. Different emperors tried to solve Rome's problems. The Emperor Diocletian divided the empire into four parts, each with its own ruler. This did not help much.

The Emperor Constantine moved the capital of the empire to Byzantium (bi ZAN tee um). This city lay where Europe and Asia met. Its location was more secure than that of Rome. Constantine renamed the new capital Constantinople (KON stan ti NOH pul) after himself. Yet the empire continued to decline.

In 395 A.D., after the death of the Emperor Theodosius, the empire was permanently divided into two parts. These were the Eastern Roman Empire and the Western Roman Empire. The Eastern Empire would survive for more than a thousand years. But the Western Empire would last for less than a century.

The Fall of the Western Empire

Various German peoples had long lived along the borders of the Roman Empire. They were called **barbarians** (bahr BAIR ee unz), which meant "uncivilized people." The barbarians constantly challenged Rome's power. They made life very difficult, particularly in the border provinces. In 378 A.D., the Visigoths, one of the German groups, defeated the Roman army

This old drawing shows the Vandals burning and looting Rome in 455 A.D.

at the Battle of Adrianople (A dree uh NOH pul). In 410 A.D., the Germans invaded Rome itself. In 455, Rome was invaded again, this time by the Vandals. The Roman army could no longer keep out the barbarians from the north. The last Roman emperor was ousted in 476. The Roman Empire had come to an end in the west.

There were many reasons for the fall of the Western Roman Empire. One reason lay in the Roman character. The early Romans had believed in serving the state and relying on themselves. But the upper-class groups in the empire became wealthy and came to own most of the land. They no longer wished to serve in the Roman army or even as officials in the Roman government. Nor did the groups below them. By the end, the Roman army was no longer made up of citizen-soldiers. It was manned by **mercenaries** (MUR suh NEHR eez), or hired soldiers. Most of these men were foreigners. They had no special loyalty to Rome.

The Roman government, itself, was a problem. Many of the later emperors were poor rulers. Because there was no clear way to pass on the right to rule, there was a damaging struggle for power whenever an emperor died. The government became more and more corrupt. Rome had given the Mediterranean world good government. Bad government undermined the very meaning of the empire.

The barbarians and the people in the provinces gradually became aware of how weak Rome was. The barbarians invaded the empire and the conquered peoples revolted. Thus, the Western Roman Empire broke up.

The Eastern Empire

The Eastern Roman Empire is also known as the Byzantine (BIZ un TEEN) Empire. This name comes from Byzantium, as Constantinople was first called. The Byzantines continued to control many of the eastern lands of the Roman Empire for many centuries. For a time in the 500s, they even reconquered Italy, North Africa, and southern Spain. Between 976 and 1025, Italy and the Balkan area north of Greece were again part of the empire.

The Byzantine Empire was largely Greek in language and culture. The Byzantines were also Christians. But the Christian church in the east gradually became the Eastern Orthodox Church. This church was different from the Roman Catholic Church in several ways. Some of its religious ideas were not the same. Most important, the Eastern Orthodox did not accept the bishop of Rome as head of their church.

The Byzantine Empire grew weaker over the centuries. Toward the end, it included only the city of Constantinople. Finally, in 1453, the Ottoman Turks conquered Constantinople. The Roman Empire had finally come to an end after 1500 years.

The Middle Ages Begin

The period in Europe after the fall of Rome is often called the Dark Ages. This was a time when civilization seemed to be going backward. Many of the ideas of Greece and Rome were lost during these years. Learning and progress almost disappeared. Cities lost population. Trade dwindled and agriculture declined. The peoples of Europe were held together by one thing—the Christian church.

After the Roman Empire fell, the leaders of the church tried to maintain order. They set up courts, collected taxes, and tried to meet people's needs. The popes turned to the Franks for help.

Around 500 A.D., a group of Germans called Franks settled along the Rhine River near the North Sea. Clovis, a Frankish king, became a Christian. The Frankish lands were expanded by the rulers who followed him. The kingdom of the Franks eventually came to cover a large area. It included what is today France, Belgium, the Netherlands, and Germany.

This old drawing shows Clovis and a bishop in 15th-century dress.

In 751, Pepin the Short seized power among the Franks. He asked the pope for support. In return, he promised to help the pope fight off the groups threatening to take over the lands that belonged to the church. From this time on, relations between the popes and the Frankish kings were close.

Charlemagne (SHAHR luh MAYN), or Charles the Great, was the next ruler of the Franks. He added to the Frankish lands and improved the government of his kingdom. In Rome, on Christmas Day in the year 800, Pope Leo III crowned Charlemagne emperor of

Charlemagne was a great ruler.

run his empire. But, at that time, few people knew how to read and write. So Charlemagne started schools. He supported the **monasteries** (MON uh STEHR eez). These were religious institutions where men lived together and devoted their lives to religion. These men, called **monks,** were also scholars. They spent their time studying and copying ancient books. The monasteries helped preserve the writings and ideas of ancient Greece and Rome.

After Charlemagne's death, his empire was divided up. The rulers who followed him were not very strong. They could not keep together such a huge territory with such different lands and peoples.

The period between Charlemagne and modern times is called the Middle Ages. During this time, the peoples of Western Europe developed a new way of life.

the Romans. Charlemagne's empire was the next important empire after the Roman Empire.

Charlemagne knew that he needed educated people to help

REVIEW

CHECK YOUR FACTS

1. Which emperor divided the Roman Empire into four parts?
2. In what year did the Western Roman Empire come to an end?
3. What is another name for the Eastern Roman Empire?
4. What is the period after the fall of Rome often called?
5. Who was Charlemagne?
6. What is the period between about 800 A.D. and modern times called?

THINK ABOUT IT

The Roman Empire lasted for 1500 years. What nearby empire that you have studied lasted, in one form or another, for 3000 years?

CHAPTER REVIEW

WATCH YOUR WORDS

1. In ancient Greece, a(n) ___ was a ruler who had all power.
   oligarch   tyrant   helot

2. Greek peasants were called ___.
   slaves   tyrants   helots

3. A ___ helps decide a case.
   jury   tyrant   helot

4. ___ devote their lives to thinking and studying.
   Juries   Oligarchs   Philosophers

5. In what order did these systems of government come in the history of ancient Greece?
   oligarchy   monarchy   democracy

6. The Roman army was made up of ___.
   consuls   tribunes   legions

7. A ___ is a ruling body made up of three men.
   triumvirate   tribute   tribune

8. A ___ is an underground tomb.
   pope   catacomb   legion

9. ___ are uncivilized people.
   Barbarians   Mercenaries   Monks

10. ___ live in monasteries.
    Barbarians   Mercenaries   Monks

CHECK YOUR FACTS

11. What city-state was the leader of the Peloponnesian League?

12. What city-state was the leader of the Delian League?

13. With what Asian empire did the Greek city-states fight a series of wars?

14. What is the Golden Age of Athens also known as?

15. From what land did Philip II and Alexander the Great come?

16. What group ruled in northern Italy before the Romans?

17. What general led the forces of Carthage against Rome?

18. What friend of Caesar's was a member of the Second Triumvirate?

19. What institution was becoming important in Europe as the Roman Empire was falling?

20. Name two German groups that invaded the Roman Empire.

USE YOUR MAPS

21. Compare the map of the Roman Empire on page 113 and the map of Europe today on page 190. Which present-day European nations were once ruled by Rome?

THINK ABOUT IT

22. Suppose you could travel in time back to ancient Greece. Who would you like to meet? What event or place would you most like to see? Give reasons for your answers.

23. How might Greek history have been different if Greece were a plain?

24. What letters of the Greek alphabet can you name? Some hints: College fraternities and honor societies usually have Greek names. Some Greek letters are used in math. The very word *alphabet* contains the names of two Greek letters.

25. Which was more important, ancient Greece or ancient Rome? Give reasons for your answer.

TRY SOMETHING NEW

26. Write a one-page report on the Olympic games in ancient Greece. Use an encyclopedia or other source suggested by your teacher.

3 EUROPE IN THE MIDDLE AGES

Lesson 1: Feudalism Begins in Europe

FIND THE WORDS

feudalism	**fief**	**lord**
vassal	**serf**	**Christendom**

The Dark Ages before Charlemagne and the early Middle Ages after him were times of disorder. There were now no Roman legions to control violence in Europe. Lawlessness spread throughout the continent. Cities were destroyed and many lost all or most of their people. Trade almost disappeared. The Germanic groups that had overrun the Western Roman Empire soon settled down and became Christians. But still there was no peace. Within each group, powerful lords battled each other for power. Still more barbarian groups invaded Europe from Asia, adding to the destruction.

Out of all this disorder, a new way of organizing and governing society arose. This system was called **feudalism** (FYOOD ul IZ um). To help restore order, the kings gave large pieces of land to important nobles. This gift of land was called a **fief** (FEEF). In return for the land, the nobles promised to fight and do other services for their king.

A noble's fief was usually too much land for him to work alone. So he would grant part of his fief to a less powerful noble in return for military and other services.

The person who granted the land was called a **lord.** The person who received the land was called a **vassal** (VASS ul). Nobles often held more than one fief. Often, too, the fiefs were scattered all over the country. This meant that a single noble might be the vassal of several lords. In turn, this noble might also be a lord to several lesser vassals. In this way, feudalism tied together all the nobles of an area.

But most people in Europe during the Middle Ages were not nobles. They were common people. Most of them lived on the land of the nobles. There were two main groups of commoners: free people and serfs.

Free people rented their land from the lord. They were free to leave the land when they chose to do so. They could travel or move to a town. **Serfs,** on the other hand, were not free. They were tied to the land. A serf needed the lord's permission to leave the land. Serfs were not exactly slaves. They were not completely owned by another person. Sometimes, a serf would get rich enough to buy his or her freedom.

Today, we think of ourselves as residents of a town or a state. We consider ourselves citizens of a country. But in the Middle Ages, people thought very differently. At first, there were very few towns. There were no unified countries as we know them today. Nobles thought of themselves as vassals of the king or of other lords. They also thought of themselves as lords of other nobles or of common people. The common people lived on the land of the nobles. No one felt loyal to any larger place, such as a country. The one institution that did unite everyone was the Roman Catholic Church. Instead of a country, the people of the Middle Ages often felt they lived in **Christendom** (KRISS un dum). This word meant the part of the world where most people were Christians.

Cooperation was what made feudalism work. Each person gave something and received something in return. But feudalism did not always work smoothly. There were constant power struggles under this system. Sometimes, a lord would try to force other nobles to do what he wanted. Often, the nobles were stronger than the king. Powerful nobles tried to control the king. When a king was strong, he tried to control the nobles. War was common in the Middle Ages.

All this fighting kept the people of Europe disunited. It weakened government and society as a whole. In addition to this violence from within, Europe was attacked by outside groups between 700 and 1000.

In the 700s, the Muslims conquered Spain and invaded France. You will read more about the Muslims later in this chapter. Beginning in the 800s, fierce warriors called Vikings (VY kingz) invaded large areas of Europe. The Vikings came from what is now Norway, Sweden, and Denmark. They were expert sailors and fighters. They used their long, low, narrow boats to sail far up rivers. They took villages, towns, and monasteries by surprise. They killed many people and robbed them of their possessions. The Vikings destroyed what they did not steal.

At last, the Vikings settled down. When the Viking raids came to an end, feudalism began to bring some peace to Europe. Kings gradually grew more powerful. The Roman Catholic Church also tried to lessen the fighting between the European nobles.

REVIEW

WATCH YOUR WORDS

1. A ____ was a peasant tied to the land.
   vassal fief serf

2. A ____ was a piece of land given by a lord.
   vassal fief serf

3. A ____ received a fief.
   vassal feud serf

CHECK YOUR FACTS

4. What system helped restore order in Europe during the Middle Ages?

5. In the Middle Ages, most people (did/did not) feel a deep loyalty to their nation.

THINK ABOUT IT

What were some of the advantages of feudalism? What were some of its disadvantages?

Lesson 2: Life on a Manor

FIND THE WORDS

**manor   castle   moat
drawbridge   knight   page
squire   tournament   joust
lance**

The place where the lord and his serfs lived was called a **manor.** A manor included a village, fields, and forests. At its center was the lord's **castle.** The castle was both a fort and a home for the lord and his family.

Castles were usually built on hills or in some other place that was easy to defend. High walls made the castle difficult to attack. A deep ditch of water called a **moat** usually surrounded the castle. The only entrance was a bridge that could be raised and lowered with chains. This is called a **drawbridge.** With the drawbridge up, attackers would have to get across the deep moat. Then they would have to climb the high walls. While they were doing this,

In the Middle Ages, most people had no need to leave the manor. As you can see in the picture, many different activities on the manor helped supply people's needs.

The lords and ladies of the manors lived well. Many servants looked after their every need.

the attackers would be easy targets for the defenders on the walls.

Today, many castles from the Middle Ages still stand. Some are a thousand years old. They are often beautiful. Since they are so old, it is obvious that they were well-built. But the castles of the Middle Ages were not really very comfortable places to live in. They were dark and cold in winter. Rugs on the walls and floors kept out some of the cold drafts of air. The only heat came from large fireplaces. Sometimes, the fires would fill the rooms with smoke.

Many people lived in the castle in addition to the lord and his family. There were many servants. The lord also took in the sons of his vassals to train them to become knights. A **knight** was a noble who knew the arts of war.

A knight's training began as early as the age of 7. At that time, the young boy was sent to the lord's castle to become a **page.** He served the lord's family and learned good manners. In his teens, the boy became a **squire.** Now he followed the lord on hunting trips and into battle. A squire did not fight, but he took care of the lord's horse and armor.

During all this time, the young man was learning how to ride and fight. He also learned to be generous, humble, and respectful of others, especially women. A knight was supposed to be more than a soldier. He was also expected to be a gentleman.

The lord carefully watched the young man's progress. When the lord thought the young man was ready, he made him a knight.

The knights held regular practices in riding and fighting. Special contests called **tournaments** were also held so knights could show off their fighting skills. One contest was called a **joust.** Knights in armor tried to knock each other off their horses with a long, sharp pole called a **lance.**

A manor was a complete community. The common people made everything needed on the manor. Food, building materials, clothes, tools, and other items were grown or were made in the village.

Life for the common people was not as interesting as it was for the knights. Both free people and serfs had to work very hard.

The common people lived in a village of small houses. The village was near the castle. That way, the villagers could take refuge there in times of danger. Beyond the village were fields planted with crops. Forests provided wood for burning and for building.

All the land of the manor belonged to the lord. The lord would rent some land to the free people.

Serfs farmed the lord's fields. They also were given a small plot of land for their own use. The common people had to give the lord a share of all they produced. This was the rent on the land.

Life was especially hard for the serfs. They had to spend most of their time working on the lord's land. This meant they had very little time to work on their own small plots.

There were, however, some good times in the villages. At special times, such as religious holidays, the whole manor would celebrate. The lord provided food for everyone. Children played games. Singing, dancing, and eating went on all day long and far into the night.

REVIEW

WATCH YOUR WORDS

1. During the Middle Ages, a young man could first become a ____, then a ____, then a ____.
   knight   page   squire   joust

2. The lord and his serfs lived on a ____.
   moat   manor   drawbridge

3. A ____ was a deep ditch filled with water.
   moat   manor   drawbridge

4. The lord's fort and home was his ____.
   castle   manor   tournament

5. ____ were special contests for the knights.
   Castles   Lances   Tournaments

CHECK YOUR FACTS

6. What did a manor usually include?

7. Castles (were/were not) usually comfortable places to live.

8. What was a knight expected to be besides a soldier?

9. Where on a manor did the common people live?

10. Life was (easy/hard) for the serfs.

TRY SOMETHING NEW

Draw a picture of a castle. Label the main parts. Use the text and pictures of this lesson as your source.

Lesson 3: Towns and Trade

FIND THE WORDS

fair   minstrel   guild   craft
master   apprentice
apprenticeship   journeyman
masterpiece   cathedral
Romanesque   gothic
flying buttress

Until around 1000, there were few towns left in Europe. For centuries, they had been raided and robbed. Towns live by trade. They have to get food from the countryside. They have to make and sell goods to pay for food. But trade almost came to a halt in the Dark Ages and early Middle Ages. The Roman roads were no longer kept up. On what roads there were, merchants could be easily robbed. But around 1000, people began traveling and trading once again.

During this time, old towns began to grow again. Also, new towns were founded. Most began as trading centers. Some were located along such trade routes as rivers and Roman highways.

The towns started slowly. Someone might build an inn for traveling merchants. Other people would open shops nearby. Free people from nearby manors would begin moving to town. Sometimes, serfs would run away and find safety in a town far from their manor.

An outdoor market was the busiest spot in town. People came to the market to shop or just to meet each other and talk.

Some towns had special events called fairs once a year. A **fair** was a special gathering where trading and other activities took place. Fairs would last for a week or more. They were planned far in advance. Merchants came from all over to these fairs.

The merchants who had traveled from far away attracted big crowds. People were curious to see the goods they brought and to listen to their stories. In the Middle Ages, most people never traveled very far from their homes in their whole lives. Merchants from, say, 320 kilometers (200 miles) away seemed like strange, fascinating people.

Far more went on at a fair than buying and selling. There was plenty of entertainment for young and old alike. Jugglers and clowns made people laugh. Singers called **minstrels** sang songs that were stories put to music. Actors put on plays based on popular religious stories.

As towns grew larger, groups called **guilds** (GILDZ) were formed to control trade. Merchants set up merchant guilds to set prices and make rules for themselves.

Skilled workers who made the same kinds of things also organized their own guilds. These were called craft guilds. A **craft** is the skill and practice of making a specific kind of product by hand. Bakers, weavers, shoemakers, candlemakers, and others all had their guilds.

The full members of a guild were called **masters.** A young person who was learning a craft was called an **apprentice** (ah PREN tiss). Apprentices lived in the homes of their masters. After a few years, a master would tell the guild that an apprentice had completed the period of training, which was called an **apprenticeship.** The apprentice then became a **journeyman.** A journeyman could go to work for another master and would be paid for the work.

A journeyman would spend several years working and practicing a craft. To become a master, a journeyman first had to complete a fine piece of work. This was called a **masterpiece.** If this work was accepted by the guild, the

Merchants became more important as towns grew. This merchant is selling fish.

This gothic cathedral is in York, England. Find the flying buttresses between the large upper windows.

journeyman became a master and could begin taking on young people as apprentices.

In most towns, each guild settled in its own neighborhood. Near their workshops, guild members built guildhalls for meetings. As the guilds became richer, they built larger and more beautiful halls. Some of these magnificent buildings still stand today.

The guilds were important, but the most important institution in each town was the church. The church was usually the largest building in the town. A large town might have a special church called a **cathedral** (kah THEE drul). This was the church of a bishop. Larger towns also had more than one church.

People in the Middle Ages were not very advanced in some ways.

Few could read or write. Travel was difficult. But these people were great builders. They showed their fine skills in the beautiful churches they built.

At first, churches were built in a style similar to later Roman architecture. This style was called **Romanesque** (ROH mun EHSK). Romanesque churches had thick stone walls and rounded arches. Since they had few windows, they were dark inside.

In the later Middle Ages, builders used a new style called **gothic** (GOTH ik). Gothic churches had pointed arches. These allowed the churches to be built taller. A new building device called the **flying buttress** (BUT riss) was invented. Flying buttresses were shaped like half of a pointed arch. They held up the walls from the outside.

They made it possible to build thin walls with many windows. Also, columns inside the church no longer had to support all the weight. They, too, could be thinner and taller.

The windows of the churches of the Middle Ages were often filled with stained glass in beautiful colors. Many of these windows had pictures. Often, they told stories from the Bible. The windows filled the inside of the church with a soft, wondrous light.

The Roman Catholic Church provided more than religion for the people of the Middle Ages. It also took care of many of the jobs that government and private businesses do today. The church provided schools, hospitals, courts, laws, and entertainment. The church also helped keep ideas from ancient times alive. Monks copied old books by hand. Remember, printing had not yet been invented in Europe. All books were written out by hand.

REVIEW

WATCH YOUR WORDS

1. ____buildings had rounded arches.
   Gothic   Buttress   Romanesque

2. ____buildings had pointed arches.
   Gothic   Guild   Romanesque

3. During the Middle Ages, a skilled worker started as a(n)__1__, then became a(n)__2__, and at last a(n) __3__.

   minstrel   master   apprentice
   journeyman

4. ____were singers.
   Minstrels   Masters   Fairs

5. Merchants and skilled workers set up____.
   cathedrals   guilds   masterpieces

CHECK YOUR FACTS

6. Between the years 500 and 1000, there were (many/few) towns left in Europe.

7. Why were fairs popular with people during the Middle Ages?

8. What did a journeyman have to do to become a master?

9. What is the church of a bishop called?

10. Romanesque churches had (many/few) windows.

THINK ABOUT IT

Europe did not have printing presses during the Middle Ages. Everything had to be written by hand. News traveled slowly. Few people could read or owned books. Few people went to school. In what ways do you think printing changed these things?

Lesson 4: The Crusades

FIND THE WORDS

Islam   Allah   Koran   Muslim
pilgrim   pilgrimage
Crusade

Christianity was the main religion of Europe in the Middle Ages. But during this time, another of the world's great religious movements was also growing strong. That faith was **Islam** (IS lam). This is the religion of the followers of Muhammad.

Muhammad was an Arab who lived around 600 A.D. in what is today Saudi Arabia. The Arabs of Muhammad's time worshiped many gods. Muhammad believed and taught that there was only one God, **Allah.** *Allah* is the Arabic word for "God." Muhammad said that Allah was good and just. He also taught that people should be good to each other.

Muhammad lived in an area that was visited by many traders from Jerusalem. He knew the teachings of the Jews and Christians. Muhammad told his people that he was following in the footsteps of Moses and Jesus.

Muhammad became a popular religious teacher and soon had many followers. After he died in 632, his teachings were written down and collected in a book called the **Koran.** It is the holy book of Islam. Muhammad's followers called themselves **Muslims,** which means "faithful" in Arabic.

The Arabs who had become Muslims now set out to spread their religion to other lands. Muhammad had taught that a holy war for spreading his faith was a good thing. So Muslim armies rode out of the desert of Arabia to expand their religion by conquest.

The Arabs quickly conquered huge areas. In less than a century, they controlled Palestine, Mesopotamia, Persia, North Africa, and Spain. By 730, it looked as if Europe might become Muslim, too.

But in 732, a very important battle took place. At Tours in France, a Christian army led by Charles Martel defeated the Muslim army. This battle came at the highpoint of the Arab conquests.

Around the year 1000, a new group came to power in the Muslim lands. These were the Seljuk Turks. They were a fierce people. The Seljuk rulers were much stricter than the Arab leaders they replaced. The Turks especially disliked Christians.

The Holy Land of Palestine and the city of Jerusalem had been part of the Muslim world for centuries. During all this time, Christians from Europe had made the long, difficult journey to the Holy Land. They were called **pilgrims.** Their trip was known as a **pilgrimage.** It was believed that making a pilgrimage to the holy places in Palestine was a good thing to do. The Muslim rulers had never bothered the Christians much. Now the Turks threatened to kill them.

The Turks also were a threat to the remaining lands of the Byzantine Empire centered in Constantinople. The Byzantine emperor sent an appeal for help to the pope in Rome.

In 1095, Pope Urban II traveled to Clermont (KLEHR MOHN), a small town in southern France. There he preached to a great crowd of knights from all over Europe. The crowd was so large that the church could not hold everybody. The meeting had to be moved to a hillside outside the town.

Pope Urban told the knights what the Turks were doing in Palestine. He asked them to form an army and conquer the Holy Land for Christendom. In a mighty roar, the knights replied to the Pope's request, saying, "God wills it!"

This was the beginning of the First Crusade (kroo SAYD). The **Crusades** were a series of wars fought by Europeans against the Muslims for control of Palestine. *Crusade* comes from a word meaning "to bear the cross." After Pope Urban's speech, the knights had crosses sewn on their shirts. This showed that they were bound for the Holy Land, where Christ had died on the cross.

Soon, a great army was on its way to Palestine. This army was not made up only of knights. Thousands of religious pilgrims went, too. These people left home without food or weapons. It was a long, hard journey. Many died along the way.

It took the main army of knights 3 years to reach Jerusalem. Once there, they surrounded

This picture shows four important leaders of the First Crusade.

the city. After a few months of fighting, the Turks surrendered. The Holy Land and Jerusalem were once again in the hands of the Christians. Most of the Christian army returned to Europe. But some knights stayed behind. They built castles in Palestine. They set up manors like those in Europe.

The Christians held Jeruselem for almost a century. Then the Turks retook the city. Other Crusades were launched from Europe, but each one failed to defeat the Turks.

The Crusades failed to hold Jerusalem for the Christians. But they changed the lives of the people of the Middle Ages.

Before the Crusades, most Europeans traveled very little. They knew very little about the outside world. The Crusaders marched off to the Holy Land expecting to find barbarians. Instead, they found beautiful cities, great riches, and educated people.

They brought back many things from the Holy Land. Among these things were fine cloth, rugs, spices, and jewelry. They also brought back some of the new Muslim knowledge about mathematics and medicine.

Below: In 1098, the Crusaders attacked the city of Antioch in Syria. *Right:* The Children's Crusade took place in 1212. Most of the children either died or were sold into slavery.

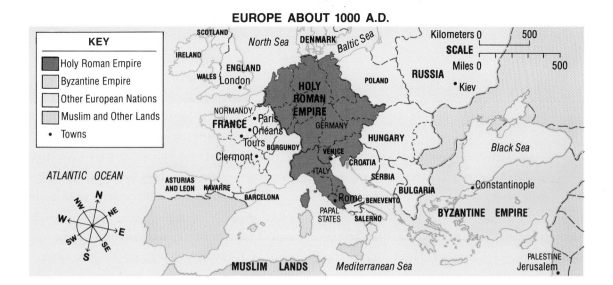

EUROPE ABOUT 1000 A.D.

KEY
- Holy Roman Empire
- Byzantine Empire
- Other European Nations
- Muslim and Other Lands
- • Towns

Most important, the Crusaders brought back a new idea. This was the idea that there was a larger world. There was a world full of new things and different people.

Over the next few centuries, Europeans began reaching out to this wider world. They started to explore far beyond the borders of Europe.

REVIEW

WATCH YOUR WORDS

1. ____ is the religion of Muhammad.
   Judaism   Christianity   Islam

2. ____ is the Muslim name for God.
   Allah   Koran   Islam

3. The ____ is the holy book of the Muslims.
   Bible   Torah   Koran

CHECK YOUR FACTS

4. List some new things the Crusaders brought back from the Holy Land.

5. What important idea did the Crusaders learn in the Holy Land?

THINK ABOUT IT

Jerusalem is still a source of religious conflict today. Tell what you know about the present-day problems there.

Lesson 5: Nations Form in Europe

FIND THE WORD

charter

In the years after the First Crusade, the nations of Europe as we know them today started to form. Each nation had its own history. But in almost every nation, there was a great struggle between the king and the powerful nobles. The king kept trying to get more power over the nobles. The nobles fought to keep the king from becoming too powerful.

Often, the new towns and cities sided with the king. Kings gave towns special favors in return for money and goods. Townspeople sometimes felt that the rules of feudalism kept their towns from growing.

It took centuries for some nations to form. Some lands had become real nations with strong central governments by the end of the Middle Ages. But others, like Germany and Italy, did not become unified nations until the 1800s.

England

England was the first European country to become a real nation. In 1066, a powerful noble, William the Conqueror, led an army across the English Channel from Normandy in northern France. William and his knights won a great victory over the king of England. The English king was killed, and William became the new king.

William the Conqueror was not only a good soldier, he was also a good ruler. He changed some of the English laws, but he kept many that seemed to work well. He began to organize a government to take care of things in a businesslike way.

The kings that followed William added to their power. In 1215, the nobles got the upper hand again. They forced King John to sign a series of promises called the Magna Carta, or Great Charter. (A **charter** is an official paper signed by a ruler.) In the Magna Carta, the king promised to protect the rights of the nobles. Out of this document came many important new ideas about the government.

The struggle in England between the king and the nobles went on over the centuries. Out of this conflict came a new kind of government. At first, only rulers had rights. But over the years, more and more people gained rights. These rights gave people greater freedom. Many of the ideas of American government came from England. The Magna Carta was the first expression of the idea that citizens have rights that their government cannot take away.

France

In the years between 1000 and 1500, France, too, was becoming a nation. One thing that held back the growth of France was that the English king owned large areas of land in France.

In the 1300s and 1400s, the French and the English fought a long series of wars. Together, they are called the Hundred Years' War, since they lasted about a century.

In the early 1400s, it looked as though the French were going to lose the war. At that time, a remarkable leader appeared in France to save the day. This leader was an uneducated peasant girl named Joan of Arc.

When the war with England ended, France had won back its land. In the years ahead, France would become one of the strongest nations in Europe.

STRANGE FACTS

Joan of Arc is a French hero. She was born in a small town in 1412. Like many girls at that time, she did not learn to read or write. She was known for being gentle and holy.

In the Middle Ages, women rarely served as soldiers. But Joan of Arc had a special calling. She journeyed from her home to the palace of the king's son. There, she told the surprised prince that she had heard voices from heaven telling her to save France. The prince was greatly impressed by Joan. He agreed to give her a suit of armor, a sword, and a great white horse.

Joan rode off to the city of Orléans (or lay AHNH), which was about to be taken by the English. She inspired the tired French soldiers with her great courage. Joan led the French in battle and won an important victory. Later, she was captured by the English and killed. Centuries after her death, the Roman Catholic Church declared Joan of Arc a saint.

Spain

Spain had long been ruled by the Muslims. In the Middle Ages, the Muslim cities of Spain were rich and beautiful places unlike any towns in Europe.

But over the centuries, Christian knights fought to reconquer Spain. Gradually, they won back more and more land. The Muslims had settled down, and perhaps they had lost their will to fight.

In the late 1400s, the two largest parts of Spain were united. This happened when King Ferdinand and Queen Isabella married. In 1492, the last Muslim outpost was taken by the Christians. In that year, Isabella and Ferdinand gave Christopher Columbus ships to sail across the Atlantic.

The End of the Middle Ages

By about 1500, the Middle Ages were over in most of Europe. In some places, the feudal system and the old ways remained strong for many years. But in the new nations, new ways of living were taking over. New inventions like the printing press helped spread new ideas. Travel became easier. Daring explorers crossed the oceans to find new lands.

It often seems that time stood still during the Middle Ages. Actually, there were many changes during that period. To be sure, change was very slow. It took a long time for new ideas to spread. But in the 1500s, the pace of life speeded up, and things began to change much faster.

REVIEW

CHECK YOUR FACTS

1. Who struggled for power in most European nations in the years after the First Crusade?
2. Who conquered England in 1066?
3. What paper was the English king forced to sign in 1215?
4. What nation owned large parts of France between 1066 and the 1400s?
5. Columbus found America in 1492. What other important event took place in that year?

THINK ABOUT IT

In the late Middle Ages, England, Spain, and France became strong, unified nations. These same countries were to explore and conquer new lands around the world. How might these two things be related?

CHAPTER REVIEW

WATCH YOUR WORDS

1. ___ was a way of organizing and governing society.
   Christendom Feudalism Serfdom

2. The areas in which most people were Christians were known as ___.
   Christendom Feudalism Monarchy

3. ___ gave fiefs to vassals.
   Serfs Feuds Lords

4. Tournaments included ___.
   moats jousts drawbridges

5. ___ crossed moats.
   Castles Jousts Drawbridges

6. Jousts were fought with ___.
   Lances Squires Pages

7. Skilled workers set up ___ guilds.
   merchant craft master

8. Journeymen first had to serve a(n) ___.
   fair guild apprenticeship

9. A ___ is the church of a bishop.
   buttress cathedral gothic

10. Followers of Muhammad are called ___.
    apostles Islams Muslims

CHECK YOUR FACTS

11. Where did the Vikings come from?

12. Describe a flying buttress and tell what it does.

13. With what religion did Christianity come into conflict during the Middle Ages?

14. What was the goal of the Crusaders?

15. What two important nations of Europe did *not* become unified during the Middle Ages?

KNOW YOUR NAMES

Match the name with the clue.

16. Queen Isabella of Spain
17. Charlemagne
18. William of Normandy
19. Vikings
20. King John of England
21. Muhammad
22. Charles Martel
23. Urban II
24. Seljuk Turks
25. Joan of Arc

A. raided Europe.
B. signed the Magna Carta.
C. founded Islam.
D. defeated the Muslims.
E. preached the First Crusade.
F. fought the Crusaders.
G. conquered England.
H. defeated the English in France.
I. was emperor of the Romans.
J. helped Columbus.

USE YOUR MAP

26. Look at the map of Europe in the Middle Ages on page 143. Why do you think the Holy Roman emperors had trouble ruling their empire?

TRY SOMETHING NEW

27. During the Middle Ages, people of the upper class were called "lords and ladies." You have read how a young boy was trained to be a knight. Find out how a young girl learned how to be a lady. Use an encyclopedia or other source suggested by your teacher.

147

CHAPTER 4 EUROPE IN THE RENAISSANCE

Lesson 1: The Renaissance Begins

FIND THE WORDS

modern   scientific method

The period that followed the Middle Ages is called the Renaissance (REN uh SAHNS). The word *renaissance* is French. It means "rebirth." This age got that name because it seemed to be a rebirth of ancient times.

As the Middle Ages were coming to an end, people began taking a greater interest in ancient times. They studied books written by the ancient Greeks and Romans. They tried to write like the ancient writers. Artists became interested in the sculpture and painting of the ancient world. Architects began to copy ancient buildings.

But the people of the Renaissance did not just copy the ways of the ancients. They also developed new ways of looking at the world that we still use today. Recent times are called **modern.** If the Renaissance was the *rebirth* of ancient civilization, it was also the *birth* of modern civilization.

The Renaissance started in Italy about 1350. Later, it spread to other parts of Europe. So the Renaissance was not taking place in

148

all parts of Europe at the same time. In Italy, the towns of the Middle Ages had grown into cities. Some of these cities had become wealthy because of the Crusades. The Crusaders brought back books from the Holy Land. Muslim scholars had preserved much of the learning of ancient times. Teachers and writers in Italy became interested in these books. They began to study the ancient learning. They began to copy the graceful Latin writing of the ancient Romans. During the Middle Ages and the Renaissance, and even later, most serious writing everywhere in Western Europe was done in Latin.

The cities of Renaissance Italy were exciting places. Proud nobles and merchants built grand palaces and beautiful homes. They paid builders, painters, and sculptors to create objects of beauty.

One of the greatest people of the Renaissance was Leonardo da Vinci (LEE uh NAHR doh duh VIN chee). Leonardo was a painter, an inventor, a scientist, and a writer. He studied the human body in great detail. Before he painted a picture, Leonardo made many sketches of each detail. The *Mona Lisa*, a painting of a woman, is his most famous work. Today, people are still fascinated by the odd smile of the *Mona Lisa*. She looks as if she has a secret that she will not share with anyone.

The artists of the Renaissance painted people and the world as they saw them. In the Middle Ages, artists had painted mostly religious subjects. Their style was usually quiet and worshipful. The

FUN FACTS

Michelangelo (MY kul AN juh LOH) was a great artist of the Renaissance. He carved beautiful sculptures out of marble. He also painted the ceiling and one wall of the Sistine (SISS TEEN) Chapel in Rome with scenes from the Bible. To paint the ceiling, Michelangelo had to lie on his back on a high platform all day long for many months. Today, his works of art are seen by millions of tourists each year. In addition to being an artist, Michelangelo was also a very important architect.

Renaissance painters also used religious themes. But their works were exciting and full of life.

Writers of the Renaissance also celebrated life. They also began writing in the language of the people. In Italy, Spain, and France, the common people spoke new languages based on Latin. People in Germany and England spoke languages descended from those of the barbarian groups that had overrun the Roman Empire. The new writers helped to set the form of these languages.

Language also began to change the way people thought of themselves. In earlier times, the Latin language and the Roman Catholic religion had led people in all parts of Europe to think of themselves as members of Christendom. Now, people in different places had their own languages. New nations were rising. People began to consider themselves as members of a particular country. The unity of the Middle Ages was breaking up.

New discoveries in science also helped make the Renaissance different from the Middle Ages. During the Middle Ages, people thought that the sun revolved around Earth. Nicolaus Copernicus (koh PUR ni kus), a Polish scientist, wrote that this idea was wrong. Copernicus figured out that Earth revolved around the sun. Later, Galileo Galilei (GAL i LEE oh GAL i LAY ee), an Italian scientist, used a telescope to prove that Copernicus was right.

Isaac Newton, an English mathematician, made many important discoveries about the laws of nature. Newton also helped develop the **scientific method.** This was a way to test the truth of ideas about science.

Unlike the people of the Middle Ages, the people of the Renaissance wanted to know how the world worked. Their spirit of curiosity is still part of our world.

REVIEW

CHECK YOUR FACTS

1. What does the word *renaissance* mean?

2. Who did the people of the Renaissance try to copy?

3. When and where did the Renaissance begin?

4. In what language was most serious writing done during the Middle Ages and the Renaissance?

THINK ABOUT IT

What things helped unite Europe in the Middle Ages? What things divided Europe in the Renaissance?

Lesson 2: Europeans Compete for Trade

Travel and trade helped Europe grow in the later Middle Ages and during the Renaissance. For centuries, Europeans had seldom gone far from their homes. Now they traveled to faraway places.

A young Italian named Marco Polo traveled a very great distance indeed. Polo was the son of a merchant family in the Italian city of Venice. In 1271, he set off with his father and uncle for China.

From Venice, they sailed east on the Mediterranean Sea to Palestine. From there, they traveled overland. They crossed valleys, deserts, mountains, and then more deserts. The trip took more than 3 years. At last, they reached China. They visited the palace of the ruler of China, Kublai Khan (KOO bly KAHN). Kublai Khan was the leader of the Mongol people who had conquered China.

The Polos stayed in China for many years. Kublai Khan liked young Marco Polo and took him along on his travels around China. Polo was very much surprised by what he saw. Like the Crusaders, he had thought that Europeans were the most advanced people in the world. He was startled by the beauty and wealth of China. He learned that China was an old and rich civilization.

This painting shows the bay of Naples in 1464. Some of the ships are warships, used to protect the trade of the Italian cities.

After many years in China, the Polos grew homesick and set out for Italy. They sailed along the coasts of China and India to the Arabian Sea. From there, they traveled overland to the Black Sea. Then they sailed home.

People in Venice had given the Polos up for dead. They had been gone for 24 years. Marco Polo wrote a book about his trip. It became a "best-seller." Europeans were eager to read about faraway lands. Some people thought that Marco Polo had made up his stories. They could not believe that a place like China really existed.

But many others, especially merchants and sea captains in It-aly, believed Marco Polo. They moved quickly to set up trade with the East. The cities of Italy were well located for such trade. All the trade routes with the East passed through the Mediterranean Sea, on which Italy borders. In the 1300s, Europeans did not know any other way to get to China.

Italian merchants and sailors had already had contacts with the Muslim world. For centuries, ship captains from Venice (VEN iss), Pisa (PEE zah), and Genoa (JEN oh ah) had ferried the armies of the Crusaders to the Holy Land. They had always charged a high fee for doing this. Then they had returned with shiploads of rice, sugar, mel-

This old map of the East was based on Marco Polo's descriptions.

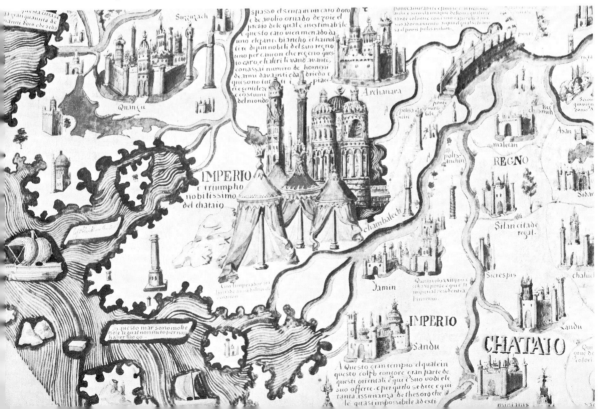

Florence, in Italy, had many rich merchants. Here a merchant is holding a banquet.

ons, lemons, and apricots from the East. These products did not grow in Europe.

The most prized new things brought back from the East were spices. Europeans did not then have refrigerators. They used salt to preserve meat. Spices gave meat a better flavor. Soon, there was a growing market for spices.

Italian merchants bought spices from Muslim merchants. The Muslims, in turn, got them from India, China, and other places in the East. The Italians traded lumber, furs, and other goods for the spices. The Italian cities that ran the spice trade grew very wealthy.

The spice trade led to great rivalries. Within Italy, cities fought each other for trade routes. Pirates roamed the seas, ready to seize richly loaded ships. Venice, Genoa, Pisa, and Florence all had armies and navies. There was almost constant fighting. Cities grew richer or poorer as a result of these wars.

Later, the new nations of Europe also began to compete for trade and wealth. The rulers and

Venice was an important trading center. This painting was done in 1338 at the end of the Middle Ages.

merchants of the nations on the Atlantic Ocean became jealous of the Italian cities. But since all trade from the East came through the eastern Mediterranean, the Italians had a stranglehold on it. The people who lived on the Atlantic began to wonder if there was another way to get to the East. What if a ship could sail around Africa to Asia? Then the Italians could be bypassed. The other Europeans would have their own source of goods like spices.

REVIEW

CHECK YOUR FACTS

1. To what distant land did Marco Polo travel?
2. What were the most important things the Italian merchants brought from the East?
3. Name some important Italian trading cities.
4. Why did the Italian cities dominate trade with the East?

THINK ABOUT IT

How many ways to preserve food can you think of?

Lesson 3: Europeans Explore the World

FIND THE WORDS

navigation **compass** **astrolabe**

During the Middle Ages, Europeans did not know how to sail long distances or go very far from land. Most people believed that Earth was flat, not round. They feared that if a ship sailed too far, it would fall off the edge of Earth. People also believed that monsters lived in the ocean. They were afraid that these sea monsters would swallow a whole ship and all its crew.

Before they could explore the world, the Europeans had to learn more about sailing. Prince Henry of Portugal was one person who saw the importance of sailing. The prince wanted to find a sea route to the East. That way, Portugal could trade directly with India, China, and other nearby lands. It could challenge the Italian cities for control of the spice trade.

In the early 1400s, Prince Henry started a school for sailors in Portugal. The prince brought together the best sailors, shipbuilders, mapmakers, and navigators in Europe. **Navigation** (NAV uh GAY shun) is the science of fig-uring out direction on the open sea. Prince Henry's school brought many improvements in sailing.

Prince Henry's school borrowed many ideas from the Muslims. Muslim sailors were more advanced than the Europeans were. The Portuguese borrowed two

Prince Henry, shown here, died before his dream of finding an all-water route to the East came true.

The astrolabe, shown here, helped sailors sail on the open sea out of sight of land.

tools that were important for navigation: the compass and the astrolabe. A **compass** has a needle that always points north. With a compass, sailors can figure out their direction on the open sea. The **astrolabe** (ASS truh LAYB) helped sailors use the positions of the stars to figure out their own position on Earth.

By the late 1400s, Portuguese sailors were sailing far out into the ocean. They used the new tools of navigation to find their way. In 1488, Bartholomeu Dias (DEE us) reached the tip of Africa, which he named the Cape of Good Hope. Ten years later, Vasco da

Gama made Prince Henry's dream come true. He and his crew sailed around Africa and across the Indian Ocean to India. Now the Portuguese could bring back spices from India. Their sea route was faster and cheaper than the land and sea route used by the Italian merchants.

Christopher Columbus was an Italian ship captain. During these years, he was trying to persuade the kings of Europe to give him money for a great voyage of discovery. Columbus believed the world was round, not flat. He reasoned that by sailing west, he would eventually reach the East. But Columbus did not know how big the world was. He did not know that North and South America were in his way!

Columbus gained the support of Queen Isabella of Spain. In 1492, Queen Isabella and her husband, King Ferdinand, decided to give Columbus three ships. Dias had made his voyage a few years earlier. The Spanish were afraid the Portuguese would beat them to India and control the spice trade.

Columbus sailed west. On October 12, 1492, he landed on the island of San Salvador in what is now the Bahamas. Columbus thought he had reached the Indies. So he called the native people he met Indians.

Christopher Columbus made three more voyages to the New World. Each time, he failed to reach the East. But Columbus had found something as good. He had discovered a whole New World that Europeans knew nothing about. The Americas were lands full of riches. In the years to come, millions of people from Europe, Africa, and Asia would settle there.

Columbus's goal of reaching the East by sailing west was achieved by another explorer, Ferdinand Magellan (muh JEL un). Magellan sailed from Spain in 1519. His ships rounded the tip of South America and crossed the Pacific Ocean. In the Philippine Islands in Asia, Magellan was killed in a battle with native people. Only one of his ships made it back to Spain.

The trip took 3 years. Along the way, Magellan and his crew claimed many lands in the Americas and Asia for Spain. So it was one of Magellan's ships that was the first to sail all the way around the world. Magellan's voyage finally proved to everyone that Earth is round, not flat.

Spain and Portugal seemed to be dividing the world between them. The nations of northern Europe did not want to be left out. Explorers from northern Europe also began to sail west. They were

This is how one European artist thought the Indians in America greeted Columbus.

looking for a northern sea route to India. Like Columbus, they failed in their search. But they found and explored the east coast of what became the United States and Canada.

John Cabot sailed from England to the coast of Canada in 1497. Jacques Cartier (KAHR tee AY), a French explorer, sailed down the St. Lawrence River in Canada. Years later, Henry Hudson discovered the Hudson River. He also claimed the area of what is now New York for the Netherlands.

But even as the northern Europeans explored North America, the

Here Spanish explorers are looking for the fountain of youth in Florida. They believed that anyone who drank from that fountain would never grow old.

Spanish continued to make discoveries there. Spanish explorers found the Mississippi River and explored the American Southwest. The Spaniard Ponce de León (PAHN suh DAY lee OHN) discovered Florida. Indians had told of a "fountain of youth." If someone bathed in its water, they would never get old. Ponce de León and his men searched for this stream. They never found it.

REVIEW

WATCH YOUR WORDS

1. Sailors used a(n) ___ to find the north.
   compass   astrolabe   thermometer
2. Sailors used the ___ to find their position on Earth.
   compass   astrolabe   computer

CHECK YOUR FACTS

3. Who founded a school for navigation in Portugal?

4. Who was the captain of the first Portuguese ship to reach India?
5. When did Columbus land in the New World?

TRY SOMETHING NEW

Long before Columbus, the Vikings reached the New World. Write a one-page report on the Viking discovery of Iceland, Greenland, and Vinland. Use an encyclopedia or other source suggested by your teacher.

Lesson 4: Empires Rise and Fall

FIND THE WORDS

colony   empire   conquistador
voyageur

The voyages of discovery excited many people in Europe. Soldiers and adventurers came to the New World in search of conquests and riches. They were followed by common people looking for freedom and a new start in life.

In the 1500s and 1600s, the nations of Western Europe set up colonies in the New World and elsewhere. A **colony** is a land ruled by another country. Great riches were shipped from the colonies back to Europe. All the colonies owned by a country came to be called an **empire.** Soon, many nations of Europe had colonial empires of their own. There was a fierce rivalry between the leading colonial empires. Often, this rivalry led to war.

The Spanish Colonial Empire

In the 1500s and 1600s, the largest colonial empire belonged to Spain. Because of the discoveries of Columbus, Magellan, and others, the Spanish rulers claimed huge areas of land in the New World. Soldiers called **conquistadores** (kohn kees tah DOR ess) were sent to explore and conquer the land for Spain.

Hernando Cortés (kor TEZ) was a conquistador who landed in Mexico in 1519. Cortés soon heard of a great city. This was the capital of an Indian people, the Aztecs. The Indians the Spanish had met so far were not as advanced as Europeans. But Cortés and his soldiers were surprised when they got to the Aztec capital. It was a great city built on an island in a lake. It had tall buildings and beautiful gardens. Gold and silver seemed to be everywhere.

The Aztecs were a very warlike people. But the Aztec emperor, Montezuma, was not sure what to make of Cortés. An old legend told of a god with white skin who had

In Mexico, the Spanish found a great Indian empire. Here they see the capital of the Aztecs on the plain below.

once visited the Aztecs and who would return. Was Cortés this god?

Cortés decided to attack the Aztecs. He was helped by other Indians who feared their powerful neighbors. The fighting was furious, but the Spanish won. Cortés had brought the first horses to the New World. The Aztecs were frightened by them. At first, the Aztecs thought that each horse and rider formed one strange animal. After Cortés and his soldiers defeated the Aztecs, they destroyed their capital. Mexico City was built on the same site.

In Peru, a conquistador named Francisco Pizarro (pi ZAH roh) found another advanced Indian people, called the Inca. Pizarro and his soldiers conquered the Inca after a long, bloody war. By the mid-1500s, huge amounts of gold and silver were being shipped back to Spain from Mexico and Peru. This treasure made Spain the richest nation in Europe.

Many Spanish people came to the New World. They built towns and set up farms and ranches. Spanish priests also came to the New World. They traveled all over the new lands, teaching Christianity to the Indians. Soon, the Spanish empire covered all of South America except Portuguese Brazil. In North America, it included Mexico and most of what is now the southwestern part of the United States. Texas and California were then Spanish.

On the the left, Spanish soldiers kill many of the leaders of the Inca. Below is a Spanish mission in California.

WHERE WE ARE IN TIME AND PLACE

THE AGE OF EUROPEAN EXPLORATION

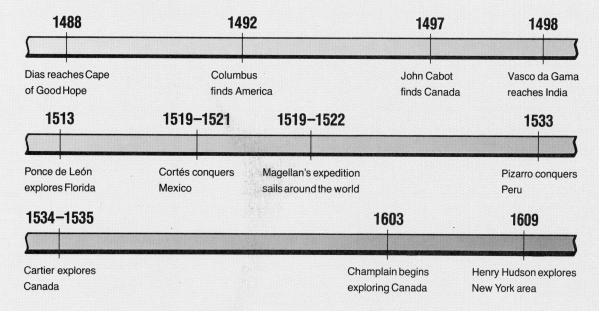

1488

Dias reaches Cape
of Good Hope

1492

Columbus
finds America

1497

John Cabot
finds Canada

1498

Vasco da Gama
reaches India

1513

Ponce de León
explores Florida

1519–1521

Cortés conquers
Mexico

1519–1522

Magellan's expedition
sails around the world

1533

Pizarro conquers
Peru

1534–1535

Cartier explores
Canada

1603

Champlain begins
exploring Canada

1609

Henry Hudson explores
New York area

EUROPEAN DISCOVERY AND EXPLORATION

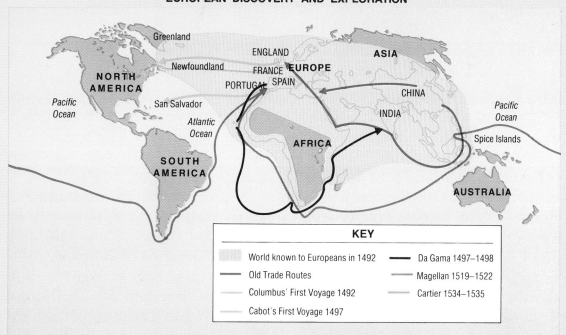

Greenland

ENGLAND

ASIA

Newfoundland

FRANCE **EUROPE**

NORTH
AMERICA

PORTUGAL SPAIN

CHINA

*Pacific
Ocean*

San Salvador

INDIA

*Pacific
Ocean*

*Atlantic
Ocean*

AFRICA

Spice Islands

SOUTH
AMERICA

AUSTRALIA

KEY

World known to Europeans in 1492	Da Gama 1497–1498
Old Trade Routes	Magellan 1519–1522
Columbus' First Voyage 1492	Cartier 1534–1535
Cabot's First Voyage 1497	

French explorers roamed over the interior of North America. This picture shows Champlain in Canada.

The English Colonies

The English also built an empire in the New World. One English group settled on Roanoke (ROH uh nohk) Island in present-day North Carolina in the 1580s. But this Lost Colony disappeared. The first permanent English settlement was made in 1607 at Jamestown in Virginia. There, the settlers had to work hard to plant crops and to survive far from England. Many of them died in the first few years. But the colony survived and began to do well. Other people came from England to Virginia. The rich soil there was very good for farming.

Settlers called Pilgrims and Puritans came to Massachusetts in the early 1600s. They had left England because of religious difficulties. In the New World, they found the freedom to worship as they pleased. The English set up 13 colonies in North America.

French Canada

A French explorer, Samuel de Champlain (sham PLAYN), founded a colony in Canada in the early 1600s. Called New France, the colony was centered around what are now the cities of Quebec (kwi BEK) and Montreal (MON tree AWL) on the St. Lawrence River. French settlers traveled deep into the Canadian wilderness to buy furs from Indian trappers. These hardy men were called **voyageurs** (vwah yah ZHURZ). They paddled large canoes up and down the rivers of Canada. Valuable furs were brought back to Quebec and then shipped from there to France.

The Clash of Empires

The rivalry between European colonial empires caused trouble in many places. In 1588, the Spanish sent a huge naval fleet, the Armada (ahr MAH duh), to invade England. English pirates had been capturing Spanish ships full of gold and silver on the high seas. But the Spanish fleet was destroyed in a battle and a storm.

In the 1700s, Great Britain and France fought a series of wars. In North America, these were called the French and Indian Wars. The British eventually won and took over all of Canada.

By the early 1800s, most of the colonies in the New World were free of rule by the Europeans. In 1776, the 13 British colonies in North America declared their independence and became the United States. In the early 1800s, most of the colonies of Latin America won their independence from Spain, Portugal, and France.

REVIEW

WATCH YOUR WORDS

1. The ____ were Spanish soldiers who conquered new lands.
   imperialists voyageurs
   conquistadores

2. The French fur traders who traveled deep into North America were called ____.
   trappers voyageurs
   conquistadores

3. A ____ is a land ruled by another country.
   kingdom empire colony

CHECK YOUR FACTS

4. What European nation had the largest colonial empire in the 1500s and 1600s?

5. What three important European nations explored and settled North America?

THINK ABOUT IT

What happened to the people who lived in the New World when the Europeans came?

Lesson 5: Europe Grows Powerful

FIND THE WORDS

protest   reform

The changes of the 1500s and 1600s made Europe the world's most powerful continent. The Middle Ages were left far behind. The voyages of discovery and the empire-building that followed them were the most important changes of this period. There were also three other major changes. First, kings and nobles struggled for power in new ways. Second, new churches appeared to challenge the Roman Catholic Church. And finally, new weapons changed the ways in which war was fought.

The quarrels between kings and nobles had been going on since the late Middle Ages. In the 1500s and 1600s, many kings began to use a new idea to try to increase their power. They did not claim to be gods themselves, as some ancient rulers had. But they claimed they got their right to rule from God. To challenge a king, they said, was to challenge God's will.

This idea of ruling was very different from the idea that had existed in the Middle Ages. In the early Middle Ages, in particular, many kings had been elected by the more important nobles.

The nobles and townspeople often objected to this new power of the kings. As you read in Chapter 3, at first the townspeople sided with the king against the nobles. But during the Renaissance, nobles and townspeople started to work together to resist the kings.

In many European nations, a council of nobles and townspeople was formed. In England, this group was called Parliament. Council members tried to get the king to let them have a say about taxes and other matters. Sometimes, the king ignored them. At other times, the king had to listen.

Democracy grew out of this long struggle for power. At first, only the nobles claimed certain rights. Gradually, the idea that all people should be free spread throughout Europe. But it was in the United States that most people first won freedom.

Religion was another area of change. You remember that in the Middle Ages, people thought of themselves as living in Christendom. The Roman Catholic Church, not the nations, united the peoples of Europe.

Toward the end of the Middle Ages, some people began to object to the ways of the Roman Catholic

Martin Luther started the Protestant churches in Germany. He opposed many practices of the Roman Catholic Church at that time.

Church. Some opposed the great wealth of the church. The printing press was invented in the mid-1400s. Now, there were more books. More people could learn how to read. People began to read the Bible for themselves. They began to think differently from the church about what the Bible meant. They began to want to worship God in new ways.

These people were called Protestants. That was because they **protested**, or spoke out, against the ways of the Roman Catholic Church. The most famous Protestant leader was a German monk named Martin Luther. Luther was thrown out of the Roman Catholic Church because of his protests. Powerful rulers got involved in the argument between Luther and the church. War broke out. In the end, Luther and other Protestants founded their own churches.

The founding of the Protestant churches is called the Protestant Reformation (REHF ur MAY shun). Protestant leaders claimed they wanted to **reform** the church, or make it better.

Sometimes, the struggles over the church really had more to do with politics than with religion. A quarrel began between King Henry VIII of England and the

Roman Catholic pope because the king wanted to remarry. King Henry then took over the church in England and formed a new church. In part, the king made the change so he could get the land and other wealth owned by the Roman Catholic Church. The new Church of England kept most of the Roman Catholic ways of worship, at least at first.

In the 1500s and 1600s, the Roman Catholic Church lost control of almost half of Europe. But at the same time, Roman Catholic beliefs were spreading around the world. Priests followed explorers into the jungles and mountains of South America, and later, into Asia and Africa, as well.

During these years, there were also very important changes in the way war was fought. In the Middle Ages, armored knights rode into battle on horses. As you read in Chapter 3, only nobles could become knights.

Toward the end of the Middle Ages, Europeans began to use gunpowder. This changed warfare forever. An armored knight was no match for a soldier with a gun or cannon. Knights became a thing of the past. Now, kings paid commoners to serve in the army. The nobles, who used to be the only armed people in Europe, had lost their special power. Thus, feudalism, which was built on the military power of the knights, also became less important.

Europe became more powerful in the 1500s and 1600s because of the new ideas of the Renaissance. Now more and more Europeans were traveling, trading, and learning. The spark of curiosity had lit a flame that still burns today.

REVIEW

CHECK YOUR FACTS

1. Besides exploration and colonization, what were three other major changes of the 1500s and 1600s in Europe?
2. In the struggles between the European kings and the nobles, whom did the townspeople support at first? Whom did they support later?
3. What was the council of nobles and townspeople called in England?
4. What group revolted against the Roman Catholic Church in the 1500s?
5. What English king took control of the church?
6. How did gunpowder change warfare?

THINK ABOUT IT

What Protestant groups have churches in your community?

CHAPTER REVIEW

WATCH YOUR WORDS

1. Recent times are called____.
   medieval   Renaissance   modern
2. The ____ was a way to prove the truth of ideas.
   navigation   scientific method   astrolabe
3. ____ is the science of figuring out direction on the open sea.
   Navigation   Scientific method   Compass
4. A(n) ____ is a land ruled by another country.
   empire   colony   nation
5. A(n) ____ included all the lands ruled by a country.
   empire   colony   territory

CHECK YOUR FACTS

6. How did the Renaissance get its name?
7. Name two important artists of the Renaissance.
8. Which emperor of China did Marco Polo visit?
9. At first, who controlled the trade between Europe and the East?
10. In the Middle Ages, what shape did most people believe Earth had?
11. What point of land did Bartholomeu Dias reach?
12. What European nation conquered Mexico and Peru?
13. What European nation first settled Canada?
14. What did many European kings begin to claim in the 1500s and 1600s?
15. What did the Protestants claim they wanted to do?

KNOW YOUR PEOPLE

Match the name with the clue.

16. Martin Luther
17. Marco Polo
18. Nicholaus Copernicus
19. Prince Henry of Portugal
20. Vasco da Gama
21. Christopher Columbus
22. Queen Isabella of Spain
23. John Cabot
24. Hernando Cortés

A. quarreled with the Roman Catholic Church.
B. landed on San Salvador.
C. figured out that Earth revolves around the sun.
D. sailed to India.
E. sailed to Canada.
F. conquered Mexico.
G. started a school for sailors.
H. visited China.
I. helped Columbus.

USE YOUR MAP

25. Look at the map on page 161. Whose expedition was the first to sail around the world?

THINK ABOUT IT

26. List some important ways in which the Renaissance differed from the Middle Ages.

TRY SOMETHING NEW

27. Look at a map of California in an atlas. The Spanish who first settled that state gave many places names beginning "San" or "Santa." These words mean "saint" or "holy" in Spanish. Find as many such places as you can.

UNIT REVIEW

WATCH YOUR WORDS

Use the words below to fill in the blanks. Use each term only once.

ancestors	City-states	dynasties	pottery
archaeologists	civilization	empires	prehistory
banks	cuneiform	fertile	ruins
bronze	delta	historic	stylus
Canals	dikes	irrigation	temples
citadels	domesticated	palaces	ziggurats

Before ___ times, there was ___. This was when people did not yet know how to write. But ___ study the ___ of their buildings to learn how they lived.

Early peoples ___ wild animals. They learned how to make ___ from clay and ___ from copper and tin. At last ___, a highly developed form of culture, arose. Ancient cultures farmed ___, or good, lands with the help of water from___.

In the ___ of the Tigris and Euphrates, Sumer, the first civilization, was founded. On the ___ of the rivers, ___ were built to hold back the floods. ___ carried the water to the fields. ___, small nations, appeared. In the center of the cities, there were ___, triangular buildings with ___, or religious structures, on top. The Sumerians used a ___ to write their ___ letters. Great nations called ___ followed them in Mesopotamia.

In China, cities had ___, or forts, at their center. Rulers lived in large buildings called ___. China had many ___, or families, of rulers. These great leaders began to worship their___.

CHECK YOUR FACTS

1. What river in India was the center of an ancient civilization?
2. What river dominated the culture of ancient Egypt?
3. When did Egyptian history begin? When did Egypt become part of the Roman Empire?
4. Name two early civilizations in Greece.
5. How was government in ancient Greece like government in Sumeria?
6. Which was more democratic, Athens or Sparta?
7. What empire did Alexander the Great conquer?
8. Where are the Apennines?
9. Who does legend say founded Rome?
10. Who fought the Punic Wars?
11. Name a Roman leader who fought in Gaul.
12. What is another name for the Emperor Augustus?
13. What was the *Pax Romana*?
14. Who founded Christianity? Who founded Islam?
15. What German group did Charlemagne rule?
16. What two groups helped preserve the learning of the ancient Greeks and Romans after the fall of Rome?
17. What two forces helped bring order to Europe during the Middle Ages?
18. What two styles of architecture were important in Europe during the Middle Ages?

19. Name three important Western European nations that became strong and unified by the end of the Middle Ages. Name two important Western European nations that were weak and divided until modern times.

20. What two meanings does the word *empire* have?

KNOW YOUR GREEKS

Match the name with the clue.

21. Ptolemies   A. conquered Persia.
22. Cleopatra   B. Athenian leader during Golden Age.
23. Solon   C. early Cretans.
24. Pericles   D. Athenian reformer.
25. Philip II   E. Greek philosopher.
26. Alexander the Great   F. Greek queen of Egypt.
27. Socrates   G. Greek goddess.
28. Herodotus   H. Greek dynasty in Egypt.
29. Minoans   I. conquered Greece.
30. Athena   J. Greek historian.

USE YOUR MAPS

31. Look at the map of ancient empires on page 103. What empires ruled Egypt?

32. Look at the map of the Roman Empire on page 113. About when did Rome reach the height of its power?

33. Look at the map of Europe in the Middle Ages on page 143. Name the Spanish kingdoms.

34. Look at the map of the world on page 161. What European nations were important in exploring new lands?

GET THE DATE STRAIGHT

Match the date with the event.

35. 753 B.C.   A. Roman Empire divided into two parts.
36. 509 B.C.   B. Jesus Christ born in Judea.
37. 264 B.C.   C. Punic Wars began.
38. 146 B.C.   D. Eastern Roman Empire ended.
39. 44 B.C.   E. Julius Caesar killed.
40. 27 B.C.   F. Etruscan king overthrown; Roman Republic established.
41. 4 B.C.   G. Charlemagne crowned emperor of Romans.
42. 313 A.D.   H. Octavian given name *Augustus*.
43. 395 A.D.   I. Punic Wars ended.
44. 410 A.D.   J. Romulus and Remus said to have founded Rome.
45. 476 A.D.   K. Christianity allowed in the empire.
46. 800 A.D.   L. City of Rome invaded.
47. 1453 A.D.   M. Western Roman Empire ended.

THINK ABOUT IT

48. Why do you think ancient Greece is so important to our lives today?

49. One modern European nation is named after the Franks. Can you guess which one?

PUT IT ALL TOGETHER

50. Make a time line called "The World in the Past." Put on it the events up to 1550 that you think are the most important. Include about 25 dates. Use this unit as your source of information.

SOCIETIES IN EUROPE

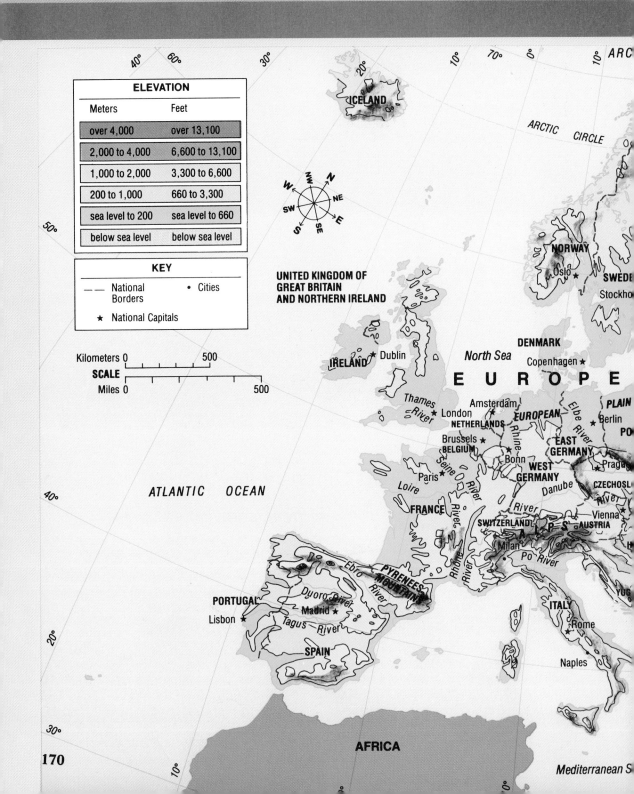

ELEVATION

Meters	Feet
over 4,000	over 13,100
2,000 to 4,000	6,600 to 13,100
1,000 to 2,000	3,300 to 6,600
200 to 1,000	660 to 3,300
sea level to 200	sea level to 660
below sea level	below sea level

KEY

– – – National Borders

★ National Capitals

• Cities

Kilometers 0   500
SCALE
Miles 0   500

40°   60°   30°   20°   10°   70°   0°   10°   ARC

ICELAND

ARCTIC CIRCLE

W NW N NE E
SW S SE

50°

UNITED KINGDOM OF
GREAT BRITAIN
AND NORTHERN IRELAND

NORWAY
Oslo ★ SWEDE
Stockho

DENMARK
IRELAND ★ Dublin   North Sea   Copenhagen ★

E U R O P E

Thames River   Amsterdam ★   PLAIN
London   EUROPEAN   Berlin ★   PO
NETHERLANDS   Rhine   Elbe River

Brussels ★   EAST
BELGIUM   Bonn   GERMANY   Prague ★
Paris ★   WEST   CZECHOSL
Loire   Seine   GERMANY   River
River   Danube

ATLANTIC OCEAN

40°

FRANCE   River   Vienna
SWITZERLAND   A L P S   AUSTRIA
Milan   Po River   YUG
Ebro River   PYRENEES MOUNTAINS   Rhone River

Duoro River   ITALY
PORTUGAL   Madrid ★   Rome ★
Lisbon ★   Tagus River

20°

SPAIN   Naples

30°

10°   AFRICA   0°   Mediterranean S

PHYSICAL MAP OF EUROPE

OCEAN

30°   40°   70°   50°   60°   70°   60°   80°

Barents Sea

URAL MOUNTAINS

50°

FINLAND

Isinki ★

• Leningrad

★ Moscow

ASIA

UNION OF SOVIET SOCIALIST REPUBLICS

Volga River

Dnieper River

40°

THIAN MOUNTAINS

CAUCASUS MOUNTAINS

Caspian Sea

ROMANIA

Bucharest ★

Black Sea

Mt. Elbrus

BULGARIA
★ Sofia

N MOUNTAINS   Istanbul

60°

E

★ Athens

30°

50°

CHAPTER 1

LOOKING AT EUROPE

Lesson 1: Introducing Europe

What does the word *Europe* mean to you? Do you think of high snow-covered mountains? Do you imagine old castles or other ancient buildings? Do you think of people dressed in colorful clothes? Do you see modern cities with tall buildings and factories, just as in the United States? Europe is all of these things.

Europe is one of the world's seven continents. Europeans have close ties with the United States. In fact, the majority of Americans are descended from European families.

Europe is not a very big continent. It covers only about 5 percent of Earth's surface. However, almost 20 percent of Earth's people live there. Europe is a crowded place in many ways.

Look at the map of the world on pages 8 and 9. Find the continent of Europe. You can see that Europe is part of the Eastern Hemisphere. You can also see that Europe seems to be part of a larger land mass. This land mass includes the much larger continent of Asia. The two continents are sometimes thought of as making up one continent. This "supercontinent" is called Eurasia (yoo RAY zhuh). In this book, however, you will study the two continents separately as Europe and Asia.

Though Europe is relatively small in area, it has many nations. Some of these nations have existed for more than a thousand years. Others were formed in this century. Today, there are both old and young nations in Europe. Nonetheless, all the cultures of Europe are very old.

Europe has two major regions. These are Western Europe and Eastern Europe. In this unit, you will study some major nations of Western Europe. These nations are the United Kingdom, France, and West Germany. You will also study two nations of Eastern Europe. These nations are East Germany and the Soviet Union. You will find out why there are now two Germanies.

REVIEW

CHECK YOUR FACTS

1. What percent of Earth's surface does Europe cover?
2. What percent of Earth's people live in Europe?
3. What is Eurasia?
4. Europe has (many/few) nations.

5. What are the two major regions of Europe?

THINK ABOUT IT

The majority of Americans are descended from Europeans. What nation or nations did your ancestors come from?

Lesson 2: The Land and Climate of Europe

FIND THE WORDS

peninsula   Meseta

If you were to fly over Europe in an airplane, you would see many different kinds of landforms. These different landforms are not just interesting in themselves. They have also affected the ways Europeans live. They have helped determine the histories of Europe's nations. They have strongly influenced the ways Europeans make a living.

Look at the map of Europe on pages 170 and 171. Find all the peninsulas that you can. A **peninsula** (puh NIN syuh luh) is an area of land almost surrounded by water. Peninsulas are very important in Europe. In the north, there is the Scandinavian (SKAN duh NAY vee un) Peninsula. Find the names of the countries that are part of this peninsula. In the west, there is the Iberian (eye BIR ee un) Peninsula. Spain and Portugal are the major nations there. To the south, there is the bootlike peninsula of Italy. Greece is on another peninsula in the south. Look at your map of Europe again. Find other peninsulas in Europe.

There are mountains throughout Europe. One of the most important groups of mountains is the Alps. Find these mountains on the map on pages 170 and 171. List the nations that the Alps are in. Another group of mountains, the Pyrenees (PIR uh neez), divide France and Spain.

Wide, fertile plains stretch across parts of Europe. Because of these, most of the European nations can feed their people. The great Central European Plain extends all the way from northern France to the Ural Mountains in the Soviet Union. Huge crops are raised on this plain. Look at the map of Europe on pages 170 and 171. Which nations seem to have the most level land in plains? Which nations seem to have the least?

Sometimes, flat lands are found at high elevations, often close to mountains. These are called plateaus. One of the major plateaus of Europe is in Spain. This high, dry land, nearly surrounded by mountains, is called the **Meseta** (muh SAYT uh). Another large plateau stretches across central Germany and western Czechoslovakia (CHEK uh sloh VAH kee uh).

174

The fertile plains of Europe produce great amounts of food.

Oceans and rivers are almost as important as landforms in Europe. The Arctic Ocean borders Europe on the north. The Atlantic Ocean is on the east. To the south is the Mediterranean (MED uh tuh RAY nee un) Sea. The Black Sea and the Caspian (KAS pee un) Sea border on Europe to the southeast. Find these bodies of water on the map of Europe on pages 170 and 171. The trade and fishing that the oceans make possible have been very important to Europe.

The great rivers of Europe have served to move people and goods across the continent. The Rhine (RYN) begins in Switzerland. It flows northwest through the heart of Europe to empty into the North Sea, an area of the Atlantic. The Danube (DAN yoob) rises near the source of the Rhine. But the Danube moves in the opposite direction. It sweeps southeast across the center of Europe to the Black Sea. It connects the western and eastern halves of the continent.

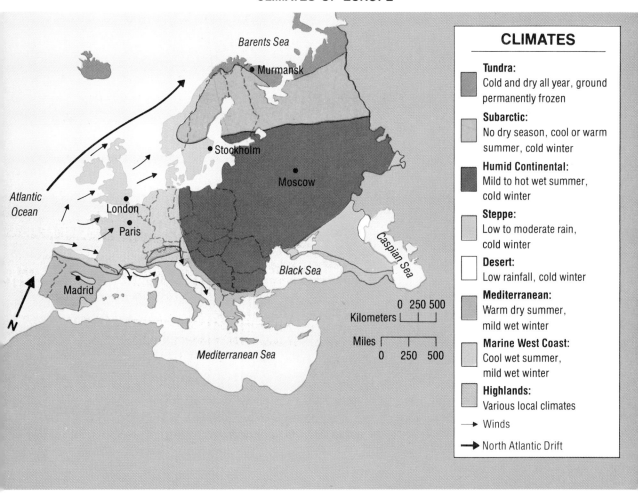

The rivers of Europe are important not only for trade. Europeans have long farmed the rich soil laid down by the rivers in their valleys. Some rivers also serve as borders between nations. Trace the Rhine River on the map of Europe. What nations does it divide? Look for other rivers that form borders.

The Climates of Europe

Which is farther north, the United States or Europe? Look at a globe or the map of the world on pages 10 and 11. Find the latitude of the southern tip of Florida. This is the southernmost part of the continental United States. Find the latitude of the southern coast of Spain. That is one of the parts of Europe that is farthest south. You will discover that Europe as a whole is north of the 48 American states that border on each other.

You know that more northerly areas tend to have colder climates. So you might guess that Europe has a colder climate than the United States. But this is not necessarily so. That is because climate depends on other things besides location on the planet.

One major factor that affects climate is water. Bodies of water tend to keep nearby land from getting too hot in summer or too cold in winter. That is because the temperature of water changes more slowly than the temperature of land.

You know that Europe is a peninsula surrounded by oceans and seas. That fact alone makes its climate milder than it otherwise might be. For example, the water of the Mediterranean Sea is very warm. It affects the climate of the nations that border on it.

Ocean currents are also important. The North Atlantic Drift is a strong and warm current that flows past the western and northern coasts of Europe. In particular, it helps keep Portugal, France, and the United Kingdom warm.

Not all of Europe is warm, of course. In all, there are three major climate regions. These are the marine, the humid continental, and the Mediterranean. There are smaller areas of subarctic, tundra, and highland climates. There are also very small areas of steppe and desert climates. Find these areas on the map on page 176.

REVIEW

CHECK YOUR FACTS

1. Name four nations of Europe that are on peninsulas.
2. Name two major mountain ranges in Europe.
3. What plain stretches across most of Europe?
4. Name two important rivers in Europe. In what direction does each of these rivers flow?

5. Why is the climate of Europe warmer than you might think?

TRY SOMETHING NEW

Using the maps in this book, find the climate in which you live. Then find a place on the same latitude in Europe. What kind of climate does it have? What reasons can you think of for any differences?

Lesson 3: The People of Europe

FIND THE WORDS

Caucasian   ethnic group

Like most continents, Europe has many nations. Most of these nations have their own cultures, or ways of living. Some have more than one. In general, however, the borders between European cultural groups follow the borders between the European nations.

Europeans belong to different cultural groups. They speak different languages. They have different lifestyles. Despite these differences, however, most Europeans have much in common. Most Europeans are **Caucasians** (kaw KAY zhunz), members of the White race. Most Europeans speak languages that are related to each other.

Most people in Europe speak one of the Indo-European languages. Indeed, about half the world's people, including the people of the United States, speak one of these languages. Most Europeans speak a language in one of

MAIN LANGUAGES OF EUROPE

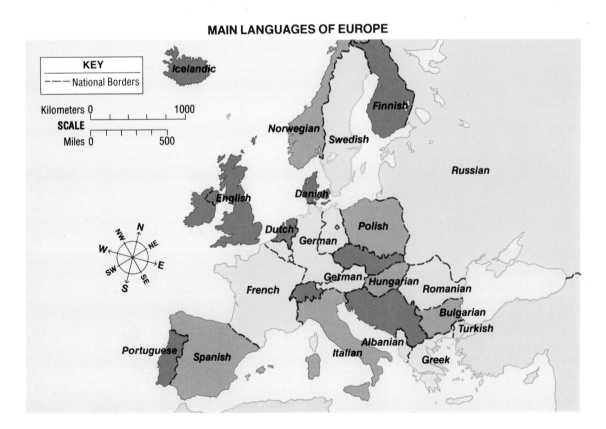

KEY
--- National Borders

Kilometers 0   1000
SCALE
Miles 0   500

Icelandic

Finnish

Norwegian
Swedish

Russian

English

Danish

Dutch   Polish
German

German Hungarian
French   Romanian

Bulgarian
Turkish

Albanian
Portuguese   Italian   Greek
Spanish

four groups of Indo-European languages. These are the Romance, Germanic, Celtic, and Balto-Slavic languages.

Most of the people of France, Spain, Portugal, Italy, and Romania speak Romance languages. Find these nations on the map of Europe on page 178.

Most of the people of northern Europe speak Germanic (jur MAN ik) languages. You might not immediately see that German, Dutch, English, Swedish, Danish, Norwegian, and Icelandic have much in common. However, all these languages began in an ancient Germanic language. On the map, find the nations where these languages are spoken.

A much smaller group of Europeans speak Celtic (SEL tik) languages. The people living in the British Isles before 450 A.D. spoke Celtic. Then, Germanic groups invaded the British Isles. Gradually, the British began to speak English. Today, some people still speak Irish Gaelic (GAYL ik), Scottish Gaelic, and Welsh. Another Celtic language, Breton (BRET un), is spoken in northwestern France.

Europeans in Eastern Europe and the Soviet Union speak Balto-Slavic languages. More Europeans speak Balto-Slavic languages than speak Romance, Germanic, or Celtic languages. The Baltic languages occur in a small area of the Soviet Union. The Slavic languages of the Soviet Union include Russian and Ukrainian (yoo KRAY nee un). Except for Romania, the other Eastern European nations speak other Slavic languages.

Greek and Albanian are Indo-European languages that do not fall into one of the four major groups. A small number of non–Indo-European languages are also spoken in Europe. These include Finnish, Hungarian, and Basque (BASK).

Language can serve to unite the people of a nation. Language can even give a common background to the peoples of different nations.

Many Religions

Most Europeans share a Christian background. But they belong to different Christian churches. Some are Roman Catholics. Some are Protestants. Some belong to other Christian churches. Most of the people who live in southern Europe are Roman Catholics. Most of the people who live in northern Europe are Protestants.

Religion is generally less strong in Eastern Europe and the Soviet Union. The Communist governments there discourage religion. Nonetheless, Roman Catholicism remains important in Eastern Europe, especially in Poland. Many of the people in the Soviet Union,

Men of the South Tyrol put on regional clothes for special holidays.

Eastern Europe, and Greece belong to Eastern Orthodox churches.

Many Ethnic Groups

Each person belongs to an **ethnic group.** This is a group of people who share many beliefs, customs, and ideas. In many European nations, most people belong to one ethnic group. Sometimes, however, there are other ethnic groups. This is particularly so near the borders of the European nations. For example, South Tyrol in Italy was originally part of Austria. The people there speak German. This area has long been a source of conflict in Eu-

FUN FACTS

You have heard of Britain, France, and Germany. But have you heard of Luxembourg and Liechtenstein? What do you know about Andorra, Monaco, San Marino, Vatican City, and Malta? These are the ministates, or small nations, of Europe.

Luxembourg is the largest. It is nestled between Belgium, France, and Germany. Luxembourg is an important producer of iron and steel. Liechtenstein lies in the Alps between Switzerland and Austria.

Andorra is in the Pyrenees Mountains between Spain and France. On France's southern coast is Monaco. Grace Kelly, an American movie actress, married the ruling prince of Monaco in the 1950s.

Italy surrounds two ministates, San Marino and Vatican City. San Marino is merely a mountaintop. Vatican City, the home of the Roman Catholic pope, covers only a few blocks in the city of Rome. South of Italy is the small island nation of Malta.

Greek children can learn about their culture by going to museums.

rope. There has been a similar problem in an area of France near Germany.

Despite the many ethnic problems in Europe, most European nations are dominated by one ethnic group. Most of the members of each ethnic group generally live in one nation. The European ethnic groups do not tend to be widely scattered, as ethnic groups are in the United States. The major exception to this rule is the Soviet Union. There are more than 100 ethnic groups in that vast nation that spans two continents.

REVIEW

CHECK YOUR FACTS

1. What are members of the White race called?
2. Name the four major groups of Indo-European languages.
3. Finnish (is/is not) an Indo-European language.
4. What part of Europe is mostly Roman Catholic? What part is mostly Protestant?
5. What is an ethnic group?
6. What European nation has more than 100 ethnic groups?

THINK ABOUT IT

Suppose people in each of the 50 states spoke different languages. How do you think life in the United States would be different?

Lesson 4: The Economy of Europe

One way to study a nation is to find out about its economy. The **economy** is the system by which people use resources to produce and distribute goods and services. **Goods** include useful products. **Services** are things people do for other people.

The economies of the European nations are often very different from one another. Europe's nations have different kinds and amounts of resources. In addition, Europe has two types of economies: capitalist and socialist.

A capitalist economy is also called a free-enterprise or market economy. Under **capitalism**, individuals and private groups own and run most businesses. People decide what goods and services they want to buy in the marketplace. These decisions determine what goods and services are produced. Each nation of Western Europe has a capitalist economy, as does the United States.

Under socialism, the government owns and runs most businesses. The government decides what goods and services will be produced. The Communist nations of Eastern Europe and the Soviet Union have socialist economies. Those nations are called Communist because they are ruled by Communist political parties. Communists believe in communism. This is an economic system in which there is no private property. Communists hope someday to go beyond socialism to communism.

Whatever the differences between the European economies, however, four things are important in each: resources, agriculture, industry, and services.

Economic Resources

Every economy is based on different kinds of resources. These include **natural resources,** such as water, fertile land, forests, and minerals. There are also **human resources.** These are the people who work on farms and in factories and offices. There are also **capital resources.** These are the sums of money needed to build machinery and factories. Each of Europe's nations has these resources in differing amounts. The nations of Western Europe have

LIVING RESOURCES OF EUROPE

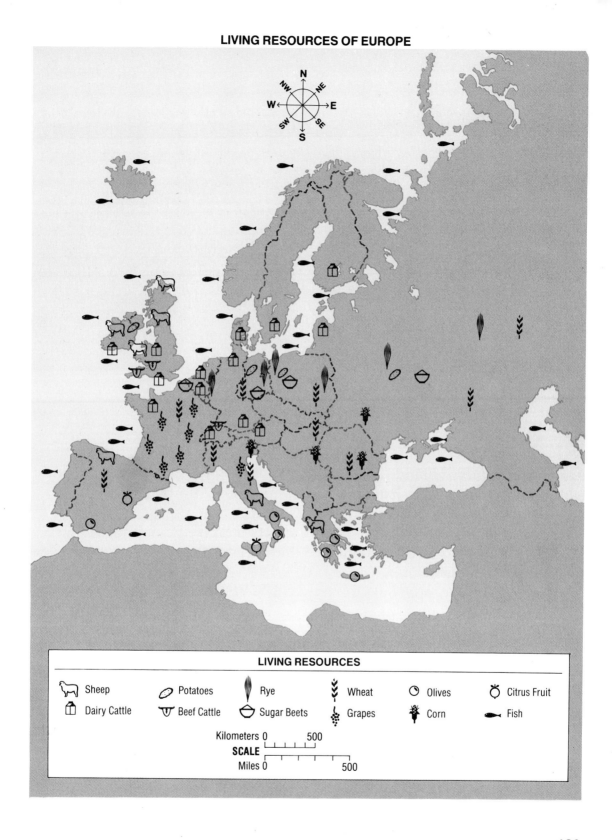

LIVING RESOURCES

- Sheep
- Dairy Cattle
- Potatoes
- Beef Cattle
- Rye
- Sugar Beets
- Wheat
- Grapes
- Olives
- Corn
- Citrus Fruit
- Fish

Kilometers 0 — 500
SCALE
Miles 0 — 500

Olives are raised on the island of Crete in Greece.

iron ore, coal, fertile land, and forests. Many Eastern European countries have mineral resources. The Soviet Union is rich in iron ore, petroleum, natural gas, and many other minerals.

Most European nations have enough people to work on farms and in factories and offices. Indeed, some nations, such as Greece, have more workers than jobs. These nations "export" people to other European nations where jobs are available.

Most Western European nations have enough money to buy the machines needed for their farms and factories. They are also able to invent new products and build whole new industries. In Eastern Europe, the Communist governments supply the capital resources for their economies.

Agriculture

One of the strengths of Europe's economy is that there is much good land for agriculture. **Agriculture** is farming—the raising of crops and livestock. It is very important in many European nations. Animals for meat, wool, and leather, and fruits and vegetables are raised in the British Isles. Various kinds of grain are grown on the Central European Plain.

NONLIVING RESOURCES OF EUROPE

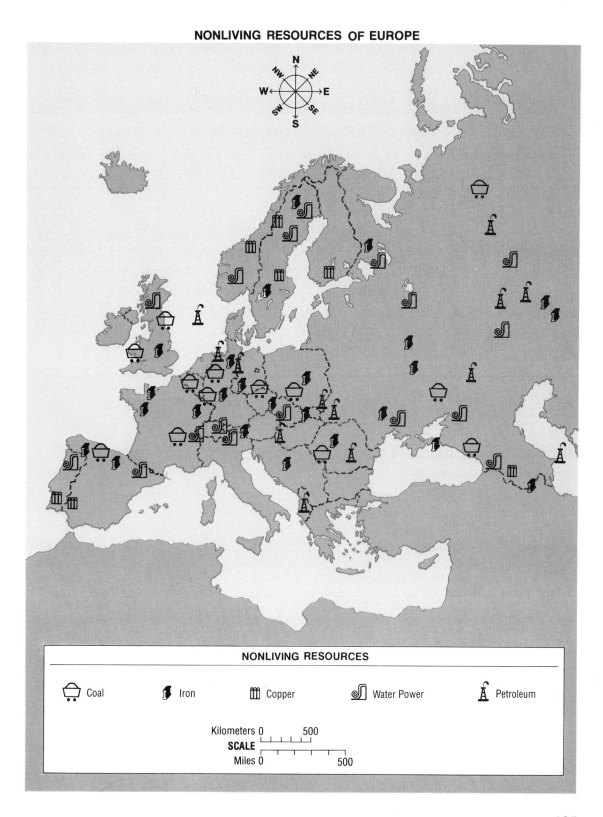

NONLIVING RESOURCES

Coal   Iron   Copper   Water Power   Petroleum

Kilometers 0   500
SCALE
Miles 0   500

Grapes are an important crop across the south of Europe from Portugal to Yugoslavia.

In most of Western Europe, farming is highly **mechanized** (MEK uh NYZD). That means that machines are used to do the work. However, in many of the poorer countries of Eastern Europe much farm work is still done by hand. Even in West Germany and in Norway you can still see people harvesting crops by hand.

The European nations **export,** or sell abroad, many of their farm products. Denmark exports dairy products. France is second only to the United States in agricultural exports. Poland also exports food.

Some European nations, such as Switzerland, must **import,** or buy from abroad, much of their food. Even great wheat producers like the Soviet Union do not always have enough food for their people's needs. In times of shortage, the Soviets must import grain from other nations.

Industry

Most European nations are more **industrial** than agricultural. This means that they earn more money from their factories than from their farms.

Europe is one of the world's most important industrial areas. All kinds of industries are located here. Machinery is made in Poland, West Germany, the Soviet

Europe has all kinds of industries. This is a steel mill in Wales.

Union, and the British Isles. Much of it is exported to other countries. Scientific instruments are made in Switzerland and West Germany and sold throughout the world. Cars are exported from Italy, Sweden, France, West Germany, and the Soviet Union. Have you ever seen cars from these nations on the streets of your community?

Southern Europe does not have as much industry as northern Europe. The nations there are not so rich. They have more trouble finding enough money to build new factories.

European nations sell goods to one another. Here, Italians buy German fruit and vegetables.

Services

European nations perform services that are used by people all over the world. Switzerland is one of the world's great banking centers. Many insurance companies also have their headquarters there. Gold is exchanged on the London gold market.

One of the most important service industries in Europe involves tourism. **Tourists** are people who visit faraway places for pleasure, usually on vacation. Many Europeans work in hotels, restaurants, travel agencies, and tourist centers. These Europeans help the millions of visitors who come to their continent each year. In many nations, tourism is a major economic activity.

Much of Europe lies close to the sea. Ships that carry people and goods around the world are another service the Europeans provide. The Greeks and Norwegians are among the great sailing peoples of Europe.

Economic Cooperation

The nations of Europe have decided that they can improve their economies by working together. In earlier times, each nation taxed goods from other nations when the goods crossed its borders. This made it more difficult for nations to sell their goods to one another. Today, the nations of both Western Europe and Eastern Europe have set up markets that cover many nations. Within these broad areas, there are no taxes on imported goods. Goods can move freely from one nation to another. In Western Europe, there is the European Economic Community, or Common Market. In Eastern Europe, there is a similar association for economic cooperation.

The Future

Since World War II, European nations have rebuilt their industries and modernized their farms. West Germany has developed one of the strongest economies in the world. If the Europeans are to remain prosperous, however, they must find dependable sources of energy. Petroleum and natural gas are not found in most European nations. These energy resources must be imported from other parts of the world. Petroleum from the North Sea is helping Norway and the United Kingdom today. Europe's economic future depends on the wise use of natural and human resources and the availability of capital resources.

REVIEW

WATCH YOUR WORDS

1. The ____ of a nation is the way its people produce and distribute goods and services.
capital resources   economy

2. Individuals and private groups own and run most businesses under ____.
socialism   capitalism
industrialism

3. Money used to build machinery and factories is a ____ resource.
capital   human   natural

4. In Western Europe, agriculture is ____.
mechanized   industrial   service

5. ____ are people who visit other places on vacation.
Exports   Human resources
Tourists

CHECK YOUR FACTS

6. What is an important difference between capitalism and socialism?

7. What four things are important to every economy?

8. List the three kinds of resources every economy needs.

9. How does agriculture in Western Europe differ from that in Eastern Europe?

10. How has the European Common Market made it easier for Western European nations to sell their goods?

THINK ABOUT IT

Why does the health of Europe's economy depend on trade? How do you think life in Europe would be affected if all trade stopped?

Lesson 5: Land of Many Nations

You have learned that Europe can be divided into western and eastern parts. It is also possible to divide the continent into northern and southern halves. In this lesson, we will do a little of both. We will study Europe in four parts: Western Europe, Eastern Europe, Mediterranean Europe, and Scandinavia. Each of these regions is made up of several nations. Most nations within each region have similar languages and customs.

Western Europe

Look at the map on page 190. Find the nations of Western Eu-rope. Did you find Ireland, the United Kingdom, West Germany, the Netherlands, France, Belgium, Switzerland, and Austria? There are also some very small nations such as Luxembourg (LUK sum BERG) and Liechtenstein (LIKH tun SHTYN). Most Western European nations have large populations. Indeed, 40 percent of all Europeans live in this region.

Eastern Europe

Look at the map on page 190. Find the nations that are part of Eastern Europe. You probably listed Poland, East Germany,

POPULATION AND INDUSTRY IN EUROPE

KEY	
___ National Borders	\\\\\ Industrial Areas

PEOPLE	
Per Square Kilometer	**Per Square Mile**
under 10	under 25
10 to 50	25 to 125
50 to 100	125 to 250
over 100	over 250

NATIONS OF EUROPE

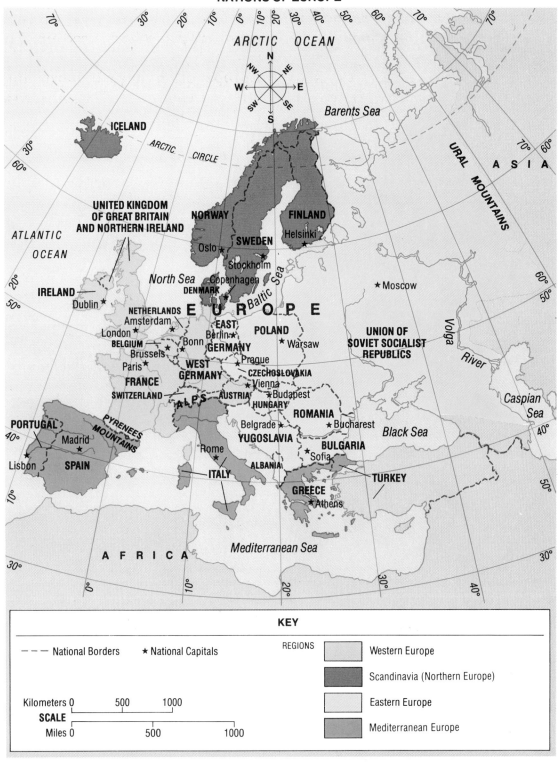

ARCTIC OCEAN

Barents Sea

ICELAND

ARCTIC CIRCLE

N
NW   NE
W   E
SW   SE
S

URAL MOUNTAINS

ASIA

UNITED KINGDOM
OF GREAT BRITAIN
AND NORTHERN IRELAND

NORWAY

FINLAND
Helsinki ★

SWEDEN

Oslo ★

ATLANTIC
OCEAN

Stockholm ★

North Sea

Copenhagen

★ Moscow

IRELAND

Dublin ★

DENMARK

Baltic Sea

E U R O P E

Volga River

NETHERLANDS
Amsterdam ★

London ★

EAST
Berlin ★

POLAND

UNION OF
SOVIET SOCIALIST
REPUBLICS

BELGIUM
Brussels ★
Paris ★

Bonn ★

GERMANY

★ Warsaw

FRANCE

WEST
GERMANY

Prague ★

Caspian
Sea

SWITZERLAND

CZECHOSLOVAKIA

Vienna ★

ALPS

AUSTRIA

★ Budapest

PORTUGAL

PYRENEES
MOUNTAINS

HUNGARY

ROMANIA

Black Sea

Madrid ★

Belgrade ★

★ Bucharest

Lisbon ★

SPAIN

Rome ★

YUGOSLAVIA

BULGARIA
Sofia ★

ITALY

ALBANIA

TURKEY

GREECE
★ Athens

AFRICA

Mediterranean Sea

70° 30° 20° 10° 0° 10° 20° 30° 40° 50° 60° 70°
30° 60° 20° 50° 40° 40° 10° 30° 0° 10° 20° 30° 40°
70° 60° 60° 50° 40° 50° 30°

KEY

– – – National Borders   ★ National Capitals

REGIONS

Western Europe

Scandinavia (Northern Europe)

Eastern Europe

Mediterranean Europe

Kilometers 0   500   1000
SCALE
Miles 0   500   1000

190

Czechoslovakia, Hungary, Romania, Bulgaria, Albania, and Yugoslavia. Did you also include the eastern part of the Soviet Union?

All these nations have Communist governments. Except for Albania and Yugoslavia, all have close ties with the Soviet Union. Like Western Europe, Eastern Europe has many people.

Mediterranean Europe

The nations of southern Europe all border the Mediterranean Sea. Look at the map on page 190. Find the nations of this region. They include Spain, Portugal, Italy, and Greece. Southern France is also on the Mediterranean, but France is part of Western Europe.

Almost one-third of all Europeans live in this fascinating part of the continent. The climate here is mild. These lands have long and colorful histories. Yet, over the years, many resources and much good soil have been used up. Today, the people of Mediterranean Europe often have a hard time growing enough food or otherwise making a living.

Scandinavia

Scandinavia is a cold region. Most Scandinavians live in the southern part of the region. Only in Denmark do many people live in all parts of the country.

Scandinavia is made up of peninsulas and islands. Look at the map on page 190. Find the nations that are part of this region. They include Denmark, Norway, Sweden, Finland, and Iceland.

The Scandinavians are surrounded by the sea. Therefore, many people make their living in fishing or shipping.

REVIEW

CHECK YOUR FACTS

Look at the Map

1. Look at the map of Europe on page 190. Name eight countries in Western Europe.
2. Name nine countries in Eastern Europe.

Look at the Lesson

3. Name the four regions of Europe.

4. The nations of Western Europe have (large/small) populations.
5. Which region of Europe has many Communist governments?
6. What kind of climate does Mediterranean Europe have?

THINK ABOUT IT

How do you think life in the United States would be different if every state were a separate nation?

CHAPTER REVIEW

WATCH YOUR WORDS

1. A ___ is almost surrounded by water.
   continent   peninsula   Meseta

2. Most Europeans are ___.
   Caucasians   Celts   Basques

3. A nation that earns more money from factories than from farms is an ___ country.
   exporting   agricultural   industrial

4. To ___ goods is to sell them in another country.
   import   export   mechanize

CHECK YOUR FACTS

5. To what larger land mass does Europe belong?

6. What two oceans border on Europe?

7. Name the three major climate regions of Europe.

8. Greek and Albanian (are/are not) Indo-European languages.

9. Name the three main groups of Christians in Europe.

10. In what ways do capitalism and socialism differ?

11. Name some important agricultural products of Europe.

12. Which European countries export cars?

13. What is another name for the European Economic Community?

14. In what manner has the sea affected the ways the people of Scandinavia earn a living?

USE YOUR MAPS

15. Look at the map of Europe's climates on page 176. Name the kind of climate each of these cities has: Paris, Stockholm, Moscow.

16. Look at the map of Europe's languages on page 178. How many nations can you find in which German is spoken?

17. Look at the map of living resources in Europe on page 183. Are citrus fruits grown in northern Europe or southern Europe?

18. Look at the map of nonliving resources in Europe on page 185. In what places is petroleum produced in Europe?

19. Look at the map of Europe's nations on page 190. What two countries are in both Europe and Asia?

THINK ABOUT IT

20. Imagine you are moving to Europe. In which region of Europe would you prefer to live? Give your reasons.

21. Many words we use in English have been borrowed from the Romance languages French, Spanish, and Italian. Which ones can you think of?

22. In which economic system, capitalism or socialism, do you think people have the most freedom? Why?

23. Why do you think many people go to Europe as tourists each year?

24. Do you think Europe will ever unite into one nation? Why, or why not?

TRY SOMETHING NEW

25. Do you know anyone who used to live in a nation in Europe? Ask the person why she or he came to this country. Ask about the differences between the two nations. Make a report to your class.

26. Many goods have labels on them that say where they were made. Look at some things in your classroom or home. Can you find any that were imported from Europe?

2 THE UNITED KINGDOM

Lesson 1: The England of Elizabeth I

Today, the United Kingdom of Great Britain and Northern Ireland is one of the most important nations of Western Europe. This nation is often called Britain or Great Britain. It began as the Kingdom of England. Gradually, the English extended their rule over Wales, Ireland, and Scotland. Britain eventually became the most powerful nation in the world. The British came to rule over a vast empire scattered across the globe. The British economy became the strongest in the

TIME LINE: MODERN HISTORY OF BRITAIN

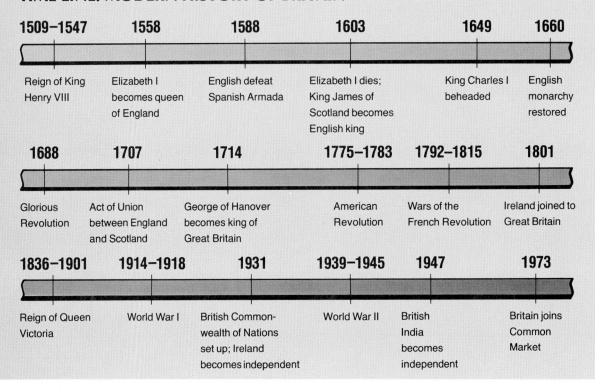

1509–1547	1558	1588	1603	1649	1660
Reign of King Henry VIII	Elizabeth I becomes queen of England	English defeat Spanish Armada	Elizabeth I dies; King James of Scotland becomes English king	King Charles I beheaded	English monarchy restored

1688	1707	1714	1775–1783	1792–1815	1801
Glorious Revolution	Act of Union between England and Scotland	George of Hanover becomes king of Great Britain	American Revolution	Wars of the French Revolution	Ireland joined to Great Britain

1836–1901	1914–1918	1931	1939–1945	1947	1973
Reign of Queen Victoria	World War I	British Commonwealth of Nations set up; Ireland becomes independent	World War II	British India becomes independent	Britain joins Common Market

world. One of the rulers who helped make England a great nation was Queen Elizabeth I. She ruled from 1558 to 1603. During her **reign** (RAYN), the time she ruled, major changes took place.

Who Was Elizabeth I?

Elizabeth I was the second daughter of King Henry VIII of England. Her mother was Queen Anne Boleyn (bu LIN), Henry's second wife.

King Henry's first wife, Queen Catherine, had given birth to a daughter, Mary. But she could have no more children. Henry wanted a son to rule after him. He asked the pope to **annul,** or declare invalid, his first marriage. The king wanted to marry Anne Boleyn. The pope refused. It was because of this dispute that England became a Protestant nation. Henry separated the Church of England from the Roman Catholic Church. He divorced Queen Catherine and married Anne Boleyn.

Queen Anne bore not a son but a daughter, Elizabeth. Henry soon had Anne executed, and he married again. His third queen, Jane Seymour (SEE mor), finally bore him a son, Edward.

194

During her childhood, Elizabeth received more education than most girls at the time. Indeed, she received training in languages like that given to a future king. By living in the king's palace, she learned much about politics and relations between nations. When Elizabeth later became queen, this education helped her to rule her people well.

When Henry VIII died, he was succeeded by his son, Edward VI. But Edward had poor health and died at an early age. His older sister, Mary I, then became queen. Mary tried to restore the Roman Catholic religion in England. Because she had some Protestants killed, she has been called Bloody Mary. Mary also died soon, and her younger sister Elizabeth I became queen. The English people welcomed Elizabeth to the throne. They hoped she would be a good ruler. She came to be so loved by her people that they called her Good Queen Bess.

Elizabeth Rules

When Elizabeth became queen, she faced many problems. The major one was religion. Elizabeth made England Protestant once again. Since her time, the ruler of England has also been the head of the Church of England.

The second major problem Elizabeth had to face was that her

Above: Henry VIII, one of England's most famous kings. *Below:* Queen Elizabeth I being carried to an important ceremony.

nation was at war with France. She helped bring the war to an end. She then kept her country at peace for many years.

Elizabeth's government also faced financial difficulties. Wars had cost much money. The nation's economy and currency were in poor shape. Elizabeth had her government take steps to make England prosperous again.

In part, Elizabeth I was a good ruler because she chose good people to help her and listened to them. Her **advisers,** the people who helped her make decisions, were excellent. The queen also worked well with the **Parliament** (PAHR luh munt), or lawmaking body. Elizabeth and her government built up a strong navy for England.

Philip II, the King of Spain, opposed Elizabeth. He had been married to her sister Mary and thought he should rule England. He also wanted to restore Roman Catholicism in England. King Philip sent the Spanish Armada (ahr MAH duh) against England in 1588. This great fleet of ships met the English fleet off the coast. The English defeated the Spanish in one of the most important sea battles in history. Elizabeth's kingdom was safe.

Elizabeth I never married. She often told foreign princes that she might marry them. This encour-

aged them to cooperate with England. Elizabeth liked having her favorites around her at the palace. But she did not want to share her power with a husband. She wanted to rule her kingdom alone.

Elizabeth sent great sailors to many parts of the world. One was Sir Francis Drake. He sailed around the world. He showed other nations that England was powerful on the seas.

Because Elizabeth kept England at peace and was careful with the government's money, most people lived better during her reign. She tried to make life easier for her people. She tried not to set high taxes. She encouraged Parliament to pass laws to help the poor.

Although the people of England loved Elizabeth, many disputes had arisen by 1600. Some members of Parliament and others were not happy with some of her actions. But no one was able to threaten her power. When Elizabeth I died in 1603, she left her country far better off than it was when she had become queen.

Literature and Shakespeare

During the reign of Elizabeth I, great writers produced works that survive today. The most important of these was William Shakespeare. He was a writer of plays who lived at Stratford-on-Avon and in

Queen Elizabeth I and members of her court often attended plays.

London. Today, the plays of Shakespeare are studied in schools all over the world. These plays are performed in many different languages. They contain some of the most beautiful poetry ever written. They have inspired much great music and art. Shakespeare's plays have lasted because they say things that still seem important.

REVIEW

WATCH YOUR WORDS

1. People who help someone make decisions are____.
   advisers   exporters   producers

2. To declare something invalid is to ____it.
   defeat   annul   advise

3. In Great Britain, laws are made by the____.
   queen   Parliament   Congress

CHECK YOUR FACTS

4. Why did England become a Protestant nation?

5. What three major problems faced Elizabeth I when she became queen?

THINK ABOUT IT

Elizabeth I was ruling a major nation at a time when few women did so. What problems do you think this might have given her?

Lesson 2: The Industrial Revolution

FIND THE WORDS

revolution   textiles
specialization   cottage industry
factory   coal   raw materials
finished goods

Through the Middle Ages and after, people in the British Isles made most things by hand or with simple tools and machines. Then in the 1700s and 1800s, many new inventions brought great changes in the ways things were made. A whole new world began. These changes are called the industrial revolution. A **revolution** is a great political or economic change. The industrial revolution gave Britain the world's strongest economy.

The Textile Industry

We will look at how the industrial revolution changed the making of just one product, **textiles,** or cloth. What happened in this one industry is similar to what happened in other industries.

In the Middle Ages, most families wove their own cloth.

Manchester is a city in England. It has many factories.

During the Middle Ages, most families had filled their own needs for cloth. Families had raised their own sheep, sheared the wool, spun the wool into thread, and woven the thread into cloth. This took a long time to do. Each family could make only enough cloth for its own needs.

Then, a great change took place. Merchants discovered that more cloth could be produced if people would do just one job. This is called **specialization.** The merchants organized the families. Each family did a specific part of the task. Some raised sheep. Others sheared the wool from the sheep. Still others spun the wool into thread. This thread was taken to other families to be woven into cloth. When each family did only one job, they produced much more cloth per family. Now there was extra cloth to sell to other people. People did these jobs in their own cottages, or homes. Thus, this was called a **cottage industry.**

At first, cloth was woven on looms powered by hand or by waterwheels. These looms worked slowly and could not be very big. To produce more cloth, the looms had to be changed.

Many British inventors and their inventions helped make the industrial revolution possible. In 1733, John Kay produced the flying shuttle. This was a weaving machine. It allowed weavers to make cloth very fast.

But spinners could not make thread fast enough to supply the new weaving machines. So James Hargreaves invented the spinning jenny in 1764. The water frame was made by Richard Arkwright in 1769. It was a spinning machine powered by water.

Samuel Crompton combined these two machines into his spinning mule in 1779.

In the 1760s, James Watt had improved the steam engine. This engine ran on coal. It could produce large amounts of power dependably.

Edmund Cartwright applied the steam engine to the loom in 1785. In 1803, John Horrocks built a metal loom. So now all parts of textile making were done in factories by large machines.

New inventions changed the ways in which people made cloth. Looms began to be made of iron instead of wood. These new looms could be much larger than the old ones. In fact, they became so big that they would not fit in people's homes. They had to be moved to special buildings. Such buildings with many machines and many workers are called **factories.** Instead of working at home, the workers now had to go to the factories to work.

The new iron looms could not be powered by hand. Waterpower was also not sufficient. Finally, steam power came to be used. Every factory had to have fuel to heat the water to make the steam. Britain had lots of **coal,** a black mineral that was an excellent fuel.

The new looms were supplied with thread by new spinning machines. More and more jobs came to be done in factories. The textile industry had changed. It was no longer a cottage industry. It was now a factory industry.

The new machines used so much wool that it had to be imported from other nations. Cotton also came to be used for cloth. The wool and cotton were **raw materials.** These are things that are grown, raised, gathered, or mined. They are then made into useful things, called **finished goods.** Typically, British manufacturers bought raw materials in other nations. They brought these back to Britain to be made into finished goods. They then sold those goods to the nations from which they had bought the raw materials. Such was the case with the cotton grown in the southern United States.

Machine-run looms increased the amount of cloth people could make.

Results of the Industrial Revolution

The changes in British industry affected everyone. Now many people worked in a big factory rather than at home. Each person had to learn to work with people from other families.

People who worked in factories had to live near them. So more and more people moved closer to where they were working. Thus, towns and cities grew up around the factories. These cities became crowded.

People could live in cities only if other people in the country

A person using a hand-operated loom could not make a large amount of cloth.

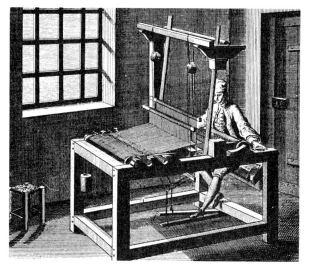

could produce food for them. Farmers began to use new methods that produced more food. This extra food could feed the people in the cities. Many farmers, too, began to specialize in one job like the factory workers.

The lives of the workers were greatly changed. No longer did they raise their own food or make their own clothing. Often, they lived in rented homes or rooms rather than in their own cottages. If they were unable to work, they had no protection. The workers might not be able to pay the rent or feed themselves. At that time, the government did not help people who were out of work.

The industrial revolution made it possible for Britain to produce many products quickly. It gave British merchants products to sell all over the world. It made these products cheaper to buy because each worker could produce more. However, the industrial revolution also created problems. Some of these problems have still not been solved.

REVIEW

WATCH YOUR WORDS

1. ___ are manufactured products.
   Finished goods   Raw Materials
   Minerals

2. A time of rapid change is called a(n) ___.
   specialization   revolution
   industrialization

3. Manufacturing done in people's own homes was called a(n) ___.
   industrial revolution   textile
   cottage industry

4. ___ occurs when people manufacture only one part of a product.
   Industrialization   Specialization
   Revolution

5. The goods needed to make finished products are called ___.
   raw materials   textiles   industries

CHECK YOUR FACTS

6. What was the industrial revolution? When did it take place?

7. How did cottage industry get its name?

8. Where did many people work after the industrial revolution?

9. How did the industrial revolution affect Great Britain's need for raw materials?

THINK ABOUT IT

Identify a problem of the industrial revolution that you think still exists today. Why do you think the problem has not been solved?

Lesson 3: The British Empire

By the 1800s, Great Britain had developed huge industries that produced a wealth of goods. Britain needed places to sell these goods. It needed sources of raw materials. One way to secure markets and materials was to build an empire. This is a group of colonies, or lands controlled by another country. Long before the industrial revolution, the English had been sailing the seas and exploring the world. They had also been founding colonies in many lands.

North America

The English began establishing colonies in North America early in the 1600s. Thirteen of these colonies later became the United States. For over 150 years, however, these colonies were part of the British Empire. Even after the United States became independent, it long remained an important British trading partner.

THE BRITISH EMPIRE IN 1900

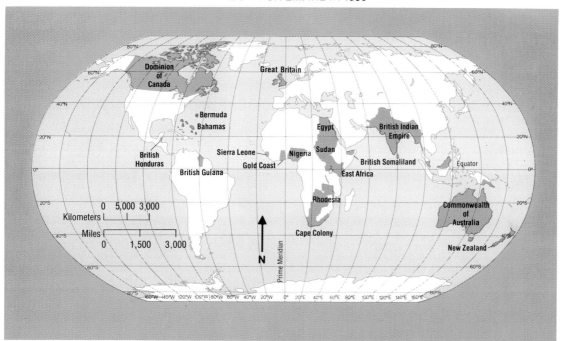

203

France had also set up colonies in North America. These lay north and west of the British colonies. The British and the French fought several wars in North America. Finally, during the Seven Years' War, or French and Indian War (1756–1763), the issue was settled. The British gained control of French Canada.

Just 20 years later, at the end of the American Revolution, the British lost their 13 original colonies. However, they kept Canada. Today, Canada is an independent nation, but it remains part of the **Commonwealth of Nations.** This group is headed by the United Kingdom. It includes many former British colonies that are now independent but wish to keep some ties with Britain.

Central and South America

The British Empire never was very strong in Central America and South America. There were a couple of British colonies along the coast and many British islands in the Caribbean (KAR uh BEE un) Sea. Many of these are now independent, but some remain British.

Asia

The British Empire was strong in Asia, particularly in India. England established claims in India through the East India Company by the end of the 1600s. However, the British had to struggle with the French for power. By the end of the Seven Years' War, the British were clearly dominant in India. Many British people came to India to make their careers in government and trade. In 1796, the British also took over the large island of Ceylon (si LON) off the coast of India.

The British government took control of India from the East India Company in 1858. From then on, Britain made the laws for the millions of Indians. The British ran the government, the army, and the schools. Many Indians learned English. Raw materials flowed from India to Britain. British manufactured goods were sold in India.

Some British people opposed ruling over colonies. In India, itself, there was a series of revolts among the people. At last, under the leadership of Mahatma Gandhi (muh HAHT muh GAHN dee), India became an independent nation in 1947. The nations of Pakistan and Burma were also carved out of British India. Ceylon became independent in 1948.

The British were also active in other parts of Asia. They were very influential in China, especially in trade. They established great trading centers at Hong Kong in China and at Singapore in Malaya. Hong Kong remains a

Above: A picture of a reception in India. The time is the late 1800s, when the British Empire was still strong in Asia. *Right:* Modern Hong Kong, which remains a British colony today.

British colony. The British also traded with Japan.

Australia and New Zealand

At first, the British used Australia as a colony for prisoners. Then gold was discovered there. Many people came from Great Britain to mine it. The various Australian colonies became a united, independent nation in 1901. Today, Australia remains a member of the Commonwealth of Nations.

In early years, New Zealand was explored by British sailors. It became part of the British Empire in 1838. The British had a lot of trouble with the native people of New Zealand, the Maoris. Finally, in 1907, New Zealand gained self-rule. Today, it is part of the Commonwealth of Nations.

Africa

Africa was the last area into which the British Empire expanded. There, as elsewhere, the British had to struggle with the French for territory. The British came to control the colonies of South Africa, Rhodesia, Nigeria, Sudan, Egypt, and others. The British mined many valuable minerals in these lands. Today, all of Britain's African colonies have become independent.

The Empire

Look at the map on page 203. Find the British colonies on each continent. At the beginning of the 1900s, the British people could say that the sun never set on their empire. It was the largest empire in history. Today, most of the British colonies are independent.

REVIEW

WATCH YOUR WORDS

1. To extend control over other lands is to build a(n)____.
   territory   state   empire
2. Lands controlled by another nation are____.
   commonwealths   colonies   states

CHECK YOUR FACTS

3. Why did Britain want to build an empire?

4. In what areas did Britain set up colonies?
5. What other nation in particular competed with Britain for control of territory?

THINK ABOUT IT

The 13 colonies became free from Britain as a result of the American Revolution. How do you think your life might be different today if the United States had not won its independence?

Lesson 4: The United Kingdom Today

FIND THE WORDS

urban   Prime Minister
immigrant   labor unions
inflation   unemployed

The United Kingdom today is made up of four areas. These are England, Wales, Scotland, and Northern Ireland. Look at the map shown below. Find each of these areas. What other nation shares the British Isles with the United Kingdom?

Resources

In part, the industrial revolution began in Great Britain because of that nation's natural resources. Coal and iron ore were particularly important. Today, Britain still has important resources, particularly sources of energy. Coal is still mined in Wales. Petroleum and natural gas come from offshore wells in the North Sea. These have been a new source of wealth for the United Kingdom.

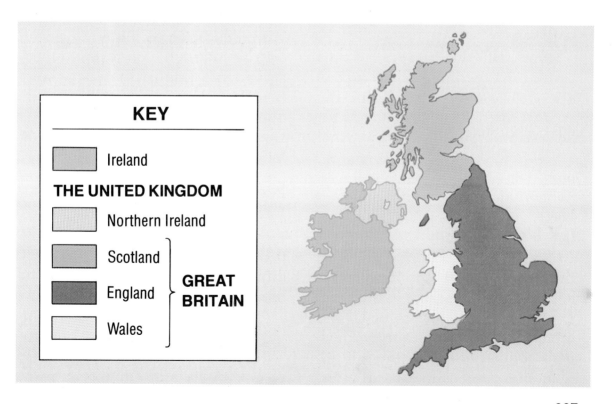

KEY

Ireland

THE UNITED KINGDOM

Northern Ireland

Scotland

England

Wales

GREAT BRITAIN

Much of the United Kingdom's land is suitable for agriculture. In addition to food crops, cattle and sheep are raised. The wool from sheep is used to make fine woolen products. Many of these products are exported.

The people of the United Kingdom include many skilled factory workers and productive farm workers. Other Britons fish the seas or build boats in Scottish shipyards.

The United Kingdom has had a major economic problem in recent years. This has been a lack of capital resources to develop more modern factories. The British hope to use their new energy resources to earn money for development.

Culture

Most of the people of the United Kingdom live in **urban** areas. These are areas in and around cities. London is one of the largest cities in the world. Other large British cities are Birmingham, Glasgow (GLASS goh), Liverpool, Manchester, Sheffield, and Leeds. More than 500,000 people live in each.

London is the cultural center of the United Kingdom. Here, there are great universities and museums, theaters, and music and dance groups. Many major business companies have their headquarters offices in London. The government of the United Kingdom conducts much of its business in London. Along the Thames River are the Houses of Parliament. The **Prime Minister,** the head of the government, lives at 10 Downing Street in London. Parts of London are filled with immigrants from all over the world. **Immigrants** are people who come from another country to live.

Most of the people of the United Kingdom have much in common. Most speak the same language, English. The Celtic languages Welsh Gaelic and Scottish Gaelic do, however, survive. Most Britons are Protestant. There are, however, many Roman Catholics, especially in Northern Ireland. British schools provide a good basic education to all.

The British Empire helped spread the English language and British culture all over the world. Many people in Asia, Africa, and the Americas speak English and follow British customs.

Problems

The United Kingdom faces major problems today. The British people must find solutions to these difficulties in order to make their future secure.

There has been much fighting between Protestants and Roman Catholics in Northern Ireland in recent years. Many innocent peo-

London is one of the largest and busiest cities in the world.

ple have died. British troops have tried to restore order. The British government has unsuccessfully sought a settlement acceptable to both sides. No end to this tragic conflict is in sight.

The United Kingdom is also faced with the problem of making its economy work. Britain is a nation that lives by foreign trade. It is true that Britain has some natural resources. But it still must import some petroleum and raw materials. It is also true that British agriculture is very productive. But Britain's population is so large that the nation must buy much of its food from abroad. To pay for petroleum, raw materials, and food, the United Kingdom must make goods and sell them to other nations.

Britain's factories and their machinery are mostly old. The United Kingdom has lacked enough capital resources to build new factories and buy new machinery. Older factories and machines produce fewer goods and cost more to run. This makes British goods more expensive. The United Kingdom also has strong labor unions, or organized groups of workers. So wage costs are higher for British manufacturers. Thus, they have to charge more for their goods. So this, too, makes British goods more expensive.

Because British goods cost more, there has been bad inflation in the United Kingdom. **Inflation** is a drop in the value of money. With inflation, people cannot afford to buy as many goods. Other nations also find British goods too expensive. Thus, fewer goods are sold. So factories have to close. Workers become **unemployed,** or lose their jobs. In recent years, unemployment has become a serious problem in the United Kingdom.

Margaret Thatcher, Britain's Prime Minister.

The United Kingdom has faced great difficulties many times in its long history. It is said that the British people always "muddle through." So perhaps today's problems will also be solved.

REVIEW

WATCH YOUR WORDS

1. ___ occurs when money goes down in value and prices go up.
   Immigration   Inflation
   Industrialization
2. An organized group of workers is a ___.
   parliament   factory   labor union
3. Cities are in ___ areas.
   rural   urban   suburban
4. The head of the British government is the ___.
   Prime Minister   queen
   Parliament
5. People who move from one country to settle in another are ___.
   immigrants   unemployed   tourists

CHECK YOUR FACTS

6. Name the four parts of the United Kingdom.
7. What raw materials are important to Britain's economy?
8. What is the main city of the United Kingdom?
9. Today, Britain rules (all/part) of Ireland.
10. Why is foreign trade so important to the United Kingdom?

THINK ABOUT IT

Does the United States have any problems similar to those of the United Kingdom?

CHAPTER REVIEW

WATCH YOUR WORDS

1. A____is a time a person rules.
   queen   reign   monarch

2. ____ is producing only one part of a finished product.
   Specialization   Industrialization   Revolution

3. Nations that were once British colonies and now share common ties belong to the____.
   League of Nations
   Commonwealth of Nations
   British Empire

4. Another name for cloth is____.
   raw material   machinery   textiles

5. The lawmaking body in Britain is the ____ . The head of the government is the____.
   Prime Minister   commonwealth
   queen   Parliament

6. Buildings with many machines and workers are____.
   factories   cottages   industries

7. An industry needs ____ to produce ____.
   finished goods
   raw materials   imports

8. A person who is jobless is____.
   unemployed   urban   annulled

9. Goods rise in price during a time of____.
   specialization   inflation
   unemployment

10. A ____ is an organized group of workers.
    Parliament   commonwealth
    labor union

CHECK YOUR FACTS

11. What problems did Elizabeth I face when she became queen of England?

12. What great writer lived during Elizabeth's time?

13. How were goods produced during the Middle Ages?

14. List some good results of the industrial revolution in Britain.

15. List some bad effects of the industrial revolution.

16. Why did people say that the sun never sets on the British Empire?

17. What are the United Kingdom's main natural resources?

18. Why has the United Kingdom been unable to build factories that are more modern?

19. Why do many people around the world speak English today?

USE YOUR MAPS AND CHART

20. Look at the time line on page 194. When did the Spanish Armada attack England?

21. Look at the map of the British Empire on page 203. What continent was entirely under British control?

22. Look at the map on page 207. What part of the British Isles is not in the United Kingdom?

THINK ABOUT IT

23. Have you seen or read any of Shakespeare's plays? If so, which ones?

24. How might Elizabeth I's reign have been different if she had married?

25. What might be some disadvantages of manufactured goods over handmade goods?

26. How would your life differ if there had been no industrial revolution?

27. Do you think it is right for one nation to make a colony of another land? Why, or why not?

3 FRANCE

Lesson 1: The World of Louis XIV.

Louis XIV became king of France in 1643. His long reign lasted until 1715. Louis believed that he ruled with the blessing of God. He thought that his ideas came from God. Because of this, Louis XIV was an **absolute monarch.** His power was not limited in any way.

Above all else, Louis tried to make sure everyone understood that he was all-powerful. He sought to weaken the power of the nobles of France. These were people with titles like prince, duke, or count. They owned most of the land. Louis XIV set up special law courts to hear complaints against the nobles. He taxed the nobles heavily. Then they did not have the money to oppose him. He expanded the number of nobles by selling titles to people who could buy them. These new nobles favored the king because he had given them their titles. Therefore, they would not oppose his power.

Louis XIV **centralized** the government of France. That means that he gathered all the government's power in one person and one place—the king and his court. Louis took complete control of the law courts, the army, and the government's money. Louis acted quickly against any person who opposed his decisions.

As king, Louis XIV made France a stronger nation. He chose advisers who helped strengthen the French economy. These advisers improved France's trade with

Louis XIV ruled France from 1643 until 1715.

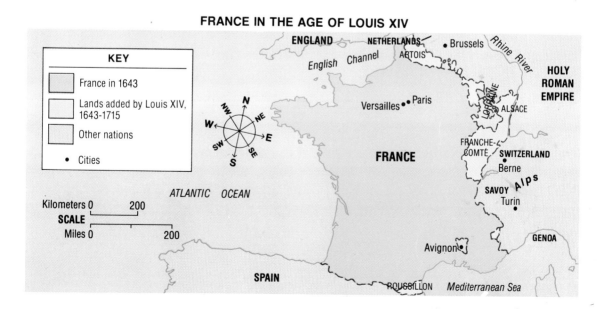

FRANCE IN THE AGE OF LOUIS XIV

KEY

France in 1643

Lands added by Louis XIV, 1643-1715

Other nations

• Cities

Kilometers 0 — 200
SCALE
Miles 0 — 200

ATLANTIC OCEAN

ENGLAND   NETHERLANDS   • Brussels   Rhine River
English Channel   ARTOIS
HOLY ROMAN EMPIRE
Versailles •• Paris
LORRAINE
ALSACE
FRANCHE-COMTÉ   SWITZERLAND
FRANCE   • Berne
Alps
SAVOY
Turin •
Avignon •
GENOA
SPAIN
ROUSSILLON   Mediterranean Sea

other nations. They helped improve French manufacturing. They organized the French East India Company. This group competed for trade with the British and the Dutch around the world.

Louis XIV encouraged the development of the French colonies. He hoped that they would provide raw materials and also markets for French products.

Louis XIV did not just make the French government stronger and more centralized. He also made it better. Once there had been much corruption. Government officials broke the law or took bribes. Louis tried to stop these bad practices.

Did Louis XIV Hurt France?

Not everything that Louis XIV did was good for France.

The beautiful palace that Louis XIV built was called Versailles (vur SY). It was very costly to build and keep up. At Versailles, the nobles surrounded the king to

This is the beautiful palace of Louis XIV. It is called Versailles.

entertain him. The French people as a whole gained nothing from all this. Yet they had to pay for it through their taxes. The palace was not in Paris, the capital city of France. Instead, it was in a village about 16 kilometers (10 miles) away. This meant that the king had little direct contact with the people he ruled.

One of the ways that Louis XIV made France stronger was by building a great army. However, this army was also a great temptation. It led the king to start a long series of wars. Louis XIV wanted to make France the strongest nation in Europe. He tried to do this by expanding France's borders. Of course, the neighboring nations resisted. Louis XIV's wars lasted for almost 50 years. The king never fully met his goal. But he spent a great deal of money trying to reach it. The taxes raised to pay for war were a great burden on the French people. Finally, even the king himself realized that war was not a good way to help his country. As Louis XIV lay dying, he told his heir that peace was better than war.

The Sun King

Louis XIV was often called the Sun King. During his reign, he shone like a star at his court. He led his people forward in many ways. But, in the end, he left the French government with huge debts. The king grew distant from the people. They, themselves, would soon turn away from their kings.

REVIEW

WATCH YOUR WORDS

1. A ruler whose power is not limited is a(n)____.
   king   noble
   absolute monarch

2. Government is ____ when its power is in the hands of one person in one place.
   centralized   democratic
   socialistic

CHECK YOUR FACTS

3. What did Louis XIV do to his nobles to protect his own power?

4. Why did France's strong army cause the nation to become weaker?

THINK ABOUT IT

Do you think Louis XIV was a success or a failure? Give some reasons for your answer.

Lesson 2: The French Revolution

FIND THE WORDS

estates   constitution   Jacobins
Directory   Consulate

The kings who ruled France after Louis XIV did not act wisely. The French people became very unhappy with their lives. At last, they decided to get rid of their kings.

The Revolution Begins

In the 1700s, the people of France were divided into three groups called **estates.** The First Estate included the bishops and priests of the Roman Catholic Church. The Second Estate was made up of the nobles. The Third Estate was all the other people of France. These included merchants, workers, and peasants, the people who farmed the land. Most members of the first two estates lived well. They were generally satisfied with the king's government. Many members of the Third Estate were very poor. Many of them did not like the way things were being run. Some members of the Third Estate decided to do something about it. They were to change France forever.

In 1789, the people of France paid heavy taxes to the govern-ment. They received few services from the government in return. The French people as a whole had little say in their government. They were not able to speak their own minds or do what they pleased. The king could put any-one in prison without a trial.

There was a lawmaking body in France. It was called the Es-tates General. But this group had not met since 1614. The king had ruled alone. But King Louis XVI was in great difficulty. He was forced to call a meeting of the Es-tates General in May 1789.

The Estates General was made up of members from the three es-tates. Each group was supposed to meet separately. However, the members of the Third Estate re-fused to agree to this. The king was forced to let all three groups meet together. This larger group was called the National Assembly. In this group, the numerous mem-bers of the Third Estate had more power.

The majority of the members of the National Assembly wanted real change in France. However, many people felt that the changes were being made too slowly. In July, the people of Paris rebelled against the king. Many people were starving. They believed the king and the nobles were responsible. On July 14, the people stormed the Bastille (bass TEEL), one of the king's prisons. They freed the prisoners inside. This became the symbol of the French Revolution. The people of France today celebrate Bastille Day just as Americans celebrate the Fourth of July.

The violence in Paris stirred the National Assembly to action. They issued the Declaration of the Rights of Man in August 1789. This document made all male citizens equal. It got rid of much of the old system. It took away much of the power of the king and gave it to the people of France. A new **constitution,** or plan of government, was written. According to this constitution, the king and the assembly would work together to govern France.

By 1791, it seemed as though the revolution had ended. The government had changed. Many people were satisfied.

The Revolution Continues

Not all the French people were happy with what had happened. The king tried to weaken the power of the new government. The National Assembly was replaced by the new Legislative (LEJ iss LAY tiv) Assembly in the fall of 1791. This group was weak and divided.

The storming of the Bastille, July 14, 1789.

Some members of the assembly wanted even greater changes in the government of France. These leaders met in clubs and were called **Jacobins** (JAK uh binz). They were led by such men as Jean Paul Marat (mah RAH), Jacques Danton (dahn TOHN), and Maximilien Robespierre (ROHBZ pee AIR). They tried to get people all over France to support their ideas. Many people did so.

Napoleon rose to power in the French army.

But it was the problem of war that finally brought down the new government. The rulers of Austria and Prussia feared that the fall of the king of France would lead to their own overthrow. Therefore, in 1792, they declared war on France. When the French armies had little success, the people revolted again in August 1792.

This time, the king lost all his power. A new National Convention replaced the Legislative Assembly. The Convention established the First French Republic. The Jacobins soon dominated the new government. The king was tried and executed in January 1793.

The Reign of Terror

The French Republic faced difficult problems. Most of the nations of Europe opposed it. The new government had to defend France. It drafted men into the armies.

The government also faced opposition within France. It set up a Committee of Public Safety to maintain control over the country. This committee was led by Maximilien Robespierre.

Robespierre used this group to find and punish enemies of Jacobin ideas all over France. Thousands of people were executed for their beliefs during 1793 and 1794. This was the Reign of Terror.

The End of the Revolution

At last, most of the French people turned against the bloodshed. A new system of government, called the **Directory,** was set up.

In 1795, Napoleon Bonaparte began his rise to power. Napoleon had risen rapidly in the French army. He was made a general at the age of only 26. In 1797, Napoleon led the French armies to victory and brought peace. He was a hero to the French people.

In 1799, Napoleon and his supporters overthrew the Directory. The French Revolution was over. Napoleon Bonaparte set up a government called the **Consulate.** He was First Consul. Napoleon was now a dictator, or a leader with absolute power. A mere 10 years after the revolution had begun, France had exchanged one ruler for another. Nonetheless, Napoleon kept many of the changes made during the revolution.

STRANGE FACTS

"Off with their heads!" That was a common cry during the French Revolution. The Reign of Terror saw the beheading of many people. King Louis XVI and Queen Marie Antoinette were killed by the guillotine.

The guillotine is a machine for cutting off heads. It has two posts joined by a beam. Suspended at the top is a heavy steel knife with a slanted edge. The executioner pulls the cord. The knife then drops down and cuts off the head.

Joseph Guillotin, a doctor and a member of the French National Assembly, suggested the guillotine. Dr. Antoine Louis actually invented the new execution machine. The guillotine is still used in France today.

REVIEW

WATCH YOUR WORDS

1. After the French Revolution began, ____ met in clubs to discuss greater changes in government.
   nobles   Jacobins   directors

2. The ____ was the government set up by Napoleon Bonaparte.
   Directory   Consulate
   National Assembly

3. The French people were divided into three groups called____.
   departments   classes   estates

4. From 1795 to 1799, the ____ ruled France.
   Consulate   Legislative Assembly
   Directory

5. A ____ is a ruler with absolute power.
   dictator   Jacobin   director

CHECK YOUR FACTS

6. Why were many of the French people unhappy with the rule of King Louis XVI?

7. What event marked the beginning of the French Revolution?

8 After the French Revolution began, what two important documents did the National Assembly approve?

9. What was the Reign of Terror?

10. Which came first, the Consulate or the Directory?

THINK ABOUT IT

Many times in history, nations have looked to generals to lead their governments. Examples are Napoleon in France, Wellington in Britain, and a number of American Presidents, including Washington, Grant, and Eisenhower. What reasons can you think of for this?

Lesson 3: Napoleon's Empire

As First Consul, Napoleon Bonaparte had a great deal of power. But he was not satisfied. In 1804, he took the title Emperor Napoleon I. Most of the French people accepted this change. Napoleon had brought them victory and a stable government. Most of the French were grateful.

Napoleon Builds an Empire

An emperor needed an empire to rule. Napoleon had made the French army very strong. He had defeated some of the major nations of Europe. He planned to take territory from the other European nations through war. Just before he became emperor, war broke out between France and Britain.

Napoleon knew that the British had a very strong navy. He could not invade Britain from France until the British navy had been destroyed. But the British defeated and destroyed the French fleet at the Battle of Trafalgar in 1805.

Napoleon had to find another way to attack Britain. He knew that Britain's prosperity and power depended on trade with Europe. If he could conquer Europe and stop this trade, he could weaken Britain indirectly.

One by one, the nations of Europe fell to Napoleon's armies. Within a few years, Napoleon controlled most of Europe.

Look at the map on page 221. You can see that only one important nation on the mainland of Europe was not controlled by Napoleon. This was Russia. Soon, Napoleon would try to conquer Russia, too.

In 1812, Napoleon finally invaded Russia. As the French army advanced, the Russian army retreated. But as the Russians drew back, they burned their villages and fields. This left the French army without food for themselves or their animals. In addition, the French were not prepared for the terrible weather of the Russian winter.

The Russians were defeated in a great battle near Moscow. They had to retreat, and the city was burned. Napoleon entered Moscow, but the Russians refused to make peace. Finally, Napoleon was forced to withdraw. The French army suffered terrible losses in the march back home.

Napoleon left his troops and raised a new army in France. He hoped to continue building the French Empire.

WHERE WE ARE IN TIME AND PLACE

AGE OF THE FRENCH REVOLUTION

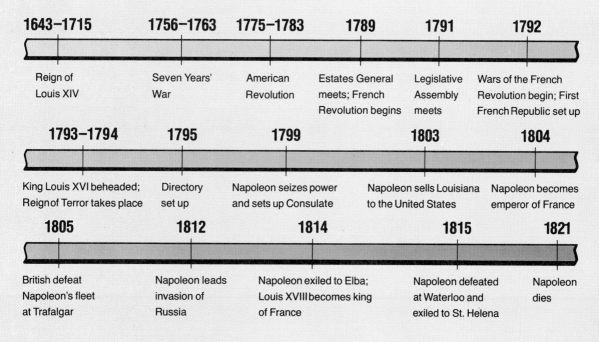

1643–1715
Reign of Louis XIV

1756–1763
Seven Years' War

1775–1783
American Revolution

1789
Estates General meets; French Revolution begins

1791
Legislative Assembly meets

1792
Wars of the French Revolution begin; First French Republic set up

1793–1794
King Louis XVI beheaded; Reign of Terror takes place

1795
Directory set up

1799
Napoleon seizes power and sets up Consulate

1803
Napoleon sells Louisiana to the United States

1804
Napoleon becomes emperor of France

1805
British defeat Napoleon's fleet at Trafalgar

1812
Napoleon leads invasion of Russia

1814
Napoleon exiled to Elba; Louis XVIII becomes king of France

1815
Napoleon defeated at Waterloo and exiled to St. Helena

1821
Napoleon dies

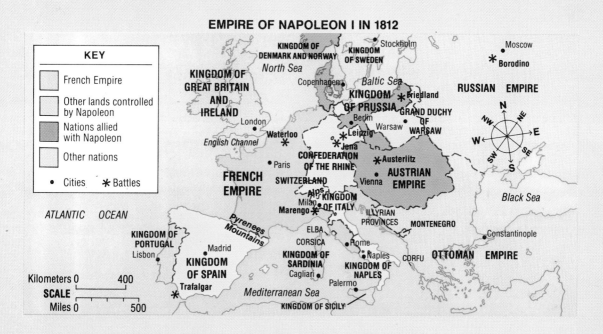

EMPIRE OF NAPOLEON I IN 1812

KEY

- French Empire
- Other lands controlled by Napoleon
- Nations allied with Napoleon
- Other nations
- • Cities   ✳ Battles

The Fall of Napoleon

The nations that had been defeated by Napoleon were encouraged by the failure of his efforts in Russia. Britain, Austria, Prussia, Sweden, and Spain united with Russia in 1813 to fight against Napoleon. The French forces were defeated in October 1813 in a battle at Leipzig (LYP sig) in Germany. Other nations deserted Napoleon. Napoleon realized he could not win, so he gave up his throne. Napoleon was sent to live on the island of Elba off the coast of Italy. He was never supposed to return to France.

But less than a year later, Napoleon escaped from Elba. Many of the people of France rose to join his army. The forces of the other nations of Europe were led by a British general, the Duke of Wellington. Near the town of Waterloo in Belgium, Napoleon met his final defeat. This time he was sent to St. Helena, an island off the coast of southern Africa. He died there in 1821.

The Results of Napoleon's Conquests

Napoleon's empire came to a quick end, but its results were lasting. Napoleon's conquests spread the influence of the French Revolution throughout Europe.

The system of laws Napoleon set up in France has lasted. In addition, many changes Napoleon made in government and education survived.

After Napoleon's defeat, Louis XVI's brother, Louis XVIII, became king of France. Other European rulers whom Napoleon had replaced were restored. But Europe was never really the same again after the French Revolution and Napoleon's empire.

REVIEW

CHECK YOUR FACTS

Look at the Map

1. Look at the map on page 221. What European nations did Napoleon control?

2. Locate Leipzig, Germany; Waterloo, Belgium; Moscow, Russia; and Elba.

Look at the Lesson

3. What was Napoleon's plan to defeat Britain?

4. Why did Napoleon's attempt to defeat Russia fail?

5. To what two places was Napoleon sent after his defeats?

THINK ABOUT IT

What do you think it means to "meet one's Waterloo"?

Lesson 4: France Today

FIND THE WORDS

bauxite   uranium

What is France like today? The answer to this question might depend on what part of France you visited. Look at the map of Europe on page 190. Find Paris, the capital city of France. If you were to go there, you would see a modern city. It is filled with cars and has

Paris has some of the most beautiful streets in the world.

a modern subway system. Paris also has some tall buildings. But some parts of Paris are much as they were hundreds of years ago.

Normandy is an area of northwestern France. In the little towns of Normandy, life is lived much as it has been for centuries. You can see many farm machines in rural France. Yet you can also see people using hand tools to cut and stack hay. Work is done in the fields with horses as well as with tractors. France today is a land of contrasts.

Resources

France has good natural resources. There is much fertile land and many forests. The nearness to the ocean encourages fishing and trade. France's mild climate favors the growth of crops.

France also has important mineral resources. There is iron ore, coal, and potash. **Bauxite** (BAWK syt) ore is mined for making aluminum. **Uranium** (yoo RAY nee um) has become an important mineral resource. This heavy metal is used as fuel in nuclear power plants. Some natural gas and petroleum are found in France. However, most of the nation's energy needs must be filled by imported petroleum. Nonetheless, France has the resources needed for industry.

The French people are good workers on farms and in factories. Farmers produce crops ranging from grapes to wheat. Farm production has been increasing, and much food is exported. French factories supply goods to many parts of the world. They make a wide variety of things, which include cars, fine perfumes, and fashionable clothing.

The French have had the capital resources to develop their industries well. The government has promoted industrial growth. In addition, France had help from the United States in overcoming the damage suffered during World War II.

Look at the maps on pages 183 and 185. Find all the different resources that France has to offer. Look for products that you have seen in your own part of the United States.

Government

Today, France has a system of government known as the Fifth Republic. All French adults have the right to vote. They choose a president. They also vote for members of the National Assembly, the lawmaking group. The officials of local governments are also elected. The government of France is more centralized than the government of the United States. That means that the central government in Paris has more power than our federal government in Washington.

In France, nuclear power plants provide a cheap source of electricity.

France's Future

France today is a nation with good resources for the future. It has recovered from the effects of two great wars in this century. It produces food and other goods for export. In 1981, the French people elected a new president and National Assembly. France's future depends in part on the policies of its new government.

REVIEW

CHECK YOUR FACTS

1. What are France's important mineral resources?

2. Name three things France exports.

3. What nation helped France after World War II?

4. The French government is (more/less) centralized than that of the United States.

THINK ABOUT IT

Some people believe that the government should own and run large companies that people depend on. These include water, electric, transportation, and oil companies. Do you think this is a good or bad idea? Give your reasons for your answer.

CHAPTER REVIEW

WATCH YOUR WORDS

1. A plan of government is a____.
   revolution constitution declaration
2. Napoleon Bonaparte had the power of a____.
   noble dictator director
3. ____ is used as fuel in nuclear power plants.
   Natural gas Uranium Petroleum
4. In the 1700s, the people of France were divided into____.
   estates castes society
5. Aluminum is obtained from____ore.
   uranium petroleum bauxite
6. To gather power in one person and one place is to____it.
   centralize display defy
7. A(n) ____ is a king or queen with unlimited power.
   director consul absolute monarch
8. The government that ruled France briefly before Napoleon was the____.
   Consulate Assembly Directory
9. Jean Paul Marat, Jacques Danton, and Maximilien Robespierre were ____.
   Jacobins directors Socialists
10. The ____ was set up by Napoleon to replace the Directory.
    empire Consulate Fifth Republic

CHECK YOUR FACTS

11. How did Louis XIV try to make France a stronger nation?

12. Why did Louis XIV encourage the development of the French colonies?
13. Why did the wars of Louis XIV not help France?
14. Who belonged to each of the three estates in France?
15. How did the Estates General and National Assembly differ?
16. What difficulties did the French Republic face in its first years?
17. Why did Napoleon's defeat in Russia lead to his downfall?
18. What were some of the results of Napoleon's rule?
19. What products does France export?
20. Describe the French government under the Fifth Republic.

USE YOUR MAPS AND CHARTS

21. Look at the map of Europe on page 221. What important nation of Western Europe did Napoleon not control? What reason can you think of for this?
22. Look at the time line on page 221. Which came first, the Consulate or Napoleon's empire?

THINK ABOUT IT

23. In what ways were the rules of Louis XIV and Napoleon similar?
24. How do you think France has benefited from its geographic location?

EUROPE ABOUT 1000 A.D.

KEY

- ■ Holy Roman Empire
- □ Byzantine Empire
- □ Other European Nations
- ▨ Muslim and Other Lands
- • Towns

CHAPTER 4 GERMANY

Lesson 1: The Holy Roman Empire

FIND THE WORD

electors

Britain and France have been strong nations in Europe for a long time. However, Germany became a unified nation only a little more than a century ago. For a long time, Germany was a disorganized collection of small states. These states were ruled by kings, dukes, and other nobles. Some were even ruled by archbishops.

At that time, most of Germany was known as the Holy Roman Empire.

This "nation" had little to do with the Roman Empire of ancient times. It is true that the old Roman Empire inspired the Holy Roman Empire. However, the two existed at different times. They covered somewhat different areas. They had different forms of government. They generally spoke different languages. They included somewhat different peoples.

What Was the Holy Roman Empire?

For a long time, much of Europe was tied together by one church and one empire. The church was the Roman Catholic Church, headed by the pope. The empire was the Holy Roman Empire. The empire was founded in the 900s. At that time, Otto, a German leader, also gained power in Italy. The pope crowned Otto the first Holy Roman emperor.

Look at the map of the Holy Roman Empire on page 227. Compare it with the map of the Roman Empire on page 113.

The Holy Roman emperors tried to rule both Germany and Italy. This was a difficult task. As a result, they gradually lost power in both areas. Eventually, the emperors ruled in name only.

In the 1300s, a group of powerful German nobles and archbishops gained the right to elect the Holy Roman emperor. These rulers were called **electors.** From the 1400s, the emperors were from the Hapsburg family. The Hapsburgs ruled Austria. They also came to control Hungary, Slavic lands east of Germany, the Low Countries, Burgundy, southern Italy, and Spain and its colonies. These areas were outside the Holy Roman Empire. Thus, the Hapsburg emperors tended to neglect the empire.

The Protestant Reformation began in Germany in the 1500s. The emperors remained Roman Catholic. So the growth of Protestantism weakened their power. In the 1600s, the emperors had a constant struggle with France. The growing power of Prussia, a kingdom in northern Germany, threatened the emperors in the 1700s.

Napoleon brought the Holy Roman Empire to an end in 1806. The Hapsburgs became emperors of Austria. After that, Austria developed separately from Germany. Napoleon united the 300 or so small German states into larger ones. But still Germany was not a united nation.

Prussia gained power over Germany in the 1800s. Finally, in 1871, Prussia led Germany to victory over France in the Franco-Prussian War. The king of Prussia was crowned emperor of Germany.

TIME LINE: HISTORY OF GERMANY

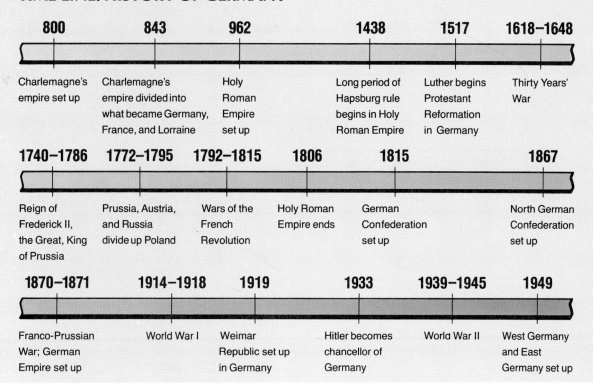

800 — Charlemagne's empire set up

843 — Charlemagne's empire divided into what became Germany, France, and Lorraine

962 — Holy Roman Empire set up

1438 — Long period of Hapsburg rule begins in Holy Roman Empire

1517 — Luther begins Protestant Reformation in Germany

1618–1648 — Thirty Years' War

1740–1786 — Reign of Frederick II, the Great, King of Prussia

1772–1795 — Prussia, Austria, and Russia divide up Poland

1792–1815 — Wars of the French Revolution

1806 — Holy Roman Empire ends

1815 — German Confederation set up

1867 — North German Confederation set up

1870–1871 — Franco-Prussian War; German Empire set up

1914–1918 — World War I

1919 — Weimar Republic set up in Germany

1933 — Hitler becomes chancellor of Germany

1939–1945 — World War II

1949 — West Germany and East Germany set up

Germany was at last united. It could now develop a strong economy and a powerful army and navy. It could now compete with Britain and France for trade and colonies.

REVIEW

CHECK YOUR FACTS

1. In what ways did the old Roman Empire and the Holy Roman Empire differ?
2. Who started the Holy Roman Empire? When?
3. What two areas did the Holy Roman emperors try to rule? How did this affect their power?
4. What group gained the power to choose the Holy Roman emperor?
5. Why did the Hapsburgs neglect the Holy Roman Empire?
6. What effect did Napoleon have on the Holy Roman Empire?
7. When did Germany unite?

THINK ABOUT IT

It has been said that the Holy Roman Empire was not holy, not Roman, and not an empire. Do you think this saying is right? Why, or why not?

Lesson 2: Germany in Two World Wars

<table>
<tr><td colspan="4" align="center">FIND THE WORDS</td></tr>
<tr><td>alliance</td><td>ally</td><td>front</td><td>trench</td></tr>
<tr><td colspan="4" align="center">armistice</td></tr>
</table>

The central theme of European history in this century has been war. Two wars that involved nations all over the world began, and were largely fought, in Europe. Germany played a central role in both these wars. In both, Germany ended up on the losing side. How did Germany get into these wars, and why did it lose?

World War I

Look at the map on page 230. Compare it with the map on page 235. You can see that Europe looked quite different before World War I than it did after World War II. The major nations of Europe before World War I were Great Britain, France, Germany, Italy, Austria-Hungary, and

EUROPE BEFORE WORLD WAR I

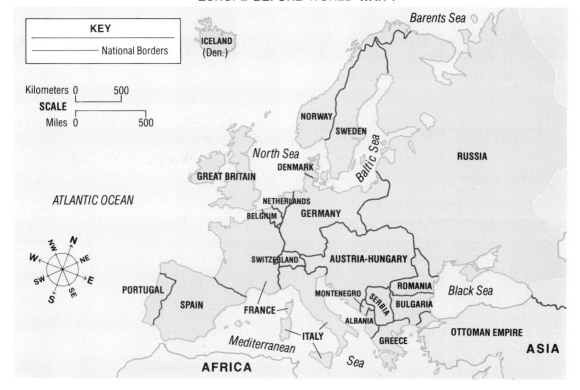

Russia. Britain and France had been strong and united nations for centuries. Britain had a strong navy, and France had a strong army. Each had huge colonial empires stretching around the world.

Both Italy and Germany had become united nations only in the second half of the 1800s. Germany, however, had been particularly successful. By 1900, it had become the major industrial nation of Europe. Germany was also building both a strong army and navy. The Germans had acquired a few colonies and were expanding their trade.

Austria-Hungary and Russia were large, weak empires. They struggled for power in Eastern Europe. Austria-Hungary included many different ethnic groups. This made it divided and weak. Russia was large but had little industry. The large, weak Ottoman Empire ruled the lands around the eastern Mediterranean.

The great European nations competed for land in Europe. They also competed for colonies and trade around the world. These struggles led to World War I. Many of the European nations tried to protect themselves by making **alliances** (uh LY un sez), or friendship agreements, with other nations. The members of each alliance were called **allies** (AL eyes). Allies agreed to help one another

in war. Before World War I, Germany, Austria-Hungary, and Italy had formed the Triple Alliance. Great Britain, France, and Russia had joined in the Triple Entente (ahn TAHNT). In French, the word *entente* means "an understanding or agreement."

The problem with the alliances was that a conflict between two nations could drag all the nations into war. That is how World War I started.

It was the murder of Archduke Francis Ferdinand that brought on the war. The archduke was the heir to the throne of Austria-Hungary. He and his wife were killed in 1914. The Austro-Hungarians blamed the Serbs. Serbia was an ally of Russia. Austria-Hungary declared war on Serbia. Russia came to the defense of Serbia. Germany supported Austria-Hungary, its ally. Britain and France backed Russia. So all the great nations of Europe were at war.

During World War I, Austria-Hungary and Germany were known as the Central Powers. They were joined by the Ottoman Empire. Russia, Britain, and France were called the Allied Powers. Italy changed sides and joined the Allied Powers. Later, the United States, too, fought on the side of the Allied Powers. Since many European nations had colonies, the war spread around the

Right: Archduke Francis Ferdinand and his wife Sophie Chotek pose with their children. It was the murder of the archduke and his wife that led to World War I.
Above: American soldiers helped turn the tide of the war against the Central Powers. Here Black Americans fight bravely in the trenches.

globe. Other nations joined in. That is why this conflict is called World War I. Of course, until World War II began, people just called it the World War or the Great War.

The war was fought in many different areas, called **fronts.** The Germans expected to win quickly on the western front. However, the French stopped them with the help of the British. The war on the western front came to be fought in **trenches.** These were deep ditches that had been dug by the troops to protect themselves.

On the eastern front, the Germans and the Austro-Hungarians fought the Russians. Both sides lost many men and neither could really win. However, the war led to the fall of the Russian government. The Russian emperor was soon replaced by a Communist government. This new government made a separate peace with Germany in 1917.

Now the Germans could use all their troops on the western front against the French and British. By this time, however, the United States had entered the war. American troops helped defeat the Germans. An **armistice** (AHR muh stis), or agreement to stop fighting, was signed on November 11, 1918.

Results of World War I

The Treaty of Versailles ended the war. It was a harsh peace. The treaty was designed to prevent Germany from ever going to war again. It limited the German army and navy and forbade the Germans from having an air force. It took away much German territory in Europe and all of the German colonies. It forced Germany to pay money to the nations that had won for the damage they had suffered in the war. The map on page 233 shows what Europe looked like between the world wars.

Between the Wars

Germany was in a difficult position after World War I. It could not afford to pay all the money the winning nations demanded. It lacked the capital resources to rebuild its economy. German money came to be worth very little.

The German people were discouraged. They were looking for a new solution to their problems. The government set up in Germany after the war did not help much. The Great Depression that spread around the world after 1929 made matters worse.

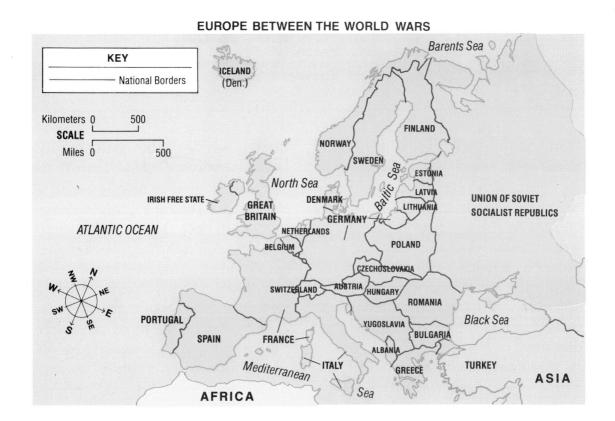

EUROPE BETWEEN THE WORLD WARS

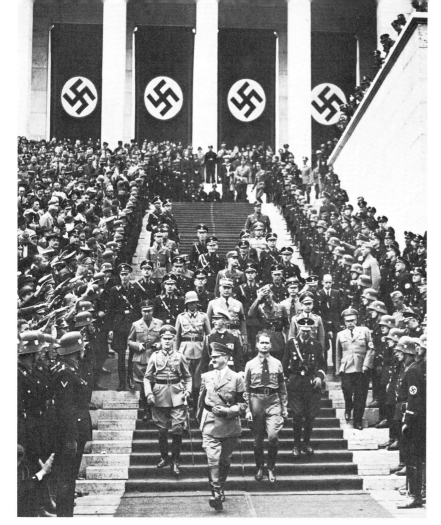

Hitler at a Nazi Party rally in Nuremberg in 1936.

A new leader arose in Germany. His name was Adolf Hitler. He was the head of the National Socialist Party, or Nazis. Hitler told the people that he would make Germany strong and prosperous once again. The Nazis used ruthless tactics against their opponents. Finally, Hitler came to power in 1933. He soon became a dictator.

Germany began to rebuild its army, navy, and air force. The Treaty of Versailles was ignored.

Hitler and the Nazis said that the Jews were responsible for all the bad things that had happened to Germany. In fact, the German Jews had been loyal to Germany. Many had fought bravely for Germany and Austria-Hungary in World War I. The Nazis began to persecute and round up the Jews. They put many of them in concentration camps. Eventually, the Nazis killed more than 6 million Jewish men, women, and children from all over Europe.

Hitler decided to seize most parts of Europe where German-speaking peoples lived. The other nations in Europe did little to stop Germany.

World War II

Germany invaded Poland in 1939. This brought Britain and France into the war. During the first part of the war, the Germans took over most of Western Europe. No nation seemed strong enough to resist them. By late 1940, Britain stood alone against Germany. In 1941, Hitler's forces invaded the Soviet Union as well.

During World War II, Germany, Italy, and Japan fought together in an alliance called the Axis. Britain, France, and the Soviet Union were called the Allies. Other nations joined both sides. The war spread around the world.

In 1941, the United States entered the war after Japanese forces attacked Pearl Harbor in Hawaii. After a long struggle, Allied troops defeated the Germans and Italians in North Africa. Then they moved slowly up the peninsula of Italy. In 1944, a huge Allied force invaded France and pushed toward Germany.

Meanwhile, Soviet forces were driving the Germans back in the

EUROPE AFTER WORLD WAR II

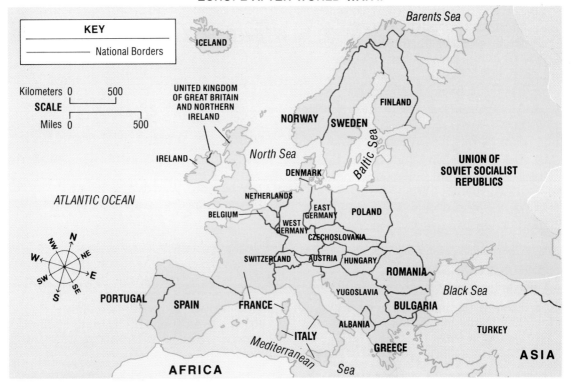

east. In addition, the Americans and British were having increasing success against the Japanese in the Pacific. Soviet troops closed in on Berlin, the German capital, in 1945. Hitler committed suicide. Germany surrendered to the Allies. American atomic bombs soon led Japan to surrender as well.

Results of World War II

Unlike after World War I, Germany was not treated badly after World War II. The Soviets did seize and carry away much machinery from their part of Germany. However, the Americans, British, and French helped the western part of Germany recover from the war. The United States gave large amounts of money to help the Germans rebuild. Today, both parts of Germany are prosperous. The map on page 235 shows what Europe has looked like since World War II.

REVIEW

WATCH YOUR WORDS

1. An agreement among friendly nations to help each other in time of war is a(n)____.
   compromise alliance armistice

2. Many soldiers during World War I tried to protect themselves in ditches called____.
   fronts tunnels trenches

3. An agreement for a temporary peace is an____.
   ally armistice allegiance

4. The place where fighting is taking place in a war is the____.
   zone district front

5. Nations that agree to help each other in time of war are____.
   competitors allies ententes

CHECK YOUR FACTS
Look at the Map

6. Look at the maps on pages 230 and 233. Name two nations that formed part of a larger nation after World War I.

7. Look at the maps on pages 233 and 235. Name four nations that greatly changed their size or shape after World War II.

Look at the Lesson

8. How did the system of alliances bring most of Europe into World War I?

9. List some terms of the Treaty of Versailles.

10. How did World War II begin?

11. When and why did the United States enter World War II?

12. When did World War II end?

THINK ABOUT IT

The Soviet Union was an ally of the United States in World War II. Germany was an enemy. How do the relations between the United States and those two nations differ today? What reasons can you think of for the change?

Lesson 3: Germany Today

FIND THE WORD

zone

Germany today is a divided nation. There are two Germanies, the German Federal Republic, or West Germany, and the German Democratic Republic, or East Germany. Austria is also a separate nation again. Germany is divided as a result of World War II.

At the end of World War II, the Allies divided Germany into four parts, called **zones.** Each was occupied by the army of one of the winning nations. The French, British, Americans, and Soviets each had their own part of Germany. Berlin, the capital of Germany, was also divided among these four nations. However, Berlin was surrounded by the Soviet zone.

After World War II, the Soviet Union did not get along with the rest of the Allies. Soon, a cold war arose between them. The parts of Germany controlled by the Americans, British, and French united to form West Germany. The Russian zone became East Germany. In 1948, the Soviets tried to cut off

East Berlin is the capital of the German Democratic Republic.

West Germany has large areas of productive farmland.

the other nations from Berlin. They stopped traffic on the railroads and highways. The three Allies then sent supplies into West Berlin by air. This was called the Berlin airlift. Later, the Soviets and East Germans built a wall around West Berlin. This wall keeps people in East Germany from fleeing to the West. Today, the two parts of Germany are still separate nations. The relations between these two nations are closer than they have been in the past. Still, it does not seem likely that West Germany and East Germany will be reunited any time soon.

West Germany

The German Federal Republic is one of the richest nations in Europe today. It has made a wonderful recovery since World War II.

West German industries have been rebuilt, in part with American help. West Germany's farms are productive. Its people work hard in factories and offices. Most West Germans live very well.

Look at the map on page 185. You can see that West Germany has most of the mineral resources of Germany. However, it does not have as much farmland as it needs. So West Germany must import some food for its people.

The West Germans are a united people. They speak the same language. They have the same customs. Only religion divides the nation. Most northern Germans are Protestants. Most southern Germans are Roman Catholics. All Germans are proud of how well they have developed their economy since World War II.

For many years, Germany has produced good scientists. Many German industries use this scientific knowledge. German scientists also came to the United States after the war. The early efforts of the United States in space were aided by German scientists.

West Germans are uncertain about their future. They would like to see the two parts of Germany united once again. They do not want a Communist government. They also do not want another war. They want to continue to live well and in peace.

STRANGE FACTS

For years after World War II, people had been "voting with their feet." They had merely walked or ridden across the border from East Berlin to West Berlin. Most had then gone on to West Germany.

The Soviets, who dominated East Germany, were unhappy. The flow of refugees made them look bad. The East German officials were also unhappy. They were losing many valuable people to West Germany.

In 1961, the Soviet government began to threaten West Berlin. Even more East Germans fled across the border. Finally, in August the East Germans started to build a wall around West Berlin.

Since then, the wall has been constantly strengthened. The flow of refugees has slowed to a trickle. But still a few brave people make it across the barrier to freedom.

East Germany

The German Democratic Republic is very different from West Germany. Its people are not quite as well off. East Germany has a great deal of farmland. Huge farms raise crops to feed the East German people and for export. East Germany's factories manufacture goods that are sold in Eastern Europe and elsewhere.

East Germany has not re- covered as completely from the ef- fects of World War II as West Germany has. The government of East Germany is Communist. The Soviet Union has given much aid to East Germany and is very powerful there.

East Germany has become one of the great sports nations of the world. East German athletes work hard to train for world events. Many win medals at the Olympic (oh LIM pik) Games and in other competitions. In this way, the

Athletes like Volker Beck have won medals for East Germany at the Olympic Games.

small nation of East Germany has won attention in the world.

Many East Germans would like to be reunited with their relatives who live in West Germany. Today, people can sometimes make visits across the border. Trade is increasing between the two nations. Yet reunion does not seem possible soon.

REVIEW

CHECK YOUR FACTS

1. Why is Germany divided into East Germany and West Germany?
2. Which of the Germanies has more farmland?
3. Which of the Germanies has more mineral resources?
4. How has East Germany claimed worldwide attention?

THINK ABOUT IT

In what ways could East Germany and West Germany cooperate without actually becoming one nation?

CHAPTER REVIEW

WATCH YOUR WORDS

1. Two or more nations that agree to support one another in time of war are ___.

   allies   electors   comrades

2. An agreement to stop fighting is called a(n) ___.

   alliance   compact   armistice

3. A ___ was part of Germany held by each of the Allies.

   trench   zone   front

4. Battles in a war are fought at the ___.

   front   border   zone

5. The nobles and archbishops who chose the Holy Roman emperor were called ___.

   allies   alliances   electors

CHECK YOUR FACTS

6. What church and what empire long united Europe?

7. How did Napoleon's conquest affect the unity of Germany?

8. What role did Prussia play in the final unification of Germany?

9. Over what did the European nations compete before World War I?

10. Which nations were the Central Powers? The Allied Powers?

11. How did the German people suffer after World War I?

12. Who became the leader of Germany during the 1930s?

13. Name three nations invaded by Germany during World War II.

14. Why is Germany divided into two nations today?

15. List three major differences between East Germany and West Germany.

USE YOUR MAPS AND CHART

16. Look at the time line on page 229. Which came first, the Franco-Prussian War or World War I?

17. Look at the map of the Holy Roman Empire on page 227. Name the large nations on which the Holy Roman Empire bordered.

18. Look at the maps of Europe on pages 230, 233, and 235. Describe the changes in the size and location of Germany over the years.

THINK ABOUT IT

19. Many people have claimed that the Treaty of Versailles caused World War II. Do you think this is true? Why, or why not?

20. Why do you think Germany has been involved in so many wars?

CHAPTER 5

THE SOVIET UNION

Lesson 1: The Rise of Russia

FIND THE WORDS

czar   boyar   famine

Today, the Union of Soviet Socialist Republics is a huge, powerful, important country. It is also called the Soviet Union. It is the largest nation in the world. It stretches from Eastern Europe across the length of northern Asia.

It extends south from the Arctic Sea to central Asia. But the Soviet Union grew from a group of small, weak, divided, and largely unimportant city-states at the eastern edge of Europe.

In 1237–1240, the Golden Horde invaded and conquered Russia. The Golden Horde was a group of Asian peoples. They demanded taxes from the Russians

WHERE WE ARE IN TIME AND PLACE

HISTORY OF RUSSIA

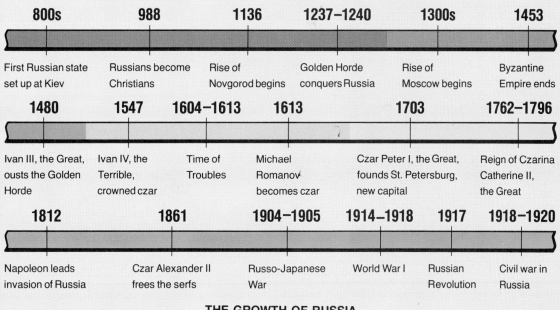

800s	988	1136	1237–1240	1300s	1453
First Russian state set up at Kiev	Russians become Christians	Rise of Novgorod begins	Golden Horde conquers Russia	Rise of Moscow begins	Byzantine Empire ends

1480	1547	1604–1613	1613	1703	1762–1796
Ivan III, the Great, ousts the Golden Horde	Ivan IV, the Terrible, crowned czar	Time of Troubles	Michael Romanov becomes czar	Czar Peter I, the Great, founds St. Petersburg, new capital	Reign of Czarina Catherine II, the Great

1812	1861	1904–1905	1914–1918	1917	1918–1920
Napoleon leads invasion of Russia	Czar Alexander II frees the serfs	Russo-Japanese War	World War I	Russian Revolution	Civil war in Russia

THE GROWTH OF RUSSIA

KEY
- Principality of Moscow in 1300
- Lands added to Moscow by 1462
- Lands added to Russia by 1533
- Lands added by 1689
- Lands added by 1801
- Lands added by 1914
- —— Present boundary of the Soviet Union
- - - - National Borders
- • Cities

Ivan the Terrible returns to Moscow.

each year. Otherwise, they left the Russians pretty much alone. During the 1300s, Moscow, in the north of Russia, became the most important city-state.

In 1462, Ivan III became grand prince of Moscow. First, he brought all the other city-states of

Russia under his rule. From this position of strength, he refused to pay any more taxes to the Golden Horde. Then, he forced them out entirely.

Ivan III was the first Russian ruler to be called **czar** (ZAHR). This is the Russian version of *caesar*. *Caesar* was a title used by rulers of the Roman Empire. Ivan was trying to make Russia the heir to the traditions of the Roman Empire.

The Eastern Roman Empire had lasted until 1453. It was also called the Byzantine (BIZ un TEEN) Empire. It had long had an important influence on Russia. Russia had adopted the Eastern Orthodox version of Christianity in 988. The Byzantines introduced monasteries into Russia. Monasteries played an important role in the Russian church and in Russian culture. Russian architecture, art, law, and government were also affected greatly by the Eastern Romans. The Russian alphabet is based on the Greek alphabet, used by the Greek-speaking Byzantines.

Ivan III dominated the Russian church and the **boyars** (boh YAHRZ), or nobles. During his time, the peasants began to be reduced to being serfs. A serf was a farm worker who had to work on land owned by a lord. Serfs were almost like slaves. Ivan III was the first real ruler of Russia. Because of his achievements, he is called "Ivan the Great."

In 1533, Ivan III's grandson, Ivan IV, became ruler of Russia. In 1547, he became the first Russian ruler to actually be crowned czar. Ivan IV was not to be called "the Great," but "the Terrible." Ivan IV may have been insane. He had many people, especially boyars, killed in a reign of terror. Ivan seized much land for himself. The peasants suffered greatly under his rule. More and more they became serfs.

In the early 1600s, a period called the Time of Troubles began in Russia. It lasted until 1613. There was a great **famine** (FAM in), or shortage of food, in 1601–1603. Then there was a struggle for the throne. Civil war broke out. Finally, in 1613, Michael Romanov (roh MAH nuf) was elected czar.

The Time of Troubles was at an end. The Romanov dynasty was to last until 1917.

The Romanov czars became absolute monarchs. That meant the czar had all the power. Democratic government did not develop in Russia as it did in Western Europe. Poor people in the cities and serfs on the farms resisted the power of the czars. However, the czars forced even more peasants to become serfs. They extended and strengthened the serf system. The czars and the boyars lived well. But the peasants had a hard life. The czars brought the Russian church under even greater control. Russia also continued to expand. This expansion brought Russia into closer contact with Western Europe. Russia began to be more strongly affected by Western European culture.

REVIEW

WATCH YOUR WORDS

1. The____were Russian nobles.
   serfs   boyars   hordes
2. A shortage of food is a(n)____.
   famine   drought   epidemic
3. A____was a Russian ruler.
   serf   boyar   czar
4. Farm workers who were tied to the land were____.
   serfs   nobles   peasants

CHECK YOUR FACTS

5. What was the Golden Horde?
6. What nation did Ivan III try to copy?
7. What dynasty ruled Russia after the Time of Troubles?

TRY SOMETHING NEW

Using an encyclopedia or dictionary, make a chart that shows the Roman, Russian, and Greek alphabets.

Lesson 2: Peter the Great

Peter I, known as Peter the Great, was one of Russia's most important czars. He ruled from 1682 to 1725. During his reign, Russia began to look west toward Europe rather than east toward Asia, as it had done in the past.

Czar Peter was a huge man, standing over 6 feet, 8 inches (203 centimeters) tall. He was a man who could become very angry without warning. When Peter was young, he studied with merchants who had come to Moscow from other nations of Europe. He began to want Russia to be more like the rest of Europe. Peter believed in learning by doing. As a result, he often tried to learn about new ways of working by doing them himself.

Peter the Great ruled Russia from 1682 to 1725.

Peter's Vision of Russia

Peter the Great was inspired by his view of what Russia could be in the future. He thought that Russia could become a strong nation by copying the other nations of Europe. He wanted to use European ways of doing things to make Russia a modern nation. Peter wanted Russia to become more European, or Western, and less Asian, or Eastern. He wanted Russia to have "windows on the West." These were ports that could be used for trading with the rest of Europe. Peter also hoped these cities would be entry points for bringing Western European ideas into his country.

What Did Peter the Great Do?

Peter the Great did many things for his country. In order to find out more about Western ideas, he made a long visit to Europe. In 1697–1698, Peter and his companions traveled through the European nations.

Peter the Great tried to get the Russians to become more European in many ways. He ordered them to wear Western clothes. He demanded that the men trim their beards like Western Europeans. He brought many Western Europeans to Russia to teach his people their ways. He sent many Russians to Western Europe to study. In order to encourage science, Peter set up the Russian Academy of Sciences. Most of his ideas, however, affected only the nobility.

Peter the Great made changes in the Russian military as well. He organized the army more efficiently and created a navy. Then he declared war on Sweden. Russia got land along the Baltic Sea from Sweden. This gave the Russians harbors that had easy access to Europe and that did not freeze over in winter. The czar now had his "windows on the West."

Peter the Great moved the capital of Russia from Moscow to a new city on the Baltic Sea. He did this to encourage his people to look more towards Europe. The new capital was called St. Petersburg (now Leningrad). There the czar built great palaces like those he had seen in Western Europe.

Peter the Great tried to bring new industries to his country. He wanted the people to manufacture goods as well as to raise crops and animals on their farms. Some new factories were begun during his rule.

It seemed to Peter the Great that the Russian Orthodox Church threatened his new ideas. As a result, he brought the church more under the control of the czar.

Peter the Great did manage to make his country more European during his reign. Russia also expanded in size during his rule.

REVIEW

CHECK YOUR FACTS

1. How did Peter the Great want to change Russia?

2. How did Peter the Great learn about Western ideas?

3. List some ways in which Peter the Great tried to make the Russians more like Western Europeans.

4. How did Peter the Great obtain "windows on the West"?

5. What city did Peter the Great make the capital of Russia?

THINK ABOUT IT

Why do you think Peter the Great thought Western European ways were better than Russian ways?

Lesson 3: Catherine the Great

FIND THE WORD

czarina

Not all the Russian rulers were men. Just as Mary I and Elizabeth I ruled in England, women ruled in Russia. The most important of these women was Catherine II, known as Catherine the Great. She ruled Russia as **czarina** (zah REE nuh), or empress, from 1762 to 1796.

Catherine was not even a Russian. She was a German princess who had married Czar Peter III. She became the ruler of Russia in his place when Peter died. Like Louis XIV, Catherine II was an absolute monarch.

Catherine the Great admired and tried to copy everything that was French. Like Peter the Great, she looked west to Europe. She, too, wanted to make her nation more European. She, too, wanted to gain "windows on the West" for Russia.

What Did Catherine the Great Do?

Catherine II expanded Russia's borders, as had Peter the Great. Russia divided up Poland with Austria and Prussia during her rule. The Ukraine (yoo KRAYN) and White Russia thus became part of the Russian Empire. Catherine led Russia into wars against the Ottoman Empire. As a result of these conflicts, the Crimea (kry MEE uh) and other lands along the Black Sea were added to Russia.

Catherine the Great also strengthened the position of the nobles. No longer were they forced to give service to the government. The nobles were allowed to do as they pleased on their own land. They could not be punished for any actions there.

Catherine the Great ruled Russia as an absolute monarch.

This is a drawing of the ceremony at which Catherine became the czarina of Russia.

Catherine the Great wrote letters to many of the important people of Europe. She was very interested in the arts. She bought French, English, and Dutch paintings to beautify the palaces of the czars.

Catherine the Great also tried to make the systems of law and local government better and more modern. She improved some schools. But not everything she did had a good result. In the lands conquered during her reign, more than a million peasants were made serfs. In these lands, there had been no serfs for a long time. Now these people were tied to the land just as other Russian peasants were.

REVIEW

CHECK YOUR FACTS

1. How did Catherine II become the ruler of Russia?

2. What lands did Catherine the Great add to Russia during her reign?

3. Catherine the Great (strengthened/ weakened) the position of the Russian nobles.

4. There were (more/fewer) serfs in Russia after the reign of Catherine the Great than before.

THINK ABOUT IT

In Western Europe, the monarchs gained power at the expense of the nobles. How was Russia different?

Lesson 4: The Russian Revolution

FIND THE WORDS

social class   abdicate
Bolsheviks
civil war   purge

Czars continued to rule the Russian people after Catherine the Great died in 1796. But the Russian people grew more and more unhappy. The serfs were freed in 1861. But most peasants remained very poor. There were a series of revolts in Russia in the 1800s and early 1900s. But these were put down. At last, the Russian Revolution brought the rule of the czars to an end in 1917. At that time Russia was fighting in World War I.

Causes of the Revolution

There were several reasons why the Russian Revolution took place in 1917. However, though the revolution occurred in 1917, its causes had roots deep in Russian history.

A chief cause of the Russian Revolution was conflict between the social classes in Russia. A **social class** is one of the groups into which society is divided by wealth and position. Most broadly, almost all societies are divided into an upper class, a middle class, and a lower class.

The main groups in Russian society before the revolution included the nobles, the clergy, the business people, the workers, and the peasants. The gap between the richest and poorest classes in Russia was very great. Though the serfs had been freed, they had been able to improve their lives very little. Most of the Russian people were peasants. They lived in small rural villages. They made a poor living by farming. Often, they lacked enough food to eat. Few knew how to read and write.

Another cause of the revolution was the bad government. The czars and their officials often governed poorly. Many government leaders were corrupt. The Russian government was not able to solve the problems of the nation.

A third cause was the fact that the Russian economy did not work well. The government and the people never seemed to have enough money. The frequent wars were expensive. The government collected too many taxes, especially from the poor.

The revolution also took place in part because groups of Russians had long been working toward it. Groups of Russian revolutionaries became very well organized, both inside and outside Russia. These people were to lead the Russian Revolution.

All these causes had long existed in Russia. Other causes of the Russian Revolution were more immediate. These included Russia's disastrous experiences in World War I and the misrule of Czar Nicholas II.

The Revolution

On March 8, 1917, the people of Petrograd (St. Petersburg) demonstrated against the government. They were seeking food for their starving families. They tried to see the czar, but he was at the war front. Finally, the people revolted. The army and the nobles refused to support the czar this time. On March 15, Nicholas II agreed to **abdicate,** or give up his throne. The czar and his family were soon arrested.

Many workers were unemployed in Moscow in the 1890s.

Police break up a workers' demonstration in St. Petersburg.

In 1917, Russian soldiers supported the revolutionaries.

A new government was formed to lead the nation. However, this government was weak. It was unable to handle Russia's problems or to meet the people's desperate needs.

On November 6, 1917, a second revolution began. It was led by the **Bolsheviks** (BOHL shuh VIKS). This was a socialist group headed by V. I. Lenin (LEN in). The Bolshevik slogan was "Peace, Land, and Bread." Many of the Russian people rebelled in support of this group. By January 1918, Lenin had become the dictator of Russia. The Bolsheviks made peace with Germany. But many Russians did not support the Bolsheviks. A **civil war,** a war within a nation, broke out in Russia.

The Bolsheviks wanted to make sure that the former czar could not return to power. Nicholas and his family were killed in July 1918.

The Bolsheviks moved the capital of Russia back to Moscow. They changed their own name to the Communist Party. This group was called the Reds because of the color of their flag.

The Russians who fought against the Communists in the civil war were called Whites. Other European nations and the United States tried to help the Whites. They were afraid that Communist ideas would spread to other countries. The Allied Powers even sent troops to Russia. However, the Red Army of the Communists had won by the end of 1920.

After the Revolution

After the civil war ended, Lenin continued in power. Right after they had come to power, the Bolsheviks had tried to set up a complete socialist system in Russia. In 1921, Lenin announced a New Economic Policy. This set up a more moderate socialist system. Russia soon began to recover from the effects of war and revolution.

STRANGE FACTS

It was the "Case of the Missing Grand Duchess." In March 1917, Czar Nicholas II and his family were arrested. Empress Alexandra was Nicholas's wife. Their son, Grand Duke Alexis, was the heir to the throne. There were also four daughters. These were the Grand Duchesses Maria, Tatiana, Olga, and Anastasia. You see two of them on the right.

The Bolsheviks had the imperial family shot in July 1918. But rumors spread that some had escaped and survived. A woman later claimed to be Grand Duchess Anastasia. No one knows exactly what happened.

In 1922, the Communists changed the name of the country to the Union of Soviet Socialist Republics. It is often called the Soviet Union for short.

Lenin died in 1924. There was a struggle for power. By the end of the 1920s, Joseph Stalin (STAH lin) had become the dictator of the Soviet Union. He remained in power until his death in 1953.

Stalin set up a ruthless dictatorship in the Soviet Union. In a **purge** in the 1930s, he got rid of many opponents. Stalin had them put in jail and killed in this so-called Great Purge. In 1939, Stalin came to an agreement with Nazi Germany. World War II soon broke out. In 1941, the Germans attacked the Soviet Union. Despite terrible losses, the Soviet armies

Lenin was one of the leaders of the Russian Revolution.

Stalin set up a dictatorship in Russia.

and people continued to struggle against the Germans. At last, in 1945, the Soviets and their American and British allies defeated Germany.

The alliance between the Soviet Union and the United States did not long outlive World War II. Soon a cold war arose between the Communist nations and the United States and its allies. The Soviet Union remains the chief rival of the United States in the world today. In the next lessons, you will read about the Soviet economy and about what life is like in the Soviet Union.

REVIEW

WATCH YOUR WORDS

1. The ____ were a socialist group led by V. I. Lenin.
   Bolsheviks   serfs
   White Russians

2. A war within a country is a(n) ____ war.
   international   civil   world

CHECK YOUR FACTS

3. Why was social conflict a chief cause of the Russian Revolution?

4. Why was the Russian government under the czars considered a bad government?

5. Who led the revolution of November 1917 in Russia?

6. What new name did the Communists give Russia?

7. Who was Joseph Stalin?

THINK ABOUT IT

What leader whom you have read about in a previous chapter led an attack on Russia in the early 1800s?

Lesson 5: The Soviet Economy

FIND THE WORDS

market economy   supply
demand   planned economy
quota   heavy industry
consumer goods

The Soviet economy is very different from the economies of the United States and the countries of Western Europe. Our nation and others have a **market economy.** In such an economy, the amounts and prices of the goods and services produced are determined by supply and demand. **Supply** refers to how much of something is available. **Demand** is how much of something people want to buy. In a market economy, most businesses are owned by private individuals. Of course, the government does make rules about the economy. For example, there are often laws about banks or the stock market. Such an economic system is also called capitalism or free enterprise.

The Soviet Union has a **planned economy.** In such an economy, the government makes all the important decisions. It decides what and how much will be produced. It decides who will produce it. It decides what it will cost. In addition to the Soviet Union, many nations of Eastern Europe and Asia have planned economies. Such an economic system is also called socialism. Socialism was set up in the Soviet Union by the Communists after the Russian Revolution.

Let's look at how economic decisions are made in the two different systems. Suppose you wanted to buy a new bicycle. In the United States, you would go to a store. Perhaps there are several stores in your community that sell bicycles. You would choose from among several different kinds of bicycles. Each would be made by a different company. Each might have different features. Each might cost a different amount of money.

In the Soviet Union, you would go to a store owned by the government that sells bicycles. There would probably be only one kind for sale. It would cost a price set by the government. There would be only as many bicycles available for sale as the government decided there should be.

How the Soviet Economy Works

The Soviet government has a central planning agency in Moscow. This group of people makes

.all the important economic decisions for the whole nation. They decide whether the country will make tractors or missiles. They decide how many of each shall be made.

The planning agency makes decisions according to the plan adopted by the Communist Party. These plans have been made every 5 years since 1928. They are called Five-Year Plans. Each plan sets production goals for the whole nation for a 5-year period.

Each Five-Year Plan lists the amount of every item that the Soviet Union expects to produce every year. This includes everything from wheat to shoes. The goals usually increase from plan to plan. The central planning agency tells the factories and farms how much to make in order to meet the plan for each year.

Each factory or farm has a **quota** (KWOH tuh), or set amount, to meet. This quota is not set by the people who operate the factory or run the farm. It is set by the agency in Moscow. Each worker in each factory or on each farm also has a quota to meet.

The quota is very important to each worker. If it is not met, the

SOVIET FIVE-YEAR PLAN: 1971-1975

Heavy industry (40%)
Farming (22%)
Housing (15%)
Transportation and communication (15%)
Light consumer goods (5%)
Consumer services (1%)
Other (2%)

worker is often penalized in some way. To encourage workers to meet their quotas, the factories and farms offer bonuses for those who do so. Workers who make more than their quotas get special rewards. These might include free vacations or various honors.

Quite often, the goals and quotas set by the Five-Year Plans are not met. That might mean that people will lack some particular foods or other goods. The Soviet government has to make choices. It has to decide what is more important to make. It has to decide how it is going to meet the needs of its people.

Sometimes, the farms do not produce enough wheat. The Soviets then often import wheat from other nations, such as the United States or Canada. At times, food is simply hard to find in the stores.

The Soviet government has long stressed **heavy industry.** This is the production of such things as steel, railroad cars, and tractors. The Soviets have put less emphasis on the production of **consumer goods.** These are goods ordinary people use directly. They include such things as food, clothing, and furniture. In recent years, the Soviet people have sought more consumer goods.

REVIEW

WATCH YOUR WORDS

1. A ____ is the set amount each factory in the Soviet Union is required to produce.
   supply   demand   quota

2. ____ is production of such things as steel, railroad cars, and tractors.
   Market economy   Heavy industry   Supply

3. ____ is how much of something people want to buy.
   Quota   Supply   Demand

4. ____ are goods ordinary people use directly.
   Quotas   Goals   Consumer goods

CHECK YOUR FACTS

5. What kind of economy does the Soviet Union have? What kind of economy does the United States have?

6. What is a Five-Year Plan in the Soviet Union?

7. The Soviet Union stresses (heavy industry/consumer goods).

8. What are consumer goods? Give some examples.

THINK ABOUT IT

Why do you think the Soviet Union has emphasized heavy industry?

Lesson 6: The Soviet Union Today

FIND THE WORDS

permafrost   taiga   subsidize
atheist   legislative   executive
judicial   cold war

What is the Soviet Union like today? Suppose you were to visit the Soviet Union. Would you find cities and towns like your own? What would the people be like? As you read this lesson, you will find some answers to these questions.

The Land

The Soviet Union is the world's largest nation. Look at the map below. You can see how the United States would fit into the Soviet Union with space left over. The Soviet Union covers about 22.3 million square kilometers (8.6 million square miles) on two continents, Europe and Asia.

The Soviet Union has four major climate areas. Look at the map on page 259 and find each of them. In the far north is the tundra. This area has mostly small plants, with few trees. In most of this area, there is **permafrost.** This is soil just below the surface that always remains frozen. It does not thaw even in summer. South of the tundra stretch the vast forests that cover much of the Soviet Union. This area is called the

UNITED STATES

SOVIET UNION

taiga (TY guh). Then come the steppes. These are great plains on which much of the food of the Soviet Union is raised. In the southwest are desert areas. There, irrigation has helped make farming possible.

Look at the map of the world on pages 10 and 11. You can see that most of the Soviet Union lies much further north than most of the United States.

Since the Soviet Union lies so far north, its climate is much colder than that of the United States. Unlike Western Europe, which is also pretty far north, the Soviet Union is not warmed by the North Atlantic Drift. In much of the Soviet Union, most of the year is wintry. Find Siberia on the map on pages 268 and 269. This area of the Soviet Union has very little summer. It is very cold there most of the year.

The Soviet Union has some of the greatest rivers in the world. Look at the maps on pages 170–171 and 268–269. Find the Dnieper (NEE pur), the Volga, the Ob, and the Lena. These rivers carry goods from one part of the Soviet Union

CLIMATES OF THE SOVIET UNION

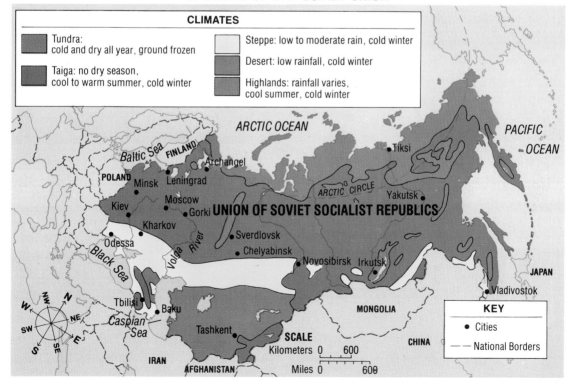

CLIMATES

Tundra: cold and dry all year, ground frozen

Taiga: no dry season, cool to warm summer, cold winter

Steppe: low to moderate rain, cold winter

Desert: low rainfall, cold winter

Highlands: rainfall varies, cool summer, cold winter

ARCTIC OCEAN

PACIFIC OCEAN

Baltic Sea FINLAND Archangel Tiksi

POLAND Minsk Leningrad

Kiev Moscow ARCTIC CIRCLE Yakutsk

Gorki **UNION OF SOVIET SOCIALIST REPUBLICS**

Kharkov

Odessa Volga River Sverdlovsk

Black Sea Chelyabinsk

Novosibirsk Irkutsk

JAPAN

Vladivostok

Tbilisi Baku

Caspian Sea MONGOLIA

Tashkent

KEY

• Cities

– – National Borders

SCALE
Kilometers 0 600

Miles 0 600

CHINA

IRAN

AFGHANISTAN

259

to another. However, they often freeze over in the winter.

The Soviet Union has large mountain ranges. The Urals divide the country in two. They separate the European part of the Soviet Union from the Asian part. Look at the map on pages 268 and 269 and find another mountain range.

The People

The European part of the Soviet Union is only about one-fourth of the country. But about three-fourths of the Soviet people live there.

The Soviet Union is still called Russia by some people. But only about half of the people of the Soviet Union are Russians. Nonetheless, the Russians are by far the largest and most powerful group. The Soviet Union has more than 100 other ethnic groups. Each group has its own culture. Many speak different languages.

These many different groups have had problems communicating with one another. The Soviet leaders have tried to solve these problems by teaching everyone to speak, read, and write the Russian language. Each group learns its own language as well. The Soviet government has sent many Russian people to work throughout the Soviet Union. In doing this, the government is trying to spread the culture of the Russians.

Lifestyle

People in the Soviet Union live better than they did before the Russian Revolution. However, the average American would not think that most of them live very well.

Imagine you lived in a large city in the Soviet Union. Your family would spend only a small part of its money on housing. The apartment in which you live would be assigned to you by the government.

In the Soviet cities, most housing is much alike. Most people live in large apartment buildings. Each apartment usually has three or four rooms plus a kitchen and a bathroom. The rooms are mostly small. A very few people have enough money to buy their own apartments. These are often larger than those the government owns.

Food is a problem in a Soviet family's life. The government food stores have only limited supplies of meat and fresh fruits and vegetables. People eat a lot of potatoes, cabbage, and carrots. They do not eat a lot of meat. Fresh fruit is rare. People form long lines to buy some when it becomes available.

Clothing is another problem in the Soviet Union. The government stores sell some items. However, these are often poorly made. The styles would seem out of date to Americans. All clothes, particularly shoes, are very costly.

The government encourages the people to read and to attend various events. Books and records are inexpensive. Seats at the theater or circus cost little. The government **subsidizes,** or pays some of the cost of, these things.

In the Soviet Union, women have the same kinds of jobs men have. Most Soviet doctors are women. Nevertheless, most directors of hospitals and clinics are men. You can see women working as police officers, construction workers, and factory workers.

In the time of the czars, most of the Russian people were members of the Russian Orthodox Church. Others belonged to other religions. Today, the government allows only a limited number of churches to remain open. In a large city such as Leningrad, there may be only two or three churches in operation. The Communist Party tries to make the Soviet people atheists. An **atheist** (A thee ist) does not believe in God.

Today, many buildings that were churches are museums. People visit them to see the works of art there, not for religious reasons.

St. Basil's Church on Red Square in Moscow is now a museum.

Government

The Union of Soviet Socialist Republics is made up of 15 republics. These are generally organized along ethnic lines. The largest and most important is the Russian Soviet Federated Socialist Republic. Despite their names, the Soviet republics are not independent nations. They are, in fact, somewhat like American states.

The Soviet Union has a constitution, just as the United States does. In fact, a new one was adopted in 1977. The constitution guarantees the people certain rights. However, it allows only one political party to exist. The Communist Party is the only one that appears on the ballot when the Soviet people vote.

The Soviet government has three branches, just as the government of the United States does. There is a **legislative** branch, which makes the laws. An **executive** branch runs the government. Courts make up the **judicial** branch. But these branches do not work as they do in the United States. The Soviet government is really run by the Communist Party. It makes all the important decisions. The government simply accepts these decisions and carries them out.

The most powerful leader in the Soviet Union is the general secretary of the Communist Party.

The premier and the president are also very important. In the late 1970s, Leonid Brezhnev (BREZH nef), the general secretary, became president as well.

Conflict with the United States

The Soviet Union and the United States were allies during World War II. But soon after the war, these two nations became enemies. For a long time, there was a period of conflict between them known as the cold war. It was called a **cold war** because the struggle took forms other than fighting.

After World War II, the Soviet Union helped bring Communist governments to power in a number of nations. These countries included Poland, East Germany, Czechoslovakia, Hungary, Romania, Bulgaria, Yugoslavia, and Albania. Look at the map of Europe on page 235. You can see that these nations lie along or near the Soviet Union's western border. These countries separate the Soviet Union from the rest of Europe. Three times since 1812, Russia has been invaded from the west. The Soviets wanted friendly nations along their border to keep this from happening again.

Many people in the Eastern European nations were not happy with Communist governments or

Yuri Gagarin was the first person to travel in space. He was called a cosmonaut. (The Russian word *kosmonaut* comes from the Greek *kosmos,* meaning "universe," and *nautēs,* meaning "sailor".) Another cosmonaut, Valentina Tereshkova, was the first woman to travel in space.

continuing Soviet influence. People tried to change the government in Hungary in 1956 and in Czechoslovakia in 1968. The Soviet leaders sent troops to those countries and put down the revolts.

The actions of the Soviet Union in Eastern Europe after World War II helped cause the cold war. The United States and the Soviet Union have also been in conflict because their political and economic systems are so different. The differences between them have helped create a lack of trust.

One area in which the Soviet Union and the United States have competed is in outer space. The Soviets were the first to put a satellite into orbit around Earth. They were also the first to send a person into space. However, only the United States has landed people on the moon.

Today, the Soviet Union and the United States have huge military forces to protect themselves and their allies. Each has thousands of nuclear missiles aimed at the other. Since the 1960s, however, the two nations have worked together to some extent to limit arms and solve disputes. Nonetheless, the conflict between the Soviet Union and the United States continues.

The Future of the Soviet Union

The Soviet Union is now one of the world's most important nations in almost every way. Its people are willing to work for their country. It has powerful military forces. Its rich natural resources support huge industries. What does the future hold for the Soviet Union?

In recent years, the peoples of some of the nations dominated by the Soviet Union have become rebellious. Soviet troops invaded Afghanistan (af GAN uh STAN) in 1979 to prevent a change of government. Workers in Poland began in 1980 to force changes in the Communist system there. Romania has become more independent of the Soviet Union in recent years.

The Soviet Union has had better relations with the nations of Western Europe recently. But it has once again come into sharp conflict with the United States.

Despite its rich resources, the Soviet Union has serious economic difficulties. These, plus its problems with other nations, threaten the stability of the Communist system. Nonetheless, it does not appear that there will be great changes in the Soviet Union in the near future.

REVIEW

WATCH YOUR WORDS

1. People who do not believe in God are _____.
   orthodox   subsidized   atheists
2. The _____ branch of government makes laws.
   legislative   executive   judicial
3. Soil that always remains frozen is _____.
   taiga   steppe   permafrost
4. A vast area of forest in the Soviet Union is called the _____.
   taiga   steppe   tundra
5. A _____ is a conflict between nations without fighting.
   cold war   armistice   civil war

CHECK YOUR FACTS

6. What are the four major climate areas of the Soviet Union?
7. Why is the Soviet Union colder than Western Europe?
8. What is the major mountain range in the Soviet Union?
9. What is the major ethnic group in the Soviet Union?
10. How many republics make up the Soviet Union?

THINK ABOUT IT

Do you think the United States and the Soviet Union will ever be able to trust one another? Give reasons for your answer.

CHAPTER REVIEW

WATCH YOUR WORDS

1. Catherine the Great reigned as ___ of Russia.
   czar   czarina   boyar

2. To give up one's throne is to___.
   purge   abdicate   abduct

3. ___ is how much of something is available.
   Supply   Demand   Quota

4. V. I. Lenin led a socialist group called the___.
   White Russians   boyars   Bolsheviks

5. ___ is how much of something people want to buy.
   Quota   Supply   Demand

CHECK YOUR FACTS

6. List two accomplishments of Ivan III.

7. Why was the period in the early 1600s called the Time of Troubles?

8. Which czar set up the Russian Academy of Sciences?

9. How did Catherine the Great show she was interested in art?

10. List three major causes of the Russian Revolution.

11. Who was czar during the Russian Revolution?

12. Who were two early leaders of the Soviet Union?

13. What is the purpose of a Five-Year Plan in the Soviet Union?

14. Name three nations the Soviets have sent troops into since World War II.

GET THE DATE STRAIGHT

Match the year or years with the event.

15. 1237–1240   A. Catherine the Great ruled Russia.

16. 1300s   B. Ivan III became ruler of Moscow.

17. 1462   C. Joseph Stalin died.

18. 1613   D. The Russian Revolution began.

19. 1682–1725   E. The Golden Horde invaded Russia.

20. 1762–1796   F. Peter the Great ruled Russia.

21. 1917   G. Michael Romanov was elected czar.

22. 1953   H. Moscow became important.

THINK ABOUT IT

23. Which Russian ruler do you think accomplished the most for the good of Russia?

24. How do you think the Russian Revolution might have been avoided?

25. Why do you think a nation the size of the Soviet Union finds it necessary to import food?

26. List some ways in which life in the Soviet Union differs from life in the United States.

UNIT REVIEW

WATCH YOUR WORDS

Use the words below to fill in the blanks. Use each term only once.

absolute	Caucasian	dictator	finished goods
monarchs	centralized	economies	Peninsula
alliance	coal	Empire	raw materials
ally	Commonwealth	Estate	revolution
armistice	Consulate	ethnic groups	serfs
Bolsheviks	czar	exports	trenches

Europe has many land areas almost surrounded by water, such as the Iberian ___. Most of the people of Europe belong to the ___ race. Europe has many ___, each of which has its own beliefs, customs, and ideas. Europe's nations have either capitalist or socialist ___. Europe ___ many goods to other nations.

Britain was one of the first European countries to feel the effects of the industrial ___. Britain had plenty of ___ to power its factories. Britain needed colonies to supply ___ and to buy the ___. At one time, the British ___ spread all over the globe. Now, many of Britain's old colonies belong to the ___ of Nations.

For many years, the kings of France ruled as ___. Louis XIV ___ the control of France in his own hands. Many people who suffered under the rule of the kings belonged to the Third ___. Soon after they overthrew the king, Napoleon took charge. He set up a system of government called the ___. Napoleon had become a ___.

Germany was at the center of two world wars in this century. A(n) ___, or friendship agreement between nations, drew Germany into World War I. Its ___, Austria-Hungary, declared war on Serbia. Soon, soldiers in ___ were facing each other across battlefields. When the ___ was signed, the fighting finally stopped.

The Soviet Union is the largest nation in the world. Before the revolution, Russia was ruled by a ___. The ___, or peasants tied to the land, lived difficult lives. In 1917, a revolution broke out. Before long, the ___, a socialist group, were in control of the nation.

CHECK YOUR FACTS

1. What is one reason the United States has close ties with Europe?
2. Name three of the major landforms of Europe.
3. To what group of Indo-European languages does English belong?
4. What is an ethnic group?
5. In what ways do capitalism and socialism differ?
6. What is the purpose of the European Common Market?
7. Name one achievement of Queen Elizabeth I of England.

8. List some ways in which the industrial revolution changed the lives of workers.

9. In what part of the world was the British Empire weakest?

10. Name a major problem facing the United Kingdom today.

11. How did Louis XIV try to make France stronger?

12. What were two causes of the French Revolution?

13. Who was Napoleon?

14. Why does France have a favorable outlook for the future?

15. The Treaty of Versailles was a (generous/harsh) peace settlement.

16. What nations belonged to the Axis? The Allies?

17. What is the meaning of the phrase "windows on the West"?

18. Catherine the Great (was/was not) originally a Russian.

19. How many political parties are there in the Soviet Union?

20. What nation is the chief rival of the Soviet Union?

USE YOUR MAPS AND CHARTS

21. Look at the physical map of Europe on pages 170 and 171. Name three seas that border on the Soviet Union.

22. Look at the map of Russia on page 243. What city was the center of Russian growth?

23. Look at the chart of the Soviet Five-Year Plan on page 256. Which is more important in the Soviet economy, heavy industry or farming?

24. Look at the map of the Soviet Union on page 258. Is the Soviet Union wider from east to west or from north to south?

25. Look at the climate map of the Soviet Union on page 259. What is the largest climate area?

THINK ABOUT IT

26. Why does the climate of Europe get colder as one goes east?

27. How would life be different if every nation could produce all that it needs?

28. Does the United States have any of the same problems faced by the European nations today? If so, which ones?

29. On the whole, has religion brought unity or conflict to Europe? Give reasons for your answer.

30. What do you consider to be the characteristics of a great leader? Do you think that Ivan III, Peter I, and Catherine II deserved to be called "great"? Give some reasons for your answer.

TRY SOMETHING NEW

31. Using pictures from magazines, make a display showing products made in Europe and imported into the United States.

32. Make a chart comparing the governments of the Soviet Union and the United States. Use this unit and an encyclopedia as your sources. For each country, show the national government and its parts. Show the name and the number of the parts into which the two nations are divided. (Hint: The United States has 50 such parts.)

267

SOCIETIES IN ASIA AND OCEANIA

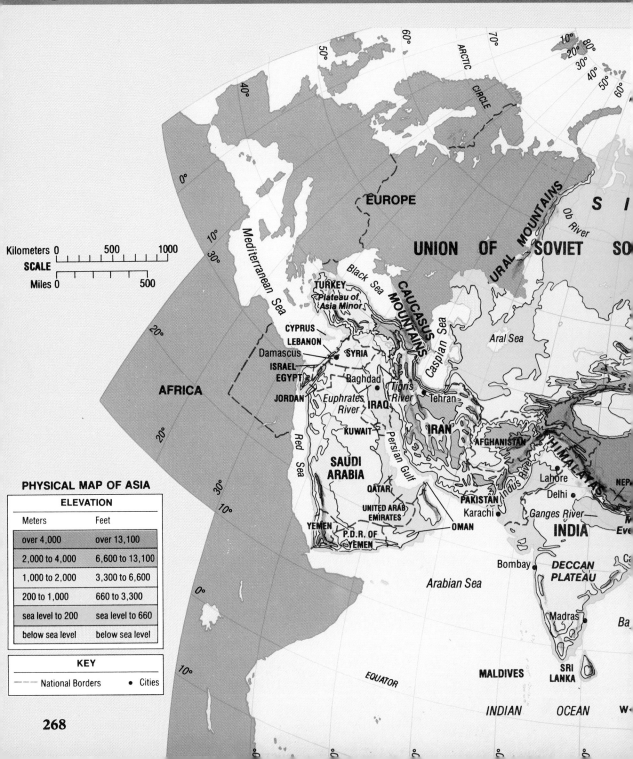

Kilometers 0   500   1000

SCALE

Miles 0   500

EUROPE

UNION OF SOVIET SO

S I

URAL MOUNTAINS

Ob River

Mediterranean Sea

Black Sea

CAUCASUS MOUNTAINS

Caspian Sea

Aral Sea

TURKEY

Plateau of Asia Minor

CYPRUS

LEBANON

Damascus

ISRAEL

EGYPT

SYRIA

Baghdad

Tigris River

Tehran

JORDAN

Euphrates River

IRAQ

IRAN

AFRICA

KUWAIT

Persian Gulf

SAUDI ARABIA

AFGHANISTAN

HIMALAYAS

Indus River

Lahore

Delhi

NEP

Ganges River

QATAR

UNITED ARAB EMIRATES

PAKISTAN

Karachi

YEMEN

P.D.R. OF YEMEN

OMAN

INDIA

M

Eve

Red Sea

Bombay

DECCAN PLATEAU

Ca

Madras

Arabian Sea

Ba

PHYSICAL MAP OF ASIA

ELEVATION	
Meters	**Feet**
over 4,000	over 13,100
2,000 to 4,000	6,600 to 13,100
1,000 to 2,000	3,300 to 6,600
200 to 1,000	660 to 3,300
sea level to 200	sea level to 660
below sea level	below sea level

KEY	
– – – National Borders	• Cities

MALDIVES

SRI LANKA

EQUATOR

INDIAN OCEAN

W

OCEAN

170°
160°
80°
150°
140°
130°
120°
110°

60°

70°

ARCTIC CIRCLE

50°

Bering Sea

40°

180°

Lena River

170°
30°

ERIA

REPUBLICS

Lake
Baikal

Amur River

20°

JAPAN

MONGOLIA

NORTH
KOREA

Sea of
Japan

Tokyo

Osaka

GOBI
DESERT

Peking

Seoul

Tientsin

PACIFIC OCEAN

SOUTH
KOREA

Hwang Ho

CHINA

Shanghai

160°

Yangtze

150°

TAIWAN

10°

HONG KONG (U.K.)

BURMA

LAOS

Hanoi

PHILIPPINES

INDOCHINA

VIETNAM

Manila

Irrawaddy River

THAILAND

South China
Sea

0°

Mekong River

ngoon

Bangkok

Ho Chi Minh City

CAMBODIA

EQUATOR

MALAY
NINSULA

BRUNEI

MALAYSIA

PAPUA

SINGAPORE

269

INDONESIA

120°

130°

140°

100°

110°

Jakarta

AUSTRALIA

CHAPTER 1

LOOKING AT ASIA

Lesson 1: Introducing Asia

FIND THE WORDS

**subcontinent   monsoon
typhoon**

Asia is by far the world's largest continent. Imagine that you are going to travel across the vast Asian land mass. You will see snowcapped mountains. You will walk through crowded cities. You will see farmers working in their fields. You will hear many different languages.

Many things you will learn about Asia will seem strange to you. But other things will seem very familiar. In Asia's cities you can see modern buildings and streets crowded with cars. You can see signs advertising products familiar to you. In many Asian

270

NATIONS OF SOUTHERN ASIA

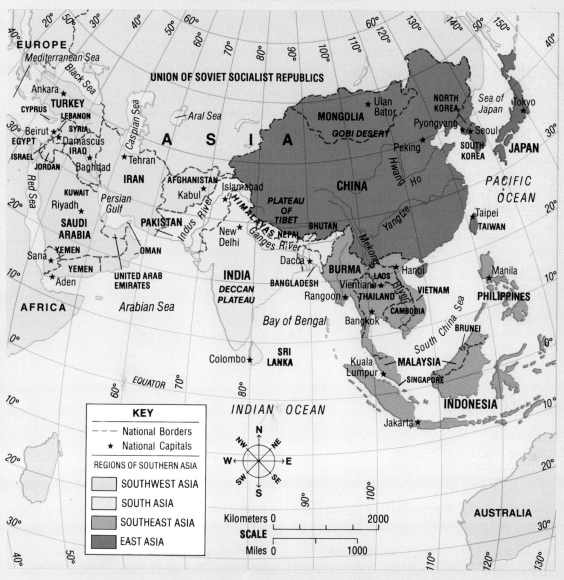

KEY

--- National Borders
★ National Capitals

REGIONS OF SOUTHERN ASIA

SOUTHWEST ASIA
SOUTH ASIA
SOUTHEAST ASIA
EAST ASIA

SCALE

Kilometers 0 — 2000
Miles 0 — 1000

271

countries, many people speak English. You can see programs from the United States on Asian television. So, in some ways, Asia will seem just like the United States.

Look at the map on pages 268 and 269. Find the Ural Mountains between Europe and Asia. Follow the land east to the Pacific Ocean. Find the Arctic Ocean in the far north. Follow the land south to the Indian Ocean. All this land is Asia. Locate the Mediterranean Sea to the southwest. Find the other seas that surround Asia and name them.

The continent of Asia can be divided into five major regions. These are North Asia, Southwest Asia, South Asia, Southeast Asia, and East Asia. Look at the map on page 271 and find these regions. North Asia consists of Siberia and the other Asian parts of the Soviet Union. You studied the Soviet Union in Unit III. Southwest Asia includes the peninsulas of Asia Minor and Arabia and extends east from the Mediterranean Sea to Afghanistan. The Indian subcontinent makes up South Asia. Southeast Asia is made up of the large peninsula of Indochina and thousands of large and small islands. East Asia includes China, Japan, and nearby nations.

In the next chapter of this unit, you will also study the continent and nation of Australia and the island nation of New Zealand. Those are the most important parts of Oceania (OH shee AN ee uh). This is a region that stretches across the Pacific west and south of Asia.

Landforms of Asia

Like Europe, Asia has many peninsulas. Look at the map on pages 268 and 269. Find the peninsulas of Asia Minor and Arabia. Find India. India is really an enormous peninsula of Asia. In the north, mountains cut India off from the rest of Asia. This makes India seem like a separate part of the continent. So India is called a **subcontinent**, a large land area on a continent that seems independent in some way. Find the peninsula of Indochina between India and China. What countries make it up? Find the peninsula on which the nations of North Korea and South Korea are located.

The main land mass of Asia is also surrounded by islands. Look at the map of Asia again. Find the island nations of Cyprus (SY prus) (south of Turkey) and Sri Lanka (SREE LAHNG kuh) (southeast of India). The nations of Indonesia, the Philippines, and Japan are made up of many islands.

Mountains are an important landform in Asia. The tallest mountains in the world, the Himalayas (HIM uh LAY uhz), are

Right: Some low hills in Asia are used for farming. *Below:* The Himalayas are the highest mountains in the world.

here. Find these mountains on the map. The Himalayas form a barrier between India and China.

Other mountains besides the Himalayas divide Asia into regions. Mountains separate the Soviet Union in North Asia from Turkey in Southwest Asia. Afghanistan in Southwest Asia and Pakistan in South Asia are also divided by mountains. Other mountains separate Indochina from India and China. Look at the map on pages 268 and 269 again. You can see that it is not only the Himalayas that isolate China. China is also ringed by other mountains along much of its land border.

Between the mountains in Asia, there are great river valleys. One of the largest of these is the valley of the Yangtze (YANG TSEE) in China. Find it on the map. The Mekong (MAY KONG) River and Irrawaddy River are important to the peoples of Indochina. On the Indian subcontinent are the great river valleys of the Indus, Ganges (GAN jeez), and Brahmaputra.

Many people live in the river valleys of Asia. There the land is good for farming. The rivers themselves provide water, transportation, and fish. Find the rivers on the map on pages 268 and 269.

Huge plains are also found in Asia. There, large crops are raised to feed the many millions of Asians. One of these plains is in northern India. Another is in northeastern China. Locate these plains on the map on pages 268 and 269.

Where there are many mountains, there usually are also high plateaus. Such lands are often too dry or too cold for many crops to grow. Asia has plateaus in Asia Minor, in Iran, in southern India, and in Tibet in China. Find these areas on your map.

The Ganges River, in India, provides water, transportation, and fish.

CLIMATES OF SOUTHERN ASIA

EUROPE
Mediterranean Sea
Black Sea
Plateau of Asia Minor
Caspian Sea
Aral Sea
A S I A
GOBI DESERT
Amur River
Sea of Japan
Euphrates River
Tigris River
Red Sea
Persian Gulf
Indus River
PLATEAU OF TIBET
HIMALAYAS
Brahmaputra River
Hwang Ho
Yangtze
PACIFIC OCEAN
Ganges River
Irrawaddy River
Mekong River
DECCAN PLATEAU
Arabian Sea
Bay of Bengal
South China Sea
AFRICA
INDIAN OCEAN
EQUATOR
AUSTRALIA
N
NE
E
SE
S
SW
W
NW
Kilometers 0
1500
SCALE
Miles 0
1500
CLIMATES
Continental: mild to hot wet summer, cold wet winter
Highlands: various local climates
Steppe: hot summer, hot to cold winter, variable rainfall
Desert: hot summer, hot to cold winter, dry all year
Humid Subtropical: hot wet summer, mild wet winter
Mediterranean: warm dry summer, mild wet winter
Tropical Grasslands: hot wet summer, hot dry winter
Rain Forest: hot and wet all year

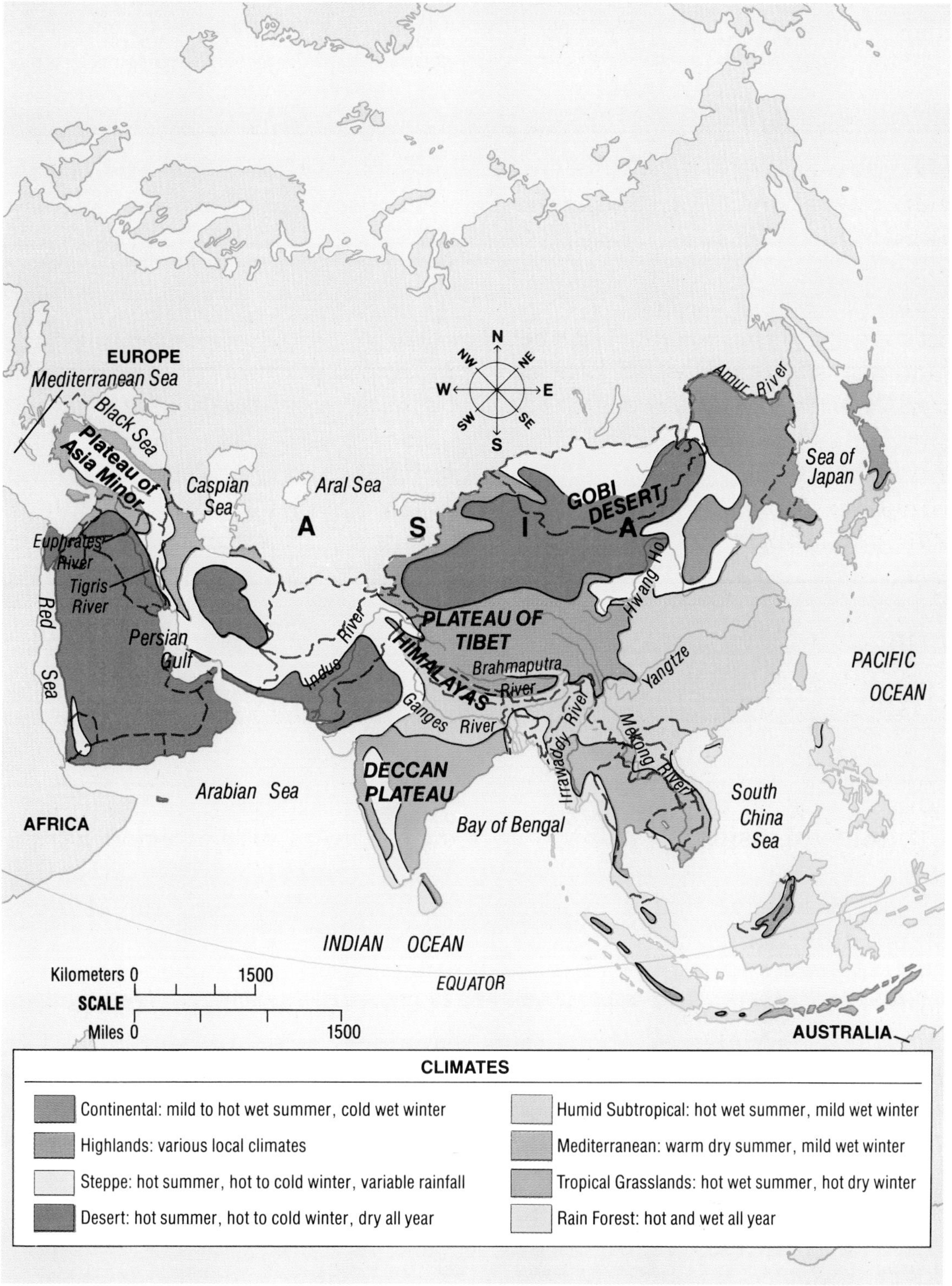

Monsoons bring heavy rains to the island of Bali, in Indonesia.

Climates of Asia

Asia is so large that it includes many different climate regions. These range from tundra in the far north to tropical rain forest in the far south. As you read about the climates of Asia, find each area on the map on page 275.

Southwest Asia is, in general, a very dry region. Much of the land is desert. There, little rain falls all year. The weather is hot during the day and cooler at night. The steppe areas of the region have a little moisture. The areas of Southwest Asia along the Mediterranean Sea, Black Sea, and Caspian (KAS pee un) Sea have a Mediterranean climate. There, the summers are hot and dry. The winters are cool and wet. Some areas have highland climates. The weather there varies greatly from area to area and changes often.

Much of South, Southeast, and East Asia has a monsoon climate. A **monsoon** is a wind that changes direction when the season changes. A monsoon climate has three seasons. The cool season lasts from October to March. Then, cool, dry air blows down from the mountains. The hot season lasts from March through May. Then, the land becomes very dry. The third season is the rainy season, or monsoon season. It lasts from June through September. Then, the weather is warm and wet. Warm, moist air blows from the oceans across the land.

Southeast Asia and East Asia also have **typhoons.** These are great wind and rain storms. They are like the hurricanes that occur in the United States. Typhoons often hit the islands off the Asian coast, Hong Kong, and the southern coast of China.

Because of their warm, wet climate, South Asia and Southeast Asia have large areas of tropical grassland and tropical rain forest. The Indian subcontinent also has desert in the west and steppe in the west and center. An area of humid subtropical climate stretches across the northern parts of South Asia and Southeast Asia.

Eastern China, the Koreas, and Japan have humid subtropical and continental climates. These are like the climates in much of our country. Northern China, the Koreas, and Japan have cold winters much like those in the northern United States. Yet all these areas can be very hot and humid during the summer.

Western China has steppes and deserts. The great Gobi (GOH bee) Desert stretches across northern China and southern Mongolia. A huge area of highland climate is in Tibet in southwestern China.

REVIEW

WATCH YOUR WORDS

1. Great wind and rain storms similar to hurricanes are____.
   typhoons   tornadoes   monsoons

2. A large part of a continent that seems independent in some way is a____.
   climate   subcontinent   zone

CHECK YOUR FACTS

3. List the five regions of Asia.
4. What landform is a barrier between India and China?
5. Describe the monsoon climate.

THINK ABOUT IT

What areas of Asia have climates like the climate of your area of the United States?

Lesson 2: Peoples of Asia

FIND THE WORD

Dravidian

The regions of Asia are divided not only by geography but also by culture. North Asia, Southwest Asia, South Asia, Southeast Asia, and East Asia all form different culture areas. You studied the Russian-dominated culture of the Soviet Union in Unit III. In this lesson, you will read about the peoples of the other four regions of Asia.

Peoples of Southwest Asia

Many different groups live in Southwest Asia. A large number of them are Semitic (suh MIT ik) peoples. These include the Arabs and the Jews. Arabs live in Iraq, Syria, Jordan, Saudi Arabia, and other nations of the region. Most are Muslims and speak Arabic. They have a common heritage and culture. The Arab nation of Lebanon is divided between Muslims and Christians. In recent years, there has been much fighting between the two groups there.

Most of the people of Iran are Persians. As in much of the rest of the region, most are Muslims. Most Iranians speak Farsi. There are a number of non-Persian groups in Iran, such as the Kurds. These people have their own cultures and languages.

The Turks of Turkey are Muslims, but not Arabs. They speak Turkish. The Turks once ruled much of the region. They spread their own culture and were, in turn, greatly influenced by Arab culture.

Apricots are one of the fruits grown in Turkey. Here, a Turkish girl is spreading apricots to dry.

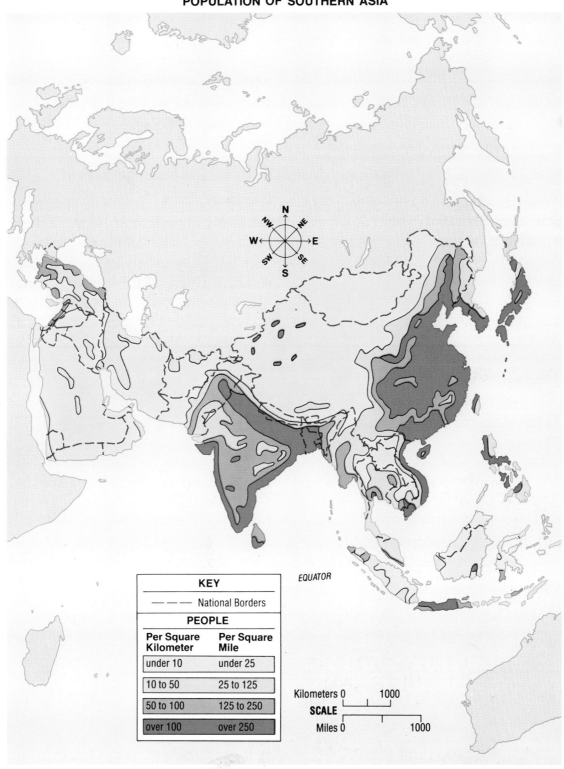

KEY

- - - - National Borders

PEOPLE

Per Square Kilometer	Per Square Mile
under 10	under 25
10 to 50	25 to 125
50 to 100	125 to 250
over 100	over 250

EQUATOR

Kilometers 0   1000

SCALE

Miles 0   1000

Many people in Israel live and work on farms.

Many Jews live in Israel. A large number practice the Jewish religion. Most speak Hebrew. The Jews of Israel fall into two groups: those of European background and those from Islamic countries. The ancestors of the European Jews, too, originally came from Southwest Asia. The Jewish people moved to other areas almost 2000 years ago. In this century, many returned to Palestine (PAL i STYN), the area of Southwest Asia at the eastern end of the Mediterranean. In 1948, they established the State of Israel in part of Palestine.

There are other groups in Southwest Asia. These include the Muslim people of Afghanistan (af GAN uh STAN) and the Christian Armenians. Like the Jews in the past, the Armenians live in a number of nations and lack a homeland of their own.

Peoples of Southern and Eastern Asia

There are many different ethnic groups in the regions east of Southwest Asia. Indeed, many different cultures and languages are often found within one nation. This is especially true in China and India, the largest nations of Asia. However, these two nations have dealt with their ethnic variety in very different ways.

China has long had many different groups within its borders. However, the Chinese have felt that any group that accepts Chinese ways is Chinese. Therefore, the ethnic groups of China have always been part of the culture and society of China as a whole. Today, the Chinese way of life is followed by all Chinese, regardless of their ethnic background. There is little conflict between the ethnic groups in China.

India, however, has long had a different kind of society. A person's ethnic group has determined her or his position in society.

Some ethnic groups have had very high positions. They have tended to be rich and powerful. Others have had very low positions. They have tended to be poor and powerless. The ethnic groups also often differ in language and religion. All these differences have led to much conflict between the various groups.

The Hindus make up the largest ethnic group in India. Many Hindus want everyone who lives in India to speak Hindi, their language. But dozens of other languages are spoken in India. When the British ruled India, the English language came to be widely spoken among all groups. It represented a common bond and a

These Chinese girls are working on a treadmill used to pump water into a field for irrigation.

sort of compromise among Indians. Now, the Hindu majority wants Hindi to take over the role of English. Many non-Hindus resent and resist this policy.

Japan and the Koreas are nations with few ethnic problems. Their peoples share a common heritage. This gives these countries much unity. Of course, Korea is now a divided nation. At present, this division is mostly political. However, if it continues for a very long time, two different cultures may develop in Korea. Then it will be difficult to reunite the two Korean nations.

Cultural Influences

In Asia, cultures have spread beyond national borders to affect nearby peoples. Chinese culture has dominated much of Indochina. The peoples affected by China incude the Khmer of Cambodia and the Laotians and Vietnamese. In addition, many people of Chinese background live in Singapore and other areas of Southeast Asia. Chinese culture also had a profound effect on Korea and Japan.

India has greatly influenced Sri Lanka and Burma. The peoples of Malaysia, Indonesia, and the Philippines have been influenced by

An Indian woman lights incense at a shrine.

Arabs have shops that sell the most modern electronic equipment.

many outside cultures. China and India have played important roles there. From Southwest Asia came the Islamic religion so important to Malaysia and Indonesia.

Western cultures have also been important in these regions of Asia. India, Pakistan, Bangladesh, Burma, and Malaysia were controlled by the British. Cambodia, Laos, and Vietnam were ruled by the French. The Dutch governed Indonesia. The Philippines was held first by the Spanish and then by the Americans. All the major Western trading nations also once had much power in China. Today, most of the Asian colonies of the Western nations are free. The Asian peoples have taken many Western ideas and made them their own.

Languages

Hundreds of languages are used in Asia. Mandarin Chinese is spoken by the most people, over 600 million. Other languages important in China include Cantonese and Shanghai (shang HY). But Mandarin is the official language. Because the Chinese use a way of writing based on pictures, all their languages are written in the same way.

Fourteen major languages are spoken in India. There are two main language groups. Hindi and other languages of northern India

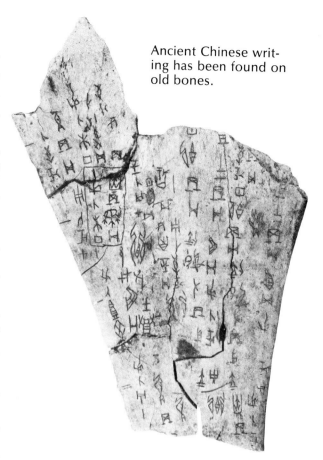

Ancient Chinese writing has been found on old bones.

are Indo-European. **Dravidian** (druh VID ee un) languages are spoken in southern India. Telugu and Tamil are the most important of these. India also has dozens of minor languages.

Nations like India and China have many different languages. But a number of Asian languages are spoken by most of the people within just one nation. These include Japanese, Korean, Malay (MAY LAY), Vietnamese, Thai (TY), and Burmese. There are many other languages in Asia. The number of people who speak each of them ranges from a few million to less than a hundred.

Asia's religions are many and varied. *Above:* Buddhist priests in traditional robes. *Left:* Hindus taking part in a sacred ceremony.

Religions

All of the world's important religions began in Asia. Southwest Asia was the source of Judaism, Christianity, and Islam. Other great religions arose in the rest of Asia. These religions are Hinduism, Buddhism, Confucianism, Taoism, and Shintoism. Many Asians practice a mixture of two or more of these religions. You will study these religions later.

REVIEW

CHECK YOUR FACTS

1. What language and religion do most Arabs share?
2. What people make up the largest ethnic group in India?
3. Western culture (has/has not) been important in Asia.
4. What language is spoken by more Asians than any other?
5. What three major religions began in Southwest Asia?
6. Name five other religions that began in Asia.

THINK ABOUT IT

Are there any people of Asian background in your community? What parts of Asia did they come from?

CHAPTER REVIEW

WATCH YOUR WORDS

1. Telugu and Tamil belong to the ___ language group in India.
   Indo-European   Celtic   Dravidian

2. A ___ climate has three seasons and a wind that changes direction with the season.
   continental   monsoon   arctic

3. A ___ is a large part of a continent that seems separate in some way.
   subway   subcontinent   valley

4. ___ are great wind and rain storms similar to hurricanes.
   Typhoons   Windwards   Savannas

CHECK YOUR FACTS

5. What land mass borders on Asia?

6. List the five major regions of Asia.

7. Name five island nations that are part of Asia.

8. Name and locate an important mountain range, river valley, and desert of Asia.

9. Which three regions of Asia have a monsoon climate?

10. What is the major religion of the people of Southwest Asia? What other two religions are practiced by minority peoples in Southwest Asia?

11. The Iranians and Turks (are/are not) Arabs.

12. Name a Semitic people other than the Arabs.

13. India has (more/less) ethnic conflict than China.

14. Name four groups of people in Asia that have been influenced by Chinese culture.

15. Name three Western nations that have influenced Asian culture.

16. In what group of languages is Hindi included?

17. Name two religions that began in Asia outside of Southwest Asia.

USE YOUR MAPS

18. Look at the physical map of Asia on pages 268–269. What sea separates Africa and Asia?

19. Look at the political map of southern Asia on page 271. What region includes Indonesia?

20. Look at the climate map of southern Asia on page 275. What kind of climate does eastern China have?

21. Look at the population map of southern Asia on page 279. In southern India, do more people live along the coasts or in the interior?

THINK ABOUT IT

22. How do you think mountains and deserts have affected the development of Asia?

23. Much of southern Asia has tropical climates. What kinds of houses and clothing might you see there?

24. How can religion be a source of unity in Asia? How can it be a source of conflict?

TRY SOMETHING NEW

25. Check the labels on your clothing and on the electrical appliances in your home. Which things, if any, were made in nations of Asia?

CHAPTER 2 SOUTHERN ASIA AND OCEANIA

Lesson 1: Southwest Asia

Southwest Asia, along with parts of northeastern Africa, is often called the Middle East. You will study the African parts of the Middle East in the next unit. In this lesson, you will read about the nations of Southwest Asia.

The most western country of Southwest Asia is Turkey. Indeed, a small part of Turkey is in Eu-

rope. South of Turkey in the Mediterranean is the island nation of Cyprus. East of Cyprus on the mainland of Southwest Asia are three nations. These are Israel, Lebanon, and Syria. Israel was created in 1948 by the United Nations. It was set up to give the Jews a homeland of their own. Israel and Turkey are the only nations in this area where most people are not Arabs.

Southeast of Israel is the oil-rich Arabian Peninsula. Saudi

Arabia occupies most of this area. Small nations ring the Arabian Peninsula along the Persian Gulf, Arabian Sea, and Red Sea. They include Kuwait (koo WAYT), Bahrain (bah RAYN), Qatar (KAH TAHR), the United Arab Emirates, Oman, and two countries called Yemen.

The Arab nation of Iraq borders Saudi Arabia on the northeast. Next to Iraq is a nation with a similar name, Iran. The most eastern nation of Southwest Asia is Afghanistan. Part of Egypt is also in Southwest Asia. But most of Egypt is in Africa.

Many of the countries of Southwest Asia were once ruled or dominated by Britain or France. Today, they are all independent nations. They began gaining their independence after World War I. The last became free in 1971.

Economy of Southwest Asia

Southwest Asia does not have many natural resources. Israel and Turkey do have some minerals. But coal and iron are generally lacking in the region.

Parts of Southwest Asia do have petroleum. More than half of the world's known oil supply is in the Middle East. Southwest Asian nations sell enormous amounts of oil to the industrial nations. This trade has made several nations of the region very rich.

Agriculture is difficult in Southwest Asia because the climate is so dry. About four-fifths of all people in Southwest Asia live by **subsistence farming.** That means they raise only enough food to feed themselves. They have little food left over to sell or trade. The region imports more food than it exports.

MIDDLE EASTERN PETROLEUM: Oil-Producing Areas of North Africa and Southwest Asia

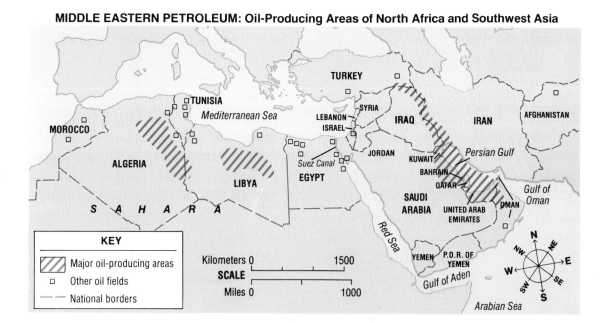

Israelis use modern machinery and irrigation to farm the desert.

There are two major kinds of agriculture in Southwest Asia: irrigated and nonirrigated. Because most areas are very dry, crops have to be watered by irrigation. In other areas, farmers depend on the rain.

Except in Israel, few modern farm machines are used in Southwest Asia. On the large Israeli farms, machinery can be used efficiently. But in the rest of the region, farms tend to be very small. The farmers cannot make good use of large machines. Few farmers can afford them.

Southwest Asia does not have much manufacturing. Only in Israel and, to some extent, in Iran and Turkey is there much industry today. In general, the region lacks the natural, human, and capital resources needed for industry.

Conflicts in Southwest Asia

Many nations of the region have disagreements with their neighbors. War often breaks out in Southwest Asia. Even when there is no open fighting, the struggles between nations often continue in other ways.

In the early 1980s, there are several trouble areas. Iraq and Iran have been at war about the border between them. Iran also has sharp arguments and fighting between groups within its borders. Lebanon is a battleground between Christians and Muslims. The two Yemens have sharp disagreements. Even more serious than these is the longstanding struggle between Israel and the Arabs.

Along with wealth, petroleum has brought problems to South-

There is much poverty in Southwest Asia, but oil has made some people there rich.

west Asia. Oil money has allowed some nations of the region to become modern. But many of these changes go against the traditional Islamic ways.

Oil money has also meant that there are now great differences in wealth among the nations of the region. The poor nations of Southwest Asia are falling farther behind their rich neighbors. The gap between rich countries and poor countries will be a problem in Southwest Asia in the future.

REVIEW

CHECK YOUR FACTS

1. What nation was set up to be a homeland for the Jews?

2. What is the most important natural resource in Southwest Asia?

3. What is subsistence agriculture?

4. There (is/is not) much manufacturing in Southwest Asia.

5. List three kinds of conflicts in Southwest Asia today.

THINK ABOUT IT

What part of Southwest Asia would you most like to visit? Why?

Lesson 2: South Asia: India

Today, the Republic of India is the seventh-largest nation in the world. It has the second-largest population. There are more than 600 million people in India. The number of people is increasing very fast in India. India's ever-growing population is a difficult problem.

India's Muslim neighbors, Bangladesh and Pakistan, also have population problems. Bangladesh, in particular, is one of the most crowded countries in the world. India is bordered on the north by the small nations of Nepal and Bhutan (boo TAN). Off India's coasts are the island nations of Sri Lanka (formerly Ceylon) and the Maldives (MAL DYVZ). Together, these seven countries make up the region of South Asia.

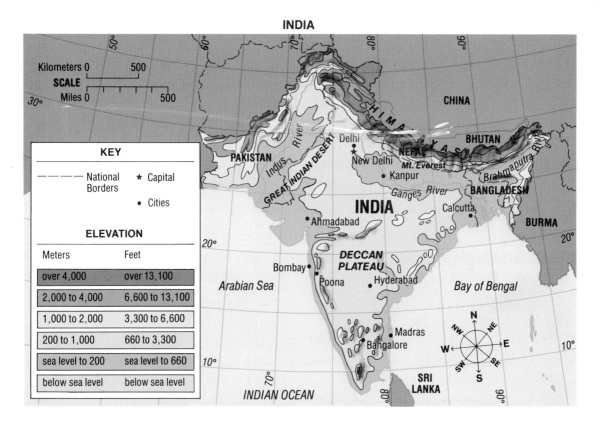

INDIA

Kilometers 0   500
SCALE
Miles 0   500

KEY

- - - - National Borders   ★ Capital

• Cities

ELEVATION

Meters	Feet
over 4,000	over 13,100
2,000 to 4,000	6,600 to 13,100
1,000 to 2,000	3,300 to 6,600
200 to 1,000	660 to 3,300
sea level to 200	sea level to 660
below sea level	below sea level

PAKISTAN   Indus River   GREAT INDIAN DESERT   Delhi   New Delhi   Kanpur   HIMALAYAS   NEPAL   Mt. Everest   CHINA   BHUTAN   Brahmaputra River   BANGLADESH   Calcutta   BURMA

Ganges River   INDIA   Ahmadabad

Arabian Sea   Bombay   DECCAN PLATEAU   Poona   Hyderabad   Bay of Bengal

Madras   Bangalore   N   NW NE   W   E   SW SE   S   10°

INDIAN OCEAN   SRI LANKA

Indian Religions

India was the birthplace of two great and ancient religions, Hinduism and Buddhism. It also became the home of many Muslims.

Hinduism is one of the oldest religions in the world. It has been part of Indian life for thousands of years. Today, more than 500 million people in India belong to the Hindu religion.

There are many gods and goddesses in the Hindu religion. Hindu temples contain many **idols,** or statues, of these gods and goddesses.

The Hindus believe in **reincarnation.** This is the idea that when a person dies, the person's soul does not die. Instead, it comes back as another person or other living thing. In addition, the Hindus believe in **karma.** This is the idea that the way a person lives influences her or his reincarnation. If a person leads a good life, she or he will be in a higher group of living things. If a person leads a bad life, she or he might be in a lower group.

The Hindus also believe in the idea of caste. A **caste** is a social class based on birth and work. The highest caste is that of the Brahmans. They are priests. The next caste is made up of rulers and warriors. The third caste includes merchants and skilled

Indians use flowers in religious ceremonies.

workers. In the lowest caste are unskilled workers and farmers. Below even these are people without a caste, the **untouchables.**

In India, the caste system long determined every person's life. You were born into your caste. You could not leave it. It had a set of special rules you had to follow. These rules told you with whom you could eat and work. They said whom you could marry.

Today, the government is trying to change the caste system. But it still exists in the villages. It still affects most people's lives.

They came from all over the East—and beyond. Architects from India, Persia, central Asia, Italy, and France were gathered together by the Mogul Emperor of India, Shah Jahan. Their job was to fashion a splendid memorial to the emperor's late wife. She had died in childbirth in 1631. She was called Mumtaz-i-Mahal. Her tomb was named the Taj Mahal for her.

In 1632, work on the Taj began. Over 20,000 workers labored every day for 11 years just to build the tomb, itself! It took another 11 to finish the whole complex. Most observers agreed that the Taj was worth it. Every part of the 12-sided tomb was made of marble, precious metals, or gems. The entrance to the Taj was once guarded with solid silver gates.

Today, many consider the Taj Mahal the world's most perfect building.

Buddhism is a religion that began in India about 2500 years ago. Siddhartha Gautama (GAUT uh muh) was its founder. He lived from 563 to 483 B.C. He wanted to know why there was pain and suffering in the world. One day, he thought he had the answer. Suffering was caused because people wanted too much pleasure from life. The pain could be stopped if a person followed the Eightfold Path. From the time that Gautama preached these ideas to others, he was called **Buddha** (BOO duh). This means the "enlightened one."

Buddha preached that if a believer followed this path, then the believer could enter **nirvana** (nir VAH nuh). This is a state of perfection in which there is no pain.

Buddhism spread far beyond India. Today, however, it is not a major religion where it began.

Indian Empires

India has one of the oldest civilizations in the world. In the past, many different empires existed in the area.

In Unit II, you read about the earliest Indian civilization. That culture was centered in the valley of the Indus River. Between 1200 and 200 B.C., the Aryan (AIR ee un) civilization flourished in the

Indian art has long been important.
Above: An ancient Buddhist statue.
Right: A modern cotton design.

Ganges River valley. It was followed by the Maurya (MAUR EE yuh) Empire in the 200s B.C. and the Gupta Empire in the 300s A.D. After the 600s, India was invaded by Muslim groups.

The Mongols were the next group to invade India. The Indians called them Moguls. The rule of the Moguls began in 1526.

The Mogul Empire declined after 1700. European traders had been coming to India since 1498. The Portuguese, Dutch, French, and English struggled for power. Eventually, the English won. You read about the British Indian Empire in Unit III.

India's Economy

Most farming in India is done on small plots of land. Hand tools or a few farm animals are used to do the work. Few modern farm machines are used in India.

Wheat and other grains are grown on the Great Northern Plain in India. Along the coasts, rice is a major crop.

India grows crops for export. It is the world's largest producer of tea. India exports cloth made from cotton grown there. **Jute,** a plant from which rope and burlap are made, is another major crop.

India has some manufacturing. Textile manufacturing is the best-developed industry. India makes fine cotton and silk cloth that is sold throughout the world. India also has factories that make things from jute. In addition, India has many steel mills. In fact, India has as many factories as some developed European countries.

Since independence, India has worked hard to improve education.

India's Future

Today, India is a crowded, poor land. There are prosperous cities, such as Bombay. But most people in India live in poverty.

Many of India's people live in small rural villages. There, life is still very much like it has been for centuries.

India has good resources that could be the basis for a strong economy. India must become self-sufficient in petroleum and make better use of its resources. Then it will be able to reduce poverty among its people. The future will tell whether India will solve its problems.

REVIEW

WATCH YOUR WORDS

1. ___ was founded by Siddhartha Gautama.
   Islam Hinduism Buddhism
2. Today, most Indians practice the religion___.
   Islam Hinduism Buddhism

CHECK YOUR FACTS

3. What name did the Indians give to the Mongols?

4. In India today, most farms are (large/small).

5. Today, most of the Indian people are (rich/poor).

TRY SOMETHING NEW

Write a report on one of the major religions of the Indian subcontinent: Hinduism, Buddhism, or Islam. Use an encyclopedia or other source suggested by your teacher.

Lesson 3: Southeast Asia

FIND THE WORDS

archipelago   terrace
plantation

Southeast Asia is a region of many cultures and religions. It is made up of peninsulas and thousands of islands that lie close to the equator. The only part of the region on the mainland of Asia is Indochina. This peninsula is called Indochina because it is between India and China. The Malay Peninsula is a long, narrow southward extension of Indochina. South and east of Indochina are thousands of islands, both large and small.

These islands have several names. They have been called the East Indies, the Malay Archipelago, and the Indonesian Archipelago. An **archipelago** (AHR kuh PEL uh GOH) is a large group of islands. Find the peninsulas and islands of Southeast Asia on the map of Asia on pages 268 and 269.

Nations of Southeast Asia

The peninsulas and islands of Southeast Asia are divided up among many nations. Burma, Thailand (TY LAND), Laos (LAH ohss), Cambodia (also called Kampuchea), and Vietnam are in Indochina. Malaysia is partly in

Thai women use parasols to protect themselves from the sun.

In Indonesia, many houses are built on supports.

Indochina and partly on the island of Borneo. Also on Borneo is Brunei (broo NY), a British protectorate. Singapore is a nation made up of one small island and many tiny islands off the Malay Peninsula. Singapore Island, the main one, is only 42 by 23 kilometers (26 by 14 miles).

East of Indochina across the South China Sea is the nation of the Philippines (FIL uh PEENZ). This country is made up of thousands of islands. These are called the Philippine Islands or the Philippine Archipelago. These islands are also considered part of the East Indies.

The rest of Borneo and the rest of the East Indies make up the nation of Indonesia. Indonesia has five large islands and thousands of smaller ones. It is about three times the size of Texas. Indonesia is more than 4800 kilometers (3000 miles) long from west to east. The most eastern part of Indonesia is included in Oceania, which you will study in the next lesson.

The nations of Southeast Asia are mostly new. Most were ruled by other nations until after World War II.

Peoples of Southeast Asia

The nations of Southeast Asia are young, but the cultures of the region are old. The peoples of Southeast Asia come from many groups. The region was settled by Asians from China and India. There are also some Black people, the Negritos.

The population in most of Southeast Asia is growing rapidly. So are the cities. The people of the cities are becoming more modern and Western. Their ways are now different from the ancient cultures in the countryside.

Throughout Southeast Asia, most people live in villages. A village may have from 20 people to several thousand. Life in the villages revolves around the family. The village houses are usually built on supports above the ground. This protects the people from water and pests.

Brunei, on Borneo, is a major oil producer.

Economy of Southeast Asia

Southeast Asia is rich in natural resources. Yet many of these resources are not being used now. About one-half of the world's tin comes from the region, most of it from Malaysia. Southeast Asia also produces bauxite, used in making aluminum. The Philippines supplies chromite. The chrome on cars comes from this ore.

Petroleum and natural gas have been discovered in Southeast Asia. Indonesia is the largest producer of petroleum in the region.

Most Southeast Asians are farmers. Most of them farm in the same way their ancestors did centuries ago.

The major crop in Southeast Asia is rice. Rice has to be carefully irrigated. It is grown on terraces. A **terrace** is a small piece of flat land cut into a hillside. Rice is also grown in river valleys. Much rice grows in fertile delta land. Some nations, such as Thailand, produce huge rice crops and export much of them.

Southeast Asia also produces pepper, sugar, coconut, rubber, and tea. These are usually raised on large farms called **plantations.**

There is not much manufacturing in most of Southeast Asia. Singapore has many industries. Indonesia is the most industrialized of the region's large nations.

Political Problems

Indochina has been the scene of fighting since the early 1940s. First, the Japanese captured the peninsula. The British and Americans opposed them. After World War II, Communist revolts broke out in Malaya and Vietnam. The Communists were defeated in Malaya. However, the Vietnamese Communists defeated the French by 1954.

In 1954, Vietnam was divided into two parts along the line of 17° north latitude. North Vietnam had a Communist government. South Vietnam had a non-Communist government. The Vietnamese Communists fought against the non-Communist Vietnamese through the 1960s and into the 1970s. The Soviet Union and China gave aid to the Communists. The United States sent troops to fight on the side of the non-Communists. This conflict was known as the Vietnam War. In the 11 years between 1961 and 1972, more than 50,000 Americans died in Vietnam.

In 1973, a peace agreement was signed. American troops were withdrawn. But in spite of the peace agreement, fighting between the Vietnamese continued. In 1975, Communists took over South Vietnam, Laos, and Cambodia. Today, there are small Communist revolts in Thailand and Burma.

The Communists at one time were very powerful in Indonesia. But in the mid-1960s, the government there changed. The Communists were thrown out. Many Communists were killed. Indonesia today is strongly anti-Communist.

REVIEW

CHECK YOUR FACTS

1. What is an archipelago?
2. Where do most Southeast Asians live?
3. What is the major crop in Southeast Asia?
4. Where in Southeast Asia did Americans fight from 1961 to 1972?

THINK ABOUT IT

Why has Communism been a strong political force in Southeast Asia?

Lesson 4: Oceania: Australia and New Zealand

FIND THE WORDS

Aborigine   Maori   dominion
mutton

South and east of Asia is a huge region of the world known as Oceania. Oceania covers much of the Pacific Ocean. It includes the continent and nation of Australia. North and east of Australia are thousands of islands. Some are parts of independent countries. Others are ruled by other nations. These islands are divided into three groups: Melanesia, Micronesia, and Polynesia.

In this lesson, you will read about Australia and New Zealand, the most important parts of Oceania. These two countries belong to the Commonwealth of Nations. Both are mostly British in culture. Most Australians and New Zealanders speak English. If you were to visit Australia and New Zealand, you might feel very much at home.

Australia

Australia is the only continent that has just one nation. The country of Australia also includes the large island of Tasmania and

MAP OF AUSTRALIA AND NEW ZEALAND

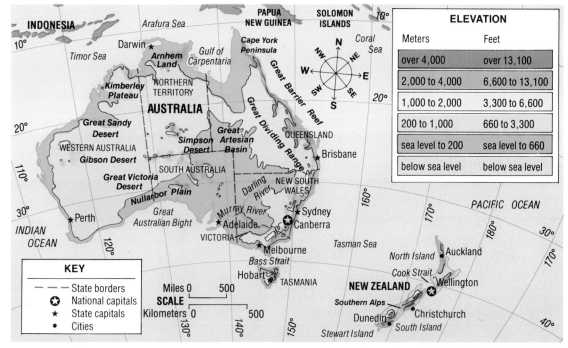

ELEVATION	
Meters	Feet
over 4,000	over 13,100
2,000 to 4,000	6,600 to 13,100
1,000 to 2,000	3,300 to 6,600
200 to 1,000	660 to 3,300
sea level to 200	sea level to 660
below sea level	below sea level

KEY
- - - State borders
✪ National capitals
★ State capitals
• Cities

SCALE
Miles 0   500
Kilometers 0   500

many small islands. It covers almost 7.7 million square kilometers (3 million square miles). Australia is the sixth-largest country in the world. Yet it has only about 15 million people. This is a small population for such a large nation.

Australia is the flattest continent in the world. Of course, there are mountains and hills in Australia. However, Australia's mountains are relatively old. They have been greatly worn down. Australia has three main regions: the western plateau, the central lowlands, and the eastern highlands.

New Zealand

New Zealand is made up of North Island, South Island, and a number of smaller islands. It is only about one-thirtieth the size of Australia. There are about 3.3 million New Zealanders.

New Zealand has much more rainfall than Australia. The west coasts of both islands, in particular, get much rain. The wet climate supports thick forests and productive agriculture. Much of New Zealand is very mountainous.

History of Australia and New Zealand

People lived in Australia and New Zealand long before the Europeans came. The first people of Australia are called **Aborigines** (AB uh RIJ uh NEEZ). The early people of New Zealand are known as **Maoris** (MOW reez).

In the 1600s, Europeans began to sail into the region of Australia and New Zealand. A Dutch ship visited Australia in 1606. In 1642, Abel Tasman, a Dutch sea captain, sighted Tasmania and New Zealand. Tasmania was later named

New Zealand is one of the world's largest exporters of lamb and wool.

Tennis star Evonne Goolagong is an Aborigine.

The kangaroo is native to Australia.

for him. Tasman, himself, named New Zealand after a part of the Netherlands.

Captain James Cook led a British group that explored New Zealand and Australia in 1769–1770. Cook claimed Australia's east coast for Britain and named it New South Wales.

The British began to settle Australia in 1788. Most of the early settlers were prisoners from British jails. The first group landed at Botany Bay on the east coast. This settlement became the city of Sydney. Soon, missionaries, merchants, and farmers began coming to New South Wales.

The British also started to settle other parts of Australia. Colonies were set up in Van Dieman's Land (now Tasmania) in 1825.

They were set up in Western Australia in 1829 and in South Australia in 1836. The new colonies of Victoria (1851) and Queensland (1859) were carved out of New South Wales.

By the 1890s, all six Australian colonies governed themselves. In 1901, the colonies united to form the independent Commonwealth of Australia. The British monarch remained head of state.

Meanwhile, in 1840, the Maoris and the British signed a treaty that brought New Zealand under British rule. In 1907, New Zealand became a **dominion.** That meant it was a self-governing area in the British Empire. Today, a dominion is a self-governing nation in the British Commonwealth of Nations.

Economy of Australia and New Zealand

Few Australians work in agriculture. But Australia's farms and ranches are very productive. Australia sells many different agricultural products around the world. It produces one-third of the world's wool. It also exports lamb and **mutton,** meat from grown sheep. Beef cattle are raised on huge ranches called cattle stations. Australian beef is shipped all over the world, including to the United States. Australian dairy farms produce butter for export.

Large areas of Australia are good for growing wheat. Australia sells much wheat to other nations, including China.

Since 1950, many mineral resources have been discovered in Australia. These include petroleum, natural gas, coal, nickel, iron, uranium, and bauxite. Australia is now the world's leading producer of bauxite. It also produces much of its own petroleum. Australia sells many minerals and other raw materials to Japan. Most of Australia's exports of manufactured goods go to New Zealand.

Australian industry is centered in the major cities. These include the state capitals Sydney, Melbourne, Brisbane, Adelaide, Perth, and Hobart. New South Wales and Victoria are the main industrial states.

The port city of Sydney is the capital of the state of New South Wales.

New Zealand's farms raise many crops for sale within the nation. These crops include wheat, barley, corn, peas, and potatoes. New Zealand exports apples and pears to other countries.

New Zealand's land and climate are good for raising dairy cattle. New Zealand efficiently produces many dairy products for export.

New Zealand's ranches raise sheep for meat and wool. Most of the production is sold abroad. New Zealand is second only to Australia in the amount of wool it exports.

New Zealand is less industrialized than Australia. One reason for this is that New Zealand has fewer mineral resources than its western neighbor. However, in recent years New Zealand's industry has been growing.

The streets of Auckland bustle with activity.

Today, most of New Zealand's industries make finished goods from the country's own raw materials. As a result, food and wood products are important. Cars are also assembled in New Zealand.

Auckland is New Zealand's largest city. It is a manufacturing center and important port.

REVIEW

WATCH YOUR WORDS

1. ____ were the first people of Australia.
   Maoris   Aborigines   British
2. ____ were the early people of New Zealand.
   Maoris   Aborigines   Melanesians

CHECK YOUR FACTS

3. Name the three groups of islands north and east of Australia.

4. Australia (is/is not) the only continent with just one nation.

5. How do Australia and New Zealand rank among the world's nations in exports of wool?

TRY SOMETHING NEW

Using an encyclopedia, write a report on the strange animals of Australia.

303

CHAPTER REVIEW

WATCH YOUR WORDS

1. ____ is growing only enough food for one's own family.

    Agriculture Irrigation
    Subsistence farming

2. ____ is a state of perfection in which there is no pain or suffering.

    Hinduism Nirvana Buddhism

3. A ____ is a social class based on birth and work.

    nirvana caste karma

4. Siddhartha Gautama was called____.

    Hindu Buddhist Buddha

5. ____ is a plant from which rope and burlap are made.

    Cotton Jute Wheat

6. In India, a person without caste is a(n)____.

    Hindu untouchable Buddhist

7. A large group of islands is a(n)____.

    peninsula oasis archipelago

8. A small piece of flat land cut into a hillside is a____.

    terrace plateau plantation

9. Today, a ____ is a self-governing country in the British Commonwealth of Nations.

    republic state dominion

10. Meat from grown sheep is ____.

    beef mutton cattle

CHECK YOUR FACTS

11. What is the most western country of Southwest Asia? What is the most eastern country in the region?

12. What are the two major kinds of agriculture in Southwest Asia?

13. Southwest Asia (does/does not) have many natural resources.

14. What seven countries make up the region of South Asia?

15. What two great religions started in India?

16. What European peoples struggled for trade and power in India?

17. The nations of Southeast Asia are (young/old). The cultures of Southeast Asia are (young/old).

18. What nation is the largest producer of petroleum in Southeast Asia?

19. There (is/is not) much manufacturing in most of Southeast Asia.

20. What is the most important culture in Australia and New Zealand?

21. What are the three major regions of Australia?

22. What land masses make up the nation of New Zealand?

USE YOUR MAPS

23. Look at the map of Middle Eastern petroleum resources on page 287. Name some nations of Southwest Asia that have much petroleum. Name some that lack this resource.

24. Look at the physical map of India on page 290. What mountains border India on the north?

25 Name three rivers on the Indian subcontinent.

26. Look at the map of Australia and New Zealand on page 299. What is the capital of Australia? Of New Zealand?

27. What oceans border on Australia?

THINK ABOUT IT

28. Why is it much more crowded in Bangladesh than in Australia? What two things make the difference?

29. Have you ever eaten any Indian foods? If so, which ones?

TRY SOMETHING NEW

30. Make a display of pictures of animals native to Australia and New Zealand.

3 EAST ASIA: CHINA AND JAPAN

Lesson 1: History of China

The Middle Kingdom

The Chinese have always thought of themselves as the Middle Kingdom, the center of the world. One reason for this was that China is cut off from the rest of the world by its geography.

Look at the map on pages 268 and 269. There are mountains and desert in the north of China. To the south are mountains and tropical rain forests. In the west are high mountains and deserts. The Pacific Ocean lies to the east.

Within these geographical barriers, China developed its own unique culture. In many ways, it was more developed than other cultures were then. China had advanced systems of government, education, transportation, and communication in very early years. The Chinese were among

Confucius is one of the most famous figures in Chinese history.

the first to use paper, silk, and gunpowder. They developed many ways of working with metal and pottery. They created great works of architecture and art.

Confucius and Confucianism

Confucius (kun FYOO shus) lived in China from about 551 to 479 B.C. Confucius was a philosopher. He spent his life thinking and studying.

Confucius thought leaders of high moral character could save society. A moral person had rules to live by. Such a person would always try to do right. Others would be inspired by the leader's example. Confucius believed that a leader's setting a good example was more important than laws.

Confucius did not write down his teachings. They were written down and spread by his followers. His ideas, plus ones added later, make up **Confucianism.** Many people think of Confucianism as a religion. But it does not have gods or priests. Confucianism is a way of living a "good" life. It tells people to respect their ancestors and the past. It stresses an orderly society. It includes a guide to behavior that is like the golden rule: Do not do to other people what you do not want for yourself.

In the 200s B.C., the rulers of China adopted Confucian ideas. In 124 B.C., a university was set up by the government to train officials in Confucianism. But Buddhism, from India, and Taoism, a Chinese religion, became important after about 200 A.D. **Taoism** (TOU IZ um) stressed withdrawing from everyday life and living in harmony with nature.

In the 600s, the T'ang dynasty came to govern China. The T'ang rulers set up a series of government examinations. People who wanted to become government officials had to pass these tests. The examinations required a knowledge of Confucian writings and teachings.

The examination system was strengthened in the 900s under the Sung dynasty. Later Sung rulers combined Confucian ideas with Buddhism and Taoism.

The changes of the Sung period affected the Chinese Empire to its end in the early 1900s. Chinese society, government, and education were dominated by the government examinations and Confucianism. Confucianism also strongly affected Korea, Japan, and Indochina.

TIME LINE: HISTORY OF CHINA

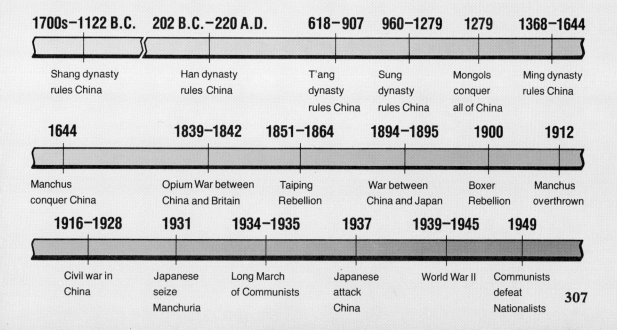

1700s–1122 B.C.	202 B.C.–220 A.D.	618–907	960–1279	1279	1368–1644
Shang dynasty rules China	Han dynasty rules China	T'ang dynasty rules China	Sung dynasty rules China	Mongols conquer all of China	Ming dynasty rules China

1644	1839–1842	1851–1864	1894–1895	1900	1912
Manchus conquer China	Opium War between China and Britain	Taiping Rebellion	War between China and Japan	Boxer Rebellion	Manchus overthrown

1916–1928	1931	1934–1935	1937	1939–1945	1949
Civil war in China	Japanese seize Manchuria	Long March of Communists	Japanese attack China	World War II	Communists defeat Nationalists

307

In 221 B.C., the Chinese had a problem—invaders. Mongols from the north had been attacking China for years. But the emperor had a bold solution. He ordered 300,000 soldiers and peasants to build a wall. Not just the kind of wall that fortified many towns all over the world. This would be a giant wall reaching across the whole north of China. The result was the Great Wall of China.

The Mongols

The Chinese people ruled themselves for many centuries. Then, in the 1200s, warriors came from Mongolia in the north to challenge them. These were the Mongols. They were led by Genghis Khan (JENG giss KAHN). In 1234, the ruler of northern China was ousted by the Mongols.

In 1260, the grandson of Genghis Khan, Kublai Khan (KOO bly KAHN), came to the throne. He was to be one of the greatest rulers of China. It was Kublai Khan whom Marco Polo visited and later wrote about. In 1279, Kublai Khan's army conquered southern China and overthrew the Sung dynasty. Kublai Khan ruled the entire nation until his death in 1294. Under the Mongols, China was part of a huge empire. The empire stretched from Eastern Europe and Mesopotamia to the Pacific Ocean.

The Manchus

In modern times, the Chinese Empire was ruled by the Manchus. The Manchus are one of China's many ethnic groups. They live in an area of northeastern China called Manchuria. In 1644, the Manchus invaded China. They established the Ch'ing dynasty of emperors. This was to be the last family of emperors to rule over China.

Many Chinese did not like the Manchus. They wanted to rule themselves. Secret societies were formed in the late 1700s. These groups plotted the overthrow of the Manchu government. The Chinese people were not very well off in the later years of Manchu rule. Most of the Chinese people were peasants. They were forced to work for landlords who demanded much of their crops in rent. Starvation was common in Manchu China.

Above: The Empress Tz'u-hsi (TSOO SHEE) controlled China from 1861 to 1908. *Right:* (From top to bottom) Sun Yat-sen, Chiang Kai-shek, Mao Tse-tung.

The Chinese Revolution

On October 10, 1911, a revolution began in China. The Manchu emperor gave up his throne. Thus, 2000 years of rule by emperors ended in China.

But the new leaders could not set up a strong government. They struggled for power among themselves. One group, the Nationalists, were strong. They wanted a democratic government in China. Sun Yat-sen was their leader.

From 1916 to 1928, the Chinese fought a civil war. The **warlords,** or local military leaders, tried to keep control of their own areas.

The Nationalists tried to gain control of the whole country.

At the same time, however, the Chinese Communist Party was also being organized. In 1921, there were only a few hundred Communists in China. The Communists and the Nationalists had very different ideas about the future of China.

In 1927, a man named Chiang Kai-shek (JYANG KY SHEK) became the leader of the Nationalists. He sent an army to destroy the Communists. The Communists fled to a place in southwest China. Then, in 1934–1935, they were forced to flee again. This time they went to the northwest. This journey is known as the **Long March.** About 100,000 Communists started north. Only about 10,000 survived. By this time, Mao Tse-tung (MOW tsay DUNG) had become the leader of the Chinese Communist Party. He was to remain so until his death in 1976.

The Nationalists were not very successful in setting up a government that worked well. Japan attacked China in 1937. The Nationalists and the Communists fought the Japanese together.

When World War II ended in 1945, the Nationalists and Communists began to fight again for power in China. Gradually, Chiang Kai-shek's Nationalists began losing the war.

In 1949, the Communists captured Peking. Chiang Kai-shek and the Nationalists withdrew to the island of Taiwan (TY WAHN). The Nationalists remain there today. The Communists rule all the rest of China. The revolution that had begun in 1911 finally came to an end in 1949.

REVIEW

CHECK YOUR FACTS

1. What group did Genghis Khan lead into China?
2. What emperor of China did Marco Polo visit?
3. Where did the Ch'ing dynasty come from?
4. In what year did the Chinese revolution begin?
5. In what year did the Chinese Communists capture Peking?

TRY SOMETHING NEW

Write a report on one of the ancient religions of China: Confucianism, Taoism, or Buddhism. Use an encyclopedia or other source suggested by your teacher.

Lesson 2: China Today

FIND THE WORDS

cooperative   commune
production brigade   paddy
nationalize   handicraft   ration
character   premier

Today, China is a huge nation with almost a billion people. Only the Soviet Union and Canada have more land. No nation has as large a population. The island of Taiwan is still ruled by the Nationalists. Today China and Taiwan are really very different nations. China is communist. Taiwan, a country of 18 million people, has a growing capitalist economy.

Two European colonies remain on the coast of southern China. These are the British colony of Hong Kong and the Portuguese colony of Macao. Hong Kong has a very prosperous economy. The Korean peninsula borders China in the northeast. It is divided between communist North Korea and capitalist South Korea. Next to Korea is the wealthy island nation of Japan. These five nations and two colonies make up the region of East Asia.

Chinese women work in the fields on cooperative farms.

Thousands of Chinese come to visit and study this model commune.

Changes since 1949

When Mao Tse-tung and the Communists won in 1949, they immediately began to change China. One of the first things they did was give land to the peasants.

At first, land was taken from the large landowners. It was then divided up among the peasants. The peasants farmed much of the land together. These large farming units are called **cooperatives.** But each peasant family also had its own small piece of land. They could farm this land as they wished.

Then, in 1958, cooperative farms were combined into **communes.** These were huge farming communities. Most included 5000 to 8000 families. Families lived in barracks, not in individual houses. All the land was owned by the commune. There were no longer any private plots. Under this new system, the peasants did not work as well or as hard. The output of farm products fell by one-third. The communes were not a success.

Further changes were made. Each commune was divided into **production brigades.** These were groups of about 100 families. They lived in settlements much like the villages of old China. Each family had its own house or apartment. Each had its own small piece of land. This new system was a compromise between the old cooperatives and the old communes. It is still in use today.

Chinese Agriculture Today

China is a very large nation. But many parts of China are not suitable for agriculture. Look at the map on pages 268 and 269. You can see that there are mountains and deserts in the north, west, and south. So most good agricultural land is in eastern China.

Only about 11 percent of China's land is used for agriculture. The Chinese people work the land very well. They produce large crops. Rice is the most important food crop in the south. Wheat is the leading grain in the north.

Today, the Chinese are beginning to use modern ways of farming. Now tractors are used as well as water buffalo to do the work in the **paddies,** or flooded rice fields. Chemical fertilizers are now used as well as other kinds. But most work on Chinese farms is still done by people using simple hand tools.

Chinese Industry Today

Since 1949, China has been trying to build up its industry. Until 1960, the Soviet Union helped the Chinese.

Since the death of Mao Tsetung in 1976, the Chinese have had more contact with the West. They have been trying to make their nation more modern. They are importing Western machines and methods. Chinese students are

China's factories belong to the whole nation.

studying abroad once again. They hope to learn new skills so they can help their country.

In China today, factories belong to the nation as a whole. After the Communist victory in 1949, all industries were **nationalized.** That means the national government took over ownership of them. In recent years, individuals have been allowed to open small businesses of their own. However, only members of the owner's family can work in such businesses.

The Chinese are building many factories to make **handicrafts.** These are goods made by hand. They include fine carvings in ivory or jade and beautiful paintings on scrolls of paper or silk. These handicrafts are sold around the world. The Chinese put the profits from these sales back into their industry.

This billboard glorifies Chinese workers.

Lifestyle in China Today

Suppose you were to visit a Chinese village or city today. You would find that most people live in much the same way.

Every Chinese family is provided with housing. This is done by the commune, the factory, or a neighborhood council. The house or apartment may have only a couple of rooms. But the rent is very low because the government pays part of it.

The Chinese wear very simple clothing. Getting enough food has long been a problem for Chinese families. Today, basic foods such as rice are **rationed** (RASH und). That means there is a limit on how much of a certain product each person can buy. Rationing is a way of making sure everyone gets some of each thing. Other foods can be bought in the normal way.

Education in China

Children begin school at a very early age in China. Most children are put in daycare centers while their parents work. These centers are provided by the factories or communes. Later they go on to nursery school and kindergarten.

Most children then go to a 4-year primary school. At this level, they are taught the Chinese language and how to read it. Chinese does not have an alphabet. Each word is written with a symbol called a **character.** The character for each word is different. It has been estimated that every child must learn more than 2300 characters to be able to read. Imagine how much harder that is than learning the 26 letters of our alphabet!

After primary school, some children go on to secondary school. There, young people prepare for college. Other students go to a vocational or technical school. There, they learn a trade. Students have to take a special examination to go to college in China.

In this class, each student has a book of the sayings of Mao Tse-tung.

Chinese Government

Since 1949, the government of China has been controlled by the leaders of the Chinese Communist Party. Mao Tse-tung was chairman of the party until 1976. The **premier** (pri MIR) is the head of the Chinese government. The Chinese people are represented in the National People's Congress, which meets each year. However, the congress only approves the decisions already made by the Communist Party.

For a long time after the Communist government was set up in China in 1949, the American government refused to accept it. The United States supported the Nationalist government in Taiwan,

American President Richard Nixon and Chinese Premier Chou En-lai met in 1972.

instead. In 1972, the Chinese and American leaders met. The two countries became more friendly. Finally, in 1979, they established normal relations. At the same time, trade has been growing between the two nations.

China's Future

What does the future hold for this giant among nations? China has many problems. It must find a way to keep its population from growing too much larger. It must find a way to provide enough food for everyone. It must find a way to maintain peace with unfriendly neighbors, especially the Soviet Union and Vietnam.

China has made much progress in recent years. If this improvement continues, China may have a brighter future. Then, the Chinese will have what they call the "Five Freedoms":

freedom to have a house
freedom to have clothes
freedom to have something to eat
freedom to have a job
freedom to have a decent burial

REVIEW

WATCH YOUR WORDS

1. A field where rice is grown is called a ___.
   ration   commune   paddy

2. To ___ a product is to place a limit on how much of it each person can buy.
   ration   premier   nationalize

3. A ___ is a huge farming community in China.
   paddy   commune   nation

4. In the Chinese language, each word is written with a symbol called a(n) ___.
   calligraphy   alphabet   character

5. To bring an industry under national government ownership is to ___ it.
   ration   publicize   nationalize

CHECK YOUR FACTS

6. What two European colonies still remain on the coast of southern China?

7. How do communes differ from co-operative farms?

8. What products does China export?

9. What is the official who heads the Chinese government called?

10. How did relations between the United States and China change during the 1970s?

THINK ABOUT IT

Why do you think farmers work harder when they have some land of their own? Give reasons for your answer.

CROSSWORD

AFRICA

Starred clues refer to the articles on Africa in this issue.

ACROSS

*1. Many people have ___ from rural areas to cities, seeking food.
5. Male children
9. Greasy
10. A single group
11. Either
12. Finish
14. Note after sol
*15. The Aswan ___ stopped the flooding of the Nile.
*17. In many areas, people must search for ___ to drink.
19. Military police (abbr.)
21. I won't.
*22. Hunger, war, and the lack of clean water

threaten many people's ___.
*25. In several countries, civil ___ is a major cause of hunger.
28. Short for advertisement
*29. Africa borders the Mediterranean ___.
31. Get ready, get set, ___
32. Held on to
34. A bit of news
36. Has a meal
37. Specific amount of medicine

DOWN

*1. Ethiopia and other countries face severe ___ shortages.
2. Italy's main unit of currency
3. Elevated (abbr.)
4. This colors hair or a fabric.

*5. Neighbor of Ethiopia where hunger is a major problem.
6. Situated atop of
*7. The ___ is the world's longest river.
8. The sun is one
13. Northwest (compass direction)
16. Two thousand and five, in Roman numerals
18. Pull along, as a disabled vehicle
*20. ___ that ravage crops are another cause of food shortages.
*22. The largest source of the Nile is ___ Victoria.
23. A thought
24. Southeast (compass direction)
26. Grows old
27. Capital of Italy
*30. More food ___ is needed for the hungry.
33. Pint (abbr.)
35. In the direction of

Previous Solution

Lesson 3: Land of the Rising Sun

FIND THE WORDS

divine   Shintoism   samurai
syllable   shogun
hereditary

Japan's Geography

Look at the map on pages 268 and 269. You can see that Japan is a chain of islands stretching along the coast of Asia. Almost a thousand islands make up Japan. But there are four main islands. Find these islands on the map. The island nation of Japan has been dominated by the sea.

Japan is also dominated by mountains. There is little flat land in Japan. Only about one-seventh of Japan's land can be used for agriculture. Japanese farmers use their land very well. They get very high yields of crops from each field. Nonetheless, they do not produce enough food for the Japanese people. Japan must import food from the rest of the world.

Japan has two major climate regions. Southern Japan has a humid subtropical climate. It is warm and wet there much of the year. Northern Japan has a humid continental climate. There, it is warm in summer and snowy and cold in winter. Like Europe, Japan is warmed by ocean currents.

Japan has few natural resources. Japan's industries are supplied by raw materials imported from other parts of the world.

Japan is a little smaller than California. However, it has about 5 times as many people. Japan's population of about 120 million is much larger than California's population of about 24 million. Thus, Japan is a very crowded nation.

Mt. Fuji, Japan's highest mountain, is thought sacred by the Japanese.

Samurai were warriors who defended the emperor.

Japan's Early History

No one really knows where the people of Japan came from. They may have come from Siberia or Korea.

By the end of the 400s, most of the people of Japan had a similar culture. Most spoke the same language. The Japanese had also become different from other Asian peoples. In this early time, the Japanese developed the idea of the emperor. According to the Japanese, he was descended from the goddess of the sun. Therefore, they thought of the emperor as **divine,** meaning that he was like a god himself. The present emperor of Japan is the direct descendant of these early emperors. The Japanese emperors are the oldest ruling family in the world. The early Japanese also developed **Shinto-ism.** This is a religion in which many things in nature are worshiped as gods.

The most important group in the society of old Japan was made up of the emperor and the nobles. These people held much of the power in the empire. The next highest group were the **samurai** (SAM yuh RY). These were mighty warriors who defended the emperor. The sword of the samurai was the symbol of the power he received from the emperor.

From about 600 to 900 A.D., the Japanese tried to copy from China. The emperor, the nobles, and the people thought everything Chinese was wonderful. Japanese art became similar to Chinese art. The Japanese language was written with Chinese characters.

Today, Japanese is written in a way that combines an alphabet with Chinese characters. Each of the main Japanese characters stands for one **syllable,** or part of a word. There are 48 of these. In addition, there are thousands of special characters like Chinese characters.

In the 500s A.D., Buddhism was brought to Japan. This Indian religion came to Japan through China and Korea. Many great Buddhist temples were built in Japan. Some of these still stand.

The Feudal System

A feudal system developed in Japan, just as it did in Europe. At first, each of the samurai warriors controlled a local area. Then, groups of samurai banded together to fight their enemies. At last, one warrior, Yoritomo, became stronger than any other. In 1192, the emperor gave him the title of **shogun.** This meant he was the commander of all the emperor's armies. From then on, until 1867, the shoguns really controlled the government of Japan. The emperors continued to reign but had no real power. In time, the position of shogun came to be **hereditary.** That means it was passed down from parent to child.

Western Contacts

From ancient times, both India and China had occasional contacts with Europe. But Japan, at the far eastern edge of Asia, had none. At last, in 1543, Portuguese sailors reached Japan. Soon, other European traders appeared in the islands. Roman Catholic priests came as missionaries.

The rulers of Japan did not like the foreigners. In 1614, the shogun ordered the Roman Catholic priests to leave. In 1639, all European traders except the Dutch were forced out. In 1646, the shogun made it illegal for any Japanese to leave Japan.

This seated Buddhist figure dates from 1099.

From 1603 to 1867, one family of shoguns, the Tokugawa, ruled Japan. Thus, this is known as the Tokugawa period. For more than 250 years, the people of Japan were alone and at peace. They fought no outside wars. Instead, they became a nation tightly controlled by their government. The people looked to the government to tell them what to do in every situation. There were few changes in Japanese life during this time.

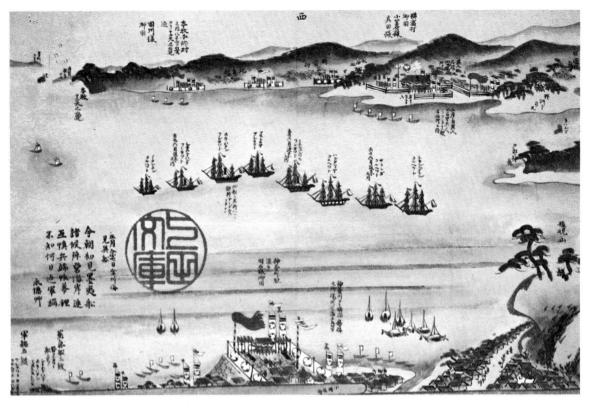

This painting shows Commodore Perry's fleet off present-day Yokohama in Japan.

Perry Comes to Japan

In 1854, Commodore Matthew Perry, an American, opened Japan to Western trade. Perry commanded a fleet of modern warships that entered the bay at Tokyo. The Japanese leaders knew that Britain had fought and defeated China in the Opium War (1839–1842). They were afraid that Japan would suffer a similar fate. As a result, they granted the United States certain trading rights in Japan.

The Meiji Restoration

Many Japanese did not like the foreigners who were coming again to Japan. They felt that the shogun should have been able to repel them. In 1867, a revolt among the samurai overthrew the shogun. The emperor was restored to power on January 3, 1868. Emperor Mutsuhito was only 15 years old. A group of new leaders held the real power in Japan. This event is called the Meiji (MAY jee) Restoration.

Changes in Japan

After the Meiji Restoration, great changes took place in Japan. The new contacts with the West gave the Japanese many new ideas. But the Japanese put their own mark on all the new ways.

The Japanese worked hard to make their new manufacturing industries successful. Groups of companies were formed to prevent competition and encourage cooperation. These groups were aided by the Japanese government.

The Japanese government modernized its army and navy. This gave Japan the power to expand its territory. Beginning in the 1890s, the Japanese went to war against other nations.

As a result of a war with China in 1894–1895, Japan took over Taiwan. In 1904–1905, Japan fought Russia for control of Korea and Manchuria. The Japanese easily defeated the Russians. The peace talks that ended the Russo-Japanese War took place in the United States. The Japanese took over Korea completely in 1910. Now all the world knew that Japan was a powerful nation.

Japan in Two World Wars

World War I began in Europe in 1914. Japan became involved in this conflict because it had an alliance with Great Britain. In the Treaty of Versailles that ended World War I, Japan was given the German lands in China and the Pacific. Look at the map on page 323. You can see how World War I helped Japan expand its lands.

Japan was involved in naval battles in a war with China in 1894–1895.

Japanese soldiers on the march in China in 1937.

The Japanese attack on Pearl Harbor, December 7, 1941.

During the 1930s, the military gained control of the Japanese government. General Tojo became a military dictator. The Japanese seized Manchuria from China in 1931. An open war between Japan and China began in 1937. By 1938, Japan controlled China's coast, major cities, and railroads.

World War II began in Europe in 1939. In 1940, Japan signed a treaty of alliance with Germany and Italy. Japan was now one of the Axis nations. The Japanese took over French Indochina in 1941. The government of the United States was deeply worried by Japan's actions. The Western nations cut off trade, including the sale of petroleum, to Japan in the summer of 1941.

On December 7, 1941, the Japanese bombed the American naval base at Pearl Harbor in Hawaii. This surprise attack brought the United States into World War II.

The Japanese continued to take more territory. By May 1942, they had conquered Malaya, Siam (now Thailand), Hong Kong, the Philippines, Burma, the Dutch East Indies (now Indonesia), and part of New Guinea. The map on page 323 shows Japan's expansion.

The Americans and British fought back. It took them 4 years to defeat the Japanese. They began recapturing the islands leading to Japan one by one.

WHERE WE ARE IN TIME AND PLACE

HISTORY OF JAPAN

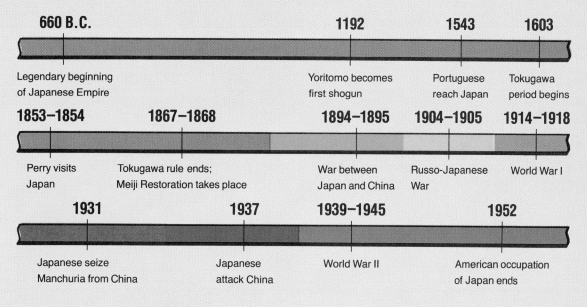

660 B.C.

Legendary beginning
of Japanese Empire

1192

Yoritomo becomes
first shogun

1543

Portuguese
reach Japan

1603

Tokugawa
period begins

1853–1854

Perry visits
Japan

1867–1868

Tokugawa rule ends;
Meiji Restoration takes place

1894–1895

War between
Japan and China

1904–1905

Russo-Japanese
War

1914–1918

World War I

1931

Japanese seize
Manchuria from China

1937

Japanese
attack China

1939–1945

World War II

1952

American occupation
of Japan ends

EXPANSION OF JAPAN

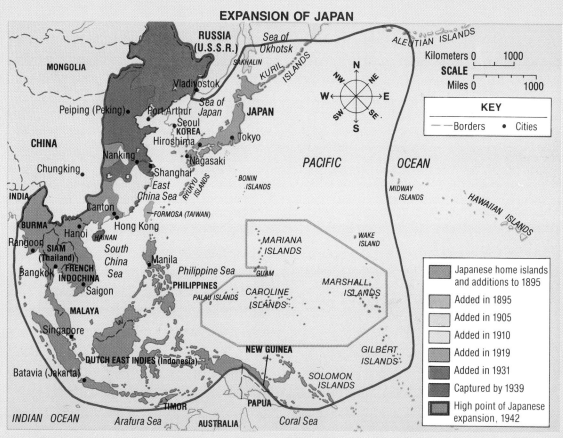

KEY
— Borders   • Cities

Japanese home islands
and additions to 1895

Added in 1895

Added in 1905

Added in 1910

Added in 1919

Added in 1931

Captured by 1939

High point of Japanese
expansion, 1942

Kilometers 0   1000
SCALE
Miles 0   1000

Above: Hiroshima, after the atomic bomb was dropped. *Right:* General Douglas MacArthur.

On August 6, 1945, Americans dropped the first atomic bomb on the Japanese city of Hiroshima (HIR uh SHEE muh). A second atomic bomb was dropped on Nagasaki (NAH guh SAH kee) on August 9. More than 100,000 people were killed by these bombs. The Japanese surrendered. The war ended on August 15, 1945.

Japan was occupied by American troops from 1945 to 1952. General Douglas MacArthur became the military governor of Japan. MacArthur and the Americans helped remake Japan.

REVIEW

WATCH YOUR WORDS

1. The ____ was the commander of all the emperor's forces.
   samurai   shogun   Diet
2. A right to rule passed down from parent to child is____.
   feudal   divine   hereditary

CHECK YOUR FACTS

3. During what years did the shoguns control Japan?

4. What Europeans first made contact with the Japanese?
5. Name three nations with which Japan has fought wars since 1900.

THINK ABOUT IT

The leaders of Japan wanted to keep their nation cut off from the rest of the world. Why did they seek isolation? Why were the Japanese unable to remain isolated?

Lesson 4: Japan Today

FIND THE WORDS

refining   crude oil

Japan is an economic giant today. It has the world's third-largest economy. Only the United States and the Soviet Union produce more goods and services. Japan has become a major industrial nation even though it lacks the natural resources that other nations have. Moreover, Japan's economy was badly damaged during World War II. The Japanese people have won out over scarce resources and war damage to build a powerful economy.

Japan's Industry

Modern industry needs energy resources, especially petroleum. Yet Japan, a great industrial nation, has no petroleum of its own. Nonetheless, Japan is one of the world's major refiners of petroleum. In **refining**, petroleum or other minerals are broken down into useful products. Japan imports **crude oil.** This is petroleum just as it comes from the ground. The Japanese then refine the crude oil into the products they need.

Japan does have one major energy resource of its own: hydroelectric power. This is produced by Japan's swift-flowing rivers. Japan is the fifth-largest producer of hydroelectricity in the world. Hydroelectric energy helps power Japan's industries.

Japan is one of the world's major producers of steel. Yet it has little iron ore, from which steel is made. Instead, Japan imports iron ore from other nations. Then it makes the raw ore into finished iron and steel products. In turn, the Japanese export these products to the world.

You can see that Japan, like Britain, lives by trade. First, the Japanese import the raw materials they do not have. Second, they manufacture these raw materials

Modern Japan is highly industrialized.

Above: An automobile production line in Japan. *Below:* A street in Tokyo.

into finished products. Third, they export these goods to other nations. This earns profits. Fourth, they use the profits to live, to improve their economy, and to buy more raw materials.

Many nations around the world are rich in natural resources. But many of these same nations lack the factories to manufacture their raw materials into finished goods. Japan trades with such nations. The Japanese also sell many goods to Europe and the United States. Japanese industry is efficient, and Japanese goods are well made. Thus, Japan can sell good products at good prices around the world.

Japanese industry has grown enormously since World War II. One reason is that the government helps business. It encourages companies to cooperate. It tries to help them avoid wasteful competition. The government also tries to protect Japanese industries from foreign imports.

Japanese Workers

Another reason for the success of Japanese industry is the attitude of the workers. The Japanese are very loyal to their companies. They do not move from job to job. In fact, most workers expect to work for the same company their whole lives. Companies are loyal to their workers, too. In Japan, when companies do not need all their workers, they still find something for them to do. Workers rarely lose their jobs in Japan. Workers who have been with a company longer get the better jobs first.

Japanese Education

Japanese workers often have to take tests to get jobs. So most Japanese are good students. Most Japanese students work very hard in school to get high grades. They know their future jobs depend on how well they do in school. Parents work with their children to help them be successful in school. Even in first grade, Japanese students have homework.

Japan's People

Today, Japan has about 120 million people. Most Japanese are young. About one-fourth are under the age of 14. There are 318 people per square kilometer (824 people per square mile) in Japan.

Tokyo (TOH kee OH) is the capital of Japan and one of the world's largest cities. It has more than 8 million people. Tokyo is a very crowded city.

Japan is a modern industrial nation. Yet, at the same time, it has an ancient culture. Many of the old Japanese traditions survive. The Japanese believe in hard work and loyalty to the group.

Many Japanese worship at Shinto temples.

They value cooperation rather than competition. They believe in excellence.

Japanese culture today shows some American influences. The most popular sport is baseball. American baseball teams often visit Japan during the winter months. Golf is another popular sport. In fact, the Japanese government has had to limit the number of golf courses. Too much valuable land needed to raise food was being used for golf.

327

Japan has the fastest railroad line in the world.

Japan's Future

In spite of its wealth, Japan has some problems today. There is a conflict between old Japanese ways and the new ways that have come since the war. Japan has disputes with its trading partners. It has a large population in a small country. Japan also must decide whether it will continue to rely completely on American military protection.

Japan has a growing economy, good workers, and a stable government. These things should help Japan solve its problems in the future.

REVIEW

CHECK YOUR FACTS

1. Japan has (much/little) petroleum and iron ore of its own.

2. What energy resource is found in Japan?

3. Foreign trade (is/is not) important to Japan.

4. Japanese workers (often/seldom) lose their jobs.

5. About how many people live in Japan today?

THINK ABOUT IT

If you were to visit Japan, what would you most like to see? Why?

CHAPTER REVIEW

WATCH YOUR WORDS

1. ___ were large Chinese farming communities.
   Paddies   Terraces   Communes

2. The journey of Mao Tse-tung and the Communists away from the forces of Chiang Kai-shek was the___.
   Trail of Tears   Death March
   Long March

3. Local military leaders in China were the___.
   Communists   Nationalists   warlords

4. The head of the Chinese government is the___.
   president   premier   prime minister

5. A way of living that stresses respect for the past and one's ancestors is___.
   Hinduism   Confucianism   Buddhism

6. A Chinese religion that stresses withdrawal and harmony with nature is called___.
   Taoism   Confucianism   Shintoism

7. The early Japanese developed a religion called___.
   Taoism   Shintoism   Buddhism

8. Gods are___.
   hereditary   samurai   divine

9. From 1192 to 1867, Japan was controlled by___.
   shoguns   samurai   warlords

10. In ___, crude oil is made into useful products.
    rationing   nationalizing   refining

USE YOUR MAP

11. Look at the map of Japanese expansion on page 323. Did the Japanese ever capture Australia?

KNOW YOUR PEOPLE

Match the name with the clue.

12. Confucius
13. Kublai Khan
14. Marco Polo
15. Sun Yat-sen
16. Mao Tse-tung
17. Chiang Kai-shek
18. Tz'u-hsi
19. Genghis Khan.

A. withdrew with the Nationalists to Taiwan.

B. opposed the Manchu emperor.

C. ruled China from 1260 to 1294.

D. encouraged respect for one's ancestors.

E. visited China and returned to Venice.

F. led Mongols into China.

G. led Chinese Communists on the Long March.

H. controlled China from 1861 to 1908.

THINK ABOUT IT

20. List as many ways as you can in which Japan and Britain are similar.

21. Why have Japan and China fought so often?

22. What things could bring Japan's prosperity to an end?

23. Why are good relations between the United States and China important?

24. China was called the Middle Kingdom. Japan was called the Land of the Rising Sun. What other names like these can you think of for cities, states, and countries of today?

UNIT REVIEW

WATCH YOUR WORDS

Use the words that follow to fill in the blanks. Use each word only once.

Archipelago	Dravidian	samurai
Buddha	hereditary	Shintoism
Buddhism	Hinduism	shogun
castes	idols	subcontinent
characters	Karma	syllables
Confucianism	nirvana	Taoism
divine	reincarnation	untouchables

Religion is very important in Asia. Southwest Asia was the birthplace of Judaism, Christianity and Islam. Two important religions began on the ___ of India. ___ is the older. This religion includes a belief in ___ , or rebirth. ___ is the idea that the way a person lives affects this rebirth. Hindu temples have many ___ , or statues of gods. The Hindus are divided into groups called ___ . The ___ are classed below the lowest of these groups. The Hindus are also an ethnic group. They speak Hindi, but many of the people in southern India speak ___ languages.

___ was founded in India by Gautama, called ___ . He told his followers they would reach perfection, or ___ .

Islam is important in Southwest Asia and on the Indian subcontinent. It is also important in the East Indies, also called the Malay ___ .

In China, Confucius developed a philosophy known as ___ . It emphasized respect for authority. Later, it blended with another Chinese religion, ___ , and with Buddhism from India.

The Japanese borrowed Buddhism from China. They also used Chinese ___ to write their language, plus new ones that stood for ___ . The early Japanese also evolved their own religion, ___ . They worshiped their ___ emperor among their gods. The ___ warriors defended the emperor. Later, a ___ took over the real power. This position became ___ .

CHECK YOUR FACTS

1. What is the world's largest continent?
2. Of what region are Australia and New Zealand a part?
3. Name the five regions of Asia.
4. What are the tallest mountains in the world?
5. Name five important rivers of Asia.
6. Name a desert located in China and Mongolia.
7. What kind of climate does much of southern Asia have?
8. What are large hurricane-like storms in Asia called?
9. What is the religion of most Arabs?
10. Name two peoples of Southwest Asia that do not have their own nations.
11. What is the area of Southwest Asia at the eastern end of the Mediterranean called?
12. What language do the Hindus of India speak?
13. Chinese culture (has/has not) spread in Asia beyond China's borders.
14. What nation of Asia was ruled by the Spanish and the Americans?
15. What is the chief language of China?

330

16. Where are Dravidian languages spoken today?

17. Name three religions that began in Southwest Asia.

18. Name four European nations that have had colonies in Asia.

19. What two areas make up the Middle East?

20. Name two religions that started in India.

GET THE DATE STRAIGHT

Match the event with the date

21. 1192	A. Tokugawa period ends.
22. 1543	B. Portuguese sailors reach Japan.
23. 1639	C. The Japanese attack Pearl Harbor.
24. 1854	D. All but Dutch traders leave Japan.
25. 1867	E. Commodore Perry opens Japan.
26. 1904–1905	F. American occupation of Japan ends.
27. 1937	G. First shogun appointed.
28. 1941	H. Japan fights Russia.
29. 1945	I. Hiroshima and Nagasaki bombed.
30. 1952	J. The Japanese attack China.

USE YOUR MAPS

31. Look at the physical map of Asia on pages 268 and 269. What body of water is west of India?

32. Look at the political map of southern Asia on page 271. What is the largest nation of Asia south of the Soviet Union?

33. Look at the climate map of southern Asia on page 275. What kind of climate does the Arabian Peninsula have?

34. Look at the population map of southern Asia on page 279. Do more Asians live west of India or east of India?

35. Look at the map of the Middle East on page 287. The Suez Canal connects the Red Sea and the Mediterranean Sea. What do you think might be an important resource shipped through that canal?

THINK ABOUT IT

36. In what ways are rivers and river valleys important to Asia?

37. In what areas of Asia has Western culture been important?

38. Why does the economy of much of Asia depend on agriculture?

39. At the time of Marco Polo, the West could learn many things from the East. What could the West learn from the East today? What could the East learn from the West?

40. If you had to describe Asia in one word, what would it be? Explain your choice.

TRY SOMETHING NEW

41. Choose one of the countries of Asia that interests you. Look it up in an encyclopedia. Write a brief report about it.

PUT IT ALL TOGETHER

42. Make a chart called "Major Nations of Asia." Include these topics: nation, capital, language(s), religion(s), ethnic group(s), resources. List India, China, and Japan. Use this unit as your source.

SOCIETIES IN AFRICA

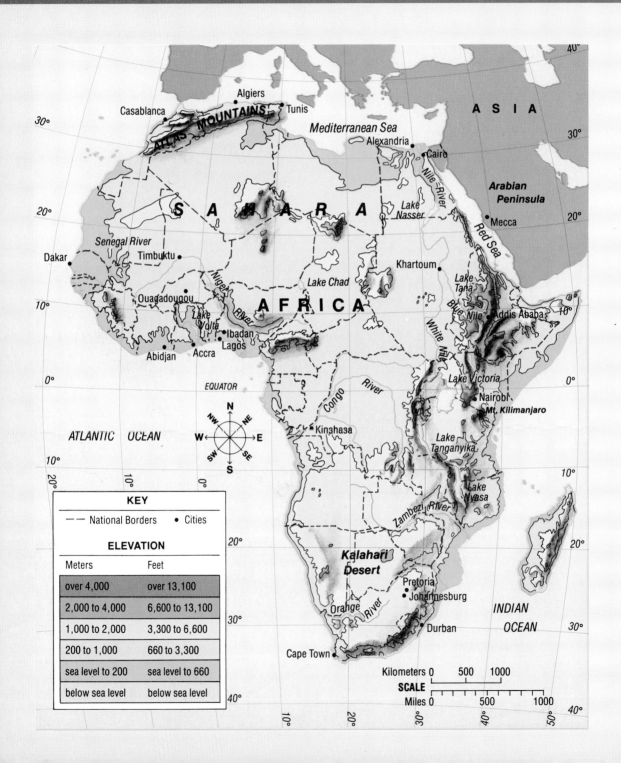

Algiers
Casablanca
Tunis
ATLAS MOUNTAINS
Mediterranean Sea
Alexandria
Cairo
ASIA
Arabian Peninsula
Mecca

S A H A R A
Lake Nasser
Nile River
Red Sea

30°
30°
20°
20°

Senegal River
Dakar
Timbuktu
Niger River
Lake Chad
Khartoum
Lake Tana
Blue Nile
Addis Ababa

A F R I C A
Ouagadougou
Lake Volta
Ibadan
Lagos
White Nile
Abidjan
Accra

10°
10°

Congo River
Lake Victoria
Nairobi
Mt. Kilimanjaro

EQUATOR
0°
0°

ATLANTIC OCEAN
Kinshasa
Lake Tanganyika

N
NW NE
W   E
SW SE
S

10°
10°

Lake Nyasa
Zambezi River

20°
20°

Kalahari Desert
Pretoria
Johannesburg
Orange River
INDIAN OCEAN
Durban

30°
30°

Cape Town

KEY

- - National Borders   • Cities

ELEVATION

Meters	Feet
over 4,000	over 13,100
2,000 to 4,000	6,600 to 13,100
1,000 to 2,000	3,300 to 6,600
200 to 1,000	660 to 3,300
sea level to 200	sea level to 660
below sea level	below sea level

Kilometers 0   500   1000
SCALE
Miles 0   500   1000

40°

10° 20° 30° 40° 50°

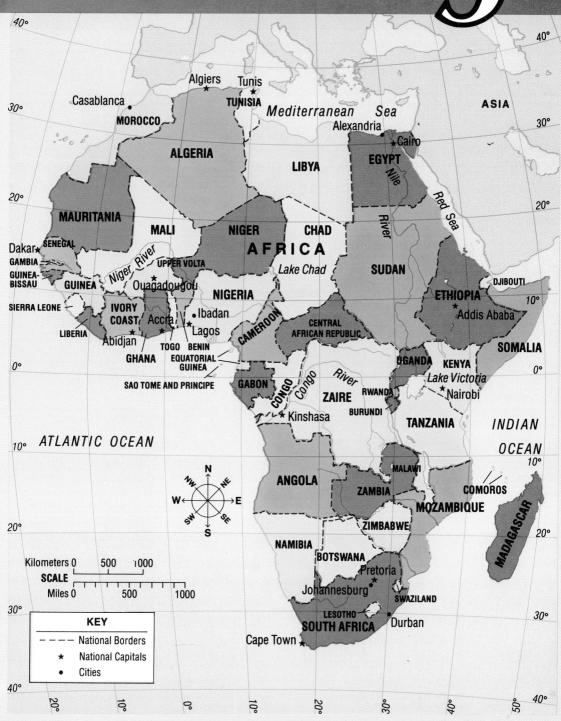

Algiers
Tunis
Casablanca
TUNISIA
Mediterranean Sea
MOROCCO
Alexandria
ASIA
Cairo
ALGERIA
EGYPT
LIBYA
Nile
MAURITANIA
Red Sea
MALI
NIGER
CHAD
River
SUDAN
Dakar
SENEGAL
AFRICA
GAMBIA
UPPER VOLTA
Lake Chad
GUINEA-
BISSAU
Niger River
DJIBOUTI
GUINEA
Ouagadougou
ETHIOPIA
SIERRA LEONE
NIGERIA
Addis Ababa
IVORY
Ibadan
COAST
Accra
SOMALIA
LIBERIA
Lagos
CAMEROON
CENTRAL
Abidjan
AFRICAN REPUBLIC
UGANDA
KENYA
TOGO
BENIN
Lake Victoria
GHANA
EQUATORIAL
Nairobi
GUINEA
GABON
River
SAO TOME AND PRINCIPE
CONGO
Congo
ZAIRE
RWANDA
BURUNDI
INDIAN
Kinshasa
TANZANIA
OCEAN
ATLANTIC OCEAN
N
MALAWI
NW
NE
ANGOLA
COMOROS
W
E
ZAMBIA
SW
SE
MOZAMBIQUE
S
ZIMBABWE
NAMIBIA
MADAGASCAR
BOTSWANA
Kilometers 0
500
1000
Pretoria
SCALE
Johannesburg
Miles 0
500
1000
SWAZILAND
LESOTHO
Durban
SOUTH AFRICA
Cape Town

KEY

- - - National Borders
★ National Capitals
• Cities

CHAPTER 1
LOOKING AT AFRICA

Lesson 1: The Land of Africa

FIND THE WORDS

source   rift valley

Africa is a continent that lies south of Europe and east of South America. Africa is almost twice as large as South America, Tunis is a city in northern Africa. It is almost 8000 kilometers (5000 miles) from Cape Town, a city at the southern tip of the continent. At their widest points, Africa is about twice as wide as the United States. Among the continents, only Asia is larger than Africa.

Like the other continents, Africa is almost surrounded by seas and oceans. The Mediterranean Sea separates Africa from Europe. The Atlantic Ocean lies between Africa and South America. The Indian Ocean borders the eastern coast of Africa. The Red Sea separates Africa from the Arabian Peninsula of Asia. Only the small Sinai Peninsula joins Africa to Asia.

Africa has a very smooth coastline compared to other continents, especially Europe. Gulfs and bays cut deeply into Europe. Thus, no European nation is very far from the sea. Some African nations are far from the sea, so they have no ports. Sailing and fishing have been less important in Africa than in Europe.

The oceans may not be so important to the people of Africa. But rivers are very significant to many Africans. The Nile River is the world's longest river. Its main **source,** or beginning, is Lake Victoria in eastern Africa. Lake Victoria lies on the equator. From there, the Nile flows more than 6400 kilometers (4000 miles) north. It empties into the Mediterranean Sea. Millions of people live along the banks of the Nile. Many use its water to irrigate their crops. The Congo River flows through Africa near the equator. It empties into the Atlantic Ocean. This river is used for transportation and fishing and to generate electricity. Rainfall is heavy in this part of Africa. Thus, the people of the area do not have to use the Congo for irrigation. In western Africa, the Niger (NY jur) River is used for transportation. In southern Africa, the Zambezi (zam BEE zee) River is used to produce electricity. Find these rivers on the map on page 332.

Mount Kilimanjaro (KIL uh mun JAHR oh) is the highest mountain in Africa. It is almost 5900 meters (19,340 feet) above sea level. Mount Kilimanjaro is near the equator. But the air gets colder at higher elevations. So its peak is covered by snow and ice all year. Several other mountains in eastern Africa are more than 4600 meters (15,000 feet) high. They, too, are covered by snow and ice.

The continent of Africa does not have many mountains. It does not have a major mountain range. There is nothing in Africa like the Rocky Mountains of North America. Instead, Africa has many plateaus. As you have learned, plateaus are areas of land that are flat, but high. Many plateaus have steep cliffs at their edges. Much of eastern and southern Africa is plateau land. At the rims of these plateaus, cliffs plunge down to the sea. Smaller and lower plateau areas cover parts of western and northern Africa, too. Though it has plateaus, Africa lacks huge plains like those of North America and Asia.

The Great Rift Valley is one of the most unusual landforms in Africa. A **rift valley** is a long valley with steep sides. It is a deep split in Earth's surface. The Great Rift Valley is very wide and deep. It is 2900 kilometers (1800 miles) long.

Egypt's Suez Canal is 162 kilometers (101 miles) long. It joins the Red Sea with the Mediterranean. Today, it is one of the world's busiest shipping lanes. Over 60 ships a day pass through its waters. Most of them are large oil tankers. The canal is the fastest route between Europe and the East.

Construction began on the Suez Canal in 1859. It took 10 years to build. The canal was officially opened on November 17, 1869.

The Red Sea fills part of the Great Rift Valley. So do Lake Tanganyika (TANG guh NYEE kuh) and Lake Nyasa (ny ASS uh) in eastern Africa. Lake Tanganyika is more than 1430 meters (4700 feet) deep. It is one of the deepest lakes in the world. Lake Victoria, Africa's largest lake, does not lie in the Great Rift Valley. It is a shallow lake. Some other African lakes do not have much water in them except after heavy rains. Many are dry for several months each year. Lake Chad is such a lake.

As you study Africa, remember what you have learned about Africa's landforms, rivers, and lakes. They have had a great influence on Africa's history and cultures.

REVIEW

CHECK YOUR FACTS

1. What four bodies of water surround Africa?
2. Name four of the important rivers of Africa.
3. What is the highest mountain in Africa?
4. What is one of the most unusual landforms in Africa?
5. Name Africa's largest lake.

THINK ABOUT IT

The Nile River flows from south to north. Some people seem to think that rivers cannot flow north because north is "up." Explain the difference between *north* and *up*.

Lesson 2: Climates of Africa

The equator passes through the middle of Africa. Thus, much of the continent receives direct, strong rays from the sun during most of the year. That is why some places in Africa are almost always warm or hot. But still there are several different climate areas in Africa. As you study these areas in this lesson, look at the climate map on page 338.

The Sahara (suh HAR uh) is a great desert in northern Africa. The world's highest temperatures occur there. Daytime temperatures sometimes reach 54°C (130°F). But nights are cool in the desert. In winter, freezing temperatures have been recorded there. Little rain falls in the Sahara. Thus, only a few plants can grow there. Parts of the desert are seas of sand. Other parts are fields of stone. It is hard for people to exist in the Sahara. Even so, some people make a living there by herding animals. Also, petroleum has been discovered in the Sahara. That will bring more people into this hot, dry land.

North of the Sahara are small areas with a pleasant Mediterranean climate. There, winters are mild and wet. Summers are warm and dry. Steppes, or dry grasslands, lie south of the Sahara. Winters on the steppes are warm. Summers are very hot. Rainfall is light. Sometimes, no rain falls for months or even years. A long period of time without rain is called a **drought** (DROWT). During a drought, crops, animals, and even people may die.

More rain usually falls south of the steppes in Africa. Savanna areas begin to appear. **Savannas** are the same as tropical grasslands. They have thick grasses and some trees. Savannas are found north and south of the equator in Africa. Temperatures in the savannas are hot throughout the year. However, savanna areas have a wet season and a dry season. As a rule, little rain falls from October through April. There is much rain during July and August.

Much of the middle of Africa is covered by tropical rain forests. In tropical rain forests, it is always hot and wet. The ground is thickly covered with trees and plants. You might think that the highest temperatures in the world would occur in this area near the equator.

CLIMATES OF AFRICA

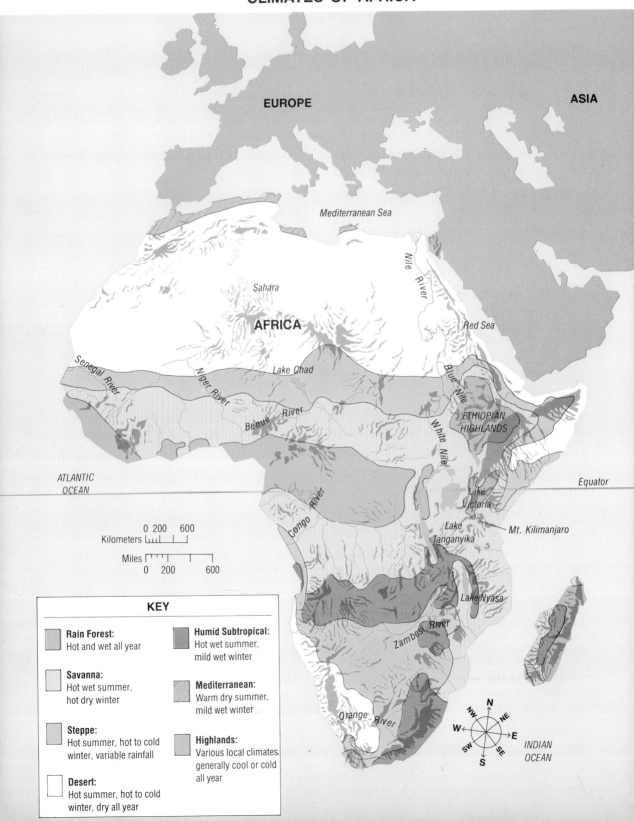

EUROPE

ASIA

Mediterranean Sea

Nile River

Sahara

AFRICA

Red Sea

Senegal River

Niger River

Lake Chad

Benue River

Blue Nile

ETHIOPIAN HIGHLANDS

White Nile

ATLANTIC OCEAN

Equator

Congo River

Lake Victoria

Lake Tanganyika

Mt. Kilimanjaro

0   200   600
Kilometers ⊔⊔⊔⊔ ⊔ ⊔

Miles
0   200   600

Lake Nyasa

Zambesi River

KEY

Rain Forest:
Hot and wet all year

Humid Subtropical:
Hot wet summer,
mild wet winter

Savanna:
Hot wet summer,
hot dry winter

Mediterranean:
Warm dry summer,
mild wet winter .

Steppe:
Hot summer, hot to cold
winter, variable rainfall

Highlands:
Various local climates,
generally cool or cold
all year

Desert:
Hot summer, hot to cold
winter, dry all year

Orange River

N
NW   NE
W   E
SW   SE
S

INDIAN OCEAN

Left: A savanna area in Zambia. *Right:* A desert landscape in Sudan.

But that is not true. Temperatures in desert areas, such as the Sahara, are often much higher.

South of the rain forests in Africa are more areas of savanna, steppe, and desert. There are also large areas with a humid subtropical climate. The weather there is much like that of the South in the United States. A small area of Mediterranean climate lies at the southern tip of Africa.

In eastern Africa, there are several areas with highland climates.

Many people prefer to live in these highlands. The weather there is cooler and drier than in nearby areas at lower elevations. Addis Ababa (AD iss AB uh buh) is a city in Ethiopia in eastern Africa. It is located just north of the equator. But it is about 2440 meters (8000 feet) above sea level. So temperatures in Addis Ababa are only around 16°C (60°F) all year. If this city were at sea level, its temperatures would be 8 to 11°C (15 to 20°F) higher.

REVIEW

CHECK YOUR FACTS

1. Why are some areas of Africa almost always warm or hot?
2. What is the weather usually like in the Sahara?
3. What two areas of Africa have a Mediterranean climate?

4. Describe two ways the savannas differ from the steppes.
5. What is a tropical rain forest like?

THINK ABOUT IT

Were you surprised to find out that Africa has many different climates? How did you picture most of Africa? Why?

Lesson 3: Peoples and Nations of Africa

Almost 500 million people live in Africa. Africa's population is not evenly distributed, or arranged, across the land. Look at the population map of Africa on page 341. You will see that many Africans live along the coasts. Many also live in the Nile River valley and in the highlands in eastern Africa. Few Africans live in the desert areas.

Some people who know little about Africa seem to think that Africa's peoples are all alike. That is not true. There are many differences among the peoples of Africa.

Many Africans have dark skin. But you can see in pictures in this unit that all Africans are not Black. Africa's population includes people of all skin colors, all kinds of hair, and all kinds of faces. The people of Africa dress in many different ways. They eat many different foods.

More than 800 languages are spoken in Africa. Some languages are used by only a few hundred people. Other languages, such as Hausa (HOU suh) and Swahili (swah HEE lee), are spoken by millions of Africans. Many Africans speak at least two languages. Some speak three or even four languages. European languages, especially French and English, are widely spoken in Africa. That is because France and Britain once controlled large areas of the African continent.

With so many languages, many Africans have trouble understanding each other. Often, many different languages are spoken in one nation. The many languages of Africa make it hard for Africans to communicate with each other. They also make it hard for some of Africa's leaders to unite their nations and make them stronger.

There are more nations in Africa than in any other continent in the world. Look at the map on page 333. You will find that there are more than 50 nations in Africa. Some African nations are very small. For example, Gambia (GAM bee uh) is smaller than the state of Connecticut. However, many African nations are large in both area and population. Zaire (zah IR) is more than four times the size of France. Nigeria (ny JIR ee uh) has more people than Italy.

Often, the people living within the borders of one African nation are very different from one another. Sudan (soo DAN) is Africa's largest nation in area. Its people speak several different languages.

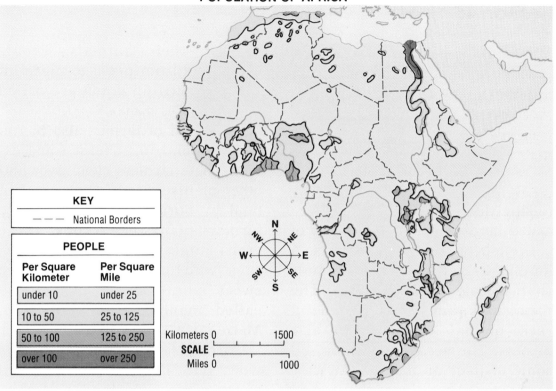

KEY

- - - National Borders

PEOPLE

Per Square Kilometer	Per Square Mile
under 10	under 25
10 to 50	25 to 125
50 to 100	125 to 250
over 100	over 250

Kilometers 0 — 1500
SCALE
Miles 0 — 1000

Islam is the most important religion in northern Sudan. However, Christianity is widespread in the southern part of the country. Most of the Sudanese people living in the north have lighter-colored skin than the southerners. The northerners are much like the Arab people who live in Egypt and Saudi Arabia.

REVIEW

CHECK YOUR FACTS

1. About how many languages are spoken in Africa?
2. Name two major African languages.
3. Why do many Africans speak English or French?

4. What problems does the existence of many languages cause in Africa?

THINK ABOUT IT

Why do people who are different from one another sometimes have trouble getting along with one another?

Lesson 4: Agriculture in Africa

FIND THE WORDS

herder   herd   nomad   yam
cassava   manioc   maize
fallow   shifting cultivation
rotate   cacao

Many Africans make a living by raising animals. These people are called **herders.** They raise herds of cattle, sheep, camels, or goats. A **herd** is a group of large animals that are all the same kind. The meat, milk, and hides of some of these animals are used by their owners. The herders trade or sell some of their animals. That way, they can get things they need but cannot make for themselves. Most herders live in dry areas. Thus, they must move often to find fresh grass and enough water for their animals. People who move from place to place instead of settling down are called **nomads** (NOH madz).

One kind of farmer also has to move around to at least some extent. These farmers clear trees and other plants from a small piece of land by burning them. Then, the farmers plant their crops. These crops might include yams, cassava, and maize. **Yams** are like sweet potatoes. **Cassava,** also called **manioc,** is a root crop. **Maize** (MAYZ) is corn.

After a few years, the land is worn out. The farmers move to another piece of land and then clear and plant it. The first field is allowed to lie **fallow,** or at rest. After a time, it recovers its fertility. Then it can be used again.

Some Africans herd cattle today just as their ancestors did.

RESOURCES OF AFRICA

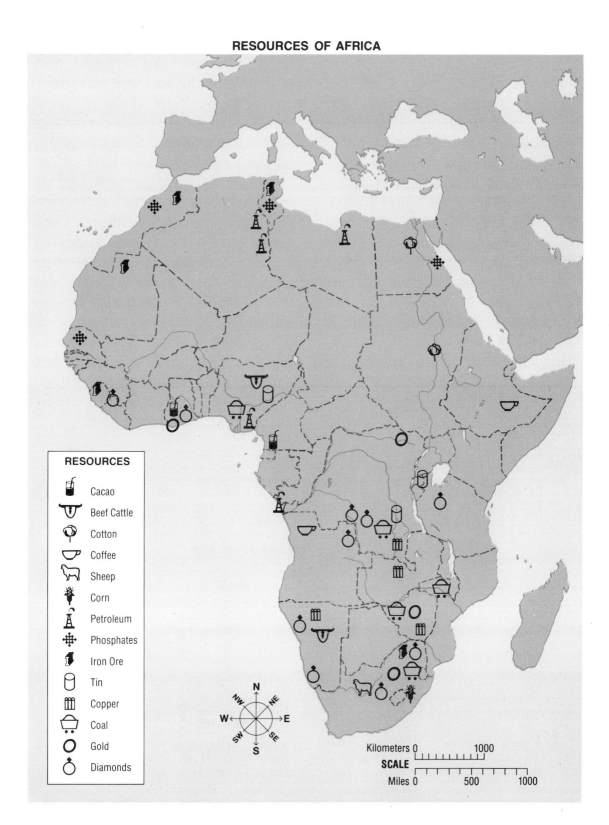

RESOURCES

	Cacao
	Beef Cattle
	Cotton
	Coffee
	Sheep
	Corn
	Petroleum
	Phosphates
	Iron Ore
	Tin
	Copper
	Coal
	Gold
	Diamonds

N
NW   NE
W   E
SW   SE
S

Kilometers 0 |||||||||| 1000

SCALE

Miles 0 |||| 500 |||| 1000

This kind of farming is called **shifting cultivation.** It produces food with not too much work. The burning fertilizes the land. The ash is good fertilizer. The fallow time also helps keep the land fertile. But shifting cultivation takes a great deal of land. That is because so much land must lie fallow. This kind of farming cannot produce enough food for a growing population.

Permanent agriculture is found in most parts of Africa. In permanent agriculture, farmers use the same fields over and over again. However, they may **rotate,** or change, the crops grown on a particular field. This method helps restore fertility, much like letting the land go fallow. That is because different crops take different minerals out of the soil and put different ones back in. Usually, more people live in areas of permanent agriculture. That is because the farmers produce more food.

Some African farmers use the most modern and efficient ways of raising crops and animals. There are huge fruit orchards and vineyards along the coasts of northern and southern Africa. Cattle and wheat are raised on large ranches and farms. Coffee, sugar cane and cacao (kuh KAY oh) are grown on giant plantations. **Cacao** trees produce seeds used to make chocolate. These crops are sold almost everywhere.

REVIEW

WATCH YOUR WORDS

1. Chocolate is made from the seeds of ___.
   cacao   yams   maize

2. To change the crops grown on a certain field is to___them.
   transfer   revolve   rotate

3. People who keep moving from place to place are called___.
   nomads   cultivators   settlers

4. A field that is not being used is lying___.
   fertile   out   fallow

CHECK YOUR FACTS

Look at the Map

5. Are diamonds mined in southern Africa or northern Africa?

6. Where is cotton grown in Africa?

Look at the Lesson

7. How do the herders supply their needs?

8. Describe shifting cultivation.

THINK ABOUT IT

Most Africans make their living by herding or farming. What does this tell you about life in Africa? How does it compare to life in the United States?

CHAPTER REVIEW

WATCH YOUR WORDS

1. Corn is another name for____.
   yams   cacao   maize
2. The beginning of a river is its____.
   source   course   bank
3. A____ is a long period of time without rain.
   savanna   famine   drought
4. A sweet potato is a____.
   plantain   manioc   yam
5. A____ is a tropical grassland.
   savanna   steppe   plateau
6. A____ is a long valley with steep sides.
   savanna   rift valley
   tropical grassland
7. ____make a living by raising animals.
   Herders   Gatherers   Hunters
8. ____ are people who move from place to place instead of settling down.
   Herders   Nomads   Hunters
9. ____ trees produce seeds used to make chocolate.
   Yam   Cacao   Maize
10. A____ is a group of large animals.
    savanna   steppe   herd

CHECK YOUR FACTS

11. Why have rivers been more important to Africans than oceans have?
12. Name two major landforms in Africa.
13. Why is it hard for people to live in the Sahara?
14. What happens during a drought?
15. List five climate areas of Africa.
16. Why is communication a problem among Africans?

17. Why do herders move from place to place?
18. What is shifting cultivation?
19. List three farm products that Africa exports.
20. Why do farmers allow their fields to lie fallow?

USE YOUR MAPS

21. Look at the physical map of Africa on page 332. Where in Africa are there highlands more than 2000 meters (6600 feet) in height?
22. Look at the political map of Africa on page 333. Name two island nations off the African coast.
23. Look at the map of Africa's climates on page 338. Where are two desert areas in Africa?
24. Look at the population map of Africa on page 341. In what parts of Africa do many people live?
25. Look at the map of Africa's resources on page 343. In what parts of Africa is gold mined?

THINK ABOUT IT

26. Why is Africa a less-developed continent than Europe?
27. How is shifting cultivation different from permanent agriculture?
28. What landforms and what climate areas in Africa would you expect to be most densely populated?
29. Africa has many cultures, languages, and religions. What kinds of problems can this cause within and between nations?
30. What do you think is Africa's most serious problem?

2 THE HISTORY OF AFRICA

Lesson 1: Europeans Come to Africa

West African Empires

Several large empires developed in western Africa south of the Sahara. These empires had governments that could enforce rules and laws fairly. They developed systems of communication so that the rulers could know what was happening in their lands. Islamic schools educated government officials and others. These educated people had broad loyalties to the Islamic religion and to their empires. Greater unity brought organized trade between the parts of western Africa.

The empire of Ghana (GAH nuh) in western Africa reached its greatest power about the year 1000. The empires of Mali (MAH lee) and Songhai (SONG GY) followed it. All three were famous throughout the Islamic world.

The Islamic empires of western Africa south of the Sahara were rich and successful. While these empires were powerful, they protected their peoples.

Europeans Arrive

European contact with Africa began again after 1415. The Portuguese started to explore the African coast. By 1445, Portuguese sailors had reached the mouth of the Senegal (SEN uh GOL) River and Cape Verde (VURD). These areas were part of Black Africa.

By 1471, the Portuguese were at the Gold Coast on the Gulf of Guinea (GIN ee). In 1488, they sailed around the Cape of Good Hope at the southern tip of Africa. Finally, between 1497 and 1499, Vasco de Gama sailed from Portugal around Africa to India and back. Soon, the Portuguese controlled the coast of Africa from the Senegal River to the Red Sea. At this time, the Spanish were exploring the New World.

At first, the Portuguese were only interested in sailing around Africa to get to India. But they soon discovered that there was gold in western Africa. They traded cloth and other goods for the gold. Ships from other European nations soon followed the routes of the Portuguese. The trade in Black slaves soon became more important than gold.

In the 1500s, ships sailed from Africa packed with Black slaves.

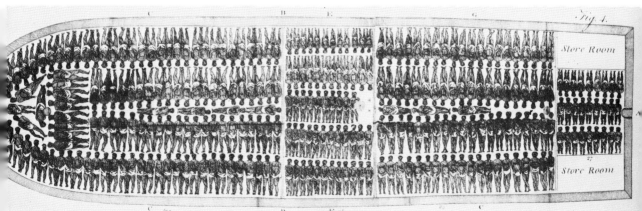

The African Slave Trade

In the 1500s, the Europeans became more interested in Africa. At that time, many European nations were developing sugar plantations in the tropical regions of the Americas. It took many workers to plant and harvest sugar cane. The Europeans were not willing to do such work. There were not many native peoples in the parts of the New World where sugar was produced. So a new source of workers was needed. About 1510, the Portuguese started trading in slaves. They would get Black slaves in western Africa. Then they would take them by force in ships to colonies in the New World. At first, these slaves were taken to the Spanish colonies in the West Indies. Later, other Europeans started shipping slaves to other colonies in the New World.

Britain may have transported more slaves than any other nation. This was because the British navy and British merchant ships controlled the seas.

Most of the slaves came from an area of western Africa that came to be known as the Slave Coast. This was the land between the Gold Coast and the Niger River. This area could provide many Black slaves because it had a large population.

How did the Europeans get slaves? They usually bought them from African kings or merchants. The Africans who lived along the Slave Coast wanted European goods. The Europeans would trade cloth, metal tools, liquor, and guns for slaves. Before, the Africans had bought these goods with gold. As the demand for workers in the New World increased, slaves were exchanged for the European goods.

At first, the slaves sold to the Europeans were probably already slaves in their own communities. Then the Europeans wanted more and more slaves. So free people from other communities were captured and sold into slavery. Some Africans who lived near the coast bought guns from the Europeans. They used the guns to capture people who lived farther inland. By the 1700s, cities along the coast were the centers of power in western Africa. These cities grew rich because of the slave trade. There was also slave trading in southern and eastern Africa.

The slave trade was very profitable to the Europeans and Africans who controlled it. At first, Europeans did not object to it. But the cruelty of the trade began to offend many people. At last, some people, especially in Britain, spoke out against it. British courts ruled in 1772 that slavery did not exist under British law. In 1807, a

African villages were raided to fill the Europeans' demand for slaves.

new British law went into effect. This law made it illegal for the British to take part in the slave trade. In 1811, another such law was passed. It imposed heavy penalties on those caught trading slaves. After 1811, the British withdrew from the slave trade.

The slave trade became illegal in the United States in 1808. It was outlawed by Denmark in 1804 and by the Netherlands in 1814. By the mid-1800s, it was against the law in almost every European nation to carry slaves across the Atlantic.

REVIEW

CHECK YOUR FACTS

1. Why were Europeans interested in getting slaves?

2. Why did Britain transport more slaves than any other nation?

3. What part of Africa did most slaves come from?

4. What part did the African kings and merchants play in the slave trade?

5. When did the slave trade become illegal in Britain? In the United States?

THINK ABOUT IT

Why did it take so long, for people to take action against the slave trade?

Lesson 2: European Colonization of Africa

Since the 1400s, there had been European trading posts along the coast of Africa. But European power rarely stretched very far inland. Then, in the 1800s, a number of European nations began to carve almost all of Africa into colonies. These European nations were Britain, France, Belgium, Germany, Italy, and Portugal.

In 1880, the French had important settlements and much power in northern and western Africa. British influence was growing along the Gold Coast and at the southern tip of Africa. Portuguese control on both coasts of southern Africa also began to expand. By 1900, almost all of Africa was under European control. Only Ethiopia (EE thee OH pee uh) and Liberia (ly BIR ee uh) were still independent nations.

At first, there was little to be gained from most of the African colonies. The European nations wanted colonies because they might be valuable in the future. They also wanted to keep rival nations from getting the colonies. In the beginning, the ideal colony was simply one that supported itself. No nation wanted a colony that would cost much money to control.

Later, the European nations started to spend more money on their colonies. More money was spent until all of the territory of each colony was under the parent country's control.

Look at the map of Africa in 1939 on page 351. You can see that almost the whole continent was then under European rule.

Though the European countries divided Africa into colonies, not many Europeans actually went there to work and live. With so few Europeans living there, the European nations could not long control their African colonies.

In this cartoon, Europeans gobble up Africa.

AFRICA IN 1939

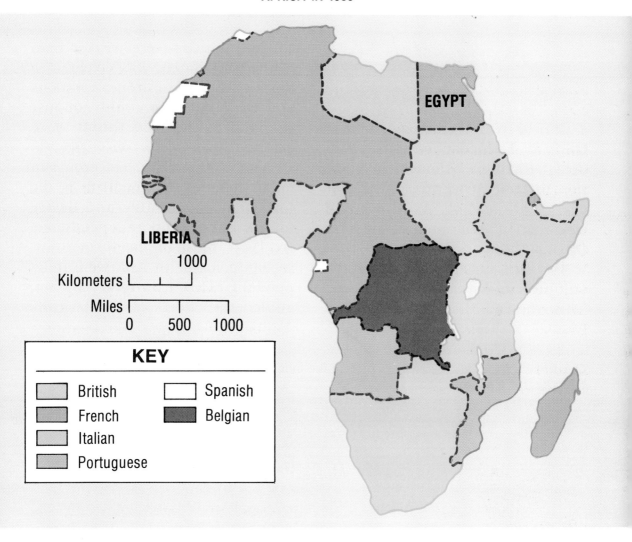

EGYPT

LIBERIA

0   1000
Kilometers

Miles

0   500   1000

KEY

British | Spanish
French | Belgian
Italian
Portuguese

REVIEW

CHECK YOUR FACTS

1. When did Europeans first establish trading posts along the coast of Africa?

2. When did European nations begin to divide Africa into colonies?

3. Which European nations set up colonies in Africa?

4. What two African nations were still independent in 1900?

5. At first, why did European countries want African colonies?

THINK ABOUT IT

Why did so few Europeans go to the middle part of Africa to live?

Lesson 3: African Independence

FIND THE WORDS

nationalism   boycott   apartheid

World War II changed forever the way European nations could deal with their colonies. In addition to their African colonies, several nations of Europe had colonies in Asia and elsewhere. During the war, Japan took control of British, French, and Dutch colonies in Asia and the Pacific. This showed that the European colonial nations were weaker than in the past. Japan was defeated in the war. But the European nations and their colonies could not just go back to the way things were before.

Also, nationalism had grown in many colonies. **Nationalism** is the love of one's country and desire for its power and independence. By 1960, most of the former European colonies in Asia were independent. This example, in part, guided the efforts of the Africans

Queen Elizabeth II at a ceremony marking the independence of Nigeria.

TIME LINE: AFRICAN INDEPENDENCE

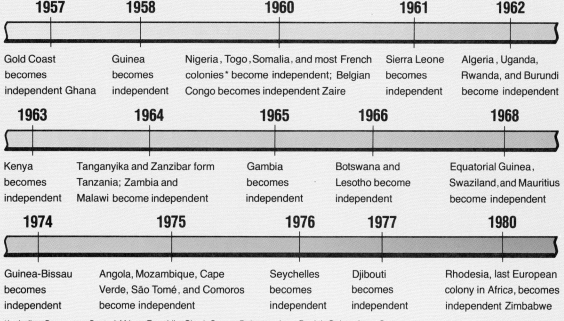

1957 — Gold Coast becomes independent Ghana

1958 — Guinea becomes independent

1960 — Nigeria, Togo, Somalia, and most French colonies* become independent; Belgian Congo becomes independent Zaire

1961 — Sierra Leone becomes independent

1962 — Algeria, Uganda, Rwanda, and Burundi become independent

1963 — Kenya becomes independent

1964 — Tanganyika and Zanzibar form Tanzania; Zambia and Malawi become independent

1965 — Gambia becomes independent

1966 — Botswana and Lesotho become independent

1968 — Equatorial Guinea, Swaziland, and Mauritius become independent

1974 — Guinea-Bissau becomes independent

1975 — Angola, Mozambique, Cape Verde, São Tomé, and Comoros become independent

1976 — Seychelles becomes independent

1977 — Djibouti becomes independent

1980 — Rhodesia, last European colony in Africa, becomes independent Zimbabwe

*Including Cameroon, Central African Republic, Chad, Congo, Dahomey (now Benin), Gabon, Ivory Coast, Madagascar, Mali, Mauritania, Niger, Senegal, and Upper Volta.

to become independent.

World War II changed the ways in which Africans viewed the Europeans and themselves. In the war, African soldiers had fought alongside European soldiers. Africa's resources brought high prices during the war. This increased Africa's prosperity and ability to buy European goods.

The United Nations was founded in 1945. This new world organization was designed to promote peace, equality, and economic development among all nations. Many Africans looked to it with hope. So the situation and attitudes of Africans had changed.

But political change was slow to come.

The British colony of the Gold Coast was the first European colony in Black Africa to gain independence. The Gold Coast became the independent nation of Ghana in 1957.

This is the story of how Ghana became an independent nation. In 1948, the people of the Gold Coast began to boycott European goods. A **boycott** is a refusal to buy something. It is a peaceful form of protest. The British government investigated the reasons for the boycott. It was clear that the Africans were tired of being ruled by

353

The flag of Guinea-Bissau is raised to celebrate the nation's independence from Portugal.

the British.

A new constitution had been put into effect in the Gold Coast in 1947. This basic law gave Black Africans a majority in the government of a colony for the first time.

But the people of the Gold Coast were not satisfied. They no longer wanted to be a colony of Britain. Another constitution was written. Ghana became completely independent in 1957.

Before independence, British officials ruled the people of Ghana. Ghana's laws were approved by the British. Ghana's government, economy, and relations with other nations were controlled by Britain.

Getting independence meant that the people of Ghana could now rule themselves. They could set up their government and make their laws. They could run their economy. They could deal with other nations as an equal.

The peoples of the other European colonies in Africa also began to think about independence. The other British colonies soon became free. The French colonies also moved toward independence.

It took some colonies longer to become free. Algeria (al JIR ee uh) had to fight a long war against the French before becoming a nation in 1962. The Belgian government had not prepared its colony in the Congo for independence. The Congo (now Zaire) became independent in 1960. But there was a lot of fighting among groups within the Congo. These groups had long distrusted each other. There was no strong central government to keep peace among them.

It was not until 1980 that Black Africans came to control Zimbabwe (zim BAHB way), formerly Rhodesia (roh DEE zhuh).

Rhodesia had been the last important European colony in Africa. Look at the time line of African independence on page 353.

One of the problems of African independence has been the relations between different Black groups in the new nations. Often, one nation contains many different culture groups. Often, too, members of one culture group are split between two or more nations.

Also, there are still problems between Whites and Blacks in Africa. South Africa is the only African nation in which there are large numbers of White people. South Africa became self-governing in the early 1900s. But the government has always been run by the Whites. This is true even though there are many more Black people than White people in South Africa.

South Africa has a system of laws that keeps Black people separate from White people. These laws deny Black people equal rights. This system of laws in South Africa is called **apartheid** (uh PAHRT HYT). This word means "apartness." Other African nations oppose South Africa. But South Africa has strong military forces. The conflict between White South Africans and the Blacks of South Africa and elsewhere will probably long continue.

REVIEW

CHECK YOUR FACTS

1. What was the first European colony in Black Africa to become an independent nation?

2. What nation controlled European colonies in Asia during World War II? What did African colonies learn from this?

3. When was the United Nations founded?

4. The European colonies in Africa (did/did not) become free all at the same time.

5. What was the last important European colony in Africa to gain its independence?

THINK ABOUT IT

Should a colonial power try to prepare its colonies for independence, step by step? Or should the colonial power grant independence quickly? Give reasons for your answer.

WATCH YOUR WORDS

1. The love of one's country and desire for its power and independence is ___.
   union apartheid nationalism
2. A ___ is a refusal to buy something.
   dispute boycott regulation
3. ___ means apartness.
   Independence Apartheid Nationalism

CHECK YOUR FACTS

4. To what religion were the West African empires loyal?
5. What three West African empires were famous in the Islamic world?
6. How were sugar and Black slavery connected?
7. Did any Africans benefit from the slave trade?
8. Africa was divided into colonies (before/after) 1800.
9. Which European nations set up colonies in Africa?
10. How did Algeria gain independence?

GET THE DATE STRAIGHT

Match the date with the event.

11. 1000 A. Portuguese started slave trade.
12. 1488 B. Modern Ghana gained independence.
13. 1510 C. Ancient empire of Ghana reached greatest power.
14. 1808 D. Black Africans gained control of Zimbabwe.
15. 1900 E. Slave trade became illegal in the United States.
16. 1957 F. Portuguese sailed around Cape of Good Hope.
17. 1980 G. Ethiopia and Liberia were the only independent African nations.

USE YOUR MAPS AND CHART

18. Look at the map of Africa in 1939 on page 351. What two nations controlled the most land?
19. Which African nations were independent in 1939?
20. Look at the time line on page 353. Which was the first African colony to become independent? Which was the last?
21. Look at the maps of Africa's nations on pages 333 and 351. What nation did the Belgian Congo become?
22. Find a nation made up of an Italian colony and a British colony.

THINK ABOUT IT

23. Why was most early European contact with Africa limited to northern and western Africa?
24. Why do you think we know little of Black Africa's history before 1415?
25. How would you feel if you lived in a colony controlled by another country?
26. How could modern communications, such as radio and television, help bring unity to Africa's nations?
27. Why is the history of Africa important to the history of our own nation?

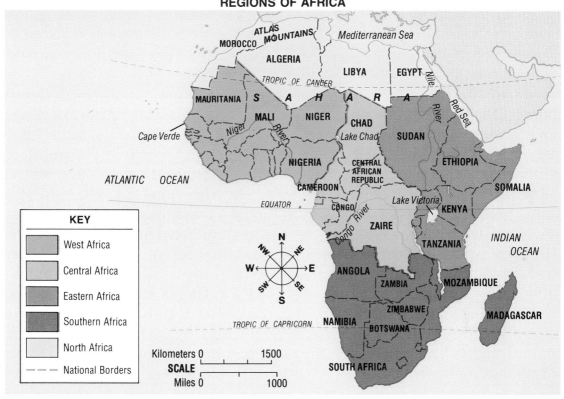

CHAPTER 3 REGIONS OF AFRICA

Lesson 1: West Africa

FIND THE WORD

erosion

Africa can be divided into five regions. They are West Africa, Central Africa, Eastern Africa, Southern Africa, and North Africa. The map on this page shows the regions and nations within each region. In this chapter, you will learn about each of the five regions of Africa.

West Africa stretches south and west from the southern edge of the Sahara to the Atlantic Ocean. Cape Verde is the westernmost point on the Atlantic coast. Lake

Chad is West Africa's eastern boundary. West Africa contains 16 nations. They range in size from the tiny island nation of Cape Verde to the large nation of Nigeria. The nations of West Africa cover about one-fifth of Africa's total area. About one-third of Africa's people live there.

Mauritania (MOR i TAY nee uh), Mali, Niger, and Upper Volta are the poorest nations in West Africa. They are also among the poorest nations in the world. Once, the rich and powerful empires of Ghana, Mali, and Songhai ruled in this area. But today, these four nations find it hard to feed, clothe, and house their peoples.

These four nations have few resources. Their environment is being made even worse by drought and erosion. **Erosion** is the washing and blowing away of the soil. Steadily, the Sahara advances south. These four nations are trying to build industries, highways, and modern cities. But their future probably depends on improvements in their agriculture. They must have better seeds, more irrigation, and better ways of selling crops. The outlook for Mauritania, Mali, Niger, and Upper Volta is not bright.

Along the Atlantic coast of West Africa between Mauritania and Nigeria are 10 small nations. Going south from Mauritania, these nations include Senegal, Gambia, Guinea-Bissau (GIN ee bi SOW), Guinea, Sierra Leone (see EHR uh lee OHN), Liberia, Ivory Coast, Ghana, Togo, and Benin (beh NEEN). The nation of Cape Verde is a group of islands. They lie in the Atlantic off a point of land in Senegal called Cape Verde.

In this part of West Africa, most of the land is tropical rain forest and savanna. Farming is the most important economic activity in the 10 small nations. Abidjan (AB i JAHN) in the Ivory Coast and Dakar (dah KAHR) in Senegal are cities on the Atlantic coast. These cities have about 1 million people each. However, in this part of West Africa, most of the people live in towns and villages. Many of the 10 small nations have been troubled by unstable governments and by poverty. As in the West African nations to the north, their future does not seem very bright.

Nigeria

Nigeria is the most important nation of West Africa. It is one of the leading nations on the whole continent. Nigeria has more people than any other nation in Africa. Indeed, Nigeria's population of more than 74 million makes it the 10th-largest country in the world. In Africa, only South Africa has a more productive economy than Nigeria. Only Libya (LIB ee

The leaders of the Yoruba in Nigeria.

uh) produces more petroleum.

Nigeria has about 250 ethnic groups. Each group has its own language and culture. The three largest groups are the Hausa, Yoruba (YOH roo bah), and Ibo (EE boh). Together, they make up more than half the population.

The Hausa live in northern Nigeria. Many also live in the nearby nations of Niger and Chad. Most of the Hausa are farmers.

The Yoruba live in southwestern Nigeria. There are also many in Benin and Togo west of Nigeria. Many Yoruba live in cities.

The Ibo dominate south-central Nigeria. Many also live elsewhere in the country. Many Ibo became very European in culture when Nigeria was a British colony. Many had important jobs in business and government.

English is the official language of Nigeria. That means it is used by the government and is taught in the schools. Most Nigerians speak one of the 250 African languages plus English. The half of the population who are Muslims also know Arabic. Arabic is the language of Islam. About one-third of the Nigerians are Christians. African religions also have a strong influence on all Nigerians.

The many different groups in Nigeria have kept the country from being truly united. In 1851, the British seized the city of Lagos (LAY GOSS). Lagos is now the capital and largest city of Nigeria. By 1914, the British united all of Nigeria under their rule. But there was conflict between the many different groups in the colony. In 1960, Nigeria became independent.

A Nigerian city with its old protective wall.

Today, Nigeria is a leading producer of petroleum. The money earned from selling petroleum is being used to build factories and schools. Nigeria's cities, especially Lagos, are becoming crowded. However, most Nigerians live in rural villages. They make a living by farming, fishing, or herding. Nigeria's farmers produce cacao, peanuts, palm oil, and rubber for export. Farms are small, and farming methods are old-fashioned. Nigeria's farmers do not grow enough food to feed the nation's people. Nigeria buys most of its manufactured goods from other nations.

Nigeria has good resources for the future. Petroleum, tin, and wood can be exported. The country has enough rain and good land to produce crops for export and for food. The Niger and Benue (BAYN WAY) rivers and Lake Chad are important water resources. Nigeria has rich sources of fish.

REVIEW

CHECK YOUR FACTS

1. Name the five regions of Africa.
2. What is the northern boundary of West Africa?
3. What two problems are making the environment worse in Mauritania, Mali, Niger, and Upper Volta?
4. Name two large cities on the Atlantic coast of West Africa.
5. What is the most important nation of West Africa?

THINK ABOUT IT

In what ways can nature be a friend or an enemy?

Lesson 2: Central Africa

FIND THE WORDS

manganese   falls   rapids
hydroelectric power

The region of Central Africa lies near the equator in the heart of the continent. Yet the region's central location has not made it as important as you might think. Today, Central Africa is probably the least known of the five regions of Africa.

Central Africa includes the large nations of Chad, Cameroon, the Central African Republic, Gabon (ga BOHN), Congo, and Zaire. The tiny nations of Equatorial Guinea and São Tomé (soun too MEH) and Príncipe (PREEN see puh) are also part of the region. Central Africa, with its eight nations, is more than half as large as the United States. That means the United States is almost twice as large as Central Africa. However, the population of the United States is almost five times larger than the population of Central Africa! Thus, you can see that Central Africa is sparsely populated. Gabon has only about 2 people per square kilometer (3 per square mile).

Much of Central Africa consists of flat and swampy plateaus. There are also hills and mountains throughout this region, especially around its edges. The Ruwenzori (ROO wun ZOR ee) Mountains stretch along the border between Zaire and Uganda. They are more than 4000 meters (13,000 feet) high. However, most of the land in Central Africa is lower than 900 meters (3000 feet).

Tropical rain forests cover much of the land in Central Africa. Wood is an important export for this region. Central Africa sells expensive woods like mahogany (muh HOG uh nee) and ebony (EB uh nee). The region also produces cheaper woods used to make plywood and paper. Minerals are even more important than wood to the economy of Central Africa. Gabon produces petroleum and manganese (MANG guh NEEZ). **Manganese** is a metal used in some steels. The Central African Republic exports diamonds. Cameroon has some bauxite (BAWK SYT), the ore from which aluminum is made. Zaire, the largest nation of the region, has the most minerals.

Zaire

The nation of Zaire has rich, vast resources. Forests cover much of the country. Zaire is one of the world's major producers of copper,

A dam on a tributary of the Congo River in Zaire.

diamonds for use in industry, and cobalt, a rare metal. However, Zaire's greatest resource is the Congo (Zaire) River. This river carries more water than any other river in Africa. It drains much of Central Africa, where the rainfall is heavy. However, the Congo has many falls and rapids. At **falls,** rivers drop suddenly as over a cliff. **Rapids** are rocky places in rivers. The Congo's falls and rapids limit its use for transportation.

The Congo River is capable of producing more hydroelectric power than any other river in the world. **Hydroelectric power** is electric energy produced by water. The river flows steadily throughout the year. There are many good places along the river for building dams like the one shown above. Electricity is produced by power plants at such dams. It will flow to Zaire's copper mines and metal industries. It will provide power to Zaire's cities, especially Kinshasa. Many years and much money will be needed to fully develop this hydroelectric power.

Kinshasa is Zaire's capital and largest city. More than 2 million people live there. Kinshasa is a modern industrial city. Clothing, chemicals, food products, and other goods are produced there.

Zaire has huge mining, forestry, and hydroelectric industries. It has a large capital city. But most of Zaire's people are still farmers who live in small villages. Most Zairians raise cassava, bananas, and corn and other grains on their own land. Some work on large plantations that produce palm oil, coffee, and cacao. Despite all this farming, Zaire still imports large amounts of food. This is because Zairian agriculture is not very productive or efficient. Zaire's government hopes to improve farming. That will make the nation more self-sufficient.

Since independence, Zaire has been a troubled nation. Producing enough food has been a problem. Transportation and communication are difficult in such a huge country. Many different groups of people live within Zaire's borders. Some groups have tried to split off from Zaire and set up their own nations. This has caused a lot of fighting. Zaire has great resources. It may become wealthy if it can survive as a united nation.

REVIEW

WATCH YOUR WORDS

1. ___ is a metal used in the production of steel.
   Bauxite Coal Manganese
2. Rivers drop suddenly at___.
   glaciers falls rapids

CHECK YOUR FACTS

3. What imaginary line runs through Central Africa?

4. Central Africa is (densely/sparsely) populated.
5. What resource is found in the tropical rain forests?
6. What important minerals are produced in Zaire?
7. What is Zaire's most valuable natural resource?

THINK ABOUT IT

Is it better for a nation to be dependent and safe or to be independent and insecure?

Lesson 3: Eastern Africa

The region of Eastern Africa has three main parts. It includes the large nation of Sudan, the nations of the Horn of Africa, and the nations of East Africa proper.

Sudan

The nation of Sudan is so large that it really does not belong in just one African region. The northern part of Sudan is much like North Africa. However, southern Sudan is more like Central Africa or parts of West Africa.

Sudan is the largest nation in Africa. Alaska, Texas, and California could almost fit inside the borders of Sudan. It is about as far from northern Sudan to southern Sudan as it is from Boston, Massachusetts, to Miami, Florida. Because Sudan is so large, it has several different geographical areas. There is desert in the north. There is a huge area of swamp and marsh in the south. Few people live in these areas. Most of the Sudanese people live in the steppe and savanna areas in between.

Northern Sudan and southern Sudan are different in other ways besides their environments. The people living in northern Sudan are Arabs and Muslims. They are much like the people of North Africa. The northern Sudanese have ruled Sudan since it became independent in 1956.

The southern Sudanese people are more like the Blacks of Central Africa. Many are Christians. The southerners have had much less political power in Sudan. The south is poorer than the north. Some southerners wish to be independent from the north. Several times in the past, these differences have led to fighting between the north and the south. Today, Sudan's leaders face two major challenges. They must bring the Sudanese people together. And they must solve the problems in southern Sudan.

The Horn of Africa

Look at the map of Africa on page 332. Find the area in the northeast that juts out into the Indian Ocean. This area is called the Horn of Africa because of its shape. The nations of Ethiopia, Djibouti (ji BOO tee), and Somalia (soh MAH lee uh) lie on the Horn of Africa.

Ethiopia is an ancient nation. It has been in existence for thou-

Workers pick tea in Tanzania.

sands of years. Somalia and Djibouti are new nations. In recent years, there has been much fighting in this area. The part of Ethiopia along the Red Sea is called Eritrea (EHR i TREE uh). People there have been struggling for independence. Ethiopia and Somalia have fought over the Ogaden area along their border. Many people in the area have fled their homes. Fighting, disease, starvation, and drought have caused many deaths. True peace is not yet in sight.

Even in times of peace, life is hard for most people living in the Horn of Africa. High plateaus and mountains cut off much of the area from the world. Transporta-

tion and communication are difficult and expensive. Most of Somalia is desert or savanna land. In Somalia, most people live by herding. Ethiopia has better climates and soils. However, poor farming methods and soil erosion have limited progress in agriculture there. Few valuable minerals have been discovered in the Horn of Africa. The area has few forests.

East Africa

There are five nations in East Africa. Rwanda (roo AHN duh) and Burundi (boo ROON dee) are tiny in both land and population. Uganda (yoo GAN duh) is small in area but has 14 million people.

365

Tanzania (TAN zuh NEE uh) and Kenya have most of the land and people of East Africa.

East Africa is an area of plateaus, mountains, and lakes. Tourists visit East Africa to see wild animals in the national parks and game preserves. Most visitors enter East Africa through Nairobi (ny ROH bee), the capital city of Kenya.

Almost all of Tanzania is savanna land. The soils are poor there. They are badly eroded in some areas. **Tsetse** (SET see) **flies** infest more than half of the country. These insects carry **sleeping sickness** to people and cattle. This disease is serious and often causes death. So far, efforts to eliminate the tsetse fly have failed. Large areas of land in Tanzania remain unused because of this pest. Water and mineral resources are scarce in Tanzania. The people and the government are trying to develop modern agriculture and industry. However, these efforts have had only limited success so far.

Kenya borders Tanzania on the north. Unlike Tanzania, Kenya has a large urban center. This is Nairobi, the capital and largest city. About half of Kenya's industry is located in the Nairobi area. Kenya's most important farming areas are north and east of the city. Farms there produce Kenya's export crops of coffee, tea, and **pyrethrum** (py REE thrum), a flower used to make insecticide. Kenya's farmers also grow corn and rice for their own people. Tourists are important to Kenya's economy. They visit game parks to see wild animals. These include lions, giraffes, leopards, zebras, and elephants.

REVIEW

WATCH YOUR WORDS

1. A flower used to make insecticide is the ——.
   marigold pyrethrum manganese
2. The——spreads sleeping sickness.
   mosquito horse fly tsetse fly

CHECK YOUR FACTS

3. How do the people of northern and southern Sudan differ?

4. What ancient nation lies on the Horn of Africa?
5. Why is East Africa popular with tourists?

THINK ABOUT IT

Do you think the most serious problems of Eastern Africa are caused by people or by nature?

Lesson 4: Southern Africa

FIND THE WORDS

**highveld   segregated   pass
shantytown**

There are 10 nations on the mainland of Southern Africa. These are Angola, Zambia, Malawi, Mozambique, Zimbabwe, Botswana, Swaziland, Lesotho, and the Republic of South Africa. Namibia (nuh MIB ee uh), or South West Africa, is controlled by South Africa. There are also four island nations in the Indian Ocean off the coast of Southern Africa. These are Madagascar, Mauritius, Camoros, and Seychelles.

Southern Africa includes the wealthiest areas of the continent as well as some very poor ones. It has Africa's richest resources. But conflict between Blacks and Whites in the region is a continuing problem.

South Africa and Its Neighbors

Southern Africa is a plateau ringed by a narrow coastal plain. The plateau is highest near the coast of the Republic of South Africa. There it blends into the Drakensberg (DRAH kunz BURG) Mountains. The plateau area northwest of the Drakensberg

Zambian high school students walk by a newly built housing development.

Johannesburg is South Africa's largest city.

Gold is South Africa's most valuable mineral and its most important export. No other nation in the world produces as much gold as South Africa. Diamonds, coal, iron ore, and the metal chromium are also important resources in this mineral-rich nation.

Johannesburg is South Africa's largest city. More than 2 million people live there. Sometimes, Johannesburg is called the City of Gold. That is because gold mining is so important to the city's economy. Most of the mines are now outside the city. Johannesburg is by far the most important industrial city in Africa. It is the banking center of Southern Africa. Most of the national government's offices are located in the nearby city of Pretoria (pri TOHR ee uh).

South Africa is a **segregated** society. That means that people of different races live separately.

There are vast differences between Black South Africans and White South Africans. White South Africans control the national government. Black South Africans cannot vote or run for public office. The government decides where Black South Africans may work and live. There is a system of laws that seeks to control the Blacks and keep them apart from Whites. This system is called apartheid.

Because of apartheid, most

Mountains is called the **highveld** (HY VELT), which means high grassland. Most of the highveld in South Africa is covered by ranches. There, South Africans raise sheep and cattle. Much of the land on the coastal plain is farmed by Black South Africans. They raise corn and other food crops. These farmers are some of South Africa's poorest people.

What is so strange about the ruins of Zimbabwe in Southern Africa? These ruins are different from any in the world. Inside a maze of high walls are several buildings—all made of stone.

Yet old stone buildings are almost unheard of in Southern Africa. The usual building materials there were mud, poles, thatch, leaves, and animal skins. In addition, the masons of Zimbabwe used stone in a special way. They did not use mortar or even mud to hold it together.

Still, they were able to build walls 10 meters (32 feet) high. They made a cone-shaped tower of solid stone. Such a design is found nowhere else in the world. They made curving walls and built beautiful patterns into the stone.

This was all done just by fitting stones together perfectly.

Who were the builders of Zimbabwe? They were Bantu-speaking groups of Africans. These people came to the area in the 200s A.D. The stone buildings date from about 1200. The round walls and conical tower came later.

Black South Africans can get only hard and low-paying jobs. Many Blacks work in the gold mines.

Black South Africans are forced to live apart from the other groups in South Africa. Some live in shantytowns. **Shantytowns** are parts of African cities where the poor live in shacks. Many live in government housing on the outskirts of the cities. Many work in the cities. But they must get permission to travel and shop there. Everyone in South Africa must carry a card called a **pass.** It shows a person's name and address. The police use these passes to tell who has permission to be in different places. Those without passes can be fined or jailed.

In recent years, the South African government has been setting up Black homelands. It considers them independent nations. It considers many Black people to be citizens of these nations, not of South Africa. But these "nations" have little land, few resources, few jobs, and many people. This policy of the South African government is condemned around the world. No country in the world except South Africa accepts the Black homelands as real nations.

Other Nations of Southern Africa

North of South Africa are Zimbabwe (once called Rhodesia), Zambia, and Malawi. Zimbabwe and Zambia have rich mineral resources. Gold was formerly Zimbabwe's leading export. Now copper, asbestos, and chromium are more important. Copper is the most significant export in Zambia.

Like South Africa today, Rhodesia was ruled by a White minority until recently. There was much fighting between the Whites and Black rebels. In 1980, a government led by Blacks came to power in Rhodesia. The nation's name was changed to Zimbabwe.

Portuguese trading posts along the west and east coasts of Southern Africa eventually became the large colonies of Angola and Mozambique (MOH zam BEEK). The Black peoples of Angola and Mozambique were forced to work on plantations and in mines. Black forces in the two colonies began to fight for independence from Portugal in the 1960s. Both Angola and Mozambique became independent in 1975. Angola has rich mineral resources, including petroleum. Both nations have good farmland. But today, most people in Angola and Mozambique remain poor.

Madagascar

The nation and island of Madagascar (MAD uh GASS kur) lies in the Indian Ocean. It is about 386

A worker holding copper wire. Copper is a major export of Southern Africa.

kilometers (240 miles) east of the mainland of Southern Africa. Madagascar is the fourth-largest island in the world.

The majority of the people of Madagascar are of Black African background. They live along the coast. The Merina people live in the highlands in the middle of the country. They are of Indonesian background. All the people speak Malagasy, a language like Indonesian and Malay. Both Malagasy and French are official languages.

Look at the map on page 338. You will see that Madagascar has several different climates. Most of the people live by farming and herding. They produce rice for their own use and coffee and vanilla for export. Madagascar has little industry. Antananarivo, in the highlands, is the capital and largest city.

These women live in Madagascar. They use hollow bamboo poles to carry water from a stream.

REVIEW

WATCH YOUR WORDS

1. A ____ society separates people of different races.
   unified   segregated   classless

2. A ____ gives a person permission to be somewhere.
   pass   highveld   resource

CHECK YOUR FACTS

3. In what region are Africa's wealthiest areas found?

4. What is the main landform of Southern Africa?

5. What was Zimbabwe formerly called?

THINK ABOUT IT

Many nations refuse to do business with South Africa because of its apartheid policy. Do you think nations have a right to try to influence what goes on within another country's borders?

Lesson 5: North Africa

The region of North Africa stretches across the northern part of the continent from the Atlantic Ocean to the Red Sea. At the northern end of the Red Sea, North Africa is joined to the Sinai Peninsula of Southwest Asia. Across the Red Sea from North Africa is the Arabian Peninsula, also in Southwest Asia. North Africa and Southwest Asia are alike in many ways. The landforms, climates, peoples, cultures, languages, and religions of the two regions are all very similar. The area stretching from Libya in North Africa to Afghanistan in Southwest Asia is often called the Middle East.

Most of North Africa, as well as most of Southwest Asia, is desert. The desert can be farmed only where there is a supply of water to irrigate the land. Sometimes, there are streams and wells in the middle of the desert. Such a place is called an **oasis** (oh A sis). People settle in an oasis and raise crops and animals. Oases are scattered across North Africa. However, most North Africans live in two areas. One of these is along the coast of the Mediterranean Sea. There, the rainfall is heavier than in the desert. Many people also live along the Nile River in Egypt. They use the river's water to irrigate their lands.

Since ancient times, only herders have lived in the deserts of North Africa and Southwest Asia. Then, in this century, petroleum was discovered in the region. The money from petroleum exports has brought many changes. Many people who were once herders and rode camels now work in oil refineries and drive automobiles. North African nations such as Libya once were among the poorest nations in the world. Now they are among the richest nations. The map on page 287 shows the major petroleum-producing areas in North Africa and Southwest Asia. About one-third of the petroleum used in the United States comes from North Africa and Southwest Asia. We would find it hard to live without this energy resource.

The peoples of North Africa and Southwest Asia have used the money earned from selling petroleum in many ways. Cities have been built in places where there were none before. Old cities have grown and changed greatly. Such

The southern part of Algeria extends into the Sahara.

cities are now a mixture of old and new. Old markets can be seen not far from modern shopping centers. Homes that are centuries old stand near suburbs built within the past few years.

Whether old or new, all North African cities have at least one mosque. A **mosque** (MOSK) is an Islamic religious building. Islam is the main religion of North Africa.

The Maghreb Nations

In the western part of North Africa are the nations of Morocco, Algeria, and Tunisia (too NEE zhuh). The northern parts of these nations form an area called the Maghreb (MUG rub), which means "western island." It is called this because the area is like a green island in the brown desert sea of the Sahara.

The Maghreb nations grow wheat, olives, grapes, citrus fruit, and other crops. These are grown on the northwestern slopes of the Atlas Mountains and along the seacoast. These crops are exported to Europe.

The southern parts of Morocco, Algeria, and Tunisia extend into the Sahara. All three of these nations were colonies of France until after World War II. Algeria, where many Europeans lived, fought a

Pipelines carry oil throughout Algeria.

hope these educated people will return to help develop their nation. Money from petroleum is also spent to improve water supplies, transportation, and health care. However, much money is also spent on weapons and military forces. Libyan forces have been involved in struggles in nearby nations. Libya has also been in conflict with Egypt, its eastern neighbor. Egypt is the most important nation of North Africa. You will learn more about Egypt next.

Egypt

The Nile has always dominated the geography, history, culture, and economy of Egypt. The Nile River valley is like a long, thin oasis. It brings life to a desert area that would otherwise be dead.

Egypt has a warm climate. The Nile brings water and new soil. These things have made farming very successful in the Nile River valley and delta.

Most Egyptians live in the Nile River valley or in the Nile delta. But this land that the people live on is only 3.5 percent of all the land in Egypt. Almost all the rest of the land is desert.

The Sinai Peninsula in Southwest Asia is also part of Egypt. The Sinai is a desert with mountains in it.

bitter war for independence. Today, Algeria is an important producer of petroleum and natural gas.

Libya

The nation of Libya is larger than any country of Western Europe. However, only about 3 million people live there. Libya was one of the poorest countries in the world. Petroleum has made it a rich nation. Libya has sent many of its young people to colleges around the world. Some study in the United States. Libya's leaders

Farming is expanding and becoming more productive in Egypt. However, Egypt's population is large, and it is growing very fast. Farming is not improving as fast as the population is increasing. Egypt does not produce enough food to feed its people.

Today, Egypt's biggest export is raw cotton. Cotton is called raw before it has been made into cloth. Egypt's second most important export is cloth.

Water is the key to Egypt's future. If Egypt has enough water, it can grow food for its people. Water power can also be used to produce electricity. In 1960, the Egyptian government began building a great dam near Aswan on the upper Nile. The dam started operating in 1968. The Aswan High Dam provides both water and electricity.

The Nile has always dominated the history of Egypt.

Some Egyptian farmers use ancient methods to plow their land.

REVIEW

CHECK YOUR FACTS

1. In what ways are North Africa and Southwest Asia similar?

2. How has the discovery of petroleum in North Africa changed people's lives?

3. Why are the northern parts of Morocco, Algeria, and Tunisia called the Maghreb, or "western island"?

4. Libya is (larger/smaller) than any country in Western Europe.

5. Where do most Egyptians live today?

6. What are Egypt's two most important exports?

THINK ABOUT IT

7. The Nile River has been called the lifeblood of Egypt. Why?

8. Why do you think progress in Egypt will probably be slow?

WATCH YOUR WORDS

1. A metal used in the production of steel is___.
   aluminum   mahogany   manganese

2. A(n) ___ is a place where there are streams or wells in the desert.
   valley   rift   oasis

3. ___ is the washing away or blowing away of the soil.
   Irrigation   Erosion   Drought

4. ___are rocky places in rivers.
   Rapids   Lakes   Valleys

5. The tsetse fly causes___.
   malaria   sleeping sickness   drought

6. South African society is___.
   integrated   segregated   socialist

7. At___, rivers drop as over a cliff.
   rapids   falls   rifts

8. The___is an area of high grassland.
   oasis   highveld   valley

9. ___is energy produced from water.
   Rapids   Hydroelectric power   Manganese

10. In many African cities, the poor live in___.
    shantytowns   rifts   oases

CHECK YOUR FACTS

11. What is the westernmost point of West Africa?

12. What are the main religious groups of Nigeria?

13. Is Central Africa densely or sparsely populated?

14. List some problems of the nations on the Horn of Africa.

15. The discovery of what nonliving resource changed Libya?

16. Where has Libya sent many of its young people? For what reason?

17. What is the key to Egypt's future?

18. In Egypt, farming is improving (faster/slower) than the population is increasing.

19. In what year did Egypt begin to build a dam near Aswan? When did the dam start operating?

20. What is Egypt's most important export product?

TRUE OR FALSE

21. Nigeria is one of the poorest countries of Africa.

22. South Africa follows a system of apartheid.

23. About 30 million people live in Libya.

24. The equator passes through Central Africa.

25. Sudan is the largest nation in Africa.

USE YOUR MAP

26. Look at the map of Africa's regions on page 357. In what region is the nation of Congo located?

THINK ABOUT IT

27. What problems do most African nations share?

28. How should nations like Libya and Nigeria prepare for the day when their petroleum runs out?

29. What would you most like to visit in Egypt?

WATCH YOUR WORDS

Use the words below to fill in the blanks. Use each word only once.

apartheid	erosion	maize	passes	segregated
boycotts	fallow	manioc	rapids	shantytowns
cacao	falls	nationalism	rift valley	shifting cultivation
cassava	herders	nomads	rotate	source
drought	highveld	oasis	savannas	yams

Africa has an interesting geography. The Nile is the world's longest river. It flows from its ____ in Lake Victoria. The Sahara is the world's largest desert. In the Sahara, there are sometimes streams and wells. Such a place is called an ____. A ____, a deep split in Earth's surface, stretches across eastern Africa. Africa has tropical areas such as rain forests and ____. An area of high grassland in South Africa is called the ____. The area south of the Sahara suffers from ____, a lack of rain. Also, ____ of the soil is taking place there. Africa has great rivers. The Congo is little used for transportation because it has ____ and ____.

Africa has many peoples and nations. Parts of Africa are very crowded. Many of Africa's cities are ringed by poor areas called ____. Most Africans make their liv-

ing off the land. Some are ____ who raise animals for a living. Many of these people are ____, people who move from place to place. Other Africans practice a simple kind of farming known as ____. They let some fields lie ____. In other fields, they raise crops like ____, or sweet potatoes, and ____, or corn. Some farmers grow ____, which is also called ____. Other farmers use the same fields over and over, but they often ____ their crops. Africa's plantations raise such crops as ____, from which chocolate is made.

After World War II, ____ increased in many African colonies. Such forms of protest as ____ helped lead to independence. But today, the Blacks of South Africa suffer from the policy of ____. They live in a ____ society and are required to carry ____.

CHECK YOUR FACTS

1. Why are rivers more important to Africa than the oceans?

2. Where could you find snow in Africa?

3. How does Africa's location on the equator affect its climate?

4. Do all Africans look alike?

5. Africa's population (is/is not) spread fairly evenly over the continent.

6. About how many languages are spoken in Africa? Which African languages are widely spoken? Which European languages are widely spoken in Africa?

7. About how many nations are there in Africa?

8. In permanent agriculture, what do farmers do with their fields?

9. List some products that are produced by modern agriculture in Africa.

10. What three large empires developed in the western part of Africa south of the Sahara?

11. What kind of school educated people in the empires of West Africa?

12. Why were the Portuguese first interested in sailing around Africa?

13. There (were/were not) many native peoples in the parts of the New World where sugar was produced.

14. To what part of the New World were the first slaves taken?

15. What goods did the Europeans trade to the Africans in exchange for slaves?

16. Why did the slave trade end?

17. (Many/Few) Europeans lived in their colonies in Black Africa.

18. Did African nations become independent before or after World War II?

19. Name the main religious and ethnic groups in Nigeria.

USE YOUR MAPS

20. Look at the physical map of Africa on page 332. What mountains are located in North Africa?

21. Look at the climate map of Africa on page 338. Where is the main area of highland climate?

22. Look at the population map of Africa on page 341. What area has the fewest people?

23. Look at the resource map of Africa on page 343. Where is copper found in Africa?

24. Look at the map of Africa's nations on page 333. What is the capital of Nigeria?

25. Look at the map of Africa's regions on page 357. In what region is the island nation of Madagascar?

THINK ABOUT IT

26. How do you think the slave trade may have influenced African views of Europeans and also European views of Africans?

27. Sometimes people overcome nature. Sometimes nature overcomes people. From what you know about Africa, give an example that you think shows each point.

28. Sometimes an African nation suddenly begins to get income from a resource such as petroleum. What do you think are the first things the nation should do with the money?

29. What are some of the problems that most African nations share? What are some of their common goals?

30. In what ways were European colonies in Africa different from the 13 colonies that became the United States?

TRY SOMETHING NEW

31. Using an encyclopedia, write a report on one of the following: the pyramids, the Suez Canal, the Aswan High Dam, the ruins of Zimbabwe, Timbuktu.

32. Look up an article on flags in an encyclopedia. Draw and color the flags of five African nations. Choose the flags you like best.

33. Plan a trip to Africa that would let you see things that interest you. Use this unit as your source.

1 LOOKING AT LATIN AMERICA

Lesson 1: Land and Climates of Latin America

FIND THE WORDS

altiplano   llanos   pampas

Latin America is known for its large bodies of fresh water. Some of the largest lakes and longest rivers on Earth are found there.

Lake Titicaca (TEE tee KAH kah) and Lake Nicaragua (NIK uh RAH gwah) are the two largest lakes in Latin America. Lake Titicaca is very beautiful. It is high up in the mountains. It is 3813 meters (12,506 feet) above sea level. Find Lake Titicaca on the map. Find Lake Nicaragua.

Havana

W E S T   I N D I E S

Caribbean Sea

20°

20°

90°

80°

70°

60°

50°

40°

30°

N
NW   NE
W ———— E
SW   SE
S

Lake Nicaragua

Caracas

10°

10°

Panama Canal

Bogotá

Orinoco River

GUIANA HIGHLANDS

ATLANTIC OCEAN

LLANOS

0°

EQUATOR

EQUATOR

0°

A N D E S

Amazon   River

10°

10°

Lima

PACIFIC OCEAN

Lake Titicaca

La Paz

ALTIPLANO

BRAZILIAN HIGHLANDS

20°

20°

ATACAMA DESERT

M O U N T A I N S

Mt. Aconcagua

Rio de Janeiro

São Paulo

Paraná   River

Uruguay River

30°

30°

Santiago

PAMPAS

Montevideo

Buenos Aires

40°

40°

50°

Kilometers 0   500
SCALE
Miles 0   500

50°

110°

100°

90°

80°

70°

60°

50°

KEY		
– – – National Borders		• Cities

ELEVATION	
Meters	Feet
over 4,000	over 13,100
2,000 to 4,000	6,600 to 13,100
1,000 to 2,000	3,300 to 6,600
200 to 1,000	660 to 3,300
sea level to 200	sea level to 660
below sea level	below sea level

The Amazon River is one of the longest rivers in the world. Find it on the map. Find where it begins and ends. Find the nations through which it flows. Suppose you were to travel from New York to San Francisco. You would still not travel as far as the Amazon River does from its source to its mouth. The Amazon River is almost 6400 kilometers (4000 miles) long.

Except for the Amazon, the rivers of Latin America are not very useful for carrying people and goods from one place to another. Find the Paraná (PAH rah NAH) River. It starts in Brazil and goes to the Atlantic Ocean. It is shallow in parts. It is also interrupted by rapids and some of the biggest falls in the world. The Orinoco River in Venezuela (VEN uh ZWAY luh) is similar to the Paraná. There is another important body of water in Latin America that was made by people. It is the Panama Canal. The canal carries ships between the Atlantic Ocean and the Pacific Ocean.

Latin America has the longest system of mountains in the world, the Andes (AN deez). These mountains run down the length of South America near the Pacific coast. The Andes are not only long, they are also high. They make east-west travel in South America very difficult. There are also many mountains in Mexico and Central America.

In eastern South America, there are two large areas of highlands. These are the Guiana (gee AN uh) Highlands in the north and the Brazilian Highlands to the south.

Latin America has many flat lands. West of the Andes Mountains, along the Pacific coast, there is a narrow plain. Part of it is the Atacama (AH tuh KAH muh) Desert. In the middle of the mountains is the **altiplano** (AHL tee PLAH noh), a high plateau. East of the mountains, much of the land is flat. The Amazon River valley is a huge area of low, flat land. In northern South America, the Orinoco River flows through plains called the **llanos** (YAH nohs). In southern South America, there are huge plains called **pampas** (PAM puz).

Climates of Latin America

The equator passes through the northern part of South America. The mouth of the Amazon River is at the equator. Much of Latin America lies in the tropical zones north and south of the equator.

You know that there are seasons in the temperate zones. In the tropics, it is always like summer. But there is a dry season and a wet season in parts of the tropics. These are the tropical grasslands. Mexico, Central America, and the northern half of South

CLIMATES OF SOUTH AMERICA

CARIBBEAN SEA

Lake Maracaibo

Orinoco River

VENEZUELA

FRENCH GUIANA

GUYANA

COLOMBIA

SURINAME

Guiana Highlands

Equator

ECUADOR

Amazon River

SOUTH AMERICA

Madeira River

PERU

BRAZIL

Brazilian Highlands

Lake Titicaca

BOLIVIA

PACIFIC OCEAN

Andes Mountains

ATLANTIC OCEAN

Altiplano

Atacama Desert

Parana River

PARAGUAY

CHILE

Uruguay River

ARGENTINA

URUGUAY

KEY

--- National Boundaries

| 0 200 400 600 |
| Kilometers |
| Miles |
| 0 200 400 600 |

N NE NW E W SE SW S

CLIMATES

Humid Subtropical:
Hot wet summer,
mild wet winter

Marine:
No dry season, mild
winter, mild summer

Steppe:
Hot summer, hot to cold
winter, variable rainfall

Highlands:
Rainfall varies, cool
summer, dry winter

Desert:
Hot summer, hot to cold
winter, dry all year

Rain Forest:
Hot and wet all year

Mediterranean:
Warm dry summer,
mild wet winter

Tropical Grasslands:
Hot wet summer,
hot dry winter

America have tropical grasslands. So do some islands in the Caribbean (KAR ub BEE un) Sea.

In some areas of the tropics, it rains almost every day. These are the tropical rain forests. The Amazon River valley is the largest area of rain forest in the world. There are also rain forests in Mexico, in Central America, and in the Caribbean area.

The tropic of Cancer passes near Mexico City. The tropic of Capricorn runs near to Rio de Janeiro (REE oh di juh NAIR oh) in Brazil. So the areas of Latin America north and south of these two cities are in the temperate zones.

The temperate regions of northern Mexico and southern South America have several different climates. There is a large area with a humid subtropical climate in Argentina, Uruguay (YUR uh GWY), Paraguay (PAR uh GWY), and Brazil. Parts of Mexico, Argentina, and Brazil have a steppe climate. Chile (CHIL ee) has Mediterranean and marine climates in places. In most of these areas, there is a wider range of temperatures than in the tropics. Also, winter is usually wetter in the temperate areas.

Argentina's cowboys, called gauchos, herd cattle on the pampas.

Large areas of Latin America are covered with tropical rain forests.

Of course, winter is at opposite times of the year north and south of the equator.

It is true that Latin America has great rivers and tropical rain forests. But it also has large areas where there is little or no rainfall.

It almost never rains in the great Atacama Desert of Chile. It seldom rains in the Sonora Desert of northern Mexico. Patagonia (PAT uh GOH nee uh), in southern Argentina, is also very dry. The highlands have their own climate.

REVIEW

WATCH YOUR WORDS

1. A plateau in the middle of the Andes is the ___.
   llanos   pampas   *altiplano*
2. The ___ are huge plains in southern South America.
   llanos   pampas   *altiplanos*
3. The Orinoco River flows through plains called ___.
   llanos   pampas   *altiplanos*

CHECK YOUR FACTS

4. What is the name of the longest mountain system in the world?
5. Name two areas of Latin America that are very dry.

THINK ABOUT IT

Would you like to live in the tropics? How would your life be different?

Lesson 2: People of Latin America

FIND THE WORDS

**peninsulares   criollos   creoles
mestizos**

In 1980, there were about 400 million people in Latin America. Latin Americans make up about 9 percent of Earth's people. Latin America covers about 20.1 million square kilometers (7.9 million square miles). This is about 15 percent of the land on Earth. You might think that Latin Americans have enough land. However, in many cases this is not true.

Look at the population map of South America shown below. Latin America's population is very unevenly spread over the region. Much of the land in Latin America is too mountainous for many people to live on it. In addition, in the center of South America is a huge tropical rain forest. Few people have managed to live there. Thus, most Latin Americans live near the coasts. There are only

POPULATION OF SOUTH AMERICA

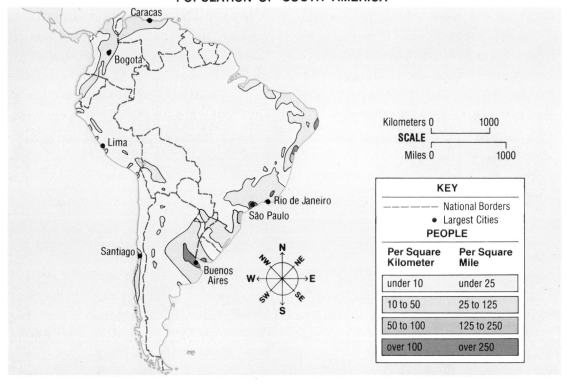

KEY

- - - - - - - National Borders

● Largest Cities

PEOPLE

Per Square Kilometer	Per Square Mile
under 10	under 25
10 to 50	25 to 125
50 to 100	125 to 250
over 100	over 250

The population of Latin America includes Indians, Europeans, and Blacks.

two places in the interior where many people live. In Mexico and Central America, people live in the mountains to avoid the heat of the coastal areas. Many people also live in the high plateau areas of Ecuador (EHK wuh dor), Peru, and Bolivia.

To understand how people live, we need to know who they are and how they got where they are. The people of Latin America include Indians, Europeans, and Blacks. Indeed, many people are a mixture of two or all three of these. Indians have lived in Latin America for many thousands of years. Europeans and Blacks from Africa started coming to Latin America after Christopher Columbus reached America in 1492.

Indians

Columbus called the people of the New World Indians because he thought he had found the East Indies. These are islands off the Asian continent. The West Indies also get their name from Columbus's mistake. However, the ancestors of the people Columbus named Indians probably did come from Asia. No one knows for sure exactly when these first peoples came to Latin America. Most scientists think they crossed the Bering Strait from Asia to North America thousands of years ago.

The ancestors of the American Indians gradually moved south from Alaska to the tip of South America. In Central America, Mexico, and Peru, important Indian

In the jungles of Central America, explorers found something fantastic—the ruins of great cities. They found giant stone pyramids, palaces, and painted temples. There were underground sewers and wide, paved roads. Hundreds of stone markers recorded dates going back 1500 years. They even found stone courts with stone hoops. There people had played a game like basketball.

From ruins like these, archaeologists learned about the civilization of the Maya Indians. The Maya left written records as early as 291 B.C. By the 400s A.D.—the Dark Ages in Europe—the Maya had formed a group of city-states. As many as 2 million people lived in them.

Astronomy, arithmetic, art, and ar-

chitecture—these the Maya knew. They wrote down their knowledge in books of paper that was made from bark and cloth.

During the 800s, the Maya left their great cities and disappeared into the jungles. No one knows why.

cultures appeared. Magnificent cities, temples, and fine roads were built by these peoples. We know something about these peoples from the writings of early European explorers. Much has also been learned about them from the remains of their cities.

Many of the Indians of Central America, Mexico, and Peru built great civilizations. But in South America east of the Andes, many just lived in small groups. They hunted and farmed and moved from place to place. Today, there are still such Indian groups living in the Amazon River valley.

After 1492, most of the Indians of Latin America were conquered by European colonists. Most became workers on farms and ranches owned by Europeans. Today, some Indians still work on large farms. Others now have their own small farms. Many have moved to the cities looking for a better life. Indians live in most Latin American nations. In South America, the largest Indian groups are in Paraguay, Bolivia, Peru, Ecuador, and Colombia. There are also many Indians in Mexico and in most of the Central American nations.

This Roman Catholic school in Brazil looks like many buildings in Spain.

Colonists and Immigrants

Europeans started coming to Latin America after the Spanish and Portuguese voyages of discovery. The Europeans had guns, horses, and large sailing ships. The American Indians did not. The Spanish and Portuguese soon gained control of at least the coasts all around Latin America. As more colonists came from Europe, new settlements were set up further inland.

Today, Spanish is spoken in all the former Spanish colonies. Portuguese is spoken in Brazil, which belonged to Portugal. English is the language of Guyana (gy AN uh), a former British colony. Dutch is spoken in Suriname (SUR uh nam), which belonged to the Netherlands. As you might guess, French is the language of French Guiana. Many Indians throughout Latin America still use their own languages. However, the European languages of the colonists are dominant in all Latin American nations.

The main religion of all of Latin America is Roman Catholicism. This was the religion of the Spanish, Portuguese, and French colonists. Many of the cities of Latin America look like cities in Spain, Portugal, and France. Forms of government in Latin America are similar to those of Europe.

Many Italians, Germans, and Poles came to southern Latin America during the late 1800s and early 1900s. British and Arab merchants settled in many cities. Japanese came to Brazil to work on the farms. These new peoples learned to speak the local language and became citizens of their new countries.

Africans

Black people from Africa were brought by force as slaves to Latin America. There were sugar plantations around the Caribbean and in Brazil. Many workers were needed to grow the sugar cane on these huge farms. There were not many Indians in the areas where sugar cane was grown. In addition, the Indians did not adapt very well to the work. Black people did the work much more successfully. For 300 years, Europeans continued to bring Black people to Latin America from Africa.

Brazilians used Black African slaves to work on their plantations.

The Black Africans greatly influenced Latin America. African words, foods, beliefs, music, and dance became part of Latin American culture. The Blacks were from tropical areas in Africa. Thus, they adjusted well to tropical Latin America. They adopted European languages and religions. However, many resisted the cruel system of slavery under which they lived.

Many Black slaves gained their freedom over the years. Slavery itself was abolished gradually in the 1800s. Today, most Black Latin Americans live in eastern South America and around the Caribbean Sea.

New Peoples

Because of the many different groups in Latin America, each was given a special name. Europeans born in Spain were called **peninsulares** (pay NEEN soo LAHR ays) because they were from the Iberian Peninsula. People of European background who were born in Latin America were called **criollos** (kree OHL yohs) in Spanish areas. In French areas, they were called **creoles** (KREE OHLZ). People who had both European and Indian ancestors were called **mestizos** (meh STEE zohz). Today, many Latin Americans have ancestors that came from two or three of these groups.

REVIEW

WATCH YOUR WORDS

1. Europeans born in Spain who lived in Latin America were called ___ .
   criollos   mestizos   peninsulares

2. ___ are people with both European and Indian ancestors.
   Creoles   Criollos   Mestizos

3. In Spanish areas, people of European background who were born in Latin America were called ___ .
   creoles   criollos   peninsulares

4. In French areas, people of European background who were born in Latin America were called ___ .
   creoles   criollos   mestizos

CHECK YOUR FACTS

5. Which areas of Latin America have sparse populations? Which areas are densely populated?

6. What three groups make up the peoples of Latin America?

7. Why did Columbus call the people of the New World "Indians"?

8. Name four European languages spoken in Latin America.

9. Why were Black slaves brought to Latin America?

THINK ABOUT IT

The culture of Latin America is a blend of many different cultures. Is the same true of the culture of the United States?

Lesson 3: The Economy of Latin America

FIND THE WORD

industrialization

Natural Resources

Latin America is very rich in natural resources. Huge amounts of petroleum have recently been found in the Gulf of Mexico near the Mexican coast. This area will be producing petroleum for many years. Another major oil-producing area is near Lake Maracaibo (MAH rah KY boh) in Venezuela. Oil fields are also found in Peru, Ecuador, Argentina, and Trinidad and Tobago (tuh BAY goh).

Latin Americans have mined other mineral resources for many years. Jamaica is one of the leading exporters of bauxite, an ore used to make aluminum. Some of the world's largest copper and tin mines are in Chile, Bolivia, and Peru. There are big iron ore deposits in Brazil. Mexico is one of the largest producers of silver in the world. Zinc and lead are also mined in the mountains of Mexico. All the large Latin American nations except Uruguay and Argentina have important mineral resources. Find as many of these mineral resources as you can on the map on the next page.

Much oil is found in the land under Lake Maracaibo in northern Venezuela.

394

RESOURCES OF SOUTH AMERICA AND CENTRAL AMERICA

RESOURCES

- Sugar Cane
- Bananas
- Petroleum
- Coffee
- Beef Cattle
- Iron Ore
- Copper
- Cotton
- Cacao
- Corn
- Sheep
- Tin
- Wheat
- Silver

SCALE

Kilometers 0 — 1000

Miles 0 — 500 — 1000

Many Latin American nations have mineral wealth, but only a few have enough good farmland. Look at your maps of Latin America. Find lands that are *not* deserts or rain forests or high mountains. These are the places where crops are planted or animals are grazed. Which nations would you guess produce more plant and animal products? If you said Argentina, Uruguay, Paraguay, Brazil, and Mexico you were right. These nations have larger amounts of flat land that are not rain forests or deserts.

Many foods come from Latin America. But most people think first of bananas and coffee. It is true that bananas and coffee are grown in large amounts in a number of Latin American nations. Look at the map on page 395. Find where these crops are grown. But there is much more to agriculture in Latin America. The southeastern part of South America produces large amounts of wheat, soybeans, and pinto beans. Wheat is also produced in northern Mexico. Beef cattle are raised in the pampas, a large area of flat land in Argentina. There are similar beef-producing plains in Uruguay, Paraguay, and Brazil. Cacao beans, from which chocolate is made, are grown in Brazil and Ecuador. The island of Grenada (gruh NAY duh) in the West Indies spe-

cializes in the spices nutmeg and mace. Sugar cane is a major crop in Cuba, Brazil, and the Dominican Republic. Find some of these products and the places they come from on the map on page 395.

Latin America has valuable resources off its shores. Fish are plentiful in the cold currents off the coast of Peru. Factories grind up fish caught there to make fish meal for fertilizer and food. Shrimp are caught in the Gulf of Mexico off Mexico and in the Atlantic Ocean off Brazil. Many of the people who live around the Caribbean Sea easily catch enough fish for their needs.

Human Resources

Latin America has a young, growing population. About one-half of the Latin Americans are under 20 years of age. More young people means more babies will soon be born. As the population multiplies, more schools, jobs, houses, hospitals, and workers are needed.

Many Latin American nations have not been able to provide education for everyone. Most schools are still in the cities. In some nations, more than half of the adults have never learned to read. These people cannot take jobs where they must read or write or work with numbers. Still, many of these people come to the cities to find

Latin America is rich in natural and human resources. *Right:* Farmers plow a field. *Below:* Fishers lower their nets for a catch.

Many people move from rural areas to cities.

work. They hope that at least their children will be able to get an education and have a better life. They see little future in the rural areas.

A number of Latin American nations do now provide schools for most people. These nations are Argentina, Uruguay, Chile, Brazil, Venezuela, Cuba, and Mexico. In most of these nations, professional people such as doctors, engineers, and teachers are well trained. However, there are usually not enough of such well-educated people to meet each nation's needs. In addition, most professional people prefer to work in the large cities. Thus, there is a shortage of such people in small cities and towns and in rural villages.

Capital Resources

Many Latin American nations are undergoing **industrialization.** This means that factories are being built. Factories produce cars, buses, electrical appliances, clothes, and many other goods. Most Latin Americans believe that industrialization is good. Factories provide jobs. Selling industrial goods brings more money into the economy. This allows even more factories to be built. Then even more jobs and goods become available. The idea is that to have more, people must produce more.

Many Latin American countries have the capital resources to buy machinery and build factories. These nations include Mexico, Venezuela, Brazil, and Argentina.

398

Modern machines like these derricks speed industrialization in Brazil.

But most Latin American nations produce mostly raw materials, such as minerals and farm products. They sell much of their raw materials to the rest of the world. Raw materials tend to sell for low prices. Their prices tend to go up and down rapidly. Agricultural production is at the mercy of good weather. Raw-material production in general provides relatively few jobs. All these things tend to weaken the economies of many Latin American nations.

REVIEW

CHECK YOUR FACTS

1. What are the important oil-producing areas of Latin America?
2. Name five other important mineral resources of Latin America.
3. Name five important agricultural products of Latin America.
4. Latin America's population is relatively (young/old).
5. What is industrialization?

THINK ABOUT IT

Why do you think most professional people prefer to live in the cities in Latin America?

Lesson 4: Land of Many Nations

FIND THE WORDS

mercantilism   viceroy

Look at the political map of Latin America on the next page. You can see that Latin America is a land of many nations.

Colonial Beginnings

Why are there so many nations in Latin America? There is no one answer. Several things helped give Latin America many nations. One important reason was the way European nations set up colonies in the area.

In the late 1400s and after, a number of European countries began to set up trading posts around the world. These nations were Portugal, Spain, France, England, and the Netherlands. These posts were run by trading companies. These companies had permission from the rulers of their nations to do business. The traders brought raw materials, such as sugar and spices, and precious metals, such as gold and silver, back to Europe. They loaded their ships with manufactured goods, such as cloth and guns, to take back and sell. The trading posts often grew into colonies. The control of most colonies passed from the trading companies to the European governments. The colonies provided raw materials, precious metals, and markets for their European owners. This system came to be known as **mercantilism.** Colonies were forced to trade only with the European nation that owned them. They were prevented from making European products. In that way, a colony could not compete with its ruling nation for money and markets.

Naturally, each European nation wanted to claim as many places as possible in the New World. Islands and good ports along the coasts of the Americas were quickly seized by the European nations. In Latin America, Spain and Portugal managed to get the most. Portugal claimed the eastern part of South America. Spain took most of the rest.

The Spanish government did not encourage traders and settlers in its colonies to work together. Instead, it gave all power in several areas to **viceroys.** *Viceroy* means "in place of the king." These officials were to rule like the king in the place of the king. They were answerable only to the king of Spain. Of course, the king chose the viceroys. The borders of their territories changed as settlements grew.

NATIONS OF SOUTH AMERICA AND CENTRAL AMERICA

Havana ★
BAHAMAS
CUBA
DOMINICAN
REPUBLIC
PUERTO RICO
(U.S.)

N
NW ⬦ NE
W ● E
SW ⬦ SE
S

GUATEMALA
BELIZE
JAMAICA
HAITI
ANTIGUA
AND
BARBUDA

HONDURAS
DOMINICA
ST. LUCIA
BARBADOS
GRENADA
ST. VINCENT AND
THE GRENADINES

ATLANTIC OCEAN

EL
SALVADOR
NICARAGUA
Lake Nicaragua
CARIBBEAN SEA

PANAMA
Caracas
COSTA RICA
VENEZUELA
TRINIDAD AND TOBAGO
Panama Canal
Orinoco River
GUYANA
SURINAME
FRENCH GUIANA

Bogotá ★
COLOMBIA

EQUATOR
0°
EQUATOR
0°

★ Quito
ECUADOR

Amazon   River

PERU

Lima ★

BRAZIL

Cuzco •
BOLIVIA
Brasília ★
Lake Titicaca
★ La Paz

★ Sucre

PARAGUAY
São Paulo •
Rio de Janeiro •

PACIFIC OCEAN
Asunción ★
River

Paraná
Uruguay River

Santiago ★
URUGUAY
Buenos Aires ★
★ Montevideo
CHILE
ARGENTINA

KEY
--- National Borders
★ National Capitals
• Cities

Kilometers 0   500   1000
SCALE
Miles 0   500   1000

401

This painting shows the entry of a viceroy into a Latin American city.

The situation was different in the Portuguese settlements in Brazil. By 1549, the city of Salvador in Bahia (bah HEE uh) was the capital. There was one governor who ruled all the settlements for the king of Portugal.

Other European nations also wanted colonies in the Americas. After about 1550, the French, English, and Dutch attacked the Spanish and Portuguese colonies. They also attacked each other's settlements. During this time, Spain and Portugal were becoming less powerful. They were not able to defend all their possessions in the New World. Some Caribbean islands changed hands several times. The island settlements were easy prey for ships from the European nations.

The Struggle for Independence

The ways in which the European colonies became independent also helped give Latin America many nations. There was not one big war for independence. Just among the Spanish colonies, there were battles in many different places at different times. Different people led these struggles. They fought against Spain for different reasons.

In New Spain (now Mexico), the struggle for independence started in 1810. Miguel Hidalgo (mee GEHL ee DAHL goh), a priest, led the fight for freedom from Spain. He was angry because the peninsulares, the people born in Spain, controlled the colony.

WHERE WE ARE IN TIME AND PLACE

LATIN AMERICAN INDEPENDENCE

1804	1811	1816	1818	1819
St. Domingue becomes independent Haiti	Paraguay becomes independent	Argentina becomes independent	Chile, part of Peru, becomes independent	New Granada becomes independent Great Colombia

1821	1822	1823	1825	1828
New Spain becomes independent Mexico; independence of Peru declared	Brazil becomes independent	United Provinces of Central America formed	Bolivia becomes independent	Uruguay becomes separate nation

1829–1830	1838	1844	1902	1903
Venezuela and Ecuador separate from Colombia	Central America breaks apart into five nations	Dominican Republic formed	Cuba becomes independent	Panama separates from Colombia

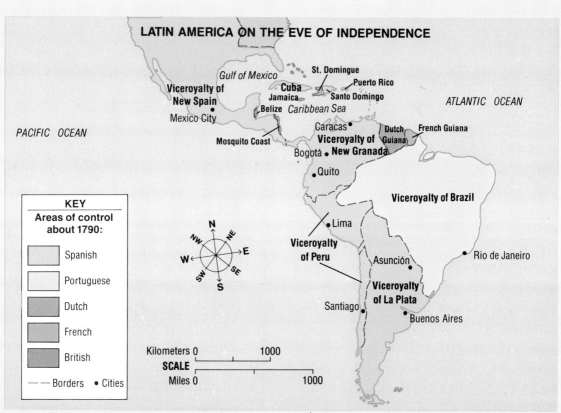

LATIN AMERICA ON THE EVE OF INDEPENDENCE

Gulf of Mexico

St. Domingue

Puerto Rico

Viceroyalty of New Spain

Cuba

Santo Domingo

Jamaica

ATLANTIC OCEAN

Belize · Caribbean Sea

Mexico City

PACIFIC OCEAN

Caracas

Dutch Guiana · French Guiana

Mosquito Coast

Viceroyalty of New Granada

Bogotá ·

Quito

Viceroyalty of Brazil

Lima

Viceroyalty of Peru

Rio de Janeiro

Asunción

Santiago

Viceroyalty of La Plata

Buenos Aires

KEY

Areas of control about 1790:

- Spanish
- Portuguese
- Dutch
- French
- British
- — — Borders • Cities

N
NW · NE
W · E
SW · SE
S

Kilometers 0 — 1000
SCALE
Miles 0 — 1000

403

Bolivia is named after General Simón Bolívar.

In New Grenada, Simón Bolívar (see MOHN boh LEE vahr) led the fight against the soldiers of the Spanish king. Bolívar felt that the people of the Spanish colonies should form their own government. Simón Bolívar was the great liberator of the Spanish colonies. He led the colonists in battles against Spanish soldiers in many areas from 1813 to 1824. Bolívar dreamed of forming one large nation. Some people wanted him to become the dictator of this new country. But other people were afraid of giving so much power to one person. Bolívar's hopes of creating a United States of South America failed. Lands Bolívar helped liberate are now the nations of Venezuela, Colombia, Ecuador, Panama, Peru, and Bolivia. Bolivia is named for him.

José de San Martín, (hoh ZAY di SAN mahr TEEN), an Argentine general, led the struggle for independence in southern South America. First, he helped free Argentina from Spain by 1816. Then, in 1817–1818, he led an army across the Andes and defeated the Spanish in Chile. Finally, he attacked the Spanish in Peru in the 1820s.

After the Spanish colonies became independent, many broke apart into several nations. At first, some of the colonies tried to stay united. For a few years, the former Spanish colonies in Central America formed the United Provinces of Central America. The members of this group are now the nations of Nicaragua, Costa Rica, Guatemala (GWAH tuh MAH luh), El Salvador, and Honduras (hon DOO russ). The nations of Panama, Colombia, Ecuador, and Venezuela were united as Great Colombia. The colonists were not used to working together. They had been very unhappy under the viceroys. Then they were part of much larger states. Most preferred to found smaller nations.

Since the early 1800s, other European colonies have become independent. Cuba won its freedom as a result of a war between the United States and Spain in 1898. Other colonies have become nations in recent years.

The United States began work on the Panama Canal in 1904.

After Independence

In the years since independence, parts of some of the Latin American nations have become independent. Brazil and Argentina agreed to the creation of Uruguay in 1828. They both wanted that area. Instead of continuing to fight over it, they agreed to make it an independent nation.

Panama was once part of Colombia. The United States wanted to build a canal through Panama from the Atlantic Ocean to the Pacific Ocean. In 1903, several leaders from the area proclaimed Panama independent. The United States government recognized Panama as a nation. Later, the United States began to dig the Panama Canal.

REVIEW

CHECK YOUR FACTS

1. Name the five main nations that colonized Latin America.

2. What was the system of European colonization called?

3. What was the official who ruled each of the Spanish colonies called?

4. Name two leaders in the fight for independence in Latin America.

5. Name two larger Latin American nations that broke apart soon after independence.

6. How did Panama become an independent nation?

THINK ABOUT IT

Imagine that it is 1527. You are standing on a dock in New Spain, waiting for a ship from Spain to unload. What items could be on that ship that would be of interest to you and your family?

CHAPTER REVIEW

WATCH YOUR WORDS

1. The building of factories is called ___.
   mercantilism production
   industrialization

2. The large plains in southern South America are the ___.
   altiplanos llanos pampas

3. The large plains in northern South America are the ___.
   altiplanos llanos pampas

4. People with both European and Indian ancestors are called ___.
   mestizos peninsulares criollos

5. ___ were people of European background born in Spanish America.
   Criollos Mestizos Peninsulares

6. Europeans born in Spain who lived in Latin America were called ___.
   creoles mestizos peninsulares

7. A ___ rules in place of a king.
   protector president viceroy

8. The ___ is a plateau that lies in Bolivia.
   llanos pampas *altiplano*

9. Under ___, colonies provide raw materials and markets for their owner.
   communism mercantilism
   industrialization

10. In French areas, people of European background who were born in Latin America were called ___.
    criollos creoles Amazons

CHECK YOUR FACTS

11. Name two waterways in Latin America that are used for transportation.

12. What is the longest mountain chain in the world? Where is it located?

13. Describe tropical grasslands.

14. What areas of Latin America are sparsely populated?

15. List some ways in which Blacks from Africa influenced Latin America.

16. Name three of Mexico's important mineral resources.

17. Name four important agricultural nations of Latin America.

18. Where are most schools located in many Latin American nations?

19. Name two benefits that come from industrialization.

20. In what way was the government of colonial Brazil different from the government of Spanish America?

USE YOUR MAPS

21. Look at the physical map of Latin America on page 383. Are the Guiana Highlands north or south of the Amazon River?

22. Look at the climate map of South America on page 385. Is there a marine climate in the north or south?

23. Look at the population map of South America on page 388. Do more people live along the coasts or in the interior of the continent?

24. Look at the map of Latin America's resources on page 395. Are sheep raised in the north or south? Is copper found in the east or west?

25. Look at the map of Latin America's nations on page 401. What are the two capitals of Bolivia?

THINK ABOUT IT

26. What difficulties lay in the way of forming a United States of Latin America?

27. In what ways have the landforms and climates of Latin America affected the patterns of settlement?

28. Why must education be improved for industrialization to take place?

2 REGIONS OF LATIN AMERICA

Lesson 1: Mexico and Central America

To get a better picture of what Latin America is like, we need to study it in smaller pieces. One way to divide Latin America is into the regions shown on the map on page 408. These are Mexico and Central America, the Caribbean and northern South America, the Indian-heritage nations, southern South America, and Brazil. In this lesson, we will study Mexico and Central America.

Landforms and Climates

Mexico and Central America lie between the United States on the north and Colombia on the south. This region is sometimes called Middle America. Much of the region is mountainous. In northern

407

REGIONS OF LATIN AMERICA

KEY: Regions of Latin America

- Mexico and Central America
- Caribbean and Northern South America
- Indian-Heritage Nations
- Southern South America
- Brazil
- — — National Borders

Mexico there are deserts. Hot, wet lowlands line the region's eastern and western coasts. Mexico and Central America form a "land bridge" connecting North America and South America. This region is more than 3200 kilometers (2000 miles) long from north to south. But it is only 48 kilometers (30 miles) wide from east to west at its narrowest point. Can you find this place on the map? It is where the Panama Canal was built.

Mountains dominate Mexico and Central America. These mountains include many volcanoes, where lava sometimes comes from the ground. There are also many earthquakes, violent shakings of the ground, in the mountains. Cities of the area have been destroyed by earthquakes.

If you look at the map on the bottom of page 409, you will see that there are many cities in the mountains of Mexico and Central America. In the lowlands in the tropics, the weather is hot all year and usually wet. But at higher elevations, the weather tends to be cooler and drier. So people prefer to live on highlands such as plateaus, hills, and mountains.

As the elevation of the land changes, the climate also changes quickly. The different climate

CLIMATES OF MEXICO AND CENTRAL AMERICA

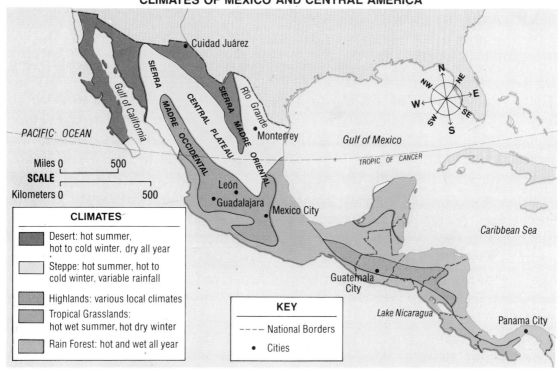

CLIMATES

- Desert: hot summer, hot to cold winter, dry all year
- Steppe: hot summer, hot to cold winter, variable rainfall
- Highlands: various local climates
- Tropical Grasslands: hot wet summer, hot dry winter
- Rain Forest: hot and wet all year

KEY

--- National Borders
• Cities

MAP OF MEXICO AND CENTRAL AMERICA

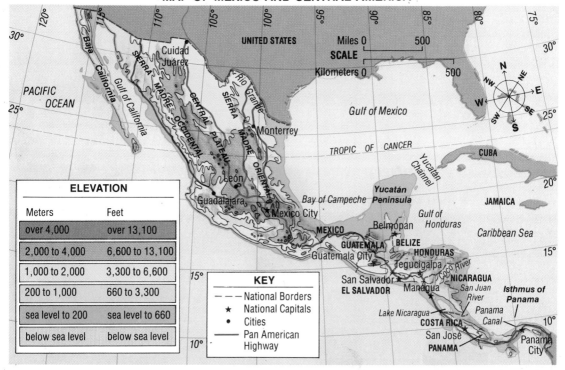

ELEVATION

Meters	Feet
over 4,000	over 13,100
2,000 to 4,000	6,600 to 13,100
1,000 to 2,000	3,300 to 6,600
200 to 1,000	660 to 3,300
sea level to 200	sea level to 660
below sea level	below sea level

KEY

--- National Borders
★ National Capitals
• Cities
— Pan American Highway

areas have different plants and animals. Rain, wind, and soil vary with the climate. Imagine you are in the lowlands along the coasts of Mexico and Central America. There you would see palms and tropical fruit trees. As you travel higher, there are forests filled with rubber trees and ferns. Above these are pine trees. In the very highest areas are grasses and other small plants. By going up in the mountains, you have gone from a tropical area to an area like the areas near the poles! Yet you are still not far from the equator. Thus does elevation affect climate. Find the climate areas of Mexico and Central America on the map at the top of page 409.

Transportation

The mountains of Mexico and Central America make it difficult to build roads and railroads. There is only one major north-south highway through the region. This road starts at four points along the border between Mexico and the United States. It extends south all the way through Panama. In Mexico, it is called the Inter-American Highway. In Central America, it is called the Pan American Highway. This highway is the most important connection between the nations of the region. Trace the Pan American Highway on the map at the bottom of page 409. It takes more than a week to

Mexico and Central America have only one major north-south highway.

drive from the northern border of Mexico to Panama City.

No railroad connects all of the region. Only Mexico has railroads that run between its northern and southern borders.

Mexico and Central America Compared

There are eight nations in this region. Mexico is by far the largest. Mexico has about three-fourths of the land area and about three-fourths of the people.

Though Mexico has much land, it has a very large number of people for its size. Mexico is one of the most densely populated nations of the Western Hemisphere. This means that the average number of persons per square kilometer or mile is quite high.

About half of Mexico's people live in the central plateau. This area lies between mountain ranges that run down the eastern and western coasts. The central plateau has some of Mexico's best farmland. Mexico City, the capital, is on this plateau. So also are many of Mexico's large cities.

Next in number of people to Mexico in the region are Guatemala, El Salvador, Honduras, Nicaragua, Costa Rica, Panama, and Belize (buh LEEZ). El Salvador has the most people for its size.

Natural resources are not evenly spread over the region.

Mexico's oil refineries employ many workers.

Mexico has important mineral resources. These include petroleum, silver, and lead. Much of the farming takes place in the valley and plateau areas. Most of the big areas of farmland are in Mexico.

Most of the goods produced in the region are used locally. Some farm products are sold to other nations. For example, most of the bananas people in the United States eat come from the region. The region also exports coffee, sugar, cacao, and cotton. Mexico sells petroleum abroad. Exports bring in money that is used to buy such things as tractors, trucks, and machines.

411

The Tourist Industry

Tourism is very important in Mexico and Central America. Many people come from the United States to Mexico and Central America. They spend a great deal of money in the region. Many people of the area have jobs taking care of the tourists. The tourists also buy many local goods.

Tourists come to Mexico and Central America for several reasons. The region's beaches and sunny weather provide relief from cold winters to the north. Many people are interested in the ruins of ancient civilizations in Mexico and Guatemala. Other tourists are fascinated by the cultures of the region.

POLITICAL MAP OF MEXICO

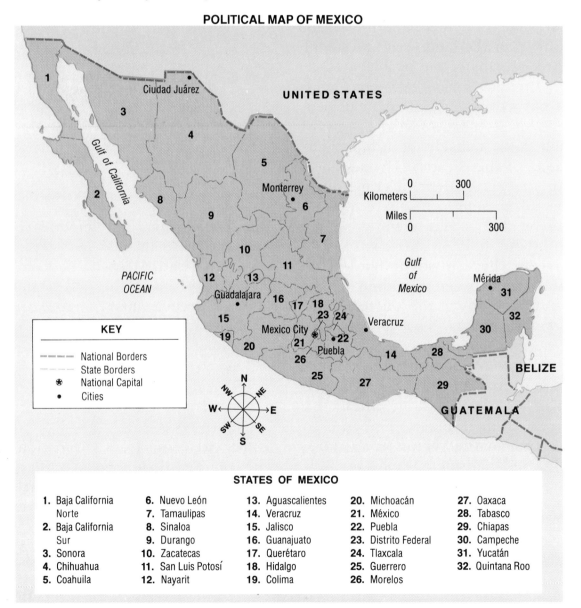

STATES OF MEXICO

1. Baja California Norte	6. Nuevo León	13. Aguascalientes	20. Michoacán	27. Oaxaca
2. Baja California Sur	7. Tamaulipas	14. Veracruz	21. México	28. Tabasco
3. Sonora	8. Sinaloa	15. Jalisco	22. Puebla	29. Chiapas
4. Chihuahua	9. Durango	16. Guanajuato	23. Distrito Federal	30. Campeche
5. Coahuila	10. Zacatecas	17. Querétaro	24. Tlaxcala	31. Yucatán
	11. San Luis Potosí	18. Hidalgo	25. Guerrero	32. Quintana Roo
	12. Nayarit	19. Colima	26. Morelos	

Social and Political Unrest

There are many problems in Mexico and Central America. Many people of the region are very poor. Rich people and the military run many of the governments of the Central American nations. These governments often do little to help poor people. They do not allow people rights.

Sometimes, all these problems have led to civil wars, fighting within the nations. In recent years, there have been civil wars in Nicaragua and El Salvador. There has been unrest in Guatemala and Honduras. It is likely that there will be much conflict in Central America in the future.

Many tourists are interested in the culture of Latin America. They spend a great deal of money in the region. But the money does not do much good for the poor.

REVIEW

CHECK YOUR FACTS

1. Name the five regions of Latin America.

2. What is another name for the region that includes Mexico and Central America?

3. There are many volcanoes and earthquakes in the mountains of Mexico and Central America. Why do many people live in those areas?

4. What is the only major highway in Central America?

5. Give some reasons why tourists visit Mexico and Central America.

THINK ABOUT IT

Many people in California live in beautiful areas with pleasant climates. But many of these same areas are threatened by serious earthquakes. Do you think it is a good idea to live in such a place? Why, or why not?

Lesson 2: The Caribbean and Northern South America

Columbus called the islands he found the Indies. People soon realized these were not the Indies of Asia, so they called the islands the West Indies. The Caribbean Sea was named after the Carib Indians of the West Indies. Europeans passed through the Caribbean to Mexico, Central America, and northern South America. The Caribbean is the gateway to the Americas.

Winds blow continuously from east to west across the Atlantic Ocean. They are called **trade winds.** The trade winds brought sailing ships to the West Indies and the northern coast of South America. These winds are wet. They bring rain almost daily from May through November. Rain clouds are always forming around the many mountains of the region. The winds get cooler and drop rain as they blow up the eastern sides of the mountains. These steady winds keep the temperature around 27°C (80°F) all year. You might expect it to be much hotter this close to the equator. But, the weather is not always perfect in the region. This saying from the Caribbean gives you a hint:

June, too soon,
July, stand by,
August, you must,
September, remember
October, all over.

Hurricanes are what this saying is about. These are great wind and rain storms that come to the Caribbean during August and September. Hurricane winds and floods do much damage to buildings and crops. Often, many people die.

The Changing Earth

Earthquakes and volcanoes have also created destruction in the Caribbean. The largest recent volcanic eruption was on the French island of Martinique (MAHR ti NEEK) in 1902. Mt. Pelée (puh LAY) sent melted rock and fiery gases running down its sides. Saint-Pierre, a town of 38,000, was destroyed. Only one man survived. He had been in an underground jail cell when Saint-Pierre was hit.

But volcanoes have not only brought destruction. The soil that comes from volcanic ash is fertile. This fine soil, together with the warm weather and dependable

Colombia's coffee is famous. Most of it is shipped to other nations.

rains, makes farming good. The best lands of the region are planted in sugar cane and coffee. Barbados (bahr BAY dohss), Colombia, Cuba, the Dominican Republic, Guyana, Haiti (HAY tee), and Jamaica all export sugar or coffee or both. Most of the crops are sold to other nations. Thus, the rich soils of the region are not much used to produce crops that the people eat. Plantation owners hire workers to plant and harvest crops. Workers rarely have jobs all year. Cuba has a Communist government. There, the large plantations are owned and run by the government.

Many Cultures

All the parts of this region are not alike. There are many nations and areas that still belong to the United Kingdom, France, the Netherlands and the United States. The people of the region speak many languages. These include Spanish, English, French, and Dutch. There are many religions. These include Roman Catholicism, Protestantism, African religions, Judaism, and Hinduism. Though there are many Black people, there are also Whites and Asians. Using the chart on page 417, find as many lands on the map on page 401 as you can.

415

Haitians battle French soldiers in this old drawing.

Colonization and Competition

After Columbus found the Caribbean region for Europe in 1492, more Spanish ships soon sailed to the New World. They brought government officials, soldiers, and missionaries. The ships carried treasure and goods back to Spain. The Spanish took gold and silver from Mexico and Peru. Often, the precious metal was first shipped to the many good ports around the Caribbean. There it was transferred into larger ships and sent on to Spain. The Spanish learned how to plant sugar cane in the fertile lowlands of the region. The sugar was shipped to Europe. Sugar cane was a very profitable crop.

All the European nations with navies wanted part of Spain's American riches. There were so many battles in the Caribbean that the people became used to them. Often, the invaders were content to take over the towns, fill up their ships, and sail away. The Caribbean became a region of constant naval struggles. It was also a region of pirates and smugglers.

In some plantation areas, the Black slaves ran away or rebelled. Often, they formed their own free settlements in the mountains. They would come down to take what they needed from the plantations and towns. Some towns, parts of islands, and whole islands changed hands many times.

416

BACKGROUNDS OF THE CARIBBEAN
AND
NORTHERN SOUTH AMERICA

French	Spanish	British	African	American (United States)
French Guiana	*Colombia	*Antigua & Barbuda	All	Puerto Rico
Guadeloupe	*Cuba	*Bahamas		United States Virgin Islands
*Haiti	*Dominican Republic	*Barbados	**Dutch**	
Martinique	Puerto Rico	British Virgin Islands	Netherlands Antilles	
	*Venezuela	Cayman Islands	*Suriname	
		*Dominica		
		*Grenada		
		*Guyana		
		*Jamaica		
		Monserrat		
		St. Christopher-Nevis-Anguilla		
		*St. Lucia		
		*St. Vincent & the Grenadines		
		*Trinidad & Tobago		
		Turks & Caicos Islands		

*independent nations as of 1982

Independence

After the United States, the French colony of Haiti was the first nation in the New World to become independent. This happened in 1804. The Dominican Republic soon also became free of Spanish rule.

Spain had gradually lost power in Europe. In the 1800s, the slave trade from Africa was stopped. The larger Spanish colonies of the region began breaking away from Spain. Great Colombia formed and then split apart into Colombia, Venezuela, and Ecuador. In 1898,

Caracas is the capital of Venezuela.

the United States fought a war with Spain. As a result of this war, Cuba became free and Puerto Rico (PWER toh REE koh) became an American possession.

In the Caribbean, most people are Blacks or of mixed racial background. On the continent, most people are Spanish or both Indian and Spanish.

Today, the people of Colombia live mostly in the mountain areas around the cities of Bogotá (BOH guh TAH), Medellín (MEHD ul EEN), and Cali (KAH lee). Most of Venezuela's people still live along the coast. Caracas (kuh RAH kuss) is the capital and main city. The interior of both these nations is settled mostly by cattle ranchers.

Recent Changes

In the 1950s, a revolution led by Fidel Castro made Cuba a Communist nation. People who did not agree with the new government fled or were told to leave Cuba. Many left to begin new lives in Florida. That American state is only 144 kilometers (90 miles) from Cuba.

Venezuela and Trinidad and Tobago have important petroleum resources. Jamaica, Suriname, and Guyana produce bauxite, the ore of aluminum. Tourism is a major source of income for the region.

REVIEW

CHECK YOUR FACTS

1. How do trade winds affect the climate of the Caribbean and northern South America?

2. What is a disadvantage and an advantage of volcanoes?

3. Name four languages spoken in the Caribbean and northern South America.

4. What crop made the Caribbean and northern South America valuable?

5. What was the second independent nation in the New World?

THINK ABOUT IT

Why do you think so many people leave Cuba when they get the chance?

Lesson 3: Indian-Heritage Nations

FIND THE WORDS

heritage   hacienda   bilingual

Geography

In four nations of South America, the Indian **heritage**, or background, has remained important. These nations are Ecuador, Peru, Bolivia, and Paraguay. These four nations are not all alike. Three of them—Ecuador, Peru, and Bolivia—are dominated by the Andes Mountains. These nations have four different areas that run in parallel strips from north to south. Along the Pacific coast is a narrow lowland. Streams run through it to the Pacific. This area is desert in Peru but wetter in Ecuador.

The next two areas to the east are the Andes and the *altiplano*, a high plateau. The fourth area is the tropical rain forest in the east. Most of the people live on the *altiplano* or in port cities on the coast. Find these four areas on the map on page 383.

The Paraguay River cuts through the middle of Paraguay from north to south. The Gran Chaco, an area of dry plains, lies west of the river. Only 4 percent of Paraguay's people live in the Gran Chaco, which covers 60 percent of Paraguay. The land near the Paraguay River is low and flat. There are some swamps there. East of the river, the land is generally low and flat.

In the mountains of Peru, many people are poor and live very simply.

THE INCAN EMPIRE

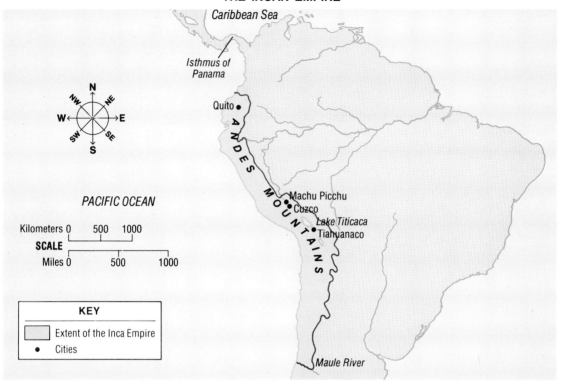

Caribbean Sea

Isthmus of Panama

Quito

PACIFIC OCEAN

Machu Picchu
Cuzco
Lake Titicaca
Tiahuanaco

ANDES MOUNTAINS

Maule River

Kilometers 0   500   1000
SCALE
Miles 0   500   1000

KEY
Extent of the Inca Empire
● Cities

Resources and People

The Andean nations have mineral resources. There is petroleum in Ecuador. Peru produces copper and silver. Bolivia has tin, petroleum, natural gas, zinc, and tungsten. Paraguay is an agricultural nation. It exports meat and wool.

Unlike in most of Latin America, more people live in small towns and villages than in large cities in this region. Most people are poor. Many cannot read and write. Many people seem to feel more attachment to their villages than to the nation in which they live.

Colonization

When the Spanish came to this region, they found two different Indian societies. The great empire of the Inca stretched over what is now Ecuador, Peru, and Bolivia. Look at the map of the Incan Empire on page 420. In what is now Paraguay, the Spanish found groups of Guaraní (GWAHR uh NEE) Indians. These people lived by hunting and fishing.

The Incan Empire was a great civilization. Farming was very complex. On the *altiplano*, there were terraced fields. There were irrigation systems in the many river valleys. Great roads and bridges crossed the mountainous land. Relay runners used these to bring goods and messages quickly to the Incan emperor from around the empire. There were great cities built of carved stone. Some still stand today. The rulers wore beautiful gold and silver ornaments. Most of the people farmed or herded animals. Some were skilled workers or builders.

In 1532, the Spanish invaded the Incan Empire. Only 168 Spaniards, led by Francisco Pizarro, brought the empire under their control. The Spanish quickly took over the land. The Indians were put to work on **haciendas** (HAH see EN duhz), great farms owned by the Spanish. The Spanish tore down the magnificent Indian temples. They used the same sites and the same stones to build Roman Catholic churches.

More Spaniards came. Silver was discovered at Potosí (POH toh SEE). This city on the *altiplano* is more than 4270 meters (14,000 feet) above sea level. So much silver was sent back to Spain that the very word *Potosí* came to mean wealth. The Indians were forced to mine the silver of Potosí.

Their Indian heritage is important to these Bolivian girls.

Cultural Problems

The Spanish and the Indians began to marry one another very early in colonial times. Today, the peoples of the four nations include many mestizos, people of a mixed Indian and Spanish background. There are also Indians and a few Whites.

Ecuador, Peru, Bolivia, and Paraguay have strong Indian heritages. However, Spanish culture is stronger in each of these nations. Spanish is generally the official language. That means it is used by the government. It is used in the schools. All educated people speak Spanish. Most jobs in the cities require a knowledge of Spanish.

Many of the Indians who live in the villages of the Andean nations speak Quechua (KEHCH uh wuh). This is an Indian language. Not many Indians in the region speak Spanish. Few can read and write in any language. This is a problem for the Indians. They have to know Spanish to deal with their governments. They have to know how to speak, read, and write Spanish to get an education. They have to know Spanish to get most jobs in the cities.

The governments of the region have set up **bilingual** (by LING gwul) schools. These are schools that first teach village children to read in their Indian languages. They then go on to learn Spanish. Classes in Spanish and reading have also been made available to many adults in the Indian villages.

The governments of these nations have a hard task in trying to make one national culture. But many government leaders feel that their nations can be made united, modern, strong, and prosperous only by extending Spanish culture.

REVIEW

WATCH YOUR WORDS

1. ___ were great farms owned by the Spanish.
   Llanos   Pampas   Haciendas
2. A group's background is its___.
   heritage   ruins   descendants

CHECK YOUR FACTS

3. Which four nations of Latin America reflect their Indian heritage?

4. Which Indian-heritage nation is not in the Andes?
5. What Indian empire ruled in Ecuador, Peru, and Bolivia?
6. What did the city of Potosí produce?

THINK ABOUT IT

What difficulties do you think are caused when a nation has two different cultures?

Lesson 4: Southern South America

FIND THE WORD

avalanche

The nations of Chile, Argentina, and Uruguay occupy the southern third of South America. These countries are alike in some ways. Their cultures and geography are somewhat similar.

Geography

The three nations of this region lie in the temperate zone. This means that they grow crops that need a cold season, such as wheat and fruits like apples.

Few trees grow in the pampas, or plains, of central Argentina. There, the soil is fertile. Wheat is grown and cattle graze. Sheep are raised in the colder, drier southern part of Argentina. This area is called Patagonia.

Buenos Aires is Argentina's capital and largest city. *Above:* An outdoor telephone in a shopping area. *Below:* The city's skyline.

Two long rivers, the Paraná and Uruguay, are used to move goods in Argentina and Uruguay. Look at the map on page 401. Find the capitals of Argentina and Uruguay. They are located on the Rio de la Plata (PLAH tuh), formed where the Paraná and Uruguay rivers join. Spanish explorers founded the city of Buenos Aires (BWAY nohss AIR eez) in 1536. Since that time, the Paraná and Uruguay rivers have been the main routes of trade and settlement. Notice that rivers form the borders between Argentina and Paraguay and between Argentina and Uruguay.

The southern part of the Andes Mountains forms the border between Argentina and Chile. There are few passes through these high mountains. A road and railroad connect Mendoza in Argentina and Santiago (SAHN tee AH goh) in Chile. They wind side by side up the mountain. Then they use the same narrow tunnel to go through the mountain. The tunnel has one lane that combines a road surface and railroad tracks. Trains and cars must wait for each other. Traffic goes one way, then the other. Avalanches (AV uh LANCH ehz) and spring floods threaten the route. An **avalanche** takes place when a great mass of snow or rock slides down the side of a mountain. The two nations built a statue called the Christ of the Andes to celebrate the connection between them.

Chile lies on the western side of the barrier created by the Andes Mountains. This nation is 4160 kilometers (2600 miles) long from north to south. But it is only from 80 kilometers (50 miles) to 320 kilometers (200 miles) wide from east to west. Because it is so long,

Snowcapped peaks in the Andes Mountains are part of Chile's natural beauty.

Chile has several different climates. The Atacama Desert in the north is one of the driest places in the world. The southern coastal areas are among the wettest places in the world. They have a marine climate. In between is an area with a pleasant Mediterranean climate.

Resources

Mineral resources are important in Chile but not in Argentina or Uruguay. The Atacama copper mines are Chile's great source of wealth. Argentina has enough petroleum to meet its own needs.

All three nations are known for their agricultural products. Chilean grapes are shipped to the United States during the northern winter. Argentine apples and pears are shipped to Brazil. Argentina and Uruguay sell meat to Europe and the rest of Latin America. Products made from cotton, wool, and leather are also important exports for Argentina and Uruguay.

Culture

The cultures of Chile, Argentina, and Uruguay are unique in Latin America. The Rio de la Plata colonies never interested the Spanish as much as Peru and Mexico. The Spanish king allowed the colonists there to go their own way. Many colonists became wealthy cattle ranchers. They took

Chile's copper mines are vital to its economy.

the land from the Indians. Most of the Indians were driven away by the Spanish settlers. Many died or were killed. As a result, few Indians live in these nations. Today, most of their peoples are descended from the Europeans who came as colonists and immigrants.

Among the region's 40 million people, 8 out of 10 live in cities. They are better educated than most people in the rest of Latin America. There are more factories and good jobs in these nations. The populations are not exploding as they are in much of Latin America. So there is not so much strain on these nations' resources. People from this region earn more per year, on the average, than people from other regions of Latin America.

The peoples of Chile, Argentina, and Uruguay have considered themselves the leaders of Latin America. They have taken pride in their schools and trade unions.

Montevideo is Uruguay's capital and largest city.

They have also been proud of their systems for taking care of the old, sick, poor, and unemployed. They have liked to think of themselves as more like Europeans than Latin Americans. Their standard of living has been higher than that of the rest of the Latin Americans.

Political Problems

During recent years, many people have left the three nations of the region. Uruguay's population has actually gotten smaller because so many people have left. People from the three nations complain about not having enough money or jobs. Many say the good times are gone. Many criticize their governments. There is an air of sadness and waiting in these nations.

All three nations are now ruled by military dictators. Groups with differing ideas about how the nations should be run continue to struggle. Some want the government to back the people who own property and industry. Others feel that the government should protect all the people by providing jobs and higher wages. Democracy is suspended as the armed forces rule.

No one knows how the political conflicts in these nations will be resolved. There may be civil war, struggles short of war, or peace. These nations will probably continue to have economic problems as long as their political problems remain unsolved.

REVIEW

CHECK YOUR FACTS

1. Name the three nations of southern South America.
2. What is the southern area of Argentina called?
3. Why does Chile have several different climates?

4. What is the major mineral resource of southern South America?

THINK ABOUT IT

Why is the culture of southern South America more European than the cultures of the other regions of Latin America?

Lesson 5: Brazil

Brazil is the giant of Latin America. It covers 8.5 million square kilometers (3.3 million square miles). Brazil has almost as much land as the United States. Brazil is more than four times larger than Mexico, the second-largest nation in Latin America. Brazil is large, important, and complex. All by itself, Brazil makes up one of the regions of Latin America.

Resources

Brazil is the giant of Latin America in other ways, too. In 1980, Brazil had 120 million people. This is about a third of the people in Latin America. It is also equal to more than half the population of the United States. Thus, there are far more Brazilians than there are Mexicans, Argentinians, or Colombians. Unlike other Latin American governments, the

São Paulo, Brazil, is the largest city in South America.

Brazilian government has not worried too much about population growth. Brazilians have felt that they have much land. The western lands of Brazil are only now being developed into ranches and farms.

Brazil is a giant in many ways. More water flows through the Amazon River system than through any other in the world. Earth's largest remaining tropical rain forest is in the Amazon River valley. Brazil has more resources of iron and manganese than any other nation.

Brazil's agricultural production is huge. Brazil is among the leading producers of coffee, soybeans, sugar, and citrus fruits. And Brazil has still more land that can be used to grow food. New farming and grazing lands are being cleared in Brazil's southwest and northwest. Older farm lands are being improved by changing crops and using fertilizer. Millions of trees are being planted to prevent more soil erosion. Soil erosion has been a bad problem in Brazil in the past.

FUN FACTS

The Amazon is the world's second-longest river. It flows for about 6400 kilometers (4000 miles) across South America. Most of the river is in Brazil. Unlike the winding Mississippi, the Amazon follows a very straight course. But 1100 streams enter into it along the way.

The mouth of the Amazon is over 400 kilometers (250 miles) across. Out of it flows one-fifth of all the moving fresh water on Earth. The river pours so much fresh water into the Atlantic Ocean that, 160 kilometers (100 miles) from shore, the water of the ocean is still fresh!

On the land around the Amazon are great rain forests. The natural plant life of the Amazon River valley is the richest and most varied in the world. In the Amazon forest, a scientist once counted 117 types of trees—all within half a mile! The most valuable are the rubber tree and the Brazil nut tree.

Animals roam these forests in great variety, too. There are large cats like jaguars, cougars, and ocelots. The shrieks of the red howler monkey keep the forests noisy. Most mammals there live in the trees. On the ground are the capybara, huge rodents. In the air fly millions of bats, including the bloodthirsty vampire. The banks of the Amazon also swarm with thousands of kinds of insects.

Brazil's leaders are having a system of roads built across the country.

Development

To help move people and goods around the country, the Brazilian government is building many paved highways. In recent years, a new highway has connected Brasília, the capital, to Belém at the mouth of the Amazon. Another highway connects Belém with areas being settled to the west. These roads cross rivers, swamps, rain forests, and hills. They are very hard and expensive to build. Brazil is also expanding its highway system in the areas that have long been settled. Brazil has more kilometers of paved highways than the rest of Latin America.

In recent years, industry has grown rapidly in Brazil. Brazil now produces and exports many manufactured goods. Factories in Brazil produce cars, buses, ships, tractors, and planes. Brazilians drive more than 7 million cars, most of them made in Brazil.

For many years, Brazilians called their country "the sleeping giant." Now the giant seems to be waking up. Many Brazilians believe that by the year 2000, their nation will be one of the most important in the world. Brazil's size and resources give Brazilians important reasons for feeling good about the future of their country.

Portuguese Heritage

Brazil is different from the rest of Latin America in several important ways. One major difference is the history of its Indian peoples. Originally, they were hunters who moved from place to place. As Europeans began to settle Brazil's coasts, only a few Indians chose to fight them. These few were killed or were caught and made to work for the Europeans. This was what happened to most of the Indians in the rest of Latin America. But in Brazil, most Indians just retreated into the interior, away from the Europeans. Many still live in the rain forests of the Amazon River valley.

The Europeans who settled Brazil were also different. Portuguese explorers landed near the present-day city of Salvador in 1500. The Portuguese began to colonize Brazil. Later, the Portuguese had to fight to keep their colony. The French, Dutch, and English tried to take Brazil from Portugal. But Portugal kept Brazil.

As you know, Spain controlled the rest of Latin America. However, the Spanish never tried to take over Brazil. This was because of a treaty these nations signed in 1494. In this treaty, Spain and Portugal divided the world between them. The lands east of the dividing line, including Brazil, belonged to Portugal. The lands west of the line, including the rest of Latin America, belonged to Spain.

The Portuguese influence is still strong in Brazil. Most Brazilians speak Portuguese. Churches, public buildings, and patterned sidewalks

This Indian boy's ancestors caught fish the way he does today.

Slaves in Brazil had to work long hours boiling sugar cane to make sugar.

are like those in Portugal. Most Brazilians are Roman Catholics. The Portuguese brought the Roman Catholic religion to Brazil.

African Heritage

Today, Brazil is not only Portuguese but also African. This is another important way Brazil differs from the rest of Latin America except the lands around the Caribbean. Beginning in the mid-1500s, the Portuguese brought thousands of Black Africans to Brazil as slaves. Slaves were captured on the Guinea Coast, in the Niger River valley, and in Angola. These places were also Portuguese colonies. Blacks worked in sugar cane plantations all along the Atlantic coast of Brazil.

The Africans were able to adjust more easily to Brazil than the Portuguese were. The hot climate was like that of Africa. The soil and plants were similar to those they knew in Africa.

Today, many foods brought from Africa by the early slaves are part of the Brazilian diet. Brazilians cook with peanuts and spices as in Africa. They fry fish in the African manner.

African religions are still practiced in Brazil. Many communities have groups that worship African gods. They practice healing and counseling in the African way. The music of these African religious services is popular. All Brazilian music is played with African musical instruments and has African rhythms.

Immigrants bring their culture to their new land.

Later Immigration

Over the years, other peoples have come to Brazil. They have come mostly from Italy, Spain, Germany, Lebanon, and Japan. Many of these peoples have married each other and the peoples already in Brazil. So today, most Brazilians have several different backgrounds. Like the people themselves, Brazilian culture is a mixture with many sources.

Brazil's Unique History

Brazil is not only different from the rest of Latin America in the way it was settled. Its history is unique in other ways, too. The Brazilians never had to fight a war to gain independence from Portugal. By contrast, the Spanish colonies of Latin America had to fight for freedom. In all the changes in Brazil's government since independence, there have been no civil wars. On the other hand, there has been much fighting since independence in much of Spanish America.

Brazil's history may continue to be different in the future. Its rich resources may someday make Brazil Latin America's only world power.

REVIEW

CHECK YOUR FACTS

1. Brazil is (larger/smaller) than the United States.
2. Name two of Brazil's major mineral resources.
3. Name three of Brazil's major agricultural products.
4. What is the capital of Brazil?
5. What have Brazilians called their country?

THINK ABOUT IT

In what way is Brazil today like the United States was many years ago?

CHAPTER REVIEW

WATCH YOUR WORDS

1. A(n) ___ is a great storm of wind and rain.
   earthquake   volcano   hurricane
2. The ___ were great farms owned by the Spanish.
   haciendas   *altiplanos*   pampas
3. ___ are great falls of snow.
   Cliffs   Volcanoes   Avalanches
4. ___ blow continuously from east to west across the Alantic.
   Trade winds   Gusts   Hurricanes
5. In ___ schools, two languages are taught.
   Indian   bilingual   elementary

CHECK YOUR FACTS

6. Why do many people in Mexico and Central America prefer to live in the highlands?
7. What important road connects Mexico and Central America?
8. Which nation has a larger population, Mexico or El Salvador?
9. Why is the weather rainy in the Caribbean area?
10. Name the two major crops grown for export in the Caribbean and northern South America.
11. What outside nations still own land in the Caribbean?
12. Name a nation of northern South America that has important resources of petroleum.
13. What Indian group lived in Paraguay when the Spanish came?
14. What two rivers are important to transportation in southern South America?
15. Why is travel between Argentina and Chile difficult?

USE YOUR MAPS AND CHARTS

16. Look at the map of Latin America's regions on page 408. In what region is Uruguay?
17. Look at the climate map of Mexico and Central America on page 409. Is there desert climate in the north or south?
18. Look at the map of Mexico and Central America on page 409. What is the capital of Nicaragua?
19. Look at the political map of Mexico on page 412. What two states lie on a long peninsula on the west coast of Mexico?
20. Are the Mexican states larger in the north or the south?
21. Look at the chart of the Caribbean and northern South America on page 417. What two areas belong to the United States?
22. Look at the map of the Incan Empire on page 420. On what ocean did it border?

THINK ABOUT IT

23. Why is agriculture in southern South America similar to that of the Mexican highlands?
24. Why do you think there are so many nations, cultures, and languages in the Caribbean?
25. What metals do you think the Inca called "the sweat of the sun" and "the tears of the moon"?
26. Do you think the Panama Canal has become more or less important since it was built?
27. How have the Andes Mountains affected the development of South America?
28. List as many things as you can that are special about Brazil.

UNIT REVIEW

WATCH YOUR WORDS

Use the words below to fill in the blanks. Use each word only once.

altiplano	hurricanes	pampas
creoles	industrialization	peninsulares
criollos	llanos	Trade winds
haciendas	mercantilism	viceroys
heritage	mestizos	

Latin America is a fascinating area of the world. The region has great mountains, the Andes, and a huge plateau, the ____. There are also large plains: the ____ in the north and the ____ in the south. Huge storms called ____ strike the Caribbean area.

____ brought ships across the Atlantic from Europe. Europeans brought the Indian cultures to an end. Latin America was soon ruled by ____ who came from Spain and Portugal. The ____ or ____ , Europeans born in Latin America, were also important. The ____ , people of Spanish and Indian blood, were less powerful. Black slaves gave Latin America an African ____.

The early Spanish kings sent ____ to govern their colonies. Soon, crops were being grown by the Indians on the large ____ owned by the Spanish. Through the system of ____ , the colonies provided raw materials and markets to Spain and the other colonial powers. Today, the economies of the Latin American nations are undergoing ____.

CHECK YOUR FACTS

1. Name some of the major areas of flat land in Latin America.

2. Name the three major culture groups of Latin America.

3. Name three major natural resources of Latin America.

4. Why did some Spanish colonies break up into several nations after they became independent?

5. Why is tourism important to Mexico and Central America?

6. Which colonial powers were important in the history of the Caribbean?

7. Which four South American nations have kept their Indian heritage?

8. Why are some people dissatisfied with the governments in Chile, Argentina, and Uruguay?

9. How does Brazil compare in size and population with Mexico?

10. How does the history of Brazil's Indian people differ from that of the other Latin American Indians?

KNOW YOUR PEOPLE

Match the person with the activity.

11. Francisco Pizarro   A. led the Cuban Revolution.

12. Simón Bolívar   B. fought for the independence of Argentina, Chile, and Peru.

13. Fidel Castro   C. defeated the Inca.

14. José de San Martín   D. struggled for the freedom of northern South America.

TRUE OR FALSE

15. Hurricanes rarely strike the Caribbean area.
16. Most of the people who live in Argentina today have an Indian background.
17. Venezuela was ruled by the Spanish.
18. French Guiana still belongs to France.
19. The Dominican Republic is an American possession.
20. The Andes lie on the border between Chile and Argentina.
21. Brazil has few natural resources, a small population, and little capital.

GET THE DATE STRAIGHT

Match the date or dates with the event.

22.	1494	A.	Bolívar led revolt against Spain.
23.	1500	B.	Uruguay created.
24.	1532	C.	Portuguese landed in Brazil.
25.	1536	D.	Spanish invaded Incan Empire.
26.	1804	E.	Haiti became an independent nation.
27.	1810	F.	Mexican Revolution began.
28.	1813–1824	G.	San Martín fought in Argentina and Chile.
29.	1816–1818	H.	Spain and Portugal divided the New World.
30.	1828	I.	Buenos Aires founded.

USE YOUR MAPS AND CHART

31. Look at the physical map of Latin America on page 383. Name two large highland areas in the eastern part of the continent.

32. Look at the climate map of South America on page 385. Is there an area of Mediterranean climate on the east coast or the west coast?
33. Look at the resource map of Latin America on page 395. Is cacao grown near the east coast or the west coast?
34. Look at the map of Latin America's nations on page 401. What is the capital of Argentina?
35. Look at the time line for Latin America on page 403. Which became independent first, Cuba or Brazil?
36. Look at the historical map of Latin America on page 403. Name the Spanish viceroyalties.

THINK ABOUT IT

37. In what ways is Brazil different from other Latin American nations?
38. Can black gold—petroleum—be more valuable than gold?
39. How does nature show its power in the Caribbean?
40. Recently, presidents of the United States and Mexico have tried to improve relations between their two nations. Why is this important to these two countries?
41. What do you consider the three most serious problems of Latin America?
42. Why is the United States concerned about the spread of Communism from Cuba?

PUT IT ALL TOGETHER

43. Many Latin Americans blame their governments for their problems. What should be done by government? What things are the responsibility of others? Write an essay on this question.

435

GLOSSARY

aborigine (AB uh RIJ uh NEE) one of a people who were native to a place before outside settlers came there (300)

absolute monarch (MON AHRK) a ruler with unlimited power (212)

adviser a person who helps a leader make decisions (196)

agriculture farming (184)

alliance (uh LY uns) an agreement between nations to work together and support each other (231)

alloy (AL oi) a mixture of metals (88)

ally (AL EYE) a person or nation that works with you, not against you (231)

altiplano (AHL tee PLAH noh) the Spanish word for a plateau (384)

ancient (AYN shunt) of a time more than 1500 years ago; very old (84)

Antarctic (ant AHRK tik) the climate area closest to the South Pole (20)

Antarctic Circle the line of latitude that is about 66° south of the equator (19)

apartheid (uh PAHRT HYT) the system of laws in South Africa that separates Black people from White people (355)

apostle (uh POSS ul) one of the first 12 followers of Jesus Christ (124)

apprentice (ah PREN tiss) a young person learning a craft from a master (137)

aqueduct (AK wuh DUKT) a raised pipe built to carry water to towns and cities (119)

archaeologist (ARH kee AHL uh jist) a person who digs up and studies old ruins (79)

archipelago (AHR kuh PEL uh GOH) a large group of islands (295)

Arctic (AHRK tik) the climate area closest to the North Pole (20)

Arctic Circle the line of latitude that is about 66° north of the equator (19)

armistice (AHR muh stis) an agreement to end a war (232)

autumnal (aw TUM nul) **equinox** the first day of fall; *see* EQUINOX (19)

axis (AK sis) an imaginary line through the center of Earth, from pole to pole, around which Earth turns (16)

barbarian (bahr BAIR ee un) an uncivilized person (125)

bilingual (by LING gwul) able to speak two languages (422)

bishop a high-ranking religious leader in some Christian churches (124)

border a line that divides two nations or parts of nations (52)

boundary a border (52)

boyar (boh YAHR) a Russian noble (244)

bronze an alloy that is a mixture of copper and tin (82)

Buddhism (BOO DIZ um) the religion based on the teachings of the philosopher Buddha (292)

Caesar (SEE zur) the title used by rulers of the Roman Empire (119, 244)

canal a waterway built by people (87)

capital a city where the government of a state or nation meets (52)

capitalism an economy in which private individuals and groups own property and run businesses; free enterprise (182)

capital resources the sums of money needed to build machinery and factories (182)

caste a social class system in the Hindu religion, based on birth and work (291)

castle the home of a king or lord during the Middle Ages, a large building, often on a hill, protected from attack by high, thick walls (133)

catacombs underground tunnels with graves in them (123)

cathedral (kah THEE drul) the main church in a bishop's district (138)

Caucasian (kaw KAY zhun) a member of the White race (178)

charter an official paper that grants a person or group special rights (144)

Christianity the religion based on the teachings of Jesus Christ (122)

citadel (SIT uh DEL) a fort in or near a city, protected by thick walls (92)

city-state a small, independent country made up of a city and the surrounding area (88)

civilization a highly developed form of culture (82)

civil war a war within a nation (252)

climate the average weather a place has over a long period of time (26)

cold war a period of conflict in which nations are enemies but are not fighting (262)

colony an area of land ruled by a foreign or "parent" country (159)

commune a huge farming community where the land is owned by the group in common (312)

communism an economy in which the government owns and runs all businesses and there is no private property (64)

compass 1 a map drawing of arrows that point north, south, east, and west **2** a tool with a magnetic needle that always points north (49, 156)

Confucianism (kun FYOO shun IZ um) the ideas and teachings of Confucius (306)

conquistador (kohn kees tah DOR) a Spanish conqueror in the New World (159)

constitution a written plan of government (217)

consul one of two rulers and chief judges in the ancient Roman Republic (114)

consumer goods goods that people buy and use, such as food and clothes (257)

continent one of the seven large masses of land on Earth (22)

cottage industry a kind of job, making goods or performing services, that hired workers can do in their own homes (199)

craft the skill and practice of making a specific kind of product by hand (137)

Crusade (kroo SAYD) one of the wars fought by European Christians against Muslims for control of the Holy Land (141)

culture a group's way of living, including beliefs, tools and skills, organization, and communication (59)

cuneiform (kyoo NEE uh FORM) wedge-shaped, as symbols used in some ancient systems of writing (90)

czar (ZAHR) a title once used by rulers of Russia (244)

delta an area of rich soil dropped by a river before it flows into the ocean (87)

democracy (di MOK ruh see) government by the people (64)

desert a very dry place, often covered with sand, where few plants can grow (25)

developed having more factories and businesses than farms (68)

dictator (DIK tay tur) a ruler with total power (114)

distribution map a map that shows how things are spread or scattered over an area (52)

domesticate (duh MESS ti KAYT) to tame (a wild animal) (80)

dominion a self-governing nation in the British Commonwealth of Nations (301)

drawbridge the only entrance to a castle; it was raised and lowered over a moat with chains (133)

dynasty (DY nuh stee) a family of rulers (94)

earthquake a quick, shifting movement of Earth's surface (35)

economy (i KON uh mee) the system by which people use resources to produce and distribute goods and services (182)

elevation (EL uh VAY shun) the height of land above sea level (24)

emperor the male ruler of an empire (91)

empire a group of lands or nations under one government (91, 159)

empress the female ruler of an empire (91)

epic a long poem that tells a story (108)

equator (i KWAY tur) the imaginary line around the middle of Earth at which latitude starts; 0° latitude (16)

equinox (EE kwuh NOKS) the first day of spring (vernal equinox) or of fall (autumnal equinox), when day and night are of equal length (19)

erosion the washing away or blowing away of the soil (37, 358)

estate (eh STAYT) **1** a large farm or country home (96) **2** formerly, one of three classes of citizens in France (216)

ethnic group a group of people of the same race, religion, or culture (180)

executive (eg ZEK yuh tiv) **branch** the branch of government that carries out the laws (262)

export *v.* (ex SPORT) to sell (a product) to another country (186)

m (FYOOD ul IZ um) the system ...anizing and governing society ...ng the Middle Ages in Europe (131)

...f (FEEF) under feudalism, a large piece of land given by a king to an important noble (131)

finished goods products that have been manufactured or made ready for use (200)

flying buttress (BUT riss) an archlike prop that supports a wall from outside (138)

free enterprise an economy in which private individuals and businesses decide what goods and services to produce; capitalism (182)

front in war, an area where fighting is going on (232)

glacier (GLAY shur) a huge, slowly moving mass of ice that grinds down the land as it moves (38)

globe a round model of Earth (40)

goods things, such as food and clothes, that can be used or sold (182)

gothic (GOTH ik) in a style of architecture marked by pointed arches, tall stone walls, and many windows (138)

guild (GILD) an organized group of merchants or skilled craft workers in the Middle Ages (136)

guillotine (GIL uh TEEN) a machine used to cut off people's heads (219)

heavy industry the production of such things as steel and large machines (257)

Hellenistic (HEHL un NISS tik) of or like the ancient Greeks (107)

helot (HEL ut) a peasant forced to work on the land in ancient Greece (102)

hemisphere (HEM uh SFIR) one of the four half circles that Earth can be divided into: the Northern, Southern, Eastern, or Western Hemisphere (16)

hieroglyphics (HY ruh GLIF iks) a form of picture writing (97)

Hinduism the main religion of India (291)

historic (hiss TOR ik) **times** the period of time since people learned to write and keep records (79)

homolosine (hoh MOL uh SYN) **projection** a map that leaves out parts of the oceans to show land areas more accurately (46)

human resources people; workers (182)

immigrant (IM i grunt) a person who comes to settle in a new country (208)

import v. (im PORT) to buy (a product) from another country (186)

industrial (in DUS tree ul) having a lot of factories (186)

industrialization the building of a lot of factories in order to produce more goods (398)

inflation a rise in the cost of goods and services, making money worth less (210)

interrupted projection a map with gaps in the ocean areas (46)

irrigation supplying land with water that comes from somewhere else (58)

Islam (IS lam) the religion of the Muslims, who follow the teachings of Muhammad (140)

journeyman a worker who has learned a craft but who is not yet a master (137)

joust (JOWST) a contest in which knights in armor tried to knock each other off their horses with a lance (134)

Judaism (JOO dee IZ um) the Jewish religion (122)

judicial (joo DISH ul) **branch** the branch of government that decides whether laws have been obeyed or broken (262)

key a list explaining the symbols and colors used on a map (49)

knight in the Middle Ages, a noble trained in the arts of war (134)

labor union an organized group of workers that tries to get better wages and working conditions (210)

lance a long, sharp pole used by knights in a joust (134)

landforms the shapes of land on Earth. Mountains, hills, plains, and plateaus are landforms (22)

legion (LEE jun) a group of about 6000 foot soldiers in the army of ancient Rome (115)

legislative (LEJ is LAY tiv) **branch** the branch of government that makes the laws (262)

lines of latitude the lines on a map that run east and west. They measure distance north and south of the equator. (42)

lines of longitude (LON juh TOOD) the lines on a map that run north and south. They measure distance east and west of the prime meridian. (42)

lord under feudalism, a powerful noble who granted land to vassals in return for military and other services (131)

manor under feudalism, a lord's castle and his village, fields, and forests (133)

map a flat drawing of Earth or of a part of Earth (44)

market economy an economy in which the amounts and prices of the goods and services are determined by supply and demand (255)

master an expert in a craft (137)

masterpiece a fine piece of work which a journeyman had to have accepted by a craft guild in order to become a master (137)

mechanized (MEK uh NYZD) using machines to do work (186)

mercantilism the system whereby colonies provided raw materials and served as markets for their "parent" countries in Europe (400)

Mercator (mur KAY tur) **projection** a map on which the lines of latitude and longitude are both parallel. This makes land areas too big near the poles. (46)

mercenary (MUR suh NEHR ee) a hired soldier (126)

meridian (muh RID ee un) a line of longitude (42)

moat a deep ditch of water surrounding a castle (133)

modern 1 of recent times **2** of times since about 1350 (148)

monarchy (MON AHR kee) rule by one person, a monarch, who inherits the position and keeps it for life (64–65)

monastery (MON uh STEHR ee) a place where men live apart from the world and devote their lives to religion (128)

monk a religious man who lives in a monastery (128)

monsoon a wind that changes direction when the season changes (276)

mosque (MOSK) a Muslim house of worship (372)

mummy a body that was preserved by ancient Egyptians (97)

Muslim a person whose religion is Islam (140)

nation an area with an independent government (22)

nationalism the love of one's country and desire for its power and independence (352)

nationalize to take over ownership of (a business or industry): said of a national government (313)

natural resources things in nature that people can use, such as water, fertile soil, forests, and minerals (182)

nomad (NOH mad) a person who moves from place to place instead of settling down (342)

North Pole the place that is farthest north on Earth (16)

oasis (oh A sis) a place in a desert where there is water (372)

ocean one of the four very large bodies of salt water on Earth (22)

oligarchy (OL uh GAHR kee) rule by a few powerful people (101)

page a young boy in training to become a squire and a knight (134)

papyrus (puh PY russ) writing paper made from reeds (97)

parallel a line of latitude (42)

Parliament (PAHR luh munt) the lawmaking group, or legislature, in some nations, such as Great Britain (196)

patrician (puh TRISH un) a Roman who belonged to a wealthy and important family (112)

peasant a person of a humble social class who farms the land (95)

peninsula (puh NIN syuh luh) an area of land almost surrounded by water (174)

pharaoh (FEHR oh) a king of ancient Egypt (96)

philosopher (fi LAHS uh fur) a person who studies ideas (109)

philosophy (fi LAHS uh fee) the study of ideas (109)

physical map a map that shows the height or shape of land (52)

pilgrimage a religious journey to a holy place (141)

plain a big, open area of flat land (25)

planned economy an economy in which the government decides what goods and services will be produced (255)

plantation (plan TAY shun) a large farm where crops are raised (297)

plateau (pla TOH) an area of high, flat land (25)

plebian (pli BEE un) one of the common people in ancient Rome (112)

political map a map that shows the borders of cities, states, or nations (52)

pope the head of the Roman Catholic Church (124)

prehistoric (PREE hiss TOR ik) of the period before people learned to write and keep records (79)

premier (pri MIR) a prime minister (315)

prime meridian the imaginary line at which longitude starts; 0° longitude (42)

prime minister the head of the government in many nations (208)

projection (pruh JEK shun) the way sizes and shapes of places on Earth are changed on a map (44)

pyramid (PIR uh mid) a triangular building with four sides (97)

raw materials natural products that can be improved by manufacturing (200)

reign (RAYN) the time a ruler is in power (194)

reincarnation (REE in kahr NAY shun) in Hinduism, the belief that, after death, a person's soul comes back in another body (291)

republic a government without a monarch (112)

revolution (REV uh LOO shun) a great political or economic change (198)

Romanesque (ROH mun EHSK) in a style of architecture marked by thick stone walls, rounded arches, and few windows (138)

samurai (SAM yuh RY) a mighty warrior of old Japan (318)

savanna (suh VAN uh) a tropical grassland (337)

scale a diagram that shows what a map distance equals in real distance (49)

scientific method a way to test the truth of ideas about science (150)

sea level the surface of the ocean (24)

serf under feudalism, a worker who was not free to leave a lord's land (131)

service an action that one person can do to fill the needs of another (182)

Shintoism an early religion of Japan (318)

shogun one of a line of military leaders who once controlled the government of Japan (319)

social class one of the groups into which society is divided by wealth and position (250)

socialism an economy in which the government owns and runs the businesses but people keep some private property (64)

society a large, organized group of people that lasts for a long time (83)

solstice the first day of summer, when the day is longest (summer solstice), or the first day of winter, when the night is longest (winter solstice) (18)

source the place where a river starts (335)

South Pole the place that is farthest south on Earth (16)

sovereignty (SOV un run tee) final authority in one's area (65)

specialization a way of working in which a worker does just one kind of job (199)

squire a young man of noble birth in training to become a knight (134)

steppes (STEPS) grassy plains (30)

stylus (STY luss) a sharp stick used to cut symbols into wet clay tablets (90)

subarctic (sub AHRK tik) just south of the Arctic Circle (30)

subcontinent a large land area on a continent that seems separate from the rest (272)

supply and demand how much of something is available and how much of it people want to buy (255)

taiga (TY guh) a subarctic climate area where there are great forests (259)

Taoism (TOW IZ um) an important religion of China (307)

tournament a contest held in the Middle Ages so knights could show off their fighting skills (134)

trade winds winds that blow continuously in one direction (414)

trench a deep ditch dug for defense (232)

tribune (TRIB YOON) an official of ancient Rome who protected the rights of the common people (114)

triumvirate (try UM vur it) a ruling group of three men (117)

tropic of Cancer a line of latitude about 23° north of the equator, the most northern place at which the sun is ever directly overhead (19)

tropic of Capricorn a line of latitude about 23° south of the equator, the most southern place at which the sun is ever directly overhead (19)

tundra (TUN druh) the climate area just south of the Arctic, a treeless plain where the ground is usually frozen (30)

typhoon a great wind and rain storm (277)

tyrant (TY runt) an all-powerful ruler, especially one who rules harshly (102)

urban area a city and its suburbs (208),

vassal (VASS ul) under feudalism, a person who received land from a lord in return for services (131)

vernal (VUR nul) **equinox** the first day of spring; *see* EQUINOX (19)

viceroy an official who rules an area for a king (400)

volcano an opening in the earth through which hot melted rock, ashes, smoke, and gases can shoot (37)

voyageur (vwah yah ZHUR) a French fur trader in Canada (163)

ziggurat (ZIG oo RAT) a pyramid-shaped temple tower, each story of which is smaller than the one below it (89)

INDEX

CREDITS

Maps by Continental Cartography (except 18, 36, 48, 51, 152, 161, 176, 203, 207, 258, 338, 351, 385). Charts and Time Lines by Function Thru Form Inc. **14:** NASA; **21:** J. Vissel/Alpha Photos; **32:** Adam Woolfitt/Woodfin Camp; **34:** Burk Uzzle/Magnum; **35:** Bruce Roberts/Photo Researchers; **36:** Wide World; **37t:** Icelandic National Tourist Office, **b:** Jim Brandenburg/Woodfin Camp; **40:** Robert Capece/McGraw-Hill; **60:** Peter Menzel; **66:** Loren McIntyre/Woodfin Camp; **76–77:** F. Schreider/Photo Researchers; **78:** Inge Morath/Magnum; **80, 81, 82:** American Museum of Natural History; **83:** Editorial Photocolor Archives/Scala; **86:** Klaus Francke/Peter Arnold, Inc.; **89:** Georg Gerster/Photo Researchers; **90:** Farrell Grehan/Photo Researchers; **91:** The Bettmann Archive; **92:** The British Museum; **94:** National Gallery of Art, Washington, D.C.; **97:** Thomas Nebbia/Woodfin Camp; **100:** Anne Sager/Photo Researchers; **105:** Hamilton Wright/Photo Researchers; **106:** Editorial Photocolor Archives; **108:** New York Public Library Picture Collection; **109:** Editorial Photocolor Archives; **111,115:** Culver Pictures; **116:** Larry Mulvehill/Photo Researchers; **110t:** Bernard G. Silberstein/Freelance Photographers Guild; **b:** Editorial Photocolor Archives; **120:** H.G. Ross/Freelance Photographers Guild; **121:** Editorial Photocolor Archives/Scala; **123:** Fototeca Unione; **124:** Editorial Photocolor Archives/Scala; **125,127,128:** Culver Pictures; **130:** The Bettmann Archive; **133, 134, 137:** Editorial Photocolor Archives; **138:** Alan Forman; **141, 142, 145:** Culver Pictures; **148, 149:** Editorial

Photocolor Archives; **151:** Museo Di San Martino, Naples; **152:** British Museum; **153:** Ufizzi Gallery, Florence; **154:** The Bettmann Archive; **155:** Culver Pictures; **156:** Museo De Fiscia, Florence; **157:** De Bry, Ocidentalis; **158:** Culver Pictures; **159:** New York Public Library Picture Collection; **160l:** De Bry, Ocidentalis, **r:** New York Public Library Picture Collection; **162, 165:** Culver Pictures; **172:** James A. Sugar/Photo Researchers; **175:** Tony Howarth/Woodfin Camp; **180:** H. Gritscher/Peter Arnold, Inc.; **181:** William Hubbell/Woodfin Camp; **184:** Margot Granitsas/Photo Researchers; **186:** Paul Conklin/ Monkmeyer; **187:** Margot Granitsas/Photo Researchers; **193:** Daniel Porges/ Peter Arnold, Inc.; **195t:** Culver Pictures, **b:** The Bettmann Archive; **197:** Culver Pictures; **198:** The Bettmann Archive; **199:** Culver Pictures; **201t:** The Bettmann Archive, **b:** Culver Pictures; **205t:** Culver Pictures, **b:** Magnus Bartlett/Woodfin Camp; **209:** Paolo Koch/Photo Researchers; **210:** Wide World; **212:** Earl Roberge/ Photo Researchers; **213:** National Gallery of Art; **214:** Adam Woolfitt/Woodfin Camp; **217, 218, 219:** Culver Pictures; **223:** Clyde H. Smith/Peter Arnold, Inc.; **225:** Werner Mueller; **232l:** National Archives, **r:** Culver Pictures; **234:** American Heritage; **237, 238:** Editorial Photocolor Archives; **239:** Jan Lukas/Photo Researchers; **240:** United Press International; **242:** Bjorn Bolstad/Peter Arnold, Inc.; **244, 246, 248, 249:** Culver Pictures; **251t:** Sovphoto, **b:** The Bettmann Archive; **252, 253t:** The Bettmann Archive, **b:** United Press International; **254:** Sovphoto; **261:** Lillian N. Bolstad/Peter Arnold, Inc.; **263:** United Press International; **270:** John Henebry, Jr.; **273t:** Ted Spiegel/Black Star, **b:** John Henebry, Jr.; **274:** John Henebry, Jr.; **276:** Robert Frerck/Woodfin Camp; **278:** Phil Carol/Monkmeyer; **280:** Camilla Smith/Rainbow; **281:** Paolo Koch/Photo Researchers; **282l:** Jehangir Gazdar/Woodfin Camp, **r:** Anthony Howarth/Woodfin Camp; **283:** East Asia House/Columbia University; **284l:** Raghubir Singh/ Woodfin Camp, **r:** Bruno Barbey/Magnum; **286:** Toge Fujihara/Monkmeyer; **288:** Camilla Smith/ Rainbow; **289:** Anthony Howarth/Woodfin Camp; **291:** Jehagir Gazdar/Woodfin Camp; **292, 293:** John Henebry, Jr.; **294:** Marc & Evelyne Bernheim/Woodfin Camp; **295:** Roland & Sabina Michaud/Woodfin Camp; **296:** Rick Merron/Magnum; **297:** Hans Hoefer/Woodfin Camp; **300:** Robert Frerck/Woodfin Camp; **301l:** Robert Bauer/Freelance Photographers Guild, **r:** Bob Strauss/Woodfin Camp; **302:** Dennis Stock, Magnum; **303:** Robert Frerck/Woodfin Camp; **305:** Mike Yamashita/Woodfin Camp; **306:** American Heritage; **308:** Fritz Henle/Monkmeyer; **309t1:** Culver Pictures, **tr:** Sunday Times, **c:** American Heritage, **b:** United Press International; **311:** V. Rastelli/Woodfin Camp; **312:** Joel Norwood/ Katherine Young Photography; **313:** Henri Bureau/Sygma; **314, 315t:** Richard Balzar/Stock, Boston, **b:** United Press International; **317:** Mike Yamashita/Woodfin Camp; **318:** New York Public Library Picture Collection; **319:** Honolulu Academy of Arts; **320:** Grehan Collection; **321:** Sekai Bunka; **322t:** Radio Times Hulton, **b:** United Press International; **324l:** United Press International, **r:** United States Army; **325, 326l:** Mitsubishi, **b:** John Henebry, Jr.; **327:** Sekai Bunka; **328:** Toge Fujihara/Monkmeyer; **332–333:** Georg Gerster/Photo Reseachers; **336:** Culver Pictures; **339, 342, 346:** Marc & Evelyne Bernheim/Woodfin Camp; **347, 349:** New York Public Library Picture Collection; **350:** Culver Pictures; **352:** Marc Ribaud/Magnum; **354:** Sygma; **359:** Bruno Barbey/Magnum; **360:** Marilyn Silverstone/ Magnum; **362:** Alpha Photos; **365:** Bernard Pierre Wolf/Photo Researchers; **367:** Marc & Evelyne Bernheim/Woodfin Camp; **368:** Monkmeyer Press Photos; **369:** J. W. Frederick/Photo Researchers; **370:** Marc & Evelyne Bernheim/Woodfin Camp; **371:** H. Uible/Photo Researchers; **313:** Thomas Hopker/Woodfin Camp; **324:** Sarah Errington/Monkmeyer; **375:** Pro Pix/Monkmeyer; **376:** Farrell Grehan/Photo Researchers; **380–381:** Bendick Associates/Monkmeyer; **382:** Loren McIntyre/Woodfin Camp; **386:** Jim Steiner/Monkmeyer; **387:** Jacques Jangoux/Peter Arnold, Inc.; **389l:** Reflejo/Woodfin Camp, **r:** Ellis Herwig/Stock, Boston; **390:** Peabody Museum; **391:** Ellis Hersig/Stock, Boston; **392:** Radio Times Hulton Picture Library; **394:** Yoram Lehman/Peter Arnold, Inc.; **397t:** Sydney Byrd/Peter Arnold, Inc., **b:** Porterfield-Chickering/Photo Researchers; **398l:** Ellis Herwig/Stock, Boston, **r:** Bruno Barbey/Magnum; **399:** David Mangurian; **402:** Museo De America, Madrid; **404:** Señor Alfredo Boulton, Caracas; **405:** Culver Pictures; **407:** Carl Frank/Photo Researchers; **410:** Frederick Ayer/Photo Researchers; **411:** Marc Bernheim/Woodfin Camp; **413:** Jacques Jangoux/Peter Arnold, Inc.; **415l:** Loren McIntyre/Woodfin Camp, **r:** Catherine Ursillo/Photo Researchers; **416:** Historical Picture Service; **418:** Murray Greenberg; **419:** Eric Simmons/Stock, Boston; **421:** Jacques Jangoux/Peter Arnold, Inc,; **423t:** Bendick Associates/Monkmeyer, **b:** Jacques Jangoux/Peter Arnold, Inc.; **424:** G. Gohier/Photo Researchers; **425:** Jacques Jangoux/Peter Arnold, Inc.; **426:** Carl Frank/Photo Researchers; **427:** Christiana Dittmann/Rainbow; **428, 429:** Loren McIntyre/Woodfin Camp; **430:** Bruno Barbey/Magnum; **431:** Radio Times Hulton Picture Library; **432:** L. L. T. Rhodes/Taurus.